D1549657

Shepherds, Sheep, Hirelings & Wolves

LORD, BLESS YE THE LORD

Shepherds, Sheep, Hirelings & Wolves

An Anthology of Christian Currents in English Life since AD 550

Tim Williams

UNICORN

Published in 2020 by
Unicorn, an imprint of Unicorn Publishing Group LLP
5 Newburgh Street
London
W1F 7RG
www.unicornpress.org

ISBN 978 1 912690 99 2

10 9 8 7 6 5 4 3 2 1

Designed by Nick Newton Design

Printed in Europe for Latitude Press Ltd

Frontispiece
Post-war English pastoral. A panel from the 'Jesse Window' in St Gregory and St Martin, Wye, Kent, which was dedicated in the Festival of Britain year, 1951. It replaced the great west window wrecked by enemy action in 1943.

CONTENTS

ACKNOWLEDGEMENTS

This book has its origins in many happy forays over the years with my wife Pam exploring churches and the wonderful heritage to be found in them. So first of all, a real appreciation for all those teams who keep these precious places open, or at least do their best to ensure a key is available. Like others on this venture, we have had the company of the fine guidebooks of Pevsner, Betjeman, Simon Jenkins, and others – and had our eyes further opened by the parishes' own booklets, often a fund of fascinating local knowledge. Taking lots of photos (in perhaps a kind of obedience to Ruskin's 'earnest request' – see p. 247) helped to deepen understanding of what has gone into their fashioning and re-fashioning. (There are two of them on the cover, and two inside.)

For broadening the sense of history, the strong tradition of scholarship in the field has offered a wealth of articles and chapters and books to learn from. If I single out Keith Thomas's *Religion and the Decline of Magic*, Eamon Duffy's *The Stripping of the Altars* and *The Voices of Morebath*, and Diarmaid MacCulloch's *A History of Christianity* for the particular notes they have struck, this is not to diminish huge learnings among the classic works.

But it was in following some of the scholars' leads, and my own literary nose, that it struck me what a rich and varied crop lay in the range of the source material I encountered, and what an interesting harvest could be made from it. In all this the resources of the London Library have been invaluable.

At an early stage of the book's development Richard Holloway was kind enough to give me important encouragement, and I thank him, and Kenneth Baker for his incisive advice towards the end that led to the professional skills of Unicorn Press. My editor Emily Lane has been unstintingly on the case, insightful, knowledgeable, and hawk-eyed: I could not have been more fortunate. My special thanks to her, along with designers Nick and George Newton, and Ian Strathcarron, and Simon Perks – who happily re-appeared from more years ago than either of us could quite believe.

The tactful interest of family and friends has helped to keep me on my toes. But my deepest thanks belong to Pam – for what we have shared, for her enthusiastic support, and her generous love in this and so much more.

INTRODUCTION

This anthology draws on material from fifteen hundred years of the English past. Its aim is to show the profound part played in people's lives – national, communal, personal – by the Christian Church as it became established and woven into the country's fabric. Separately, each piece has been chosen for what it has to reveal about its particular moment. Together and in their chronological sequence, they form a gallery of the unfolding story and its shifting currents. The familiar and the less familiar sit side by side, a deliberately diverse 'cloud of witnesses'.

Sources for the earlier centuries come mostly from the chronicles and biographies that the monastic age recorded in Latin of the lives and legendary deeds of their great figures – the abbots and bishops whose faith, courage, and administrative skills planted new values in the struggles of their times. Through accounts of the foundations they laid, their buildings and centres of learning, their missions and systems of pastoral care, something of the immensity of what was achieved over these centuries can be sensed, if only rudimentarily.

With the parish coming to the fore as a social unit from the Middle Ages on, the old image from the Bible of shepherd and flock grew its own local roots among the priests and the townspeople and villagers they served. Chaucer's 'poor parson' in the General Prologue to his *Canterbury Tales* is an exemplar, humbly and devotedly carrying out his calling, practising what he preached, helping the poor from his own slender means, and refusing to use his powers of excommunication to squeeze tithes out of people; he was not one to leave his flock struggling in the mire while he chased after a sinecure in London, but stayed at home and kept the wolf from the fold. In short, 'he was a shepherd and no mercenary' – and also under as few illusions about some of his colleagues as everyone else.

Chaucer's near contemporary John Mirk, in his *Instructions for Parish Priests*, presents a different facet of the authority of office encouraged in the clergy over this period. His directions for putting parishioners through the Service of Excommunication 'twice or thrice a year', with bell tolling to 'shake their hearts', culminates in a catalogue of sinfulness that even in abbreviated form speaks volumes about pastoral care of a different order.

The parish priests, who since early Norman times had been charged with offering education to the promising young, lay behind the gradual spread of literacy that broadens the range of material there is to draw on. Latin may have remained the medium of learning, but the people's tongue is palpably emerging from its shadow, so that by 1362 the Statute of Pleading established English as the official language of the law courts. During the calamity of the Black Death the priest of Ashwell, Hertfordshire, may have despairingly scored the stonework of the church tower in his basic Latin (in translation, '1350 wretched ... savage ... distraught ... there survive only the worst of the people as witnesses' can still be made out), but only decades later Chaucer and Langland were putting together the first great works of literature in their Middle English. The battle, however, to give the people access to an English Bible had a long and bitter way to go. The sheep were not free to roam these pastures unsupervised yet.

At the secular level, though, once the print medium became established (after 1476), the channels began to open for a new wealth of experience and viewpoint. Essays, poems, memoirs, diaries, satires, conversations, anecdotes, letters, articles, journals and fiction have all been drawn on here for what they convey of the spirit of their age. The cast of leaders and led, exploiters and predators find their next manifestations.

The selection intermingles the everyday tempo of people's lives with the periods of upheaval as they broke over them – the Reformation, the break with Rome and establishment of the Anglican Church, religious persecutions and martyrdoms, puritanism, Civil War, dissent and the spread of Nonconformism, to name only some. Analysis of all such issues and arguments belongs to a different undertaking: what is presented here is, as far as possible, the evidence of first-hand witnesses speaking in their own unmediated voices.

The clergy themselves could naturally be relied on for having things to say: they were men, after all, who had the education and vantage point, not to mention the leisure, to develop a keen if sometimes eccentric eye. The sons and daughters of the rectory make another interesting group to consider: they often went on to develop striking positions of their own (Addison, Wesley, Austen, Tennyson, the Brontës, Lewis Carroll ...).

One such was Matthew Arnold, son of Thomas Arnold, Headmaster of Rugby and proponent of a broad programme of Christian reform. In the quietly intimate poem 'Dover Beach', dating from his honeymoon (1851) though not published for another sixteen years, he wrote:

The Sea of Faith
Was once, too, at the full, and round earth's shore
Lay like the folds of a bright girdle furled.
But now I only hear
Its melancholy, long withdrawing roar ...

The great Anglican, Catholic and Nonconformist themes, with their sectarian and doctrinal variations, would continue to play on, and they certainly left their mark on the immense social and educational reforms of the Victorian era. But Arnold's sense of the tide running out on the old certainties is a note that sounds throughout much of the last part of the selection. The early Roman Church might have forcibly deprived the word 'heretic' of its original Greek meaning, 'able to choose', for a millennium and a half, but now 'freethinking' was abroad, whether the conservatives liked it or not. The constraints of dogma and obedience found their ancient grip loosening, whatever reluctance, or fear, too, there was in throwing off their embrace.

If the traditional hierarchies still clung on to their paternalistic grip over much of the country at large, it was badly shaken, like so much else, by the Great War; and this in turn was only the first of the twentieth century's further blows to the old deferences to class and establishment. In short, the days when ordinary people were willing to submit to being shepherded as if they were sheep, however benevolently or seemingly for their own good, were on their way out. They have found their way to different pastures, holy or unholy. Whether the churches can draw them back is yet to be seen.

Opposite
St George and the Dragon, on the screen in St Andrew, Wellingham, Norfolk, dated 1532 and defaced in the Reformation not many years afterwards. The widespread cult of the saint, brought back by Crusaders from the Middle East, found national status when Edward III instituted the Order of the Garter in 1348, with St George as its patron, leading to his becoming the patron saint of England. Only a few years before this painting, Erasmus wrote of the veneration of St George: 'They paint the saint on horseback, and drawing the horse in splendid trappings, very gloriously accoutred, they scarce refrain in a literal sense from worshipping the very beast' (*In Praise of Folly*, 1511: see p. 79).

From the autobiographical *Confession* of St Patrick (*c.* 390–461)

Patrick's Confession *is the earliest writing to come down from Christian Britain as a whole. His work was in Ireland, but he was British born, and this episode gives insight into some of the conditions of the age.*

About AD 400, in the disturbed wake of the Romans withdrawing from Britain, a sixteen-year-old boy, grandson of a priest and son of a deacon and town councillor, was captured by Irish raiders and, along with thousands of others, taken to Ireland as a slave. 'We deserved this, because we had gone away from God, and did not keep his commandments. We would not listen to our priests and their advice on how we could be saved.' He describes how, during six solitary years tending his owner's sheep, his spiritual fervour grew, until 'One night in my sleep I heard a voice saying to me: "You have fasted well. Very soon you will return to your own country." And soon I heard a voice, again, saying to me, "See – your ship is ready." It was nowhere near, but a good two hundred miles away, where I had never been and knew nobody. So, in the strength of God, I ran away from the man with whom I had been for six years.'

The ship's crew of 'pagans' was distinctly reluctant to take him on board. After three days at sea and twenty-eight days on a wilderness of coastline their food ran out, and 'The captain turned to me and said, "What about this, Christian? You tell us how great and all-powerful your God is – so why don't you start praying since we're all facing starvation? There's not a sign of another human being anywhere!" So I spoke to them with confidence: "Turn to the Lord my God with faith in all your hearts, because for him there is nothing impossible, so that he may set food in your way."' Sure enough a herd of pigs appeared, on which they feasted for two nights; and the famished Irish hunting-dogs they had as a prized part of their cargo were also saved. They gave the greatest thanks to God, and he was honoured in their eyes.

The sins of the British priests, from Gildas the Wise (*c.* 500–*c.* 570), *Concerning the Destruction and Conquest of Britain* (*c.* 540)

Gildas was a British monk at the time of the Saxon invasions. In his diatribe, British failure in the face of the heathens stemmed from God's wrath at the immorality of its princes, and, here, those who have usurped the priesthood and ecclesiastical dignity while 'wallowing like swine in their old and unhappy puddle of intolerable wickedness'.

Britain hath priests, but they are very unwise; very many that minister, but many of them that are impudent; clerks she hath, but certain of them are deceitful raveners; pastors (as they are called) but rather wolves prepared for the slaughter of souls (for they provide not for the good of the common people, but covet rather the gluttony of their own bellies), possessing the houses of the church, but obtaining them for filthy lucre's sake; instructing the laity, but showing withal most depraved examples, vices, and evil manners; seldom sacrificing, and seldom with clean hearts standing at the altars; not correcting the commonalty for their offences, while they commit the same sins themselves; despising the commandments of Christ, and being careful with their whole hearts to fulfil their own lustful desires, some of them usurping with unclean feet the seat of the apostle Peter; but for the demerit of their covetousness falling down into the pestilential chair of the traitor Judas; detracting often, and seldom speaking truly; hating verity as an open enemy, and favouring falsehoods, as their most beloved brethren; looking on the just, the poor, and the impotent with stern countenances, as if they were deprecated serpents, and reverencing the sinful rich men without any respect of shame, as if they were heavenly angels, preaching with their outward lips that alms are to be disbursed upon the needy, but of themselves not bestowing one halfpenny, concealing the horrible sins of the people, and amplifying injuries offered unto themselves, as if they were done against our Saviour Christ; expelling out of their houses their religious mother, perhaps, or sisters, and familiarly entertaining strange women, as if it were for some more secret office, or rather, to speak truly, though fondly (and not fondly to me, but to such as commit these matters) debasing themselves unto such bad creatures; and after all these seeking rather ambitiously for ecclesiastic dignities, than for the kingdom of heaven ...

Bede's *History of the English Church and People*

The Venerable Bede (c. 672–735) seems not to have ventured much out of his monastic world of Wearmouth and Jarrow in Northumbria, but his reputation was Europe-wide in his lifetime. Six hundred years later he was the only Englishman to find a place in Dante's Divine Comedy (Paradiso X). *He was the author (in Latin) of some sixty books. In his dedicatory epistle to the King of Northumbria, who would himself end his life as a monk on Lindisfarne, he wrote: 'In order to avoid any doubts in the mind of yourself, or of any who may listen to or read this history, as to the accuracy of what I have written, allow me briefly to state the authorities upon whom I chiefly depend.' He worked from copies of documents, and built up a network of correspondents. Hence his reputation as 'the Father of History'. In concluding his* History, *he wrote the following:*

With God's help, I, Bede, the servant of Christ and priest of the monastery of the blessed Apostles Peter and Paul at Wearmouth and Jarrow, have assembled these facts about the history of the Church in Britain, and of the Church of the English in particular, so far as I have been able to ascertain them from ancient writings, from the traditions of our forebears, and from my own personal knowledge.

I was born on the lands of this monastery, and on reaching seven years of age I was entrusted by my family first to the most reverend Abbot Benedict and later to Abbot Ceolfrid for my education. I have spent all the remainder of my life in this monastery and devoted myself entirely to the study of the scriptures. And while I have observed the regular discipline and sung the choir offices daily in church, my chief delight has always been in study, teaching, and writing.

Pope Gregory's letter to Abbot Mellitus on his departure for Britain in 601, from Bede's *History of the English Church and People*

Gregory sent Mellitus to Britain following Augustine's appeal for further support, and by 604 he was appointed the first bishop of London. The gradual approach to conversion advocated here did not prevent Mellitus having to take refuge in Gaul for a time. He became Canterbury's third archbishop in 619 and died in 624.

To our well-loved son Abbot Mellitus: Gregory, servant of the servants of God.

Since the departure of those of our fellowship who are bearing you company, we have been seriously anxious, because we have received no news of the success of your journey. Therefore, when by God's help you reach our most reverend brother, Bishop Augustine, we wish you to inform him that we have been giving careful thought to the affairs of the English, and have come to the conclusion that the temples of the idols among that people should on no account be destroyed, but the temples themselves are to be aspersed with holy water, altars set up in them, and relics deposited there. For if these temples are well built, they must be purified from the worship of demons and dedicated to the service of the true God. In this way, we hope that the people, seeing that their temples are not destroyed, may abandon their error and, flocking more readily to their accustomed resorts, may come to know and adore the true God. And since they have a custom of sacrificing many oxen to demons, let some other solemnity be substituted in its place, such as a day of dedication or the festivals of the holy martyrs whose relics are enshrined there. On such occasions they might well construct shelters of boughs for themselves around the churches that were once temples, and celebrate the solemnity with devout feasting. They are no longer to sacrifice beasts to the Devil, but they may kill them for food to the praise of God, and give thanks to the Giver of all gifts for the plenty they enjoy. If the people are allowed some worldly pleasures in the way, they will more readily come to desire the joys of the spirit. For it is certainly impossible to eradicate all errors from obstinate minds at one stroke, and whoever wishes to climb to a mountain top climbs gradually step by step, and not in one leap. It was in this way that the Lord revealed himself to the Israelite people in Egypt, permitting the sacrifices formerly offered to the Devil to be offered thenceforward to Himself instead. So He bade them sacrifice beasts to Him, so that, once they became enlightened, they might abandon one element of sacrifice and retain another. For, while they were to offer the same beasts as before, they were to offer them to God instead of to idols, so that they would no longer be offering the same sacrifices. Of your kindness, you are to inform our brother Augustine of this policy, so that he may consider how he may best implement it on the spot. God keep you safe, my very dear son.

The sparrow in the banqueting hall, 627, from Bede's *History of the English Church and People*

King Edwin of Northumbria holds a 'witan' about accepting Christianity, and his high priest destroys his own pagan altars.

While King Edwin hesitated to accept the word of God at Paulinus' preaching, he used to sit alone for hours, as I have said, earnestly deliberating what he should do and what religion he should follow. On one of these occasions, the man of God came to him and, laying his right hand on his head, enquired whether he remembered this sign. The king trembled and would have fallen at his feet; but Paulinus raised him and said in a friendly voice: 'God has helped you to escape from the hands of the enemies whom you feared, and it is through His bounty that you have received the kingdom that you desired. Remember the third promise that you made, and hesitate no longer. Accept the faith and keep the commands of Him who has delivered you from all your earthly troubles and raised you to the glory of an earthly kingdom. If you will henceforward obey His will, which He reveals to you through me, He will save you likewise from the everlasting doom of the wicked and give you a place in His eternal kingdom in heaven.'

When he heard this, the king answered that it was his will as well as his duty to accept the faith that Paulinus taught, but said that he must still discuss the matter with his principal advisers and friends, so that, if they were in agreement with him, they might all be cleansed together in Christ the fount of life. Paulinus agreed, and the king kept his promise. He summoned a council of the wise men, and asked each in turn his opinion of this strange doctrine and this new way of worshipping the godhead that was being proclaimed to them.

Coifi, the chief priest, replied without hesitation: 'Your Majesty, let us give careful consideration to this new teaching; for I frankly admit that, in my experience, the religion that we have hitherto professed seems valueless and powerless. None of your subjects has been more devoted to the service of our gods than myself; yet there are many to whom you show greater favour, who receive greater honours, and who are more successful in all their undertakings. Now, if the gods had any power, they would surely have favoured myself, who have been more zealous in their service. Therefore, if on examination you perceive that these new teachings are better and more effectual, let us not hesitate to accept them.'

Another of the king's chief men signified his agreement with this prudent argument, and went on to say: 'Your Majesty, when we compare the present life of man on earth with that time of which we have no knowledge, it seems to me like the swift flight of a single sparrow through the banqueting hall where you are sitting at dinner on a winter's day with your thegns and counsellors. In the midst there is a comforting fire to warm the hall; outside, the storms of winter rain or snow are raging. This sparrow flies swiftly in through one door of the hall, and out through another. While he is inside, he is safe from the winter storms; but after a few moments of comfort, he vanishes from sight into the wintry world from which he came. Even so, man appears on earth for a little while; but of what went before this life or of what follows, we know nothing. Therefore, if this new teaching has brought any more certain knowledge, it seems only right that we should follow it.' The other elders and counsellors of the king, under God's guidance, gave similar advice.

Coifi then added that he wished to hear Paulinus' teaching about God in greater detail; and when, at the king's bidding, this had been given, he exclaimed: 'I have long realised that there is nothing in our way of worship; for the more diligently I sought after truth in our religion, the less I found. I now publicly confess that this teaching clearly reveals truths that will afford us the blessings of life, salvation, and eternal happiness. Therefore, Your Majesty, I submit that the temples and altars that we have dedicated to no advantage be immediately desecrated and burned.'

In short, the king granted blessed Paulinus full permission to preach, renounced idolatry, and professed his acceptance of the faith of Christ. And when he asked the chief priest who should be the first to profane the altars and shrines of the idols, together with the enclosures that surrounded them, Coifi replied: 'I will do this myself; for now that the true God has granted me knowledge, who more suitable than I can set a public example and destroy the idols that I worshipped in ignorance?' So he formally renounced his empty superstitions and asked the king to give him arms and a stallion – for hitherto it had not been lawful for the chief priest to carry arms or to ride anything but a mare – and, thus equipped, he set out to destroy the idols. Girded with a sword and with a spear in his hand, he mounted the king's stallion and rode up to the idols. When the crowd saw him, they thought he had gone mad; but without hesitation, as soon as he reached the shrine, he cast into it the spear he carried and thus profaned it. Then, full of joy at his knowledge of the worship of the true God, he told his companions to set fire to the shrine and its enclosures and destroy them. The site where these idols once stood is still shown, not far east of York, beyond the river Derwent, and is known today as Goodmanham. Here it was that the chief priest, inspired by the true God, desecrated and destroyed the altars that he had himself dedicated.

The Easter Controversy: King Oswy calls a synod of English and Irish clergy at Abbess Hilda's community in Whitby, 664, from Bede's *History of the English Church and People*

Wilfrid (634–709), the key figure at the Synod of Whitby, was a bishop for forty-six years, although twenty-six of them were spent in exile, and Abbot of Ripon; after his death he was considered a saint. The traditions and influence of the Celtic Church in Northumbria had run from St Columba's Iona through St Aidan to Lindisfarne Priory and his successor Colman; here, Wilfrid wins dominance for the Roman orthodoxy now being established in York.

When Wilfrid had received the king's command to speak, he said: 'Our Easter customs are those that we have universally observed in Rome, where the blessed Apostles Peter and Paul lived, taught, suffered, and are buried. We have also seen the same customs generally observed throughout Italy and Gaul when we travelled through these countries for study and prayer. Furthermore, we have learned that Easter is observed by men of different nations and languages at one and the same time, in Africa, Asia, Egypt, Greece, and throughout the world wherever the Church of Christ has spread. The only people who stupidly contend against the whole world are those Irishmen and their partners in obstinacy the Picts and Britons, who inhabit only a portion of these the two uttermost islands of the ocean.'

In reply to this statement, Colman answered: 'It is strange that you call us stupid when we uphold customs that rest on the authority of so great an Apostle as John, who was considered worthy to lean on our Lord's breast, and whose great wisdom is acknowledged throughout the world.' ...

To which Wilfrid answered: 'With regard to your father Columba and his followers ... I do not doubt that they are true servants of God and dear to Him, and that they loved Him in primitive simplicity but in devout sincerity. Nor do I think that their ways of keeping Easter were seriously harmful, so long as no one came to show them a more perfect way to follow. Indeed, I feel certain that, if any Catholic reckoner had come to them, they would readily have accepted his guidance, as we know that they readily observed such of God's ordinances as they already knew.

'But you and your colleagues are most certainly guilty of sin if you reject the decrees of the apostolic see, indeed of the universal Church, which are confirmed by holy writ. For, although your fathers were holy men, do you imagine that they, a few men in a corner of a remote island, are to be preferred before the universal Church of Christ throughout all the world? And even if your Columba – or, may I say, ours also if he was the servant of Christ – was a saint potent in miracles, can he take precedence before the most blessed prince of the Apostles, to whom our Lord said: 'Thou art Peter, and upon this rock I will build my Church, and the gates of hell shall not prevail against it, and I will give unto thee the keys of the kingdom of heaven'?'

When Wilfrid had ended, the king asked: 'Is it true, Colman, that these words were spoken to that Peter by our Lord?' He answered: 'It is true, Your Majesty.'

Bishop Wilfrid (634–709) and his companions are rescued from the sea and from the Vikings, 666, from Stephen of Ripon's *Life of St Wilfrid*

The Life *was written soon after the death of Wilfrid.*

While they were crossing the British sea on their return from Gaul with Bishop Wilfrid of blessed memory, and the priests were praising God with psalms and hymns, giving the time to the oarsmen, a violent storm arose in mid-ocean and the winds were contrary, just as they were to the disciples of Jesus on the sea of Galilee. The wind blew hard from the south-east and the foam-crested waves hurled them on to the land of the South Saxons which they did not know. Then the sea left the ship and men high and dry, fled from the land, and, laying the shores bare, withdrew into the depths of the abyss.

Forthwith a huge army of pagans arrived intending to seize the ship, to divide the money as booty for themselves, carry off the captives whom they vanquished and incontinently put to the sword all who resisted them. The holy bishop spoke to them soothingly and peaceably, and sought to purchase the lives of his companions by the promise of a large sum of money. The enemy however were fierce, and, hardening their hearts like Pharaoh, were unwilling to let the people of God depart, proudly declaring that they treated as their own possessions all that the sea cast up on the land. The chief priest of their idolatrous worship also took up his stand in front of the pagans, on a high mound, and like Balaam attempted to curse the people of God, and to bind their hands by means of his magical arts.

Thereupon one of the companions of our bishop took a stone which had been blessed by all the people of God and hurled it from his sling in the manner of David. It pierced the wizard's forehead and penetrated to his brain as he stood cursing; death took him unawares as it did Goliath, and his lifeless body fell backwards onto the sand. The pagans then got ready for battle, but in vain did they draw up their array against the people of God. For the Lord fought for the few, even as when Gideon with his 300 warriors at the bidding of the Lord slew 120,000 Midianite warriors at one onslaught. In the same way these companions of our holy bishop being well-armed and brave at heart though few in number (there were 120 of them, equal in number to the years of the age of Moses), formed a plan and made a compact that none should turn his back upon another in flight, but that they would either win death with honour or life with victory, God being able with equal ease to bring either event to pass. So St Wilfrid the bishop and his clergy on bended knees lifted their hands again to heaven and gained the help of the Lord. For as Moses continually called upon the Lord for help, Hur and Aaron raising his hands, while Joshua the son of Nun was fighting against Amalek with the people of God, so this little band of Christians overthrew the fierce and untamed heathen host, three times putting them to flight with no little slaughter, though, marvellous to relate, only five of the Christians were slain.

Then the great bishop prayed to the Lord his God, who straightaway bade the tide return before its usual hour and, while the pagans, on the coming of their king, were preparing with all their strength for a fourth battle, the sea came flowing back and covered all the shore, so that the ship was floated and made its way into the deep. They returned thanks to God for the glorious way He had honoured them, and with a south-west wind they prosperously reached a port of safety at Sandwich.

Abbot Ceolfrid sends church architects to the king of the Picts, c. 710, from Bede's *History of the English Church and People*

Abbot Ceolfrid survived an attack of plague at Monkwearmouth (In-Gyrwum) along with the seven-year old Bede, and became his mentor.

At this time, Nechtan, king of the Picts, living in the northern parts of Britain, convinced after assiduous study of church writings, renounced the error hitherto maintained by his nation about the observance of Easter and adopted the Catholic time of keeping our Lord's resurrection with all his people. In order to do this more smoothly and with greater authority, the king asked help from the English people, whom he knew to have based their practice long previously on the pattern of the holy Roman apostolic Church. So he sent messengers to the venerable Ceolfrid, abbot of the monastery of the blessed Apostles Peter and Paul, which he ruled most illustriously as successor of the above-mentioned Benedict. This monastery stands at the mouth of the river Wear, and also close to the river Tyne at a place called In-Gyrwum [Monkwearmouth]. The king requested Ceolfrid to write him a letter of guidance that would help him to refute those who presume to keep Easter at the wrong time; and although he was relatively well informed on these matters himself, he also required information about the form and reason for the tonsure that clergy should wear. In addition, he asked that architects be sent him in order to build a stone church for his people in the Roman style, promising that he would dedicate it in honour of the blessed prince of the Apostles and that he and his people would follow the customs of the holy apostolic Roman Church, as far as they could learn them in view of their remoteness from the Roman people and from Roman speech. The most reverend abbot Ceolfrid complied with his devout wishes and requests, sending him the architects he asked.

Alcuin (*c.* 732–804) writes to King Ethelred of Northumbria following the sack of Lindisfarne on 8 June 793

Alcuin was a product of the York school and then its librarian and leading figure until he was enlisted by Charlemagne to bring his scholarship and other skills to Aachen for the revival of learning on the Continent. Lindisfarne in 793, and Iona two years later, were among the earliest targets of the Scandinavian raids to come. Ethelred's marriage to the daughter of Offa, the powerful King of Mercia, seems to have brought him limited security, but he was assassinated in 796. Lines copied into a manuscript by an Irish monk read:

Bitter is the wind tonight
It tosses the ocean's white hair:
Tonight I fear not the fierce warriors of Norway
Coursing on the Irish Sea.

To his beloved lord, King Ethelred, and all his nobles, Alcuin, a humble deacon, sends greetings.

It is because I remember your tender affection, my brothers, fathers and Christian lords, and desire that divine mercy may long keep prosperous this country of ours, which by his grace he generously gave us long ago, that I constantly give you my counsel, dear comrades ...

We and our fathers have now lived in this fair land for nearly three hundred and fifty years, and never before has such an atrocity been seen in Britain as we have now suffered at the hands of a pagan people. Such a voyage was not thought possible. The church of St. Cuthbert is spattered with the blood of the priests of God, stripped of all its furnishings, exposed to the plundering of pagans – a place more sacred than any in Britain. Suffering and disaster have started in the very place where, after the departure of St. Paulinus from York [633], the Christian religion began in our nation.

Consider closely and carefully, brothers, in case this unprecedented, unheard-of disaster is due to some unheard-of evil practice. I do not say that the sin of fornication has not existed among our people in the past. But since the days of King Aelfwald, fornication, adultery and incest have flooded the land to such an extent that these sins are committed without any shame even among nuns. Why should I mention greed, robbery and judicial violence when it is as clear as day how these crimes have increased everywhere. A plundered people is proof of it. He who reads Holy Scripture and studies ancient history and considers the way the world develops will find that kings have lost kingdoms and peoples their lands for sins of this kind, and when powerful men have wrongly seized the property of others, they have rightly lost their own.

Consider the luxurious dress, hair and behaviour of leaders and people. See how you have wanted to copy the pagan way of cutting hair and beards. Are not these the people whose terror threatens us, yet you want to copy their hair? And why this wasteful clothing, beyond the needs of man and beyond the practice of our ancestors? Luxury in princes means poverty for the people.

In conduct be upright, pleasing God and winning praise from men. Be rulers, not ravagers, of the people, pastors, not predators. You received your honours at God's hand: keep his commandments that he who has been your benefactor may be your saviour. Obey God's priests. They must give account to God for their advice to you, and you for your obedience to them.

Alfred the Great (849–899): preface to his translation from the Latin of Pope Gregory's *Cura pastoralis (Pastoral Care)*

Gregory's celebrated treatise was written c. 590 *to give guidelines to all priests and bishops on how to be pastors to their flocks and 'physicians to their hearts'.*

King Alfred sends words of greeting lovingly and amicably ... And I would have it known that very often it has come to my mind what men of learning there were formerly throughout England, both in religious and secular orders, and how there were happy times then throughout England; and how the kings, who had authority over the people, obeyed God and his messengers; and how they not only maintained their peace, morality and authority at home but also extended their territory outside, and how they succeeded both in warfare and in wisdom; and also how eager were the religious orders both in teaching and in learning as well as in all the holy services which it was their duty to perform for God; and how people from abroad sought wisdom and instruction in this country; and how nowadays, if we wished to acquire these things, we would have to seek them outside. Learning had declined so thoroughly in England that there were very few men on this side of the Humber who could understand their divine services in English, or even translate a single letter from Latin into English: and I suppose that there were not many beyond the Humber either. There were so few of them that I cannot recollect even a single one south of the Thames when I succeeded to the kingdom. Thanks be to God Almighty that we now have any supply of teachers at all! Therefore I beseech you to do as I believe you *are* willing to do: as often as you can, free yourself from worldly affairs so that you may apply that wisdom which God gave you wherever you can. Remember what punishments befell us in this world when we ourselves did not cherish learning nor transmit it to other men. We were Christians in name alone, and very few of us possessed Christian virtues.

When I reflected on all this, I recollected how – before everything was ransacked and burned – the churches throughout England stood filled with treasures and books. Similarly, there was a great multitude of those serving God. And they derived very little benefit from those books, because they could understand nothing of them, since they were not written in their own language. It is as if they had said: 'Our ancestors, who formerly maintained these places, loved wisdom, and through it they obtained wealth and passed it on to us. Here one can still see their track, but we cannot follow it.' Therefore we have now lost the wealth as well as the wisdom, because we did not wish to set our minds to the track.

When I reflected on all this, I wondered exceedingly why the good, wise men who were formerly found throughout England and had thoroughly studied all those books, did not wish to translate any part of them into their own language. But I immediately answered myself, and said: 'They did not think that men would ever become so careless and that learning would decay like this; they refrained from doing it through this resolve, namely they wished that the more languages we knew, the greater would be the wisdom in this land.' Then I recalled how the Law was first composed in the Hebrew language, and thereafter, when the Greeks learned it, they translated it all into their own language, and all other books as well. And so too the Romans, after they had mastered them, translated them all through learned interpreters into their own languages. Similarly all the other Christian peoples turned some part of them into their own language. Therefore it seems better to me – if it seems so to you – that we too should turn into the language that we can all understand certain books which are the most necessary for all men to know, and accomplish this, as with God's help we may very easily do provided we have peace enough, so that all the free-born young men now in England who have the means to apply themselves to it, may be set to learning (as long as they are not useful for some other employment) until the time that they can read English writings properly. Thereafter one may instruct in Latin those whom one wishes to reach further and wishes to advance to holy orders.

When I recalled how knowledge of Latin had previously decayed throughout England, and yet many could still read things written in English, I then began, amidst the various and multifarious afflictions of this kingdom, to translate into English the book which in Latin is called *Pastoralis*, in English 'Shepherd-book', sometimes word for word, sometimes sense for sense, as I learned from Plegmund my archbishop, and from Asser my bishop, and from Grimbald my mass-priest and from John my mass-priest. After I had mastered it, I translated it into English as best I understood it and as I could most meaningfully render it; I intended to send a copy to each bishopric in my kingdom; and in each copy there will be an *aestel* [a pointer] worth fifty mancuses. And in God's name I command that no one shall take that *aestel* from the book, nor the book from the church. It is not known how long there shall be such learned bishops as, thanks be to God, there are now nearly everywhere. Therefore I would wish that they [the book and the *aestel*] always remain in place, unless the bishop wishes to have the book with him, or it is on loan somewhere, or someone is copying it.

The famous Alfred Jewel, now in the Ashmolean, Oxford, may be the socket-head of one of these very aestels *or pointers. A 'mancus' was a gold coin. In his biography of Alfred (893) Asser told of the King's fostering of 'craftsmen who were skilled in every craft' and the 'incomparable treasures' they fashioned, and the story of his comparatively late acquisition of literacy.*

The re-founding of the monastery of Peterborough, from the *Anglo-Saxon Chronicle* (Peterborough text), 963

In the late ninth century several monasteries received copies of a manuscript chronicle outlining British history from the time of the birth of Christ, and then kept their own chronicles of the years' events. The decline of Latin literacy meant that the monks turned to the vernacular Anglo-Saxon for their accounts; in the case of the Peterborough text *this was maintained until 1137. The monk-scribe records Aethelwold's rebuilding of destroyed churches, notably the re-founding of the monastery of Peterborough from the ruins left by the Danes, its independent status, and the details of its endowments.*

In the same year King Edward appointed Abbot Athelwold to the bishopric of Winchester; and he was consecrated on the vigil of St. Andrew, which happened on a Sunday. On the second year after he was consecrated, he made many minsters, and drove out the clerks from the bishopric, because they would hold no rule, and set monks therein. He made there two abbacies, one of monks, another of nuns. That was all within Winchester.

Then came he afterwards to King Edgar, and requested that he would give him all the minsters that heathen men had before destroyed; for that he would renew them. This the king cheerfully granted; and the bishop came first to Ely, where St. Etheldritha lies, and ordered the minster to be repaired; which he gave to a monk of his whose name was Britnoth, whom he consecrated abbot: and there he set monks to serve God, where formerly were nuns. He then bought many villages of the king, and made it very rich.

Afterwards came Bishop Athelwold to the minster called Medhamsted [Peterborough], which was formerly ruined by heathen folk; but he found there nothing but old walls, and wild woods. In the old walls at length he found hid writings which Abbot Hedde had formerly written; – how King Wulfhere and Ethelred his brother had wrought it, and how they freed it from king, bishop and all worldly service; and how Pope Agatho confirmed it with his writ, as also Archbishop Deusdedit. He then ordered the minster to be rebuilt, and set there an abbot who was called Aldulf, and made monks where before was nothing.

He then came to the king, and let him look at the writings which before were found; and the king then answered and said: 'I Edgar grant and give to-day, before God and before Archbishop Dunstan, freedom to St. Peter's minster at Medhamsted, from king and from bishop; and all the thorps that thereto lie; that is, Eastfield, and Dogsthorpe, and Eye, and Paston. And so I free it, that no bishop have any jurisdiction there, but the abbot of the minster alone. And I give the town called Oundle, with all that thereto lieth, called Eight Hundreds, with market and toll; so freely, that neither king, nor bishop, nor eorl, nor shire-reeve, have there any jurisdiction, nor any man but the abbot alone, and whom he may set thereto. And I give to Christ and St. Peter, and that too with the advice of Bishop Athelwold, these lands; – that is, Barrow, Warmington, Ashton, Kettering, Castor, Ailsworth, Walton, Werrington, Eye, Longthorpe and a minster in Stamford. These lands and all the others that belong to the minster I bequeath clear; that is, with sack and sock, toll and team, and infangthief [the right to arrest and try a thief caught in one's domain]: these privileges and all others bequeath I clear to Christ and St. Peter.

'And I give the two parts of Whittlesey Mere, with waters and weirs and fens, and so through Meerlade along to the water that is called Nene; and so eastwards to Kingdelf. I will that there be a market in the town itself, and that no other betwixt Stamford and Huntingdon. And I will that thus be given the toll; – first, from Whittlesey Mere to the king's toll of Norman Cross Hundred, then backward again from Whittlesey Mere through Meerlade along to the Nene, and as that river runs to Crowland; and from Crowland to Must, and from Must to Kingsdelf and to Whittlesey Mere. And I will that the freedom, and all the privileges, that my predecessors gave, should remain; and I write and fasten this with the rood-token of Christ.'

Then answered Dunstan, the Archbishop of Canterbury, and said: 'I grant that all the things here given and spoken, and all the things that thy predecessors and mine have given, shall remain firm; and whosoever breaketh it, then give I him God's curse, and that of all saints, and of all hooded heads, and mine, unless he come to repentance. And I give expressly to St. Peter my mass crozier and my stole and my vestments, to serve Christ.'

The reign of King Edgar 'the Peaceable', following the Danish Wars, 959–975, from Henry of Huntingdon, *History of the English People*

Henry (c. 1088–1155), Archdeacon of Huntingdon, benefited from the wealth and patronage of the bishops of Lincoln, and was commissioned to write a 'History of the English to the present day' from sources. From a period when there was the constant threat of warfare, he offers here a model combination of ruler and religion.

Edgar the peaceable, brother of King Eadwig, reigned for sixteen years. In his days this land received many benefits, and by the grace of Almighty God, which as far as he could he earned by his devotion, he reigned in peace for the whole of his life. For he very energetically extended the faith of Christ in his kingdom, and very clearly promoted the works of salvation by his own example. Beloved of God and of men, he sought always to pacify the peoples of his land, and none of his predecessors had been able to maintain the kingdom in such great peace and joy. Indeed, he himself honoured God's name, and often searching into God's law, he gladly learned and joyfully taught it, and in word and deed was quick to encourage his people to perform good works. The omnipotence of the Lord rewarded His servant Edgar for his good deeds not only in the future world but also in the present, for he subjugated to his will all the petty kings, earls, and people of the whole country, with fear and love, without battle or any other mental anguish. The repute and famous name of the king were widely spread throughout all lands, and foreigners came to see his glory and to hear his teaching from his own mouth. But he erred in giving too much security to the pagans who were settled in his country under him, and was eager to favour foreign visitors more than was right. For nothing is quite perfect in human affairs.

In Edgar the Peaceable's fifth year, the venerable Aethelwold auspiciously received the bishopric of Winchester. In the second year of his episcopate he ejected the canons living in the Old Minster at Winchester, who were observing their rule indolently and negligently, and implanted monks. In our own time this church has been removed from the place because it was too closely joined to the mother church which is the bishop's see. With the consent of the bishop and abbot of that monastery, therefore, it was placed outside the walls of the city. Now Bishop Aethelwold was a builder of fences, who diverted the paths of iniquity and planted the roots of charity. He was a sower of the best counsel. On his advice, King Edgar founded new plantations and the trees of tenderness most gratifying to God. He founded the abbey of Glastonbury. He built the abbey of Abingdon on the Thames. He established the abbey of Peterborough, near Stamford. He set up the abbey of Thorney, near that of Peterborough, in a very beautiful site in the middle of the fens. It was on the advice of Bishop Aethelwold, indeed, that Aethelwine, the king's ealdorman, founded the abbey of Ramsey on a very pretty island in the midst of the same fens. The marshland of which I am speaking is very wide and beautiful to behold, washed by many flowing rivers, adorned by many meres, great and small, and green with many woods and islands, among which are the church of Ely, the abbey of Ramsey, the abbey of Chatteris, the abbey of Thorney, the abbey of Crowland, and on its edge are the abbey of Peterborough, the abbey of Spalding, the church of St Ives on the river Ouse at Huntingdon, the church of St Giles on the river Granta at Cambridge, and the church of Holy Trinity at Thetford.

In the eleventh year of his reign [969] King Edgar ordered the Isle of Thanet to be ravaged, because they had scorned the royal rights, not, however, raging wildly like an enemy, but rather as a king, punishing evil with evil.

In the thirteenth year of his reign, King Edgar was consecrated at Bath on Whitsunday. Then after Whitsun he led his army to Leicester [in fact Chester], where six kings came to meet him. They all submitted to his authority and pledged the loyalty that was owed to him as lord, to serve him by land and sea according to him overlordship.

Edgar the Peaceable, the magnificent king, the second Solomon, in whose time a foreign army never came into England, to whose dominion the kings and princes of England were subject, and to whose power even the Scots bent their necks, after he had ruled for sixteen years and two months, died as happily as he had lived. For he who had lived well could not die badly, he who had founded so many churches for God and in a brief time, had established so many good deeds for eternity.

Exeter Book, No. 26, *c.* 995

The Old English manuscript that this riddle comes from, in Exeter Cathedral Library, is a unique survival – worn, battered, leaves missing, stained, burnt in places – and the chief source for what remains of Anglo-Saxon poetry. It includes nearly a hundred riddles, often as highly informative as they are charming. They seem to have been intended for live performance before the community.

No. 26 shows the whole process of creating a book, from the preparation of the parchment to its decoration and binding. And not just any book, of course, but the Word of the Protector of Men. The symbolic importance of the book as vehicle of the Word is visible in the manuscript's artistic magnificence, and can be further inferred from the less visible economies that supported the monastic scriptoria. *The* Lindisfarne Gospels *alone required the hides of a hundred young cattle, and excavations on Holy Island have uncovered the remains of many hundreds of their bones.*

An enemy ended my life, deprived me
of my physical strength; then he dipped me
in water and drew me out again,
and put me in the sun where I soon shed
all my hair. After that, the knife's sharp edge
bit into me and all my blemishes were scraped away;
fingers folded me and the bird's feather
often moved over my brown surface,
sprinkling meaningful marks; it swallowed more wood-dye
(part of the stream) and again travelled over me
leaving black tracks. Then a man bound me,
he stretched skin over me and adorned me
with gold; thus I am enriched by the wondrous work
of smiths, wound about with shining metal.
Now my clasp and my red dye
and these glorious adornments bring fame far and wide
to the Protector of Men, and not to the pains of hell.
If only the sons of men would make use of me
they would be the safer and the more victorious,
their hearts would be bolder, their minds more at ease,
their thoughts wiser; and they would have friends,
companions and kinsmen (courageous, honourable,

trusty, kind) who would gladly increase
their honour and prosperity, and heap
benefits upon them, ever holding them
most dear. Ask what I am called,
of such use to men. My name is famous,
of service to men and sacred in itself.

Colloquy 28, A thief is punished, from the *Colloquies of Aelfric Bata*, c. 1000

In his own words: 'In short, one called Aelfric Bata, a very short monk, wrote these suitably varied pieces for boys, so as students they might absorb some introduction to speaking Latin.' The forty-two conversations range over everyday topics of monastic life – rising, washing, students arguing, preparing writing materials, clothing – in a style that suggests they may have been written for classroom performance. The boys, initially probably only twelve years old, will have had to give up both their families and the language they grew up with for an all-male institution and its requirement of Latin.

My boys, who among you stole the apples of this monastery yesterday? Speak to me – let me know whether any of you stole them.

We don't know, father. We think that thief of ours might have stolen them, along with his accomplice.

I think so too. You bad boys! Why did you two steal our apples?

No, sir, no!

Don't believe them. They're not telling the truth. They were the only ones in the apple orchard at dawn. They stole a lot of apples and filled up their robes with them. Then they went to their beds and put the apples in their lockers for safekeeping. They gave me a few to eat.

Believe, me, you're lying and accusing us falsely, God knows, you devil's brat. Who teaches you to speak falsely like this, if not the evil devil? You slander and never stop lying. You're the guilty one, and we're innocent.

You tell lies against us because you're a liar and an apostate from God and man. You steal anything you find in the cloister, oratory, refectory or dormitory, you ravening wolf. You often steal our belts and coins, and the purses and money of our brothers – not to mention their sheepskins, hoods, cowls, combs, cups, wine jugs, wine cups, nets, books, parchment, cheeses, loaves, morsels, hams, poultry and fish. Among your classmates you're nothing but a devil and the greatest thief of all who now live on earth. That accomplice of yours always behaves badly like you do. You're always covering up your evil designs and sinfulness. Everything you get with your wickedness you give to the peasants who pay you back with butter, milk, or chickens. But it shouldn't happen again the way you and your comrade think it will. Tell us now, you villainous boy, what do you think about this deed of yours that you commit almost every day? Is what we're saying against you true or false?

I can't deny it. What you say is true. But from now on I want to stop and do penance.

That's what you always say, but you always do it again. Our master will take care of all this in the way that seems best to him.

I certainly won't hesitate to deal with it. Do you have any canes here?

No, but we'll get some for you.

Get me some good canes right away.

Here, we've got some canes now, sir.

Do you want to beat him?

Yes, sir, right now, if we ought to.

Take two canes. One boy stand on the right of his arse and one on the left. Take turns like this beating his arse and his back. First you two beat him well, and then I will.

Be lenient this time, father, and spare me. That's enough!

Hit harder, you fool. He's making fun of your strokes. He doesn't feel them at all.

Father, from this moment I'll stop the lying I'm suffering for. I've been beaten and punished enough this time. Show me some kindness and leniency. I'm about to die.

You're not dead yet – you're still alive.

Wulfstan (d. 1023), from 'Sermon of the Wolf to the English'

Wulfstan was Archbishop of York. This sermon was probably delivered on 16 February 1014, before the 'witan' at York, on the English humiliations at the hands of the Danish army brought on by their own sinfulness. During the failures of 1009 he had drafted King Ethelred II's edict of three days of barefooted, bread-and-water national penance and prayer on pain of punishment. He continued to serve as both elder statesman and lawmaker under the new regime of King

*Cnut until his death. In this extract he invokes the perils of Gildas's time over four hundred years earlier (**see p. 2**).*

But oh, in the name of God let us do as is necessary for us, protect ourselves as we most eagerly may, lest we all perish together. There was a wise man of the nation in the time of the Britons called Gildas. He wrote about their misdeeds, how they angered God overmuch with their sins so that at last he allowed the English army to conquer their land and destroy the host of the Britons entirely. And that happened, as he said, through great theft and through greed for ill-gotten property, through a lawless people and through unjust judgments, through the laziness of bishops and through the evil cowardice of God's preachers who were silent about the truth all too often and who mumbled in their jaws where they should call out. Also through the foul lust of the people and through gluttony and manifold sins they forfeited their land and destroyed themselves.

From the *Life* of St Wulfstan (*c.* 1008–1095)

This Wulfstan was Bishop of Worcester under Edward the Confessor, an envoy for Harold before Hastings, and one of the few Anglo-Saxons to continue to hold high office after the Conquest. His chaplain and companion Coleman (d. 1113) wrote his Life *in English; the original has long been lost, but William of Malmesbury's Latin version, written sometime between 1124 and 1143, has come down to us. (Wulfstan was canonized in 1203.)*

There was in the city of Worcester a wife, whose house was well provided above what is needful for life, and whose comely person was apt to draw the curious eyes of them that looked on it. She came often to the Church, but rather to be gazed at that to hearken to the oracles of God, as was proved by her daring to court Wulfstan, then the Prior, with words of flattery. It was vain, for Wulfstan's modesty was far above her beauty and her promises. For a while she nursed her hidden wound, and was afraid to show it; but at last her desire grew stronger than her shame, and as the Prior chanced to be standing near her in the Church, she took hold of his garment. He checked her with a stern glance – but she begged him in God's name not to reject what she had to say. Wulfstan, supposing she wished to make her confession, went aside with her. But the woman, seizing her opportunity, began to whisper in the holy man's ears words of evil counsel savouring of the wiles of woman and the cunning of the serpent. For a long time she had thought of speaking to him of a thing which might well be of profit to them both. She had a home abounding in riches, but with no man to govern it. Both her parents were dead, and her husband far away. Wulfstan's wisdom should take upon it the charge. He should rule the household at his will: and order the spending of the money. On that he bade her give her money to the poor, and herself take the veil: but she replied, not so: what she desired and implored was that he should lay aside for a moment his priestly strictness and consent to share her bed. 'Twas but a little fault to enjoy the embraces of a woman: even if it were a grave fault he could redeem the guilt of a venial sin by almsgiving from her wealth. She had enough and to spare, and she would not grudge it.

The Prior endured no more: but breaking in upon her speech, and making the sign of the Cross on his forehead, Away, he cried, with the hatred thou dost deserve, thou fuel of lust, thou vessel of Satan. His stern words were followed by a blow with his open hand, which, in his zeal for chastity, he laid so heartily on the cheek of the snarling woman that the sound of it was heard outside the doors of the church.

The story of this deed ran through the town, and was for many days spoken of wherever men met together – how this second Joseph rejected a wanton woman in his heart, and smote her with his hand.

A ship was miraculously rescued at the height of a storm by the succouring presence of Wulfstan's image in spirit form, rousing its crew from despair.

This miracle had such power with the men of Bristol that they were wholly minded to do whatsoever Wulfstan bade them. And at the last he removed from among them a very ancient custom, which was so rooted in their hearts that neither the love of God nor the fear of King William had yet prevailed to do away with it. For they used to buy men from all England and carry them to Ireland in the hope of gain; nay, they even set forth for sale women whom they had themselves gotten with child. You might well groan to see the long rows of young men and maidens whose beauty and youth might move the pity of a savage, bound together with cords, and brought to market to be sold. It was a damnable sin, a piteous reproach, that men, worse than brute beasts, should sell into slavery their own womenfolk, nay, their own blood.

This long-established custom, come down from their forefathers, Wulfstan, as I have said, blotted out little by little. He knew them for a stiff-necked generation, hard to bend; so he would sojourn in their coasts two months or three together. Each Sunday he would come to Bristol, and by his preaching sow the good seed, which in due time sprang up and bore fruit – so that not they not only forsook their sin, but were an example to all England. One of them, who stubbornly transgressed the counsel of the Bishop, they cast out of the city and blinded his eyes. Therein I praise their goodwill, but blame their deed. But when the minds of rough men are once stirred, no force of reason can withstand them.

Relics from Laon on tour in England, from the *Autobiography* of Guibert, Abbot of Nogent sous Coucy, *c.* 1113/14

Guibert (1053–1124) says of the holy relics at Laon: 'Now there was a splendid amulet that was carried with a casket of great note which contained part of the shift of the Virgin Mother and of the sponge lifted to the lips of the Saviour and of His Cross and, I believe, some of the hair of the Virgin Lady.' At Easter 1112, when the Bishop of Laon had blocked the granting of a charter to the town, the leading citizens had him murdered and his palace was set on fire. The fire spread, and the cathedral was badly damaged. Months later, the famous miracle-working relics were taken on fund-raising tours in neighbouring France and in England.

After that they determined to journey to the parts overseas, and having travelled down to the ocean straits and found certain wealthy merchants with fleets for that voyage, they were carried across with good fortune, as far as the weather was concerned. But behold, they see the vessels of fierce pirates, whom they much feared, coming on directly against them. And as they steered towards them with oars sweeping the waters and their prow cutting through the waves and were now scarcely a furlong off, the carriers of the relics, being in great fear of the pirates, there rose in their midst one of our priests, who, lifting on high the casket in which the relics of the Queen of Heaven were kept, forbade their approach in the name of the Son and of the Mother. At once at that command the pirate craft fell astern, driven off as speedily as they had with eagerness approached. Then was there thanksgiving among the delivered and much glorification, and the merchants with them offered many gifts to the gracious Mary.

They had a fair voyage then to England, and when they were come to Winchester, many miracles done therein brought renown. At Exeter events not unlike these occurred and produced many gifts. Let me pass over the ordinary healing of sickness and touch only on exceptional cases. For we are not writing a Pyrrhic ode on them; let them do that for themselves; nor what happened to each person, but are culling outstanding examples. In almost all places they were received with reverence, and according to the means of the people, but when they came to a certain village, they were not admitted by the priest within the church, nor by the people within their dwellings. Two houses they found without inmates, and in one they bestowed themselves and their baggage, and fitted up the other for the holy relics.

And so, as that wicked people persisted in their obstinacy against the holy things, on the morrow the clergy left that place, and behold the sound of terrible thunder was accompanied by lightning from the clouds, and this, falling on their town, burnt everything to ashes. And oh, wonderful distinction made by God! Whereas those two houses were in the midst of those that were burnt, they remained for a manifest testimony by God that, for their irreverence shown towards the Mother of God, those unhappy men had suffered from the burning. But that wicked one who had inflamed the cruelty of the barbarians, when he ought to have taught them, after collecting the furniture saved (to his satisfaction) from the heaven-sent fire, carried it away either to the river or the sea, intending to cross over. But there all the property he had gathered together was destroyed on the spot by lightning. Thus these people of the country, being uninstructed in understanding of the mysteries of God, were taught by their own punishment.

They came to another town in which there was a great fervour of offerings to the sacred relics both by reason of the fame and certainty of the miracles and for many reasons. A certain Englishman standing in front of the church said to his companion, 'Let us go and drink.' But the other said, 'I have not any money.' 'I,' said the first, 'will get some.' 'How will you get it?' said he. 'I think,' said the first, 'from those clerics, who by their lying and their tricks get so much money out of the silly people. I will certainly manage in some way or other to get out of them the cost of my drink.'

After saying that, he entered the church and went to the consistory, in which the relics were placed, and pretending he wished to show his reverence for them by kissing them, putting his mouth against them with his lips open, he sucked up some coins that had been offered. Then, going back to his companion, he said, 'Come and let us drink, for we have money now for our draught.' 'How did you get it,' said he, 'since you had none before?' 'I got it by carrying away in my cheek some of the money given to those cheats in the church.' 'You have done ill,' said the other, 'in taking that from the holy offerings.' 'Silence,' he replied, 'and get along to the nearest tavern. Why so much talk?'

They drank the sun down into the ocean. But when evening came on, he who had stolen the money from the holy altar, mounting his horse, said he was going home. And when he had reached a wood near, he made a noose and hanged himself on a tree. There dying a miserable death, he paid the penalty for his sacrilegious lips. Out of the many things which the queenly Virgin did in England let it be sufficient to have culled these.

William of Malmesbury (*c.* 1095–1143): two extracts from his *Chronicle of the Kings of England*

William of Malmesbury's father was Norman and his mother English, which gives a particular interest to what he writes about the Norman Conquest and its aftermath. He spent his life as a monk and librarian at Malmesbury Abbey, where he wrote his Chronicle of the Kings of England. *Bede was his declared model: 'Though born in a remote corner of the world, he was able to dazzle the whole earth with the brilliancy of his learning.'*

The old church at Glastonbury

The church of which we are speaking, from its antiquity called by the Angles, by way of distinction, 'Ealde Chirche', that is the Old Church, of wattle-work, savoured somewhat of heavenly sanctity even from its very foundation, and exhaled it over the whole country, claiming superior reverence even though the structure was mean. Hence, whole tribes of the lower orders came here, thronging every path; here assembled the opulent, divested of their pomp, and it became the crowded residence of the religious and the clerical. For, as we have heard from men of old time, here Gildas – a historian neither unlearned nor inelegant, to whom the Britons are indebted for whatever notice they obtain among other nations – captivated by the sanctity of the place, took up his abode for a series of years.

This church, then, is certainly the oldest I am acquainted with in England. In it are preserved the mortal remains of many saints, some of whom we shall notice in our progress, nor is any corner of the church lacking in the ashes of the holy. The very floor, inlaid with polished stone, the sides of the altar and even the altar itself, above and beneath, are laden with the multitude of relics.

Moreover, in the pavement may be remarked on every side stones designedly interlaid in triangles and squares, and figured with lead, under which if I believe some sacred enigma to be contained, I do no injustice to religion. The antiquity, and multitude of its saints, have endued the place with so much sanctity that, at night, scarcely anyone presumes to keep vigil there, or, during the day, to spit upon its floor. He who is conscious of pollution shudders throughout his whole frame: no one ever brought hawk or horses within the confines of the neighbouring cemetery who did not depart injured either in them or in himself. Within the memory of man, all persons who, before undergoing the ordeal of fire or water [i.e. enduring red-hot iron or boiling water to prove innocence], there put up their petitions, exulted in their escape, one only excepted: if any person erected a building in its vicinity, which by its shade obstructed the light of the church, it forthwith became a ruin.

Effects of the Norman Conquest

This was a fatal day to England, a melancholy havoc of our dear country, through its change of masters. For it had long since adopted the manners of the Angles, which had varied considerably over the years: for in the first period after their arrival they were barbarians in their looks and manners, warlike in their habits, heathens in their rites; but, after embracing the faith of Christ, by degrees, and in process of time, from the peace they enjoyed they came to regard weapons merely in a secondary light, and gave their whole attention to religion. I say nothing of the poor, the wretchedness of whose fortune often restrains them from overstepping the bounds of justice: I pass over men of ecclesiastical rank, whom sometimes respect for their profession and the fear of shame prevent from deviating from the truth: I speak of princes, who from the greatness of their power might have full liberty to indulge in pleasure – some of these, in their own land, others when in Rome, adopted the monk's habit, obtained a heavenly kingdom, and a saintly intercourse. Many others lived their whole lives embracing the present world in outward appearance only, in order to pour out their treasures on the poor, or share them amongst monasteries. What shall I say of the great numbers of bishops, hermits and abbots? Does not the whole island blaze with such numerous relics of its natives that you can scarcely pass a village of any consequence without hearing the name of some new saint, let alone all those whose names are lost through lack of records?

Nevertheless, in process of time the desire for religion and the written word had fallen into decay for several years before the arrival of the Normans. The clergy, contented with a very slight degree of learning, could barely stammer out the words of the sacrament, and a person who understood grammar was an object of wonder and astonishment. The monks mocked the rule of their order by wearing fine vestments, and indulging in every kind of food. The nobility, given up to luxury and wantonness, went not to church in the morning after the manner of Christians, but merely, in a careless manner, heard matins and masses from a hurrying priest in their chambers, amid the blandishments of their wives. The commonalty, left unprotected, became a prey to the powerful, who amassed fortunes by either seizing on their property or selling them into slavery abroad – although it is a more native trait of this people to incline to revelry than the accumulation of wealth. There was one custom, repugnant to nature, which they adopted, that is, to sell their female servants when pregnant by them and after they had satisfied their lust, either to public prostitution or into foreign slavery.

Drinking in sessions was a universal practice, in which occupation they passed entire nights as well as days. They consumed their whole substance in mean and despicable houses – unlike the Normans and French, who in their noble and splendid mansions lived with frugality. The vices attendant on drunkenness followed, enervating the human mind: thus it turned out that, engaging with William with more rashness and hasty fury than military skill, they doomed themselves and their country to slavery by a single, simple victory. 'For nothing is less effective than rashness, and a violent start will either come to a halt or be rebuffed.'

In sum, the English at that time wore short garments reaching to mid-knee; they had cropped hair and shaven beards, gold-braceleted arms and tattooed skin. They were accustomed to eat till they became surfeited, and to drink till they were sick – habits that were adopted by their conquerors. I would not, however, concur with a universal application of such behaviour in every Englishman. I know that many of the clergy of that time trod the path of sanctity in blameless lives, and many of the laity too, of all sorts and conditions, were well-pleasing to God. ...

The Normans too, if I may also talk about them, were at that time (as they are nowadays as well) proud in their apparel and fastidious in their food, though not excessively so. They are a race inured to war, and can hardly live without it, ferocious in attack, and where sheer strength does not work, ready to resort to other devices, or bribery. As I have told, they live, economically, in large buildings, envious of their equals and competitive with their superiors. They plunder their subjects, yet protect them from others.

They are loyal to their lords, though a slight offence can lead to perfidy. What constitutes treachery is measured by its chance of success, and money alters opinions. They are, though, the kindest of people, and hold strangers in equal honour with themselves. They also intermarry with their vassals.

Their arrival revived religious observances, which everywhere in England had fallen lifeless. You could see churches being built in every village, and monasteries in the towns and cities, in a style of architecture not previously encountered; you could observe the country flourishing with renewed practices, so that any man of wealth considered it was a lost day if he had failed to mark it with some magnificent deed. But having enlarged on these points, let us follow William's course of actions.

When his victory was complete, he arranged for his dead to be buried with great pomp, allowing his opponents the liberty of doing likewise if they thought fit. He sent Harold's body to his mother, who begged it unransomed, though she had proffered large sums by her emissaries. Once obtained, she buried it at Waltham, a church which Harold had built at his own expense, in honour of the Holy Cross, and had endowed four canons.

From the *Life of Anselm* by Eadmer (d. *c.* 1124)

Eadmer was a monk at Christ Church, Canterbury. When Anselm (1033/34–1109) was appointed archbishop there he became his close associate, and eventually wrote his biography. In this passage he expands Anselm's teaching on the three 'estates' of society, clerics, warriors and labourers.

Exemplum of the sheep, the oxen and the dogs. The purpose of sheep is to provide milk and wool; that of oxen is to work the ground, and that of dogs is to defend sheep and oxen from wolves. If each type of animal performs its duty, God protects them ... Similarly he has set up orders which he has established in view of the various duties which must be fulfilled in this world. He has established some – clerks and monks – so that they may pray for the others and so that, full of gentleness, like sheep, they may give others the milk of preaching to drink and may inspire in them a fervent love of God by the wool of good example. God has established the peasants to sustain their own lives and other people's, as the oxen do by their work. God has established yet others – the warriors – to show force in so far as it is needful, and to defend those who pray and those who till the land from enemies such as wolves.

A Dominican friar's version of the 'three estates'

This trope of the three estates found regular usage among the clergy.

God has ordained three classes of men, namely, labourers such as husbandmen and craftsmen to support the whole body of the Church after the manner of feet, knights to defend it in the manner of hands, clergy to rule and lead it after the manner of eyes. And all the aforesaid who maintain their own status are of the family of God. The Devil, however, finds a certain class, namely the slothful, who belong to no Order. They neither labour with the rustics, nor travel about with the merchants, nor fight with the knights, nor pray and chant with the clergy. Therefore they shall go with their own Abbot, of whose Order they are, namely, the Devil, where no Order exists but horror eternal.

From the *Life of St Godric* by Reginald of Durham (d. 1190)

Reginald's exceptionally full account of the Life *was written before Godric's death in 1170, and was evidently based on notes from their conversations. It gives a fascinating insight into the social mobility possible in his time.*

Godric was born in the township of Walpole in Norfolk, to a couple of slender rank and wealth. ... As he grew to manhood, he began to follow more prudent ways of life, and to learn carefully the teachings of worldly forethought. Wherefore he chose not to follow the life of a husbandman, but rather to study, learn and exercise the rudiments of more subtle notions. For this reason, aspiring to the merchant's trade, he began to follow the pedlar's way of life, first learning how to gain in small bargains and things of insignificant price; and thence, while still a youth, his mind advanced little by little to buy and sell and gain from things of greater cost. ... For, early on, he was wont to wander with small wares around villages and farmsteads of his own neighbourhood, but in time he entered into deals with city merchants. Thus it was not long before the youth ... who had trudged for weary hours from village to village and farm to farm, did so profit by his increase of age and wisdom as to travel with associates of his own age through towns and boroughs, fortresses and cities, to fairs and all the various stalls of the market-place in pursuit of his trade. ...

Yet in all things he walked with simplicity; and, in so far as he yet knew how, it was always his pleasure to following the steps of the truth. For, having learned the Lord's Prayer and the Creed from his very cradle, he often turned them over in his mind, alone on his longer journeys. …

After four years as a pedlar in Lincolnshire, Godric travelled to St Andrews in Scotland and then Rome, after which he began trading by sea, the constant perils of which 'led him to worship certain of the Saints with more ardent zeal, venerating and calling upon their shrines, and giving himself up by wholehearted service to those holy names'.

At last his great labours and cares bore much fruit of worldly gain. For he laboured not only as a merchant but also as a shipman, to Denmark and Flanders and Scotland; in all of which lands he found certain rare, and therefore more precious, wares, which he carried to other parts where he knew them to less familiar, and coveted by the inhabitants beyond the price of gold itself. …

For he was vigorous and strenuous in mind, whole of limb and strong in body. He was of middle stature, broad-shouldered and deep-chested, with a long face, clear and piercing grey eyes, bushy brows, a broad forehead, long and open nostrils, a nose of comely curve, and a pointed chin. His beard was thick, and longer than the ordinary, his mouth well-shaped, with lips of moderate thickness; in youth his hair was black, in age as white as snow; his neck was short and thick, knotted with veins and sinews; his legs were somewhat slender, his instep high, his knees hardened and horny with kneeling; his whole skin rough beyond the ordinary, until all this roughness was softened by old age. … He knew, from the aspect of sea and stars, how to foretell fair or foul weather. In his various voyages he visited many saints' shrines, to whose protection he was wont most devoutly to commend himself; more especially the church of St. Andrew in Scotland, where he most frequently paid his vows. On the way thither, he often touched at the island of Lindisfarne, where St. Cuthbert had been bishop, and at the isle of Farne, where the Saint had lived a hermit's life – and where Godric (as he often used to say himself) would meditate on his life with tears. From this he began to yearn for solitude, and to hold his trading life in lower esteem.

After sixteen years as a merchant Godric took the cross as a pilgrim to Jerusalem, returning to England via Compostela, and on his second pilgrimage to Rome

his mother besought his leave to bear him company, which he gladly granted, and willingly paid her every filial service that was her due. They came therefore to London; and they had scarcely departed from thence when his mother took off her shoes, going thus bare-footed to Rome and back to London. Godric, humbly serving his parent, was wont to bear her on his shoulders.

With his parents' blessing, he distributed his wealth among the poor and finally embarked on an austere life as a hermit. The remains of Finchale Priory, near Durham, mark where he spent his last forty years.

The nineteen years of King Stephen's reign, from the *Anglo-Saxon Chronicle* (Peterborough text), 1137

This extract summarises the 'Anarchy' of Stephen's reign from the perspective of the Benedictine monastery at Peterborough.

I neither know nor can tell all the horrors they did to the unhappy people in this land, that lasted nineteen years while Stephen was king; and ever it was worse and worse. They laid taxes on the towns all the while, and called it 'tenserie', protection money; when poor men had no more to give, they plundered and burnt all the towns, so that though you might journey all day, never would you find a man staying in a town, nor land tilled. Then was corn dear, and meat, and cheese and butter, for there was none in the land. Poor men died of hunger, some went out for alms who were once powerful men, and some fled out of the land.

Never yet was more wretchedness in the land, nor ever did heathen men do worse than they did, for against all custom they spared neither church nor churchyard, but seized all the goods therein, and later burnt the church and all together. Nor did they spare in the land either abbots or priests, but plundered monks and clerics – and every man robbed another if he could. If two or three men came riding to a town, all the township fled before them, believing they were robbers. Bishops and clergy did not cease from cursing them, but it was nothing to them, for they were all utterly forsworn and lost.

Whenever the soil was tilled, the earth bore no corn, for the land was all ruined with such deeds; and they said openly that Christ slept, and his saints. Such, and more than we know how to say, we suffered nineteen years for our sins.

In this evil time abbot Martin held his abbey twenty years, half a year and eight days with great toil, provided the monks and the guests with all that was needed, and kept much cheer in the house. Notwithstanding this, he worked on the church, added thereto lands and rents, and enriched it very much, and bestowed vestments upon it. And he brought them into the new minster on St. Peter's mass day with much ceremony; this was in the year, from the incarnation of our Lord, 1140, and in the twenty-third from the destruction of the place by fire. He journeyed to Rome, and was there received by pope Eugenius, from whom he obtained privileges – one for all the lands of the abbey, another for the land belonging to the office of sacrist; and had he lived longer, he meant to do the same for the treasurer's office.

He regained lands that powerful men held by force: from William Malduit, who held the castle of Rockingham, he won Cottingham and Easton Maudit; from Hugo de Waterville he won Irthlingborough and Stanwick, and sixty shillings a year from Aldwinkle. He made many monks, planted a vineyard, constructed many buildings, and changed the layout of the town to better than it was before. He was a good monk and a good man, therefore God and good men loved him.

The meeting at Northampton between King Henry II and Archbishop Thomas Becket before the Constitutions of Clarendon, 1164

Henry II's convention at Northampton in October 1163 was called with the aim of curbing Church privileges and legal powers and restricting papal authority. Becket resisted. The following year he was tried, accused of treason, and sentenced; he took refuge in France. This extract, from one of the many biographies of Becket that came out after his murder in 1170, is generally accepted as the work of the Cistercian monk Roger, of Pontigny Abbey, where Becket spent the first two years of his exile.

The king, for the present frustrated of his intent, not long after when he was at Northampton called the archbishop to him, wishing to try his constancy, if perchance he might turn him and bend him to his will. When the archbishop drew nigh and his approach was made known to the king, he – it is not known with what design – sent certain men to meet him and say, 'The king is lodged in the town with many men and you are come with a great company. There is not room to hold you both, and so the king commands you to await him here. Here he will come to speak with you.'

And when the archbishop had turned aside into a field, straightaway without delay came the king, to whom the archbishop sped in order to give him the due salutation of reverence. But when because of the neighing and kicking of their lusty steeds on which they rode they could not come close to each other, they changed their horses and withdrew together. Thus began the king: 'Have I not raised you from a humble and poor man to the height of honour and dignity? It seemed but a small thing to me unless I also made you father of the kingdom, with precedence even to myself. How is it that so many benefits, so many proofs of my love towards you, known to all, have so soon passed from your mind that you are not only ungrateful but now oppose me in everything?'

The archbishop answered: 'Far be it from me, my lord. I am not unmindful of the favours which, not you alone, but God who is the giver of all things deigned to confer on me through you. Far be it from me, therefore, to have the ingratitude to resist your will in anything, so long as it accords with the will of God. Your Grace knows how faithful I have been to you, from whom I long only for a worldly reward. How much more then must I do faithful and true service to Almighty God, from whom I have received temporal and look for spiritual benefits? You indeed are my lord, but He is both your Lord and mine, and to ignore His will so as to obey yours would be fitting neither for you nor for me. For at His awful judgment we shall both be judged as servants of one Lord, where neither of us can answer for the other, and each of us, all pretences failing, will receive according to his deeds. We must obey our temporal lords but not go against God. As St. Peter says, 'We must obey God rather than men.'

To this the king replied, 'I want no sermon from you. Are you not the son of one of my peasants?'

'It is true,' said the archbishop, 'I am not "sprung from royal race." But neither was St. Peter, the chief of the Apostles, on whom the Lord deigned to confer the keys of heaven and the headship of the whole church.'

'True,' said the king, 'but he died for his Lord.'

The venerable prelate replied, 'And I will die for my Lord when the time is come.'

Then said the king, 'You trust too much to the ladder you have mounted by.'

And the archbishop answered, 'I trust and lean upon God, for cursed is the man who puts his hope in man. Nevertheless, whatever you may say and answer, I am ready for your honour and good pleasure, saving my order. But on these things which concern your honour and the salvation of your soul you would do better to consult one whom you have always found faithful and useful in your counsel than those who, under pretended concern for your honour, have kindled this flame of envy, and strive to take revenge on me, who has never hurt them. You will not deny that I was ever your faithful servant before I took on holy orders: how much more ought you to believe me faithful in all things when raised to the office of the priesthood?'

Bishop Hugh of Lincoln performs a miracle, 1198/99, from Adam of Eynsham's *Life of St Hugh of Lincoln*

This episode has been dated to 1198 or early 1199. Adam (c. 1155–1233) was one of the witnesses who testified to the event as a miracle before the commission on Hugh's canonization in 1219.

At dawn one Sunday Bishop Hugh was journeying through the township already mentioned, which since the olden days has been called Cheshunt. Most of his people had gone on ahead, and when he with a few attendants reached the centre of the township he was suddenly surrounded by a throng of people giving vent to loud lamentations. They rushed up to him, and besought him to bless with the sign of the holy cross one of their neighbours who was possessed by a terrible demon. The door of his house was open, and when Hugh saw him lying bound inside, he groaned in spirit, and not content to bless him from a distance, he dismounted from his horse, exclaiming 'Alas, this is not as it should be.' He saw the possessed man lying prostrate with his head tied to a post and each of his hands to great stakes fixed in the ground. His feet also were bound to a beam. The unhappy wretch was rolling his eyes, and his mouth kept twisting now in this direction and now in that with a ghastly leer. At one moment he stuck his tongue out, and at the next gnashed his teeth, and then opening his mouth wide he showed the whole back of this throat which appeared to the spectators like some horrible cavern.

The bishop hastened to him, and after signing him with the cross, bent down, and kept his outstretched right hand for a little while over his mouth, at the same time reciting in a low voice the chapter of the gospel 'In the beginning was the Word'. Whilst this was happening he saw that the poor fellow was holding his head still and motionless, which had been turning all the time this way and that, and like dogs when they fear a beating, and was moving his eyes fearfully and furtively in various directions. Having continued the gospel up to the words 'full of grace and truth', the bishop raised himself and looked silently at the sufferer for some time, who suddenly turned away his face from him and derisively put out his tongue. Then the valiant assailant of the powers of darkness waxed indignant, and rapidly mixed water and salt and blessed them in the form prescribed by the Church, and sprinkled it upon him. He ordered the bystanders to put some of the water in his mouth, and after giving them all his blessing, mounted his horse and rode away. They one and all blessed him, declaring that the demoniac's own bishop had passed that way a little while before, and when he saw him had in panic dug his spurs into his horse and had not merely passed by the sufferer without helping him, but galloped away as if pursued by the Furies. The man, who was from then onwards delivered from the demon, did his best to reform his life in every way. He spent much time in pious pilgrimage to the shrines of saints, and after living devoutly for some years, finally made a good and peaceful end.

I learned about his death recently from his neighbours in the township I have mentioned, who said they had been present at his cure. There I also heard how he came to be possessed by the demon. Early one morning he was sleeping near London in a ship which had brought wood to be sold. Suddenly the evil spirit had entered into him, and he had begun to tear and rend his fellow sailors and his own limbs with his hands and teeth. It was only with difficulty and the assistance of a large number of people that he was secured and tied to a great beam in the ship, and so brought home.

The Bishop's great rebuilding of Lincoln Cathedral was still in its early stages when he was buried there in November 1200. 'The grandeur of his funeral defies description', wrote Adam. 'It was attended by three archbishops, fourteen bishops, over a hundred abbots, many earls and two kings, not to mention a multitude which no-one could number of humbler folk' – testimony to Bishop Hugh's recognition as one of the great figures of his age.

Walter Map (*c.* 1130–*c.* 1210), from *Courtiers' Trifles*

Walter Map went from boyhood in the Welsh Borders to become a secular clerk in the service of Gilbert Foliot, Bishop of Hereford (later Bishop of London), and finally Archdeacon of Oxford. Such a career was possible for a learned and witty secular man of talent. Here he mocks Bernard of Clairvaux and the habits of the Cistercian Order.

Two White abbots [i.e. Cistercians] were conversing about Bernard in the presence of Gilbert Foliot, bishop of London, and commending him on the strength of his miracles. After relating a number of them, one of the abbots said: 'Though these stories of Bernard are true, I did myself see that on occasion the grace of miracles failed him. There was a man living on the borders of Burgundy who asked him to come and heal his son. We went, and found the son was dead. Dom Bernard ordered his body to be carried into a private room, turned everyone out, threw himself upon the boy, prayed, and got up again: but the boy did not get up; he lay there dead.' 'Then he was the most unlucky of monks', said I; 'I have heard before now of a monk throwing himself upon a boy, but always, when the monk got up, the boy promptly got up too.' The abbot went very red, and a lot of people left the room to have a good laugh. ...

As to the Cistercians' clothing, their food and their long hours of work, the people to whom they are kind (because they cannot do them any harm) say that their clothing is insufficient to keep off cold, their food to keep off hunger, and the work they do is enormous, and from this they argue to me that they cannot be covetous because their acquisitions are not spent on luxuries. But oh how simple is the answer! Do not usurers and other slaves of avarice clothe and feed themselves most poorly and cheaply? Misers crouch over their treasures on their deathbeds; they do not amass them for delicacies, but for their delight; they mean not to use them but to keep them. If you make a point of toil, cold and food, why, the Welsh lead a harder life in all these respects. ...

Now in this regulation about clothing I find cause for surprise in regard of the breeches, in that they are obliged to wear them at the service of the altar, and they are taken off when they go thence. This is the privilege of the sacred vestments; but this garment is not sacred, is not reckoned among those of the priests or Levites, and is not blessed. It has, however, its meaning: it hides that which is better hid, 'tis Venus' privy seal, her barrier against publicity. A reason why the Cistercians do not use it was given me by someone, namely to preserve coolness in that part of the body, lest sudden heats provoke unchastity. But I say, No. It would be better to shorten the inner tunic from the belt downwards, keeping the upper part, and not discarding the breeches, which are a respectable garment and approved by every other order, from the privy regions.

The lord king, Henry the Second, of late was riding as usual at the head of all the great concourse of his knights and clerks, and talking with Dom

Reric, a distinguished monk and an honourable man. There was a high wind, and lo! a white monk was making his way on foot along the street and looked round, and made haste to get out of the way. He dashed his foot against a stone and was not 'being borne up by angels' at the moment, and fell in front of the feet of the king's horse, and the wind blew his habit right over his neck, so that the poor man was candidly exposed to the unwilling eyes of the lord king and Reric. The king, that treasure-house of all politeness, feigned to see nothing, looked away, and kept silence; but Reric said, sotto voce, 'A curse on this bare-bottom piety.' I heard the remark and was pained that a holy thing was laughed at, though the wind had only intruded where it was rightfully at home. However, if spare diet and rough clothing and hard work (and all these they claim) cannot tame them, and if they must have ventilation too to keep Venus at bay, let them go without their breeches and feel the draught. I know that our flesh – worldly and not heavenly though it be – does not need such defences: with us, Venus, apart from Ceres and Bacchus, is cold: but perhaps the Enemy attacks those more fiercely whom he knows to be more stoutly fenced in. Still, the monk who tumbled down would have got up again with more dignity had he had his breeches on.

From the *Chronicle* of Jocelin de Brakelond (1173–1202)

The Chronicle *records events in the Benedictine abbey dedicated to St Edmund, King and Martyr, which by then had grown into one of England's wealthiest monasteries, its liberties virtually identical to the whole of present-day West Suffolk. Jocelin served successively as chaplain to Abbot Samson, guest master and later almoner. Abbot Samson built the abbey's enormous Norman west front (which does not survive); among his actions, he had outwitted the Bishop of Ely over a whole stand of oaks that each had earmarked for his building programme. The two extracts below convey something of the relations between the monastery and the town – Bury St Edmunds – that had grown up in its orbit.*

Brawl and penitence

On the day after Christmas people gathered in the abbey burial ground, and there were wrestling matches and contests between Abbot Samson's servants and the burgesses of the town; words turned into blows, and commotion into wounds and bloodshed. On hearing about it, the Abbot quietly summoned some of the people who had joined in watching the events while keeping their distance and demanded from them the names of the miscreants in writing; then he had them all brought before him in the Chapel of St. Denys on the day after the feast day of the Blessed Archbishop Thomas; and he invited none of the burgesses to his table as was his custom over the first five days of Christmastide. So on the appointed day, after sixteen men of legal standing had taken the oath and all the evidence had been heard, the Abbot spoke:

'It is clear that these miscreants have breached the canon law with *sententia lata* [with automatic penalty]. But because they are laymen and therefore have no understanding of the enormity of their crime of sacrilege, in order to ensure that everybody else feels a proper sense of fear I will publicly name and excommunicate them. And, for the justice carried out here to be undeniable, I will commence with my servants and the members of my own household.'

And so it was done. We put on our stoles and lit our candles, and all the men obediently trooped out of the church, undressed and, entirely naked except for their underclothes, prostrated themselves before the church door. When the Abbot's staff – monks and clerks – came weeping to him to tell him that there were more than a hundred naked men lying out there, the Abbot too was in tears. His word and face expressed the rigour of the law while he covered up the pity in his heart; he wished his counsellors would compel him to pardon the penitents, knowing that mercy is a higher virtue than justice, and that the Church takes back all who are penitent.

So after they had all been severely flogged and absolved, every man swore that he would stand by the Church's judgment of sacrilege, and the next day they were given penances according to canon law. Thus it was that the Abbot restored all to the harmony of agreement, making terrible threats to all those who in either word or deed showed any sign of trouble. But he publicly banned any gatherings or spectacles from being held in the burial ground. In this manner everyone was returned to the blessing of peace, and over the days that followed the burgesses feasted with their lord abbot amid great rejoicing.

The Abbot was not above criticism

A wise man has said, 'There is no one who is blessed from every aspect,' and neither was Abbot Samson. [Jocelin cites two instances of his taking bribes for appointments, and how he told his critic, 'I shall not desist from doing what I want, for you any more than for some boy.'] There is another stain of wrong-doing that he will wash away with penitential tears, God willing, and prevent one bad deed dragging down such a heap of good ones. The fish-pond next to the new mill at Babwell, he raised its level so much that, because of the damming up of the stream, there is not a man, rich or poor, with land along the water from the Town Gate to the East Gate, who hasn't lost his garden and his orchards. The Cellarer's pasture over on the other bank is ruined, the neighbours' arable grounds have been spoilt. The Cellarer's meadow is wrecked, and the orchard belonging to the Infirmarer is under water from the overflow, and all the neighbours are complaining. The Cellarer actually spoke about his huge loss in full Chapter meeting, but he got the angry reply that his fish-pond was not going to be lost for the sake of our meadow.

Gerald of Wales (*c.* 1147–*c.* 1223) sees the lavish refectory of Canterbury Priory

Gerald was known in Latin as Giraldus Cambrensis because he came from a Welsh-Norman family. He travelled, studied and wrote extensively. He was chaplain to Henry II for a time, and Archdeacon of Brecon, but his hopes of becoming Bishop of St David's were never realised. Here he describes in his autobiography a visit to Canterbury Priory on his return from the Continent.

Proceeding therefore on his journey and crossing the sea of Flanders Gerald came to Canterbury, and ate on the day of the Holy Trinity with the monks of that monastery in their refectory at the Prior's bidding. Sitting then in that hall with the Prior and the greater monks at the high table he noted there, as he was wont to relate, two things; that is to say, the excessive use of gestures, and the profusion of the dishes. For the Prior sent so many gifts of meat to the monks who served him, and they on their part to the lower tables, and the recipients gave so many thanks and were so extravagant in their gesticulations of fingers and hands and arms and in the whisperings whereby they avoided open speech, (wherein all showed a most unedifying levity and licence), that Gerald felt as if he were sitting at a stage play or among a company of actors and buffoons; for it would be more appropriate to their Order and to their honourable estate to speak modestly in plain human speech than to use such a dumb garrulity of frivolous signs and hissings.

Of the dishes themselves and their multitude what can I say but this, that I have often heard him relate how six courses or more were laid in order (or shall I say in disorder?) upon the table, and these of the most sumptuous kind. At the very last, in the guise of being the principal course, masses of herbs and greens were brought to all the tables, but they were scarcely touched in the face of so many kinds of fish, roast and boiled, stuffed and fried – so many dishes tricked out by the cook's art with eggs and pepper – so many savouries and sauces composed by that same art to stimulate gluttony, and to excite the appetite. Add to this, there was such abundance of wine and strong drink – of piment and claree, of new wine and mead and mulberry wine, and all intoxicating liquors in such plenty – that even beer, which the English brew excellently (especially in Kent), found no place; but rather beer stood as low in this regard as the pot-herbs among the other dishes. You could see such an excessive and sumptuous superfluity here of meats and dishes as was enough to weary not only the guest but also the onlooker. What would Paul the Hermit have said to this? or Anthony? or Benedict, father and founder of monastic life?

Dreams, pigs, tithes and bets, from *Vitae Patrum* by Peter, Prior of Aldgate, London (1139/40–1221)

Tithes – the annual payment to the priest of a tenth of all parish produce – were a constant source of argument and ill-feeling, and did not formally end until 1836.

There was once a devout and well-respected man from Orpington called John who told me the following story. 'One night, as I was sleeping at home, it seemed that I rose from my bed early one Saturday and ordered my horse to be saddled. Then (so it seemed) I mounted him and rode to my own church at Cray to hear mass, left my servant-lad outside with the horse, and went inside just as they were singing the *Alleluia Veni Sancte Spiritus*, for Gilbert the parish priest had already begun. After hearing the Gospel and the whole service, I went out to my horse just at the moment when Gilbert's groom appeared to come for him too. When I asked the lad where his master was going, he said, 'To the Chapter at Eynsford.' So I waited for a while until the priest left the church and came towards me. When he said he was indeed going to Eynsford, I said, 'Let's ride together, if you agree, as I am going to my sister's house, which is on the way.'

'So off we rode until we came to a field where (so it appeared) I saw a fine-looking sow, fat and white with black spots, and behind her a litter of fine sucking-pigs with the same markings. Father Gilbert, riding alongside me, said, "Do you see those piglets running after their mother, Sir John? Now mark my words, although there are ten of them and their master is my own parishioner, he won't give me a single one for tithe."

'So I reined in my horse to count the piglets, but when there only appeared to be nine I turned to the Father and said, "You priests are all far too greedy, seeing everything through the eyes of your own advantage rather than sober judgment. Count them again, please, Sir Priest, and you will not find the ten you need for your legal entitlement."

'The priest was very surprised, counted them again, still found ten, and we ended up in a sort of friendly disagreement – the upshot of which was (as it seemed in my dream) that we both made a solemn promise that whoever was proved to be wrong would pay the other a forfeit of four gallons of wine. We made a very careful count together, and I won my wager – and just as I was celebrating my victory I woke up!

'In the course of time the whole dream slipped from my mind. But the very next day every jot and tittle of what I had seen in my sleep actually happened with my eyes wide awake – Saturday morning ride, Cray church, sung mass, the priest's groom, agreeing to ride together, seeing the litter of pigs in the field; and my dream suddenly came back to me as everything was vividly the same: in fact I solemnly swear that I recognised mother and litter better than my own pigs at home. This all made me rein in my horse and laugh with amazement. The priest, wondering at my sudden change of behaviour, asked what I was laughing at, and I dodged his questions as vaguely as I could.

'And now, looking at the piglets, he spoke exactly the words I had heard in my dream, and I too said my piece about greedy priests and their dubious arithmetic, and we pledged that the winner would have four gallons of wine off the loser – and after a careful count I won. Which', said John, 'delighted me much more by what I learnt from it than for any earthly gain, because I was taught from my very own experience that the soul has something of the divine in it, and I have been firmly convinced of the immortality of the soul ever since.'

'Woe unto the world because of scandals!': the Prior of Thetford and his murder in 1248, related by Matthew Paris

Matthew Paris (c. 1200–1259) was a Benedictine monk at St Alban's Abbey, the large and wealthy foundation much used by king and nobles as the first day's staging-post north of London (it is said to have had stabling for the horses of three hundred guests), and was consequently full of opportunities for information gathering. He was a vivid chronicler of the events of his own times, and a fine illustrator too.

In order to fulfil what is written in the gospel, 'It must needs be that scandals come; woe unto the world because of scandals!', in the same year, in December, the prior of Thetford, who was a Savoyard by birth, a monk of Cluny who claimed to be a blood relative, or kinsman, or at least compatriot, of the queen and who rode the high horse as a result, summoned his brothers, a knight called Bernard and a beastly cleric called Guiscard, to come to his house at Thetford. There, forgetful of matins, he remained all night till cock-crow with them, indulging in immoderate feasting and drinking. He seldom went to mass, was rarely present at the canonical hours, and in the morning, drunk, he vomited forth his nocturnal potations. If the cries of the hungry poor came to him, 'These things were a minor care to his mind'. And if one of the aforesaid brothers, Bernard, went away, the other, Guiscard, whose belly was like a bladder in frosty weather and whose body was a cart-load, stayed longer; and all the monks' provisions were engulfed in the Charybdis of his belly. Afterwards, thoroughly gorged, he poured insults on them.

While this prior was entertaining his brothers in this unbecoming manner, disgracefully squandering the substance of his little church and, so it is said, exceeding the bounds of moderation in his cups, a dispute arose between him and a certain monk, Welsh by birth. The prior was spitefully and uncharitably trying to send this monk, summoned by him from Cluny not long before, back there against his will and in spite of his perfectly reasonable excuses for not wanting to go. But when the prior yelled at him fearfully, swearing that, willy nilly, he should go on pilgrimage, pilgrim's wallet and all, this devil of a monk, in a fit of violent temper or madness, drew a knife and disembowelled him, with no regard for committing such a crime within the church precincts. When the wounded prior, with the death-rattle sounding in his throat, tried by shouting to summon the monks, or at least to arouse them, he could not do so because his windpipe had closed. Again the monk rushed at him and with frantic blows, three or four times repeated, buried the knife right up to the hilt in his lifeless body. Thus this wretch, not without great dishonour and harm to the monastic order, and with the anger and vengeance of God on both sides, sent another wretch to Tartarus.

I have narrated all this in full so that the reader, warned and prevented, will steer clear of such crimes, lest he be precipitated into a similar confusion by an angry God. The author of the crime was seized by those arriving on the scene and taken into custody tightly bound.

When this came to the notice of the lord king, urged by the queen's complaints, be ordered the miscreant to be committed to the lowest dungeon of Norwich Castle, where he would be deprived of all light, notwithstanding the cause of the blessed Thomas Becket, the martyr, who constantly held to and maintained, even to the shedding of his own blood and brains, on behalf of a certain homicidal priest, the principle that a cleric, and especially a priest, should not be condemned by the judgement of a secular court nor hanged after being deprived of holy orders. He accepted martyrdom for the principle that God does not punish twice for the same offence, mitigating the punishment of sinners and rewarding them beyond merit, and that a single misdeed ought to be adequately reprieved by a single reasonable penalty.

'Howe Angell in bodily shappe is peynted', from Bartholomew the Englishman, *On the Property of Things* (*c.* 1250)

Bartholomew's text was translated from the Latin in 1397 by John Trevisa, a Cornishman who became Vicar of Berkeley.

Although angels' kind have no substance, or lineaments, or bodily shape, yet angels are depicted with a bodily likeness, and scripture makes mention of various limbs and shapes. But by the denomination of limbs that are visible, the invisible workings of heavenly intelligences are to be understood. So, when angels are painted with long locks and curling hair, this represents their pure affections and measured thoughts. For the hair of the head betokens thoughts and affections, which spring from the root of thought and mind. ... And they are depicted beardless so as to indicate and pay heed to how they never pass the stage of youth, or wax feeble in virtues, or fail from old age. Feet they do have, but they are always barefoot, as the movement of their affections God-wards is sequestered from all sinful desire. And truly, they are portrayed with feathers and wings since their spirit is alien and clean of all earthly cogitation; they are loftier in power and intelligence, and enraptured with the deepest contemplation of the love of god. Their dress is fiery red because they have been wrapped in the light and the mantle of the knowledge and love of god (Psalm 103: 'They are clothed with light as with a garment'). They are arrayed with arms and weapons of war, for with their aid good men are often given succour, and defended in war, and the battle of between body and soul. And they are shown playing the harp because those deserving of comfort, by their help and prayers, do not fall into the sorrow of despair and hopelessness. They bear trumpets in their hands to signify the way that they sound out and comfort us, and stir us to take profit always in goodness. Many suchlike things are written of the dress and doings of angels, betokening their wonderful works.

A late thirteenth-century Dominican friar-preacher has a story at the expense of the parish priest

When a certain very rich rustic, who was hard-hearted towards both the poor and his own soul, had amassed so much wealth that he had a chest filled with money and other treasures, he had it set in front of him as he lay on his deathbed. By the time that the priest could be summoned to make his Will, the sick man had already lost the power of speech. The priest, accordingly, suggested a plan to his wife and brother whereby a 'Ha!' from the patient might be taken to indicate approval of what was proposed to him, and silence the mark of disapproval. Having won agreement for this plan, our priest said to the testator –

'Do you wish to bequeath your soul to God after your decease, and your body to Mother Church for burial?', and the latter replied, 'Ha!' Then said the priest to him – 'Do you wish to leave twenty shillings to the fabric of your church, where you have chosen to be buried?' But the other made no reply and kept a complete silence. Forthwith the priest pulled him violently by the ear, whereat the man cried – 'Ha!' Then said the priest, 'Write down twenty shillings for the church fabric, for see, he has granted it with his "Ha!"'

After that the priest pondered how he could get for himself the chest with the aforesaid treasure. So he said to the sick man – 'I have some books, but I have no chest to keep them in. That coffer over there would be most useful to me. Would you like me, therefore, to have that coffer to put my books in?' But the other said nothing to these remarks. Then the priest pinched his ear so hard that those who were present declared afterwards that the pinch drew blood from the man's ear. Then the enfeebled rustic, in a loud voice, said to the priest before them all – 'Oh you greedy priest, by Christ's death never shall you have from me so much as a farthing of the money that is in that chest!' Having thus spoken, he turned to his devotions and expired. Accordingly, his wife and relatives divided the money between them. This happened in England, so it is said.

The Months

The routines of the agricultural year and its labours are often to be found in details in churches such as bench-ends, misericords and capitals. The Church calendar's recognition of the country seasons begins with Plough Sunday ('God speed the Plow!') on the Sunday after Epiphany, then celebrates Rogation Sunday, blessing the crops and beating the parish bounds after Easter; Lammas (1 August), 'Loaf Mass' for the blessing of the first loaf made from the new harvest; and Martinmas (11 November), when autumn sowing ended and the cattle were slaughtered.

January: By this fire I warm my hands,
February: And with my spade I delve my lands.
March: Here I set my crop to spring,
April: And here I hear the fowles sing.
May: I am light as bird on bough,
June: And I weed my corn well enow.
July: With my scythe my grass I mow,
August: And here I shear my corn full low.
September: With my flail I earn my bread,
October: And here I sow my wheat so red.
November: At Martinmas I kill my swine,
December: And at Christmas I drink red wine.

'A certain most unhappy calamity' at Norwich, from Bartholomew de Cotton, *Historia Anglicana*, 1271

Bartholomew was a monk from Norwich of whom nothing is known beyond his writings.

This year, in the month of August, there befell at Norwich a certain most unhappy calamity, and one hitherto unheard of by the world, as among Christians; for the Cathedral Church in honour of the Holy Trinity, which had been founded there from of old, was burnt by fire, purposely applied, together with all the houses of the monks built within the cloisters of the said church. And this took place through the pride of the person who at that time was Prior of this Convent; as from the following facts may be ascertained. For by assent and consent of this same Prior, the grooms and servants of the monks very frequently went into the City, beating and wounding men and women, both within their houses and without, and doing much mischief. ... Also, whereas the monks have a fair by ancient custom each year, it happened this year, about the Feast of the Holy Trinity, that after the citizens had come with their merchandise there, and the greater part of them, at the end of the fair, had returned home, the servants of the monks, wickedly assaulting those who remained, beat and wounded them, and slew some ... The citizens, however, no longer able to endure so many evils, and such violence as this, assembled together and had recourse to arms, in order that they might repel force by force; which this most wicked Prior understanding, brought over a great multitude of malevolent persons from Yarmouth, who had been robbers, plunderers, and malefactors, during the disturbances in the realm. All these persons, coming by water to the Convent, ascended to the belfry where the bells were hung, fortified it with arms, just as if it were a castle, and took aim with their bows and arbalests [crossbows] therefrom, so that no one could pass along the streets or lanes near the Convent without being wounded. The citizens, seeing these acts of violence, were of opinion that these miscreants were acting manifestly against the peace of his lordship the King, in thus setting up a spurious castle in his city. Accordingly, meeting together, and coming to a determination to seize these persons and to bring them to judgment in the King's name, they provided themselves with arms; and, approaching the closed gate of the courtyard, on being unable to enter it by reason of the armed men by whom it was defended, set fire to it, and ruthlessly burned the gate. The fire spreading, however, the belfry was burnt, and all the dwellings of the monks, as well as, according to what some say, the Cathedral Church alas! together with all the relics of the saints, books, and ornaments of the church; so that whatever could be burnt was reduced to ashes, a certain chapel only excepted, which remained unburnt. The monks, however, and all who were able, took to flight and made their escape; though still, some persons on either side were slain.

From the *Exeter Constitutions*: Bishop Quivil of Exeter decrees tithe payments, 1287

Seeing that contention ariseth oftentimes between rectors of churches and their parishioners – since it is sometimes doubtful how much should be given for tithes when there are so few cows or sheep that no cheese can be made from their milk, or when in like manner there are too few calves, lambs, kids, chickens, piglings, geese, or fleeces, to be divided by ten, since there are not ten in all – therefore it is our will to hand down a certain rule in these matters; for in leaving them to local custom we should rather increase than remove the matter for quarrels, since the customs themselves are disputed and denied. We therefore decree that one farthing should be given as tithe for each lamb, kid, or pigling below the number of seven. If there are seven, let one be given for tithe; and next year whatsoever is lacking from the number ten shall be allowed for in tithing. ... For the milk of each cow, if no cheese be made, let a penny be given; for that of each milch-ewe a farthing and for each she-goat a halfpenny. ... Again, seeing that certain persons, for their tithe of milk (which hath hitherto been given in cheese, according to the custom hitherto approved in our diocese) maliciously bring the milk itself to church, and – what is more wicked still – finding no man there to receive it, pour it out before the altar in contumely to God and His Church; and others [practice many similar frauds and subterfuges]. We therefore, by the authority of God the Father Almighty, and of St Peter Prince of the Apostles, our patron saint, with the approbation of the present holy synod, excommunicate all such evildoers with their aiders and abettors, until they shall have made competent satisfaction for their misdeeds.

From the *Exeter Constitutions*: Bishop Stapeldon receives sidesmen's reports on parish priests, 1301

The Bishop keeps tabs on his parish priests through reports from their leading parishioners.

Clyst Honiton. They say that their parish priest is of honest life and good conversation, and has been there 22 years honestly fulfilling his priestly office in all that belongs to a parish priest; but he is now broken with age and inadequate for the cure of the parish.

Colyton. They say that sir Robert Blond, their Vicar, is an honest man and preaches to them as best he can, but not well enough in their opinion. They also say that his predecessors used to call in the Friars to instruct them for the salvation of their souls, but this Vicar does not care for them, and if they do happen to come he does not welcome them or help them on their way. For this, they request that he be given a reprimand.

Branscombe. They say that Thomas, their Vicar, bears himself well in all things, and preaches willingly, visits the sick, and carries out his priestly office with diligence. Of the clerk and the other parishioners, they know nothing but what is good and honest.

St Marychurch (Torquay). The parishioners say that, before the present Vicar came, the custom was that they paid for the total upkeep of the Chancel, with immunity from paying tithes for church restoration. But the present Vicar compels them to pay the tithe, but fails to maintain the Chancel. *Item.* They say that Agnes Bonatrix left five shillings in pollard [base or foreign] coins for the upkeep of St Mary's church, which the Vicar received and keeps. *Item.* Master Roger le Rous left a certain sum of money for the same purpose, which the Vicar is said to have received in part. *Item.* They say that the Vicar feeds his beasts of all kinds in the churchyard, which is evilly trodden down by them, and vilely befouled. *Item.* The Vicar has made personal use in his own building of trees blown down in the churchyard. *Item.* He has his own malt malted in the church, and stores his wheat and other goods there, and so his servants are constantly going in and out and leaving the door open, and the wind blows in when there are storms and keep damaging the roof. They say besides that he is a good preacher and carries out his office laudably in all respects, when he is present. But he often goes to stay in Moretonhampstead, sometimes for a week, sometimes for a fortnight, which means that they then have no Chaplain, except when sir Walter, the Archdeacon's Chaplain, is there, or some other chance Chaplain is procured. It is also presented that the church is in bad repair, one of the three dependent chapels is in ruins, and the other two dilapidated.

From *The Pricke of Conscience*, early to mid-1300s

This anonymous poem from the North of England depicts the fifteen days of the end of the world. More than a hundred copies of it survive in manuscript, an indication of its widespread use as an aid to personal prayer and penitence. It is strikingly illustrated in a stained-glass window of 1410 in All Saints, North Street, York. The verses below come from a version by Sebastian Evans (1830–1909), a lawyer and man of letters who was for one period of his life a designer of stained-glass windows. He became a friend of Burne-Jones.

Day III

On the third day, o'er the seething
Of the leprous ocean writhing,
Whale and dragon, orc and kraken,
And leviathan, forsaken
His unfathomable eyrie,
To and fro shall plunge – the dreary
Dumb death-sickness of creation
Startling with their ululation.
Men shall hear the monsters bellow
Forth their burden as they wallow;
But its drift? – Let none demand it!
God alone shall understand it!

Day V

On the fifth day, Judgement-stricken,
Every green herb, from the lichen
To the cedar of the forest,
Shall sweat blood in anguish sorest!
On the same, all fowls of heaven
Into one wide field, fear-driven,
Shall assemble, cowed and shrinking,

Neither eating aught, nor drinking;
Kind with kind, all ranked by feather,
Doves with doves aghast together,
Swan with swan in downfall regal,
Wren and wren, with eagle, eagle!
Ah! when fowl feel such foreboding,
What shall be the Sinner's goading?

On Day XV, the Archangel Michael summons all souls to gather at the footstool of the Almighty Father to be weighed in the scales 'without revenge or pity':

Sinner! Dost thou dread that trial?
Mark the shadow on the dial!

John Bromyard (d. *c.* 1352): preaching aids

A friar of the Dominican Priory in Hereford, he left extensive compilations in Latin. These are two 'exempla' for use in homilies and sermons.

Gargoyles and corbels

At times, on these great buildings, we see a stone displaying a grinning open mouth, and from other hints looking as if he supports the whole building. Nonetheless, a plain stone, sometimes hidden in a corner, does a lot more of the work – for the other is much more for show than doing a job. Some people are just like these, like the ones who, when they hear poor beggars crying for alms, or when actual friends tell them their bad luck, for example what they have lost through fire or flood or thievery, their mouths open with cries of sympathy for their suffering, and they say, 'I'm so sorry! May God help you', but give them neither help nor money, and don't even lend them provisions or things they really need.

Women in their fancy finery

In the woman wantonly decked out to ensnare souls, the garland she wears on her head is like a burning coal or firebrand of Hell aiming to set men on fire; equally the horned headgear of another woman, or a bare neck, or a brooch on a breast, or any of their fine bodily display. How else could any of it be considered than as a spark breathing out hell-fire, which this wretched

Devil's arsonist breathes out to such good purpose that in just one day, by her dancing or promenading through the town, she inflames with the fire of lust it could be twenty of those whose eyes are drawn to her, damning souls created by God and redeemed at such cost for their salvation. It's for this purpose that the Devil has dressed these women up, and sent them out through the town as his apostles, stuffed full with every iniquity and malice and fornication. ... They are the Devil's nets, and he fishes in God's fish-pond with them, trying to lure His fish into the lake of Hell.

The 'crimes' of the priest John Ball and the Peasants' Revolt in 1381, from Thomas of Walsingham's *Chronica Maiora*

Thomas of Walsingham recorded events between 1376 and 1422; he was in charge of the scriptorium at the monastery of St Albans, where Ball's sentencing and execution took place. The tripling of the poll tax in 1381 led to uprisings in Kent, headed by Wat Tyler and the hedge priest John Ball, and in Essex; by mid-June they were converging on London. The courage of fourteen-year-old Richard II in confronting them was instrumental in their dispersal, but not without a number of casualties, including Archbishop Sudbury and the Treasurer. The crisis continued to spread further afield but by mid-July was under control.

When vespers was over, the abbot and monks went in solemn procession to the west door of the monastery to meet the king [Richard II]. He was greeted with the full honours of a peal of bells and the chants of reverence that were his due. About a thousand archers and armed men came with the king, among them the knight Sir Robert Tresilian, a justiciar of the greatest experience, and a man of great courage and the wisdom of a serpent. Sitting next day on his seat of justice at the Moot hall ... Sir Robert sentenced the priest, John Ball, to be drawn, hanged, beheaded, disembowelled and quartered, to use the common expression.

He had been taken prisoner at Coventry and brought to St Albans the previous day into the presence of the king. Having stated his case and confessed his most shameful crimes, he was found guilty of treason on an enormous scale. His death was put off until the following Monday at the intervention of William Courtenay, bishop of London, who in concern for the salvation of his soul, had obtained for him this space for repentance. For twenty years and more he had continually preached up and down the land those things that he knew would please the people, attacking both ecclesiastics and secular lords, and seeking to gain the goodwill of the people more than merit in the eyes of God. He even taught the people that tithes should not be paid to a curate, unless the person paying the tithe was richer than the vicar or rector who received it. Also that tithes and offerings should be taken away from a curate, if it was found that that his parishioner was a man of better life than his priest. He also taught that no one was fit for the kingdom of God unless he had been born in wedlock. He also taught the perverse doctrines and opinions and crazy heresies of the perfidious John Wyclif, and still more things which it would take too long to enumerate.

Because of all this the bishops, in whose parishes he had dared to say such things, stopped him from preaching in their churches in the future, and so he took his sermons out into the squares and marketplaces and even the fields. He was never short of hearers from among the common people, whom he always took good care should be attracted to his preaching by his attacks on prelates and his pleasing words. In the end, when, even after excommunication, he did not stop preaching, he was put in prison where he prophesied that he would be set free by twenty thousand friends. This afterwards came true during the trouble in the kingdom which I have described, when the commons unbarred all the prisons and forced the prisoners to depart. Freed in this way, John followed along with them, spurring them on to commit further crimes and declaring that they were completely right to do all these things. So that he might infect still more people with the poison of his preaching, at Blackheath, where two hundred thousand of the commons had assembled together, he began a sermon with the words

When Adam delved, and Eve span,
Who was then a gentleman?

Proceeding from this beginning and using the words of the saying which he had taken for his text, he tried to introduce and to prove the argument that in the beginning all men had been created equal by nature, and that servitude had been brought in by the unjust oppression of wicked men contrary to the will of God. Further, that if God had wanted to create slaves, he would have established right at the beginning of the world who was to be master, and who a slave. And so they should realise that a time had now been given to them by God, in which they could, if they desired, put off the yoke of long endured slavery and enjoy the liberty which they had long desired. His advice therefore was that they should behave sensibly, and, showing the love of a good father for his family, who in tilling his fields roots out or cuts back the harmful weeds which can damage his crops, they themselves likewise at the present time should hurry to do the same thing, first by killing the senior lords of the kingdom, secondly by murdering the lawyers, justiciars and jurors of the land, and finally by uprooting from the soil of England all those whom they knew would do harm to the commons in the future. Thus in the end they would secure peace for themselves and security for the future, if, having done away with the important people, there was equal freedom and the same nobility for all of them, together with honours and powers in which all shared alike.

Having heard this sermon and several other similar ravings, the common people supported him with such enthusiasm that they shouted out that he should be archbishop and the chancellor of the kingdom; he was the only man worthy of the position of archbishop, for the archbishop, who was then still alive, had been a traitor to the commons and the kingdom and should be executed, wherever in England he could be found.

John Ball had also sent to the rebel leaders in Essex a letter, full of riddles, to encourage them to carry through what they had begun. The letter was found in the sleeve of a man being hanged for his share in the revolt. ... John Ball confessed that he had written this letter and sent it to the people of Essex. And for this and many other crimes which he had committed and confessed, as I have said, he was drawn, hung and beheaded at St Albans on 15 July in the presence of the king. His body was cut in four and sent to four cities of the kingdom.

Geoffrey Chaucer (*c.* 1342–1400), from the General Prologue *to the Canterbury Tales*

Of the thirty characters who gathered one April day at the Tabard Inn in London to make their pilgrimage to St Thomas Becket's shrine, besides the Parson there are six other figures connected with the Church: Madame Eglentyne the Prioress, with her smiling manners and lapdogs; a horse-loving Monk who couldn't give a plucked hen for the monastic Rule; 'wanton' Friar Huberd, adept at finding favours and raising money; the Oxford Clerk with his head full of books and Aristotle; the Summoner of delinquents to the Ecclesiastical Court, loud-mouthed and venal; and the openly fraudulent Pardoner with his bag of spurious relics. The simple sincerity of the Parson and his ploughman brother stands in idealized contrast.

A holy-minded man of good renown
There was, and poor, the PARSON to a town,
Yet he was rich in holy thought and work.
He also was a learned man, a clerk,
Who truly knew Christ's gospel and would preach it
Devoutly to parishioners, and teach it.
Benign and wonderfully diligent,
And patient when adversity was sent
(For so he proved in much adversity).
He hated cursing to extort a fee,
Nay rather he preferred beyond a doubt
Giving to poor parishioners round about
Both from church offerings and his property;
He could in little find sufficiency.
Wide was his parish, with houses far asunder,
Yet he neglected not in rain or thunder,
In sickness or in grief, to pay a call
On the remotest, whether great or small,
Upon his feet, and in his hand a stave.
This noble example to his sheep he gave
That first he wrought, and afterwards he taught;
And it was from the Gospel he had caught
Those words, and he would add this figure too,
That if gold rust, what then will iron do?
For if a priest be foul in whom we trust
No wonder that a common man should rust;
And shame it is to see – let priests take stock –
A shitten shepherd and a snowy flock.
The true example that a priest should give
Is one of cleanness, how the sheep should live.
He did not set his benefice to hire
And leave his sheep encumbered in the mire
Or run to London to earn easy bread
By singing masses for the wealthy dead,
Or find some Brotherhood and get enrolled.
He stayed at home and watched over his fold
So that no wolf should make the sheep miscarry.
He was a shepherd and no mercenary.

Holy and virtuous he was, but then
Never contemptuous of sinful men,
Never disdainful, never too proud or fine,
But was discreet in teaching and benign.
His business was to show a fair behaviour
And draw men thus to Heaven and their Saviour,
Unless indeed a man were obstinate;
And such, whether of high or low estate,
He put to sharp rebuke, to say the least.
I think there never was a better priest.
He sought no pomp or glory in his dealings,
No scrupulosity had spiced his feelings.
Christ and His Twelve Apostles and their lore
He taught, but followed it himself before.

From *Piers Plowman* by William Langland (*c.* 1332–1390s)

Nothing certain is known about the author. In its longest form the poem comprises 23 Passus, or 'Steps', opening with the Dreamer viewing 'a fair field full of folk', of all manner of men, high and low, 'working and wandering as the world asketh'. There follows a cycle of visions, surveys of his fourteenth-century English society, and the individual's relation to its temptations and weaknesses. He returns again and again to corruption in the Church and its abuses of power and privilege, and the cynical betrayal by many friars of the Christian ideals they claim to embody.

• An autobiographical passage

In the following extract, from a prose translation of what is known as the C text of the poem, the idle life and enlightenment of a minor cleric in the London of his time are vividly portrayed.

I met Reason one hot harvest-time, just as I was passing by Conscience. And though, at the time, I was as fit as a fiddle, and my muscles were in good shape for work, I was fond of an easy life, and had nothing better to do than drink and sleep. And so I roamed along content with the world, and lost in daydreams of times past, I heard a voice, the voice of Reason, rebuking me and saying:

'Why can't you serve at Mass or sing in the choir, or rake the corn for the harvesters, or help them to mow and stack it, or bind up the sheaves?

Or why don't you get up early and join the reapers, or find yourself a job as a head-reaper or a hayward, and stand with a horn in your hand, and sleep out at night to guard the corn in my fields from thieves and pilferers? Or why couldn't you cobble shoes, or watch the sheep or the pigs, or get some hedging or harrowing done, or drive the hogs and geese to market? At all events, you ought to do *something* that's useful to the community, and play your part in feeding the old and infirm.'

'Well, to be perfectly honest,' I said, 'I just haven't the strength. I'm no good with a scythe or a sickle, and God knows I'm far too tall to bend down to a labourer's job – honestly, I should never stand the pace!'

'Then have you got an estate of your own to live on?' asked Reason, 'or a wealthy family to provide for you? For you certainly look an idle fellow – one of those spendthrifts, I should think, who can't resist wasting their time and money. Or maybe you beg for your living, and hang around buttery-doors and squat in the churches on Fridays and fast-days, telling some yarn or other. That's not the kind of life that will gain you much credit when you come to where Justice deals out men's deserts – "For God rewards every man according to his work" [Psalm 62]. – But perhaps you're lame in one of your limbs or maimed by some accident, and are excused from working?'

'Many years ago, when I was a boy,' I answered, 'my father and friends found the means to send me to school, so that I came to understand Holy Scripture, and was taught all that's best for my body and safest for my soul – provided, of course, that I persevere in it. And though the friends who helped me then have since died, I have never found any life that suited me, except in these long, clerical robes. If I'm to earn a living, I must earn it by doing the job that I've learnt best, for it is written, "Let every man abide in the same calling wherein he was called."

'So I live in London, and also on London, and the tools that I work with are my Paternoster and Prayer Book, and sometimes my Book of Offices for the Dead, and my Psalter and Seven Penitential Psalms. And with these I sing for the souls of those who help me; and I expect the folk who provide me with food, to make me welcome when I visit them once or twice a month. So I go on my rounds, now to his house and now to hers, and that is how I do my begging – with neither bag nor bottle, but only my stomach to carry all my supplies!

'What is more, Sir Reason, I am convinced that you should never force a man in Holy Orders to do manual work. For it says in Leviticus, the Law of God, that men whose natural gifts lead them to take Orders should not toil or sweat, or serve on juries, or fight in the front line or attack an enemy – "Do not render evil for evil," says the Scripture. For all who wear the tonsure are heirs of Heaven and ministers of Christ, and their job is to serve Him in the churches and choir-stalls. For it is written, "The Lord himself is the portion of mine inheritance," and again, "The life of meekness does not constrain a man."

'So a cleric's duty is to serve Christ, and leave carting and labouring to ignorant serfs. And no one should take Holy Orders unless he comes from a family of freemen, and his parents are married in church. Serfs and beggars' children and bastards should toil with their hands, while men of noble blood should serve God and their fellow men as befits their rank – some by singing Masses, and others by book-keeping and advising men how to spend their money.

'But nowadays, bondmen's children are made into Bishops and bastards into Archdeacons; and soap-makers and their sons buy themselves knighthoods, while the sons of true noblemen toil and sweat for them – for they mortgage their estates to ride out against our enemies and to fight for king and country in defence of the people. And the monks and nuns, who should feed the poor, buy up the incomes of knights and make noblemen of their relatives. Even Popes now, and ecclesiastical patrons, are refusing noble blood, and appointing the sons of Simony to keep God's sanctuary. No wonder charity and holy living have disappeared – and will not return till this new fashion wears out, or someone uproots it.

'So pray do not rebuke me, Reason, for my conscience tells me what Christ would have me do. Our Lord loves the prayers of a perfect man and penance done with discretion, more than any other work in the world. ...'

'But I don't see how this applies to you', interrupted Conscience. 'To beg in cities is not the life of perfection – not unless you're appointed to beg by a Prior or Abbot.'

'True enough,' I replied, 'and I confess that I have frittered away my time. But consider: a merchant may lose money again and again, yet if at last he makes some wonderful bargain which sets him up for the rest of his life, what does he care about his previous losses?' ...

'Then I suggest you get a move on,' said Reason, 'and begin a more reputable life at once, and treat your soul with some respect.'

'Yes, and persevere in it too,' added Conscience – so off I went to church, to worship God.

• From Passus V, The Seven Deadly Sins – Gluttony

The dreamer sees Reason preaching to the whole field full of people, urging them to confess their sins, and each of the Deadly Sins is brought to meet with Repentance – Pride, Lechery, Envy, Anger, Avarice, and, here, Gluttony; he is on the way to Friday Mass and Confession when Betty the ale wife entices him to join the company in her pub – Cissie the shoemaker, Wat the warrener and wife, Tim the tinker and his apprentices, Hick the hackneyman, Hugh the haberdasher, Clarice the whore of Cock Lane, with the parish clerk, Father Peter of Priedieu Priory with Parnel the Flemish wench, Davy the ditcher, and a dozen more – a fiddler, a ratcatcher, a Cheapside street sweeper, a rope-maker, a thatcher (?), Rose the dish-seller, Godfrey of Garlickhithe, Griffin the Welshman, and a bunch of old-clothes dealers. They all make a game of getting Glutton drunk –

And grete Sire Glotoun with a galoun ale.	*greet him with a gallon of ale*
There was laughyng and louryng 'Let go the cuppe!'	
Bargaines and beverages bigan to arise	*bets and rounds of drinks*
And seten so til evensonge and songen umwhile	*sat singing till evensong*
Tyl Glotoun had y-globbed a galoun an a gille.	*had glugged 8½ pints*
His guttis gunne to gothelen as two gredy sowes;	*gut began to grumble*
He pissed a potel in a Paternoster while,	*pissed half a gallon*
And blew the rounde ruwet at his rigge-bone ende	*blew a backside fanfare*
That alle that herde that horne held her nose after	*held their noses*
And wissheden it had be wexed with a wispe of firses.	*wiped with a wisp of gorse*
He hadde no strengthe to stonde er he his staffe hadde,	
And thanne gan he go liche a glewmannes bicche	*like a street-minstrel's bitch*
Somme tyme aside and somme tyme arrere,	*backwards*
As whoso lyeth lynes forto lacche with foules.	*like one setting lines to catch birds*
Ac whan he drowgh to the dore, thane dymmed his eighen;	*drew; his eyes dimmed*
He thrumbled on the thresshewolde an threwe to the erthe.	*stumbled*
Clement the cobelere caught hym bi the myddel	
Forto lifte hym alofte and leyde him on his knows.	*laid him on his knees*
Ac Glotoun was a gret cherle and a grym in the liftynge,	*a load*
And coughed up a caudel in Clementis lappe.	*a 'custard'*
Is non so hungry hounde in Hertfordschire.	
With al the wo of this worlde his wyf and his wenche	
Baren hym home to his bedde and brought hym therinne.	
And after al this excesse he had an accidie	*attack of sloth*

That he slepe Saterday and Sonday til sonne yede to reste.
Thanne waked he of his wynkyng and wiped his eyghen,
The fyrste worde that he warpe was, 'Where is the bolle?' *uttered; drinking-bowl*
His wyf edwyted hym tho of wykkednesse and synne,
And Repentance righte so rebuked hym that tyme.
'As thow with words and werkes hast wrought yvel in thi lyve,
Shryve the and be shamed therof, and shewe it with thi mouth.' *confess yourself*
'I, Glotoun,' quod the gome, 'gylti me yelde; *admit I am guilty*
That I have trespassed with my tonge, I can noughte telle how ofte;
Sworen Goddes soule and his sydes and 'so God me help!' *taken God's name in vain*
There no need ne was nyne hundredth tymes
And overseye me at my sopere and sometime at nones, *stuffed myself; noon*
And y-spilte that myghte be spared and spended on somme hungrie; *spoilt*
Overdelicatly on feste days drunken and eten bothe; *feast days*
And sat sometime so longe there that I slepe and ete at ones; *slept and ate at the same time*
For love of tales in tavernes to drinke the more I hyed; *gossip and more drink ...*
Fedde me bifor none whan fastyng days were.' *eaten before noon on fast-days*
'This shewyng shrift,' quod Repentance, 'shal be meryte to the.' *open confession; merit*

The Service for Excommunication, from *Instructions for Parish Priests* by John Mirk (late fourteenth–early fifteenth century)

The mighty statement I make here
That twice or three times in a year
You shall pronounce, no bar or let,
When your parish is together met,
You shall pronounce this fearful thing,
With cross and candle and bell tolling,
Speak readily, no hesitation,
That everyone may understand.

Then let him say in such a manner: By authority of god almighty, father and Son and holy ghost, and of all the saints of heaven, First, we curse all those who have broken the peace of the holy church, or disturbed it ...

Mirk's catalogue of sins incurring excommunication, to be publicly pronounced, consists of: those who rob the church, or withhold their tithes; all slanderers, fire-raisers, thieves, handlers of stolen goods; all heretics, usurers, forgers of papal bulls, clippers of the king's coin, users of false weights and measures; those who bear false witness against marriages or wills; all traitors, and disturbers of the English peace; all those who steal holy goods or church property; anyone who assists Jews or Saracens in acting against Christendom; those who destroy children, the newborn or the unborn, with potion or with witchcraft; all those who spy at night behind walls, doors or windows, housebreakers and those who commit murder; anyone who knowingly has dealings with the excommunicated; those who traffic in witchcraft or black magic; anyone who holds back his tithes or lays violent hands on a priest; all defilers of the sanctuary of church and churchyard; also all those who act falsely as executors of wills, and anyone who abandons a child at a church door or in any other public place.

We curse them by the authority of the court of Rome, whether indoors or out, asleep or awake, moving and sitting, on foot or riding, above ground and below, speaking, and crying, and drinking; in woodland, on water, in field, in town: may Father, Son, and Holy Ghost curse them, angels and archangels curse them, and all the nine orders of heaven [etc., etc.]. And their lives be struck from the Book of Life until they come to amendment, full satisfaction made. Amen. Amen.

Then you cast the candle to the ground, spit on that place, and have the bells rung to further shake their hearts ...

Margery Kempe (*c.* 1373–after 1439) saves St Margaret's Church in King's Lynn from fire, from *The Book of Margery Kempe*

Margery Kempe was the daughter of a brewer who was five times mayor of Bishop's – now King's – Lynn in Norfolk, one of medieval England's most important ports. Her book survived in a single copy that resurfaced in the 1930s. It is the story of 'a creature set in great pomp and pride of the world, who later was drawn to our Lord by great poverty, sickness, shame, and great reproofs in many countries'; several priests transcribed it for her. Pilgrimages took her to Assisi, the Holy Land, Compostela, and – late in life – Danzig. Records show the date of this fire as 23 January 1421.

On one occasion there happened to be a great fire in Bishop's [King's] Lynn, which burned down the Guildhall of the Trinity. The same terrible and serious fire was very likely to have burned down the parish church

– dedicated in honour of St Margaret, a stately place and richly honoured – and also the whole town as well, had there been no grace or miracle.

The said creature being present there, and seeing the dangerous plight of the whole town, cried out very loudly many times that day, and wept most abundantly, praying for grace and mercy for all the people. And notwithstanding that at other times they could not endure her crying and weeping because of the plentiful grace that our Lord worked in her, on this day, in order to lessen their physical danger, they allowed her to weep as much as she liked, and nobody would order her to stop, but instead begged her to continue, fully trusting and believing that through her crying and weeping our Lord would take them to mercy.

Then her confessor came to her and asked if it were best to carry the sacrament towards the fire, or not.

She said, 'Yes, sir, yes! For our Lord Jesus Christ told me it will be well.'

So her confessor, parish priest of St Margaret's Church, took the precious sacrament and went before the fire as devoutly as he could and afterwards brought it back into the church again – and the sparks of the fire flew about the church. The said creature, desiring to follow the precious sacrament to the fire, went out at the church door, and as soon as she saw the terrible flames of the fire, she immediately cried with a loud voice and much weeping, 'Good Lord, make everything all right!'

These words worked in her mind, inasmuch as our Lord had said to her before that he would make everything all right, and therefore she cried, 'Good Lord, make everything all right, and send down some rain or storm that may through your mercy quench this fire and ease my heart.'

Afterwards she went back into the church, and then she saw how the sparks were coming into the choir through the lantern of the church. Then she had a new sorrow, and cried very loudly again for grace and mercy, with great abundance of tears. Soon after, three worthy men came in to her with snow on their clothes, saying to her, 'Look, Margery, God has shown us much grace and sent us a fair snowstorm to quench the fire with. Be now of good cheer, and thank God for it.'

And with a great cry she gave praise and thanks to God for his great mercy and his goodness, especially as he had said to her before that everything would be well, when it was most unlikely to be well, except through a miracle and special grace.

And now that she saw that all was well indeed, she thought she had great reason to thank our Lord.

Then her confessor came to her and said he believed that because of her prayers God granted them to be delivered out of their great danger, for without devout prayers it could not happen that the air, being bright and clear, should so soon be changed into clouds and darkness, and send down great flakes of snow, through which the fire was hindered in its natural work – blessed may our Lord be.

Notwithstanding the grace that he showed for, still, when the dangers were past, some people slandered her because she cried, and some said that our Lady never cried. 'Why do you cry in this way?' – and she said, because she could not do otherwise.

Then she fled from people into the Prior's Chapel, so that she should give them no further occasion. When she was there, she had such intense recollection of the Passion of our Lord Jesus Christ, and of his precious wounds, and how dearly he bought her, that she cried and roared amazingly, so that she could be heard a great way away, and she could not restrain herself from doing so. …

Afterwards there came a parson who had taken a degree, and who would preach both morning and afternoon. And as he preached most holily and devoutly, the said creature was moved by devotion during his sermon, and at last she burst out with a cry, and people began to grumble about her crying. … Then the parson stopped for a while from his preaching and said to the people, 'Friends, be quiet, and do not complain about this woman, for … I dare say it is a most gracious gift of God, blessed may he be.'

Some of a mother's instructions to her daughter in how to be 'a ful good womman', *c.* 1430

Daughter, see that you act wisely if you would become a wife,
Look attractive, love god and holy church, and lead a good life.
Go to church when you may, see you don't use rain as an excuse,
For you fare best when you have seen god that same day.
He must needs well thrive
That lives well all his life,
My dear child.

Give both tithes and offerings with a good heart;
On the old and the bedridden hold your care not apart;

Give of your own goods, without being mean,
For where god runs the household poverty is seldom seen.
He prospers more
Who loves the poor,
My dear child.

When sitting in church, your beads you will tell,
And not chatter to friends and family as well.
Laugh scornfully at neither the old nor the young,
But keep your manner fair, and be kindly of tongue.
Through your fair behaviour
Your standing will grow,
My dear child.

Jolly Jankin, early fifteenth century

Alison has fallen for Clerk Jankin as he sings the Yuletide office; his 'Kyrie Eleison' ('Lord have mercy upon us'), which comes near the opening of the Mass, seems to be ringing with her own name. The celebration of the Nativity is eclipsed by her own more mundane drama.

Kyrie, so kyrie,
Jankin singeth merye,
With 'Aleison'.

As I went on Yole Day
In oure prosession,
Knew I joly Jankin
By his mery tone –
Kyrieleyson.

Jankin began the offis
On the Yole Day,
And yet me thinketh it dos me good,
So mery gan he say
'Kyrieleison!'

Jankin red the pistil*
Ful faire an ful wel,

And yet me thinketh it dos me good,
As ever I have sel.
Kyrieleyson.

Jankin at the *Sanctus*
Craketh a mery note,
And yet me thinketh it dos me good –
I payed for his cote.
Kyrieleyson.

Jankin craketh notes
An hunderid on a knot
And yet he hakketh hem smallere
Than wortes to the pot.†
Kyrieleyson.

Jankin at the *Agnus*
Bereth the pax-brede;††
He twinkeled, but said nought,
And on myn foot he trede.
Kyrieleyson.

Benedicamus Domino,
Christ fro shame me shilde!
Deo gracias therto – ‡
Alas, I go with childe!
Kyrieleyson.

* *epistle*
† *Jankin trills the notes a hundred in a cluster, and chops them smaller than vegetables for the pot.*
†† *The pax-brede is the osculatory, a tablet to be kissed, which he carries round during the Mass when the kiss of peace is exchanged.*
‡ *Let us bless the Lord, Thanks be to God.*

Going to Hell, fifteenth century

All backbiters, they are going to Hell,
And thieves and robbers and murderers as well,
Lechers and harlots thither shall wend,
And there they shall dwell time without end.

All these false traders the devil will grab,
Bakers and brewers more than all men they gab,
Sell the gallon-can short and fill it with froth
And always conjuring silver from purse;
They both bake and brew weak bread and beer,
But as long as they coin it, they just don't care.

Good people, for God's sake leave off such sin
Or the riches of Heaven you never will win.

All priests' wives, I know they are lost and damned,
And these parsons too will meet the same end,
Those young men in their pride who chase after Moll,
And the proud young maidens too, hot after Col.
At church and market when they meet up and gather,
It's nothing but whispers and secrets together.
When they come to church on Sunday for Mass
All they're on the look-out for is their lad or their lass.
She stares at Watkin with the gladdest eye
But her prayer-book's at home behind lock and key.
For Masses and Matins she cares not as she ought –
It's Wilkin and Watkin who have all her thought.
Robin takes Gill out to the inn
And they'll sit there together love-making,
Then he'll pay the bill, and they're off on that game,
For being out at night with him she feels no shame.
Her mother and father threaten to beat her
But she'll not given up Robin however they treat her.
She'll keep swearing to them that no man's been at her
Till the swell of her belly makes no doubt of the matter.

Good people, for God's sake leave off your sin
Or the riches of Heaven you never will win.

Letter from Margaret Paston, at Oxnead in Norfolk, to her husband John in London, 28 September 1443

From the unique survival of family correspondence of the period, the Paston Letters. John and his heiress-wife had five sons and two daughters, and he lived from 1421 to 1466.

Margaret Paston's will of nineteen years later (1482, prepared before her death in 1484) specifies in detail her funeral arrangements and the marble tomb to be erected in Mauteby church 'rehearsing these words: "Here lieth Margret Paston, late the wif of John Paston, doughter and heire of John Mawteby, squier." There are numerous bequests to other Norfolk parish churches as well, her tenants, the clergy, the poor, the hermits, the friars, the lepers and others.

Right worshipful husband, I recommend me to you, desiring heartily to hear of your welfare, thanking God of your a-mending of the great dis-ease that ye have had; and I thank you for the letter that ye sent me, for by my troth my mother and I were not in heart's ease from the time that we wost of your sickness, till we wost verily of your a-mending. My mother behested another image of wax of the weight of you to our Lady of Walsingham, and she sent IIII nobles to the IIII Orders of Friars at Norwich to pray for you, and I have behested to go on pilgrimage to Walsingham, and to Saint Leonard's [Norwich] for you; by my troth I had never so heavy a season as I had from the time that I wost of your sickness till I wost of your a-mending, and yet mine heart is in no great ease, nor shall not be, till I wot that ye be truly hale. Your father and mine was this day se'nnight at Beccles for a matter of the Prior of Bromholm...

I pray you heartily that ye will vouchsafe to send me a letter as hastily as ye may, if writing be not dis-ease to you, and that ye will vouchsafe to send me word how your sore doth. If I might have had my will, I should 'a' seen you ere this time; I would ye were at home, if it were your ease, better even than a gown of scarlet cloth, if your sore might be as well looked to here as it is where ye been. I pray you, if your sore be healed, and so ye may endure to ride, when my father come to London, that ye will ask leave, and come home when the horse shall be sent home again, for I hope ye should be kept as tenderly here as ye been at London. I may none leisure have to write half a quarter so much as I should say to you if I might speak with you. I shall send you another letter as hastily as I may. I thank you that ye would vouchsafe to remember my girdle, and that ye would write to me at the time, for I suppose that writing was not easy to you. Almighty God have you in his keeping, and send you health. Written at Oxnead in right great haste on Saint Michael's Even. Yours, M. Paston.

My mother greets you well, and sends you God's blessing and hers, and she prayeth you, and I pray you also, that ye be well dieted of meat and drink, for that is the greatest help that ye may have now to your health-ward. Your son fareth well, blessed be God.

Lollards in the Ecclesiastical Court, Buckden Manor, Huntingdonshire, 27 May 1457

The radical academic John Wyclif, the instigator of the first English Bible, died in 1384, but his ideas, with their appeal to pious but anti-clerical feeling, found followers among so-called Lollards ('mutterers') through to the Reformation. This judgment by an ecclesiastical court (preserved in the Lincoln Diocese Documents) shows what the Church authorities found subversive and how they dealt with it.

William and Richard Sparke, of Somersham in the diocese of Lincoln, publicly acknowledge before the Bishop the following heretical beliefs:

1. Crosses and Images set up in Churches ought not to be worshipped; and offerings should not be made at them, since they are nothing but stocks and stones. A human being would be better to worship a man with arms outstretched, since that is a true cross and image of God.
2. Pilgrimages ought not to be made to places where the bodies of saints rest. Expenses on pilgrimages are a waste of money, and the trouble is profitless.
3. A child whose parents have been baptized has no need of baptism, and ought not to be baptized, since its parents' baptism is sufficient.
4. Laymen who are married or who engage in manual labour do not have to fast. Christ is nowhere found to have instituted fastings of this sort. This is a Canonical Rule and binding only on clerics and those in monasteries.
5. To bury a corpse in consecrated ground does the soul of the dead person no more good than if the corpse has been thrown into a bog. Funeral solemnities were invented to provide fees for money-loving priests. Rather than enriching the priests, it would be better if these expenses went as alms to the poor.
6. A priest has no more power to make 'the body of Christ' than a stalk of wheat has. Bread remains bread, and is in fact debased by such spell-words.

7. 30 communion breads are sold for a halfpenny, but Christ was sold for 30 pieces of silver. Such a sacrament is a device for enriching priests.
8. Confession made to a Lollard believer is more soul-healing than to a priest.
9. Inasmuch as God searches all hearts and knows all secrets, an unspoken prayer is just as good as a spoken one, and if it is made in a field or other unconsecrated place, it is just as valid as one made in a church.
10. Mutual consent between a man and woman is all that is needed for a valid marriage, and no other solemnity is needed to justify their living together. The marriage-service was instituted only for priests to get the fees.
11. Extreme unction benefits no man's soul. This anointing is just a vile 'greasing' of the person's body.
12. The Pope is Antichrist, and priests the disciples of Antichrist. All persons in Holy Orders are incarnate devils. ...

The Penance: William Sparke and Richard Sparke shall, each of them, clad only in his breeches and his shirt, bearing a faggot on his neck and shoulders, and carrying a penny wax-candle alight in his hand, walk once, meekly as a penitent, round the public market-place of the town of Huntingdon, in full market-time, and once round the market-place of St Ives in the same way; and once on a Sunday or Holy-Day (when the processions take place and therefore there is a great attendance of people) round the Churchyard of Somersham in the same manner, and once round the Churchyard of Ramsey. And when his penance has been fully done, each shall, on bended knees, humbly offer what remains of his wax-candle as an offering to the altar of that church where his penance is concluded.

Their priests, under threat of punishment for neglect of this mandate, each duly attired in surplice and stole, and having a rod in his hand, are to follow them as they walk round market-place and churchyard, and to beat and discipline them (with the rod) at each corner of the market-place or churchyard, proclaiming, publicly, and in the vulgar tongue, the cause of this penance, and to certify in writing, under seal, what each of them has done.

An 'amusing story' from a Latin sermon of Master Rypon of Durham, early fifteenth century

Fifty-nine of Robert Rypon's sermons survive.

A certain bailiff was particularly oppressive in the way he collected rents from the poor. One day, riding out to a certain village in pursuit of his duties, he met with the Devil in human form. Said the Devil to him, 'Whither are you going?' He replied, 'To the next village on my master's business.'

Mephistopheles then enquired if he was willing to take whatever was freely offered to him. The bailiff answered in the affirmative, and asked in his turn who the questioner might be, and what was his errand. The latter replied that he was the Devil, busy like him in quest of gain, only willing, though, not just to take whatever men gave; but only 'whatsoever they would gladly bestow with their whole heart and soul, that will I accept.'

'You do most justly', said the relentless bailiff.

Proceeding on their way together, as they approached the village, they beheld a ploughman angrily commending to the Devil his half-tamed oxen that repeatedly strayed from the furrow. Says the bailiff to his companion, 'Behold, they are yours!' 'No,' says the other, 'they are in no wise given from the heart.'

Then as they entered the village, the strains of a weeping child reached their ears. Its mother, powerless to correct its faults, was wishing it to the Devil. Then says our bailiff, 'This is yours indeed!' 'Not at all,' replies the Devil, 'for she has no desire to lose her son.'

At length they came to the end of the village. A certain poverty-stricken widow, whose only cow the bailiff had seized the day before, espied him coming, and with knees bent and hands outstretched at him shrieked at him – 'To all the devils of hell I commend thee!'

Whereupon remarked the Devil – 'To be sure, this one *is* mine. Because thus cordially you have been bestowed upon me, therefore I am willing to have you.' And snatching up the bailiff, he bore him away to hell.

God speed the plow

'Plough Monday' marked the return to work after the Twelve Days of Christmas.

The merthe of alle this londe — *mirth*
Maketh the gode husbonde — *husbandman*
With erynge of his plowe. — *tilling*
I-blessyd be Cristes sonde, — *ordaining*
That hath us sent in honde
Merthe & joye y-nowe.

The plowe goth mony a gate, — *track*
Bothe erly & eke late,
In wynter in the clay.
Aboute barly and whete,
That maketh men to swete, — *sweat*
God spede the plowe al day!

Browne, morel, & sore — *Brown, Dark, & Sorrel*
Drawen the plowe ful sore, — *laboriously*
Al in the morewenynge.
Rewarde hem therefore
With a shefe or more, — *sheaf (of corn)*
Alle in the evenynge.

Whan men bygyne to sowe,!
Fful wel here corne they knowe, — *their*
In the mounthe of May.
Howe ever Janyuer blowe,
Whether hye or lowe,
God spede the plowe all way!

Whan men bygyneth to wede
The thistle fro the sede,
In somer whan they maye;
God lete hem wel to spede — *grant them*
& longe gode lyfe to lede,
All that for plowemen pray.

Last will and testament, from the *Hundred Tales*, later fifteenth century

This particular 'Hundred Tales' collection for aristocratic entertainment is Burgundian, but the characters range over a broader sphere of action, including England.

Listen, please, to what happened the other day to an ordinary village priest, not poor, whom his bishop fined the sum of fifty good gold crowns for his simplicity.

This good priest had a dog he had raised and looked after since a puppy. The animal surpassed all the other dogs of the neighborhood in going into the water to fetch a stick, or in retrieving the priest's cap, if his master forgot it or just thought he had left it somewhere. In brief, everything which an obedient and intelligent dog should know how to do, he was an expert in. Whenever the dog did something like this, his master became so much more attached to him that he never tired of singing his praises.

Nevertheless it came to pass – how, I don't know, whether he was too hot or too cold, or whether he had eaten something which upset him – that the dog became very ill and died, and from this earthly life went straight to the paradise for dogs.

And what did this good priest do? When he saw his dog depart this world, he thought that so good and intelligent an animal should not be left without a proper burial. Therefore he dug a grave in the churchyard adjoining, pretty close to the door of his house or presbytery, and there interred and buried him. I don't know if he set up a marble tombstone for him with an engraved epitaph – I keep silent about that.

It wasn't long before the death of this good dog of the priest was noised about in the village and vicinity. The whole story of the Christian burial which his master had given him spread so far that it reached the ears of the bishop of the diocese, who sent a marshal with a summons ordering the priest to appear before him.

'Alas!' said the priest to the marshal. 'What have I done, and who has sent me this official summons? I couldn't be more amazed that the court has sent for me.'

'For my part,' replied the other, 'I don't know what it's all about, unless it's because you've buried your dog in the consecrated ground reserved for the bodies of Christians.'

'Ah!' mused the priest. 'So that's what it is.'

Now for the first time it dawned on him that he had done wrong, and he knew that if he went there he would be imprisoned and fleeced, for the lord bishop, God bless us, was the most avaricious prelate in the kingdom, and was surrounded by people who knew all the tricks of bringing grist to his mill.

'Since it's inevitable I lose something, it may as well be soon as late,' the priest thought to himself.

On the day appointed he went and straightway presented himself before the lord bishop, who, as soon as he saw him, launched into a long diatribe on the holy burial given to the dog, interpreting the affair so fantastically it seemed the priest had done worse than deny God. After all this harangue, he ordered that the priest put in prison.

When the priest saw they were going to incarcerate him, he begged to be heard, and the lord bishop consented. Now you must know that a lot of men of great importance were watching this interrogation, like the judge, the prosecutors, the scribe, notaries, advocates, and attorneys, all of whom were highly amused at this unusual hearing of a simple priest who had given his dog Christian burial.

Speaking in self-defence the priest said: 'In truth, my lord, if you had known my good dog, God rest his soul, as I did, you wouldn't be so surprised as you are at the burial I arranged for him, for his equal never was and never shall be.'

Then he related the wonders his dog had done, and continued: 'If he was indeed good and intelligent while alive, he was even as much or more so at his death, for he left a handsome will, and because he knew your need and poverty, he set aside for you fifty gold crowns, which I am bringing to you.'

The priest reached into his cassock, and handed them over. The bishop accepted them very readily, and then praised and approved the good sense of this valiant dog, as well as his testament and the burial the priest had given him.

When Sir Thomas Champneys died in 1796, the devoted master arranged for his dog Azor, who had once saved him from drowning, to be buried with him in the family vault. The furious Bishop of Bath and Wells insisted that the dog be removed from consecrated ground, and there is an eighteenth-century monument to a dog originally in the Champneys' family grounds and now in the churchyard of St Mary, Orchardleigh, on an island in a lake in the landscaped park. But repair work in the 1980s found the skeleton of the dog at Sir Thomas's feet in the vault.

The Second Shepherds' Pageant, from the Wakefield Mystery Plays, early to mid-fifteenth century

The Feast of Corpus Christi, falling close to Midsummer, became the occasion in many towns for the performance of Miracle or Mystery plays, that is, dramatisations of biblical events with different trade guilds taking on their particular story. This Nativity *is taken from one of the most complete surviving cycles. The local and comic ends up transcended by the marvellous miracle.*

Three shepherds, Coll, Gib and Daw, tending their flocks one wintry night on the Wakefield moors, have been joined by Mak, and he has made off with one of their sheep while they were sleeping, taken it home for his wife Gill to hide, and re-joined them. Following their suspicions, they have just been searching his cottage, and at last approach the cradle where Mak and Gill have bundled up their stolen sheep as if it's their newborn.

Daw Mak, with your leave,
Let me give your bairn
But sixpence.
Mak Nay, go away! He's sleeping.
Daw Methinks he is peeping.
Mak When he wakens he'll be weeping.
I pray you go hence!
Daw Give me leave him to kiss
And lift up the clout.
What the devil is this?
He has a long snout!
Coll He is marked amiss.
We wait ill about.
Gib Ill-spun weft, I wys,
Ay comes foul out.
Aye, so!
He is like to our sheep!
Daw How, Gib, may I peep? …
Will you see how they swaddle
His four feet in the middle?
Saw I never in a cradle
A horned lad ere now.
Mak Peace, I say, what!
Let be your fare!

I'm he that him begot,
And yon woman him bore.
Gill A pretty child is he
As sits on a woman's knee,
A dilly-down, pardee,
To make a man laugh.
Daw I know him by the ear-mark –
That is a good token –
Gill He was taken with an elf,
I saw it myself –
When the clock struck twelve
Was he misshapen.

They seize Mak and toss him in a blanket for his trickery, then crash out exhausted – to be woken by an Angel singing 'Gloria in excelsis' and directing them to Bethlehem, for the final scene, and a genuinely miraculous birth.

***Lyke-Wake Dirge*, a traditional North Country song addressed to the dead, traced back to the fourteenth century**

This song is advice to the deceased. John Aubrey in 1686 preserved a version that he had noted down from a Mr Mawtese, who recalled it being sung 'at country vulgar Funeralls': 'At the funerals in Yorkshire to this day they continue the custom of watching & sitting up all night till the Body is interred. In the interim some kneel down and pray (by the corpse), some play at cards, some drink & take Tobacco; they also have Mimical plays and sports.' It was also collected, in the early nineteenth century, by Sir Walter Scott: 'This is a sort of charm sung by the lower ranks of Roman Catholics in some parts of the north of England, while watching a dead body previous to interment. The tune is doleful and monotonous, and joined to the mysterious import of the words has a solemn effect.' It was set by Benjamin Britten in his Serenade for Tenor, Horns and Strings.

This ae night, this ae night,
Every night and all,
Fire and fleet and candle light,
And Christ receive thy soul.

When thou away from hence art passed,
Every night and all,
To Whinny Muir *[gorse moor]* thou com'st at last,
And Christ receive thy soul.

If ever thou gavest hosen and shoon *[stockings and shoes]*,
Every night and all,
Sit thee down and put them on;
And Christ receive thy soul.

If hosen and shoon thou ne'er gave none,
Every night and all,
The whins shall prick thee to the bare bane,
And Christ receive thy soul.

From Whinny Muir when thou may'st pass,
Every night and all,
To Brig o' Dread thou com'st at last;
And Christ receive thy soul.

From Brig o' Dread when thou may'st pass,
Every night and all,
To Purgatory fire thou com'st at last;
And Christ receive thy soul.

If ever thou gavest meat or drink,
Every night and all,
The fire shall never make thee shrink
And Christ receive thy soul.

If meat or drink thou ne'er gav'st none,
Every night and all,
The fire will burn thee to the bare bone;
And Christ receive thy soul.

This ae night, this ae night,
Every night and all,
Fire and fleet and candle light,
And Christ receive thy soul.

The Love-Letter, c. 1500

Go, little bill, and commend me heartily
Unto her that I call my truelove and lady,
By this same true tokening,
That she saw me in church on a Friday morning,
With a sparrow-hawk on my hand,
And my man did by her stand,
And an old woman sat her by
That little knew of courtesy
And often turned on her a smile
To look upon me for a while.
And yet as well, another token,
To the church she came with a gentlewoman,
And right behind the church door
They both knelt down on the floor,
And fast they did pitter-patter –
I hope they were saying Matins together!
Yet once or twice, at the least,
She did on me her eye cast,
Then stepped I forth privily
And greeted them with full courtesy.
By all the tokens, truly,
Commend me to her heartily!

The Demaundes Joyous, from a collection of riddles printed by Wynkyn de Worde, 1511

a) Who was Adam's moder? *The erthe*
b) What space is from the hyest space of the sea to the deepest? *But a stone's cast*
c) How many calves' tayles behoveth to reche from the erthe to the skye? *No more but one if it be long ynough*
d) Which parte of a sergeaunte love ye best towarde you? *His heles*
e) Which is the moost profitable beest, and that men eteth leest of? *That is bees*

f) Which is the brodest water and leest jeopardye to passe over? *The dewe*
g) Why dryve men dogges out of the chyrche? *Bycause they come not up and offre*
h) Why come dogges so often to the churche? *Bycause when they se the aulters covered they wene theyr maysters goo thyder to dyner*
i) What beest is it that hath her tayle bytweene her eyen? *It is a catte when she lycketh her arse*
j) Wherfore set they upon chyrche steples more a cock than a henne? *Yf men sholde sette there a henne, she wolde laye egges, and they wolde fall upon mennes hedes*
k) Which was first, the henne or the egge? *The henne, whan God made her*
l) Why doth an ox or a cowe lye? *Bycause she can not sytte*
m) What tyme in the yere bereth a gose moost feders? *Whan the gander is upon her back*

A feast day, from John Stow (1524/25–1605), *A Survey of London*, 1598

The historian and antiquarian John Stow gives accounts of how some of the festivals were celebrated. The Feast of St Bartholomew falls on 24 August. The three-day fair in Smithfield, ostensibly raising funds for the Priory there, was originally licensed by Henry I in 1133. It became a somewhat notorious event.

In the month of August, about the feast of St. Bartholomew the Apostle, before the Lord Mayor, aldermen and sheriffs of London, placed in a large tent near unto Clarkenwell, of old time, were divers days spent in the pastime of wrestling, where the officers of the city, namely the sheriffs, sergeants, and yeomen, the porters of the king's beam or weigh-house, now no such men, and other of the city, were challengers of all men in the suburbs, to wrestle for games appointed, and on other days, before the said mayor, aldermen, and sheriffs, in Fensburie field, to shoot the standard, broad arrow, and flight, for games; but now of late years the wrestling is only practised on Bartholomew's day in the afternoon, and the shooting some three or four days after, in one afternoon, and no more. What should I speak of the ancient daily exercises in the long bow by citizens of this city, now almost clean left off and forsaken? – I overpass it; for by the mean of closing in the common grounds, our archers, for want of room to shoot abroad, creep into bowling alleys, and ordinary dicing houses, nearer home, where they have room enough to hazard their money at unlawful games; and there I leave them to take their pleasures.

Some of the fools, from Desiderius Erasmus (*c.* 1466–1536), *In Praise of Folly*, 1511

The Dutch humanist scholar wrote his Moria *while living in England and teaching Greek and Divinity at Cambridge; he dedicated it to his friend and fellow-Catholic Thomas More.*

The next to be placed among the regiment of fools are such as make a trade of telling or inquiring after incredible stories of miracles and prodigies. Never doubting that a lie will choke them, they will muster up a thousand several strange relations of spirits, ghosts, apparitions, raising of the devil, and suchlike bugbears of superstition; which the farther they are from being probably true, the more greedily they are swallowed, and the more devoutly believed. And these absurdities do not only bring an empty pleasure, and cheap divertissement, but they are a good trade, and procure a comfortable income to such priests and friars as by this craft get their gain.

To these again are nearly related such others as attribute strange virtues to the shrines and images of saints and martyrs, and so would make their credulous proselytes believe, that if they pay their devotion to St. Christopher in the morning, they shall be guarded and secured the day following from all dangers and misfortunes. If soldiers, when they first take arms, shall come and mumble over such a set prayer before the picture of St. Barbara, they shall return safe from all engagements. Or if any pray to [St] Erasmus on such particular holidays, with the ceremony of wax candles, and other fopperies, he shall in short time be rewarded with a plentiful increase of wealth and riches. The Christians have now their gigantic St George, as well as the pagans had their Hercules; they paint the saint on horseback, and drawing the horse in splendid trappings, very gloriously accoutred, they scarce refrain in a literal sense from worshipping the very beast.

What shall I say of such as cry up and maintain the cheat of pardons and indulgences? That by these compute the time of each soul's residence in purgatory, and assign them a longer or shorter continuance, according as they purchase more or fewer of these paltry pardons and saleable exemptions?

Or what can be said bad enough of others, who pretend that by the force of such magical charms, or by the fumbling over their beads in the rehearsal of such and such petitions, which some religious impostors invented, either for diversion, or, what is more likely, for advantage; they shall procure riches, honour, pleasure, health, long life, a lusty old age, nay, after death a sitting at the right hand of our Saviour in his Kingdom.

Though as to this last part of their happiness, they care not how long it be deferred, having scarce any appetite toward a tasting the joys of heaven; till they are surfeited, glutted with, and can no longer relish the enjoyments on earth. By this easy way of purchasing pardons, any notorious highwayman, any plundering soldier, or any bribe-taking judge, shall disburse some part of their unjust gains, and so think all their grossest impieties sufficiently atoned for. So many perjuries, lusts, drunkenness, quarrels, bloodsheds, cheats, treacheries, and all sorts of debaucheries shall all be, as it were, struck a bargain for, and such a contract made, as if they had paid off all arrears, and might now begin upon a new score.

And what can be more ridiculous, than for some others to be confident of going to heaven by repeating daily those seven verses out of the Psalms, which the devil taught St. Bernard; thinking thereby to have put a trick upon him, but that thereby he was over-reached in his cunning.

Several of these fooleries which are so gross and absurd, as I myself am even ashamed to own, are practised and admired, not only by the vulgar, but by such proficient in religion as one might well expect should have more wit.

From the same principles of folly proceeds the custom of each country's challenging their particular guardian-saint. Nay, each saint has his distinct office allotted to him, and is accordingly addressed upon the respective occasions. As one for the toothache, a second to grant an easy delivery in child-birth, a third to help persons to lost goods, another to protect seamen in a long voyage, a fifth to guard the farmer's cows and sheep, and so on. For to rehearse all instances would be extremely tedious.

There are some more catholic saints petitioned to upon all occasions, as more especially the Virgin Mary, whose blind devotees think it manners now to place the mother before the Son.

And of all the prayers and intercessions that are made to these respective saints the substance of them is no more than downright Folly. Among all the trophies that for tokens of gratitude are hung upon the walls and ceilings of churches, you shall find no relics presented as a memorandum of any that were ever cured of Folly, or had been made one dram the wiser.

One perhaps after shipwreck got safe to shore; another recovered when he had been run through by an enemy; one, when all his fellow-soldiers were killed upon the spot, as cunningly perhaps as cowardly, made his escape from the field; another, while he was a-hanging, the rope broke, and so he saved his neck, and renewed his licence for practising his old trade of thieving; another broke gaol, and got loose; a patient, against his physician's will, recovered of a dangerous fever; another drank poison, which putting him into a violent looseness, did his body more good than hurt, to the great grief of his wife, who hoped upon this occasion to have become a joyful widow; another had his waggon overturned, and yet none of his horses lamed; another had caught a grievous fall, and yet recovered from the bruise; another had been tampering with his neighbour's wife, and escaped very narrowly from being caught by the enraged cuckold in the very act.

After all these acknowledgments of escapes from such singular dangers, there is none, as I have before intimated, that return thanks for being freed from Folly. Folly, being so sweet and luscious, that it is rather sued for as a happiness, than deprecated as a punishment.

On the need for translation of the Bible, from William Tyndale (*c.* 1494–1536), *The Obedience of a Christian Man*, 1528

In the gathering storm of Protestant challenges to Church authority, providing lay people with translations in their own language grew to be one of the most insistent concerns. Tyndale became a master of seven languages; like Erasmus and Miles Coverdale he took seriously the importance of reaching behind Jerome's Vulgate version to the original Hebrew and Greek. Betrayed while in exile in Antwerp, he was convicted of heresy, and after death by strangulation at the stake his body was burnt. But three years later Coverdale used his work as the basis of Henry VIII's Great Bible, and seventy years later King James's learned committee owed Tyndale's work a similar debt.

They [that is, those opposed to a Bible in the common tongue] will say haply, the scripture requireth a pure mind and a quiet mind; and therefore the lay-man, because he is altogether cumbered with worldly business, cannot understand them. If that be the cause, then it is a plain case that our prelates understand not the scriptures themselves: for no lay-man is so tangled with worldly business as they are. The great things of the world are ministered by them; neither do the lay-people any great thing, but at their assignment.

'If the scripture were in the mother tongue,' they will say, 'then would the lay-people understand it, every man after his own ways.' Wherefore serveth the curate, but to teach him the right way? Wherefore were the holy days made, but that the people should come and learn? Are ye not abominable schoolmasters, in that ye take so great wages, if ye will not teach? If ye would teach, how could ye do it so well, and with so great profit, as when the lay-people have the scripture before them in the mother tongue? For then should they see, by the order of the text, whether thou jugglest or not: and then would they believe it, because it is the scripture of God, though thy living be never so abominable. Where now, because your living and your preaching are so contrary, and because they grope out in every sermon your open and manifest lies, and smell your unsatiable covetousness, they believe you not when you preach truth. But, alas! the curates themselves (for the most part) wot no more what the new or old Testament meaneth, than do the Turks: neither know they of any more than they read at mass, matins, and evensong, which yet they understand not: neither care they, but even to mumble up so much every day, as the [mag]pie and popinjay speak, they wot not what, to fill their bellies withal. If they will not let the lay-man have the word of God in his mother tongue, yet let the priests have it; which for a great part of them do understand no Latin at all, but sing, and say, and patter all day, with the lips only, that which the heart understandeth not.

The Case of the Poor Man and the Priest, from Sir Thomas More (1477–1535), *Dialogues*

Lawyer, humanist, statesman, author of Utopia *and numerous other works, and eventually martyr, More's wit was also part of his perspective.*

'Such witnesses shall indeed not speak falsely,' he said, 'as in the case of the poor man and the priest – if I may be down to earth and tell you an amusing story.'

'A merry tale to my mind never comes amiss,' I said.

'The poor man,' he said, 'had found the priest being over-familiar with his wife, and because he talked about it in public and couldn't prove it, the priest had him up before the bishop's official for defamation; and the poor man was ordered, upon pain of excommunication, to stand up in his parish church, on Sunday at high mass, and say, 'Mouth, you lie.' So to fulfil his penance, the poor soul was set up in a pew, for the people to have a good look at him and hear what he said. And there, after he had repeated the story he had spread about the priest, he put his hands over his mouth and out loud said, 'Mouth, mouth, you lie.' And straight after he put his hands over both his eyes, saying 'But eyes, eyes, by the mass ye lie not a jot.'

Sir Thomas More visited in prison by his wife, from William Roper (1495/96–1578), *The Life of Sir Thomas More*, 1534

More's fall from favour was complete when he refused to swear to the Act of Succession, and in 1534 he was committed to the Tower of London, where his wife Dame Alice visited him. Roper, who wrote this account, was married to their daughter Meg. More was executed as a traitor on 6 July 1535, insisting that he was dying for his faith.

When Sir Thomas More had continued a good while in the Tower, my lady, his wife, obtained licence to see him. Who, at her first coming, like a simple ignorant woman, and somewhat worldly too, with this matter of salutation saluted him:

'What the good year, Master More,' quoth she, 'I marvel that you, that have been always hitherto taken for so wise a man, will now so play the fool to lie here in this close, filthy prison, and be content thus to be shut up amongst mice and rats, when you might be abroad at your liberty. And with the favour and good will both of the King and his Council, if you would but do as all the bishops and best learned of this realm have done. And seeing you have at Chelsea a right fair house, your library, your books, your gallery, your garden, your orchard and all other necessaries so handsome about you, where you might be in the company of me your wife, your children and household be merry, I muse what a God's name you mean here still thus fondly to tarry.'

After he had a while quietly heard her, with a cheerful countenance he said unto her, 'I pray thee, good Mistress Alice, tell me one thing.'

'What is that?' quoth she.

'Is not this house,' quoth he, 'as nigh heaven as my own?'

To whom she, after her accustomed homely fashion, not liking such talk, answered, 'Tilly-vally, tilly-vally!'

'How say you, Mistress Alice,' quoth he, 'is it not so?'

'Good God, good God, man will this gear never be left?' quoth she.

'Well, then, Mistress Alice, if it be so,' quoth he, 'it is very well. For I see no great cause why I should much joy either of my gay house or of anything belonging thereunto when, if I should but seven years lie buried under the ground, and then arise and come thither again, I should not fail to find some therein that would bid me get out of doors, and tell me it were none of mine. What cause have I then to like such an house as would so soon forget his master?'

So her persuasions moved him but a little.

From 'A Dialogue between Cardinal Pole and Thomas Lupset, Lecturer in Rhetoric at Oxford', by Thomas Starkey (*c.* 1495–1538)

Thomas Starkey was Chaplain to Henry VIII. Reginald Pole (1500–1558) was Henry VIII's cousin (through his mother Margaret Pole), and was under repeated pressure from the King to use his influence in the Church as an international scholar to support his pursuit of a divorce from Catherine of Aragon. Thomas Starkey's dialogue may have been based on an actual meeting between the two men at Bisham Abbey in 1529. It seems to have been an attempt to establish Pole's position as both loyalist to the King and principled man of the Church. He was reluctantly made a cardinal in 1536, and Papal Legate to England in 1537.

Corruptions and Diseases in the English Body Politic

POLE Well, then, let us consider and behold how that, beside this lack of people, there is, also, in this politic body, another disease and sickness more grievous than this, and that is this (shortly to say): A great part of these people which we have here in our country, is either idle or ill occupied, and a small number of them exerciseth themself in doing their office and duty pertaining to the maintenance of the common weal; by the reason whereof this body is replenished and overfulfilled with many ill humours, which I call idle and unprofitable persons, of whom you shall find a great number, if you will a little consider all states, orders, and degrees, here in our country.

First, look what an idle rout our noblemen keep and nourish in their houses, which do nothing else but carry dishes to the table and eat them when they have done; and after, giving themself to hunting, hawking, dicing, carding, and all other idle pastimes and vain, as though they were born to nothing else at all. Look to our bishops and prelates of the realm, whether they follow not the same trade in nourishing such an idle sort, spending their possessions and goods, which were to them given to be distributed among them which were oppressed with poverty and necessity. Look, furthermore, to priest, monks, friars, and canons, with all their adherents and idle train, and you shall find also among them no small number idle and unprofitable, which be nothing but burdens to the earth. In so much that if you, after this manner, examine the multitude in every order and degree, you shall find, as I think, the third part of our people living in idleness, as persons to the common weal utterly unprofitable; and to all good civility, much like unto the drone bees in a hive, which do nothing else but consume and devour all such thing as the busy and good bee, with diligence and labour, gathereth together.

LUPSET Master Pole, me seemeth you examine this matter somewhat too shortly, as though you would have all men to labour, to go to the plough, and exercise some craft, which is not necessary. For our mother the ground is so plenteous and bountiful by the goodness of God and of nature given to her, that with little labour and tillage she will sufficiently nourish mankind, none otherwise than she doth all beasts, fishes, and fowls, which are bred and brought up upon her; to whom we see she ministreth food with little labour or none, but of her own friendly benignity. Wherefore if a few of our people busy themselves, and labour therein, it is sufficient; the rest may live in triumph, at liberty, and ease, free from all bodily labour and pain.

POLE This is spoken, Master Lupset, even as though you judged man to be born for to live in idleness and pleasure, all thing referring and applying thereto. But, Sir, it is no thing so; but contrary, he is born to labour and travail, after the opinion of the wise and ancient antiquity, none otherwise than as a bird to fly; and not to live (as Homer saith some do) as an unprofitable weight and burden of the earth. For man is born to be as a governor, ruler, and diligent tiller and inhabitant of this earth, as some, by labour of body, to procure things necessary for the maintenance of man's life; some, by wisdom and policy, to keep the rest of the multitude in good order and civility. So that none be born to this idleness and vanity, to the which the most part of our people is much given and bent; but all to exercise themselves in some fashion of life convenient to the dignity and nature of man. Wherefore, though it be so that it is no thing necessary all to be labourers and tillers of the ground, but some to be priests and ministers of God's Word, some to be gentlemen to the governance of the rest, and some servants to the same; yet this is certain, that overgreat number of them, without due proportion to the other parts of the body, is superfluous in any commonalty. It is not to be doubted but that here in our country of those sorts be over-many, and specially of them which we call serving-men, which live in service to gentlemen, lords, and other of nobility. If you look throughout the world, as I think, you shall not find in any one country, proportionable to ours, like number of that sort.

LUPSET Marry, Sir, that is troth, wherein, me seemeth, you praise our country very much; for in them standeth the royalty of the realm. If the yeomanry of England were not, we should be in shrewd case, for in them standeth the chief defence of England.

POLE Oh, Master Lupset, you take the matter amiss. In them standeth the beggary of England; in them is nourished the common theft therein, as hereafter at large I shall declare. Howbeit, if they were exercised in feats of arms, to the defence of the realm in time of war, they might be much better suffered. But you see how little they be exercised therein, insomuch that, in time of war, it is necessary for our ploughmen and labourers of the country to take weapon in hand, or else we were not like long to enjoy England; so little trust is to be put in *their* [i.e. yeomen's] feats and deeds. Wherefore doubt you no more but of them (like as of other that I have spoke of before, – as of priests, friars, monks, and other called religious) we have over-many, which altogether make our body politic unwieldy and heavy, and, as it were, to be grieved with gross humours; insomuch that this disease therein may well be compared to a dropsy in a man's body.

'That all daunsynge is nat to be reproved', from Sir Thomas Elyot (*c.* 1499–1546), *The boke named The Governour* (1531)

In his dedication to Henry VIII Sir Thomas wrote: 'I have now enterprised to describe in our vulgar tongue the form of a just public weal: which matter I have gathered as well of the sayings of most noble authors (greeks and latins) as by mine own experience. ... This present book treateth of the education of them that hereafter may be deemed worthy to be governors of the public weal under your highness.'

I am nat of that opinion that all daunsing generally is repugnant unto virtue: although some persons excellently learned, specially divines, so do affirm it, which alway have in their mouths (whan they come into the pulpit) the saying of the noble doctor St. Augustine, That better it were to delve or to go to the plough on the Sunday than to daunse: which might be spoken of that kind of daunsing which was used in the time of St. Augustine, when every thing with the empire of Rome declined from their perfection, and the old manner of daunsing was forgotten, and none remained but that which was lascivious, and corrupted the kinds of them that daunsed, and provoked sin, as semblably some do at this day. Also at that time Idolatry was nat clearly extinct, but divers fragments thereof remained in every region. And perchance solemn daunses, which were celebrate unto the paynyms' false gods, were yet continued; for as much as the pure religion of Christ was nat in all places consolidate, and the pastors and curates did wink at such recreations, fearing that if they should hastily have removed it, and induced suddenly the severity of God's laws, they should steer the people thereby to a general sedition; to the imminent daunger and subversion of Christ's whole religion, late sown among them, and nat yet sufficiently rooted. But the wise and discreet doctor St. Augustine, using the art of an orator, wherein he was right excellent, omitting all rigorous menace or terror, dissuaded them by the most easiest way from that manner ceremony belonging to idolatry; preferring before it bodily occupation; thereby aggravating the offence to God that was in that ceremony, since occupation, which is necessary for man's sustenance, and in due times virtuous, is nat withstanding prohibited to be used on the Sundays. And yet in these words of this noble doctor is nat so general dispraise to all daunsing as some men do suppose. And that is for two causes. First in his comparison he ... annexeth it with tilling and digging of the earth, which be labours incident to man's living, and in them is contained nothing that is vicious. Wherefore the pre-eminence thereof above daunsing qualifying the offence, they being done out of due time, that is to say, in an holy day, concludeth nat daunsing to be at all times and in every manner unlawful or vicious, considering that in certain cases of extreme necessity men might both plough and delve without doing to God any offence. Also it shall seem to them that seriously do examine the said words that therein St. Augustine doth nat prohibit daunsing so generally as it is taken, but only such daunses which (as I late said) were superstitious and contained in them a spice of idolatry, or else did with unclean motions of countenances irritate the minds of the dauncers to venereal lusts, whereby fornication and adultery were daily increased. Also in those daunces were interlaced ditties of wanton love or ribaldry, with frequent remembrance of the most vile idols Venus and Bacchus, as it were that the daunce were to their honour and memory, which most of all abhorred from Christ's religion, savouring the ancient error of paganism. I would to God those names were nat at this day used in ballads and ditties in the courts of princes and noble men, where may good wits be corrupte with semblable fantasies, which in better wise employed might have been more necessary to the public weal and their prince's honour. But now will I leave this serious matter to divines to persuade or dissuade herein according to their offices.

Decree of Henry VIII abolishing several festival days, 1537

The King ordered John Longland, Bishop of Lincoln, to issue a printed copy of this decree to every church in his diocese for public proclamation.

Forasmuch as the number of holidays is so excessively grown, and yet daily more by men's 'devotion' (yea, rather, 'superstition') was like further to increase, that the same was (and should be) not only prejudicial to the common weal by reason that it is occasion as well of much sloth and idleness ... as of decay of good mysteries and arts ... and loss of man's food ... but also pernicious to the souls of many men, which, being enticed by the licentious vacation & liberty of those holidays, do upon the same commonly use and practise more excess, riot and superfluity than upon any other days ... It is therefore, by the king's highness' authority, as supreme head on earth of the church of England, with the common assent of the prelates and clergy of this his realm in convocation lawfully assembled and congregate, (among other things) decreed, ordained, and established –

First, that the feast of Dedication of the church shall in all places throughout this realm be *celebrated* and kept on the first Sunday of the month of October for ever, and upon no other day.

[Item: parishioners from now on legally to work on their church's feast day.]

Also, that all those feasts or holidays which shall happen to fall or occur either in the harvest time (which is to be counted from the first day of July unto the 29th day of September), or else in the term time at Westminster, shall not be kept or observed from henceforth as holidays, but that it may be lawful for every man to go to his work or occupation upon the same, as upon any other work day (Except always the feasts of the apostles, of our Blessed Lady and of Saint George, And also such feasts wherein the King's judges at Westminster Hall do not use to sit in Judgment, All which shall be kept holy and solemn of every man, as in time past have been accustomed).

Provided always that it may be lawful to all priests and Clerks, as well secular as Regular, in the foresaid holidays now abrogate, to sing or say their accustomed service for those holidays in their churches, So that they do not the same solemnly, nor do ring to the same after the manner used in high holidays, nor do command or indict the same to be kept or observed as holidays.

Finally, the feasts of the Nativity of our Lord, of Easter, of the Nativity of St. John the Baptist, and of St. Michael Archangel, shall from henceforth be counted, accepted, and taken for the four general offering days.

Long Melford, Suffolk, in its Catholic days, from Roger Martin (*c.* 1527–1615), Memoir (*c.* 1590)

Roger Martin recalls some of the parish rituals from the time of his Catholic youth as churchwarden of Holy Trinity in the time of Queen Mary (1553–58). There are brasses of him and his two wives in the floor of the church.

On Corpus Christi day they went likewise with the Blessed Sacrament in procession about the church green in copes, and I think also they went in procession about the said green, with handbells ringing before them, as they did about the bounds of the town in Rogation Week, on the Monday one way, on the Tuesday another way, on the Wednesday another way, praying for rain or fair weather as the time required, having a drinking and a dinner there upon Monday, being fast day; and Tuesday, being a fish day, they had a breakfast with butter and cheese etc., at the parsonage and a drinking at Master Clopton's by Kentwell at his manor of Lutons near the ponds in the park, where there was a little chapel, I think of St. Anne, for that was their longest perambulation. Upon Wednesday, being fasting day, they had a drinking at Melford Hall. All the choir dined there three times in the year at least, namely, St. Stephen's day, mid-Lent Sunday, and I think upon Easter Monday. On St. James's day, mass being sung then by note, and the organs going in St. James's Chapel (which were brought into my house with the clock and bell that stood there, and the organs that stood upon the rood loft) that was then a little way from the road, which chapel had been maintained by my ancestors. And therefore I will that my heirs, when time serve, shall repair, place there, and maintain all these things again. There were also fair stools on either side, such as are in the church, which were had away by John King's means, who was Sir William Cordell's bailiff; about which chapel there was paled in round about a convenient piece of the green for one to walk in.

On St. James's Even there was a bonfire, and a tub of ale and bread then given to the poor, and before my door there was made three other bonfires, namely, on Midsummer Even, on the Even of St. Peter and St. Paul, when they had the like drinkings, and on St. Thomas's Even, on which, if it fell not on the fish day, they had some long pies of mutton and peasecods, set out upon boards with the aforesaid quantity of bread and ale. And in all these bonfires, some of the friends and more civil neighbours were called in, and sat at the board with my grandfather, who had at the lighting of the bonfires wax tapers with balls of wax, yellow and green, set up all the breadth of the hall, lighted then and burning there before the image of John the Baptist.

The countryside after the dissolution of the monasteries, from Thomas Beccon (*c.* 1511–1567), *The Jewel of Joy*

Thomas Beccon was a Protestant, chaplain to Thomas Cranmer and later to Lord Protector Somerset. Under the Catholic Queen Mary as a married priest he lost his living, and was imprisoned in the Tower of London for seditious preaching. He fled the country on release, but was able to return to Canterbury under Elizabeth. Although he had suffered under Mary, he finds that after the dissolution of the monasteries the towns and villages have emptied, the countryside has been given over to rich 'gentlemen', morals have lapsed, and church wealth has been dispersed and its welfare system lost.

Truth it is. For I my selfe know many townes and villages sore decayed, for that whereas in times past there were in some town an hundred housholdes there remain not now thirty, in some fifty there are not now ten, yea (which is more to be lamented) I knowe townes so wholly decayed, that there is neyther sticke nor stone standying as they use to day.

Where many men had good livynges, and maynteined hospitality, able at times to helpe the kyng in his warres, and to susteyne other charges, able also to helpe their pore neighboures, and vertuously to bring up their children in Godly letters and good scyences, now sheepe and conies devoure altogether, no man inhabiting the aforesaid places. ... Those beastes which were created of God for the nouryshment of man doe nowe devoure man. The Scripture sayeth that God made both shepe and oxen wyth all the beastes of the fielde subject unto man, but nowe man is subject unto them. Where man was wonte to beare rule there they now beare rule. Where man was wont to have hys living, there they nowe onely live. Where man was wont to inhabyt, there they now raign and graze.

And the cause of all thys wretchednesse and beggary in the common weale are the greedy Gentylmen, which are sheepmongers and graziers. Whyle they study for their owne private commoditie, the common weal is like to decay. Since they began to be sheepe Maysters and feeders of cattell we nyther had vittayle not cloth of any reasonable pryce. ... For they are touched with no pity toward the poore. It is founde true in them that S. Paul wrighteth. All seke their own advantage and not those thynges which belong unto Jesu Christ. They which in times past wer wont to be fathers of the contry, are now pollers and pyllers [robbers and despoilers] of the contry. They which in times past wer wont to be the defenders of the poore, are now become the destroiers of the same. They by whom the common weale sometimes was preserved, are now become the Caterpillers of the common weale ... They are right brothers of Cain, which had rather slay his brother Abel, than he should have any part with him of worldly possessions. ... They abhorre the names of Monkes, Friars, Canons, Nunnes &c. but their goods they gredely gripe. And yet where the cloysters kept hospitality, let out their farmes at a reasonable pryce, norysshed schools, brought up youth in good letter, they did none of all these thinges. They lightlie esteme and in a maner contemne Priestes, parsons, vicares, Prebendaries, &c., yet their possessions they gladly embrase and niggardly retain ... And yet how vainly those goods be spent, who seeth not? The state of England was never so miserable, as it is at this present.

The practice of the longbow, from the sixth sermon of Archbishop Latimer (*c.* 1487–1555) before King Edward VI, 1549

Deeply scored stones on church walls where arrow-heads were sharpened, e.g. at Mugginton (Derbyshire), are evidence of parish butts being set up in churchyards.

Men of England in times past, when they would exercise themselves (for we must needs have some recreation, our bodies cannot endure without some exercise) they were wont to go abroad in the fields a-shooting, but now it is turned into glossing [cheating], gulling, and whoring within the house. The Art of Shooting hath been in times past much esteemed in this realm, it is a gift of God that he hath given us to excel all other nations withal, it hath been God's instrument whereby he hath given us many victories against our enemies. But now we have taken up whoring in townes, instead of Shooting in the fields. A wondrous thing, that so excellent a gift of God should be so little esteemed.

I desire you, my Lords, even as ye love the honour and glory of God, and intend to remove his indignation, let there be sent forth some proclamation, some sharp proclamation to the Justices of Peace, for they do not their duty. Justices now be no Justices; there be many good acts made for this matter already. ... Charge them upon their allegiance, that this singular benefit of God may be practised, and that it be not turned into bowling, glossing, and whoring within the towns: for they be negligent in executing these laws of Shooting.

In my time, my poor father was as diligent to teach me to Shoot, as to learn me any other things, and so I think other men did with their children. He taught me how to draw, how to lay my body in my bow, and not to draw with strength of arms as other nations do, but with strength of the body. I had my bows bought me, according to my age and strength: as I increased in them, so my bows were made bigger and bigger: for men shall never Shoot well, except they be brought up in it. It is a goodly Art, a wholesome kind of exercise, and much commended in Physick.

Reprisals after the Prayer Book Rebellion, from John Hooker (1526–1601), *History of Exeter* (1549)

Hooker, also known as John Vowell, wrote of the Prayer Book Rebellion that it was 'The last most troublesome commotion Anno 1549 whereof I was an eye wyttnes and can testifie it to be true'. It was a popular uprising among the men of Cornwall and Devon against the newly enforced use of Cranmer's English Prayer Book and the banning of Catholic ritual. After a five-week siege of Exeter and several pitched battles fought against an army of largely foreign mercenaries under the command of Lord John Russell it ended in ruthless anti-Catholic reprisals.

Among the many to be executed and put to death there was no one so exalted as was Welsh, the Vicar of St Thomas near the Exe bridge at Exeter ... This man had many good things in him; he was of no great stature, but well set and mightily compact; he was a very good wrestler, shot well, both in the long bow as also in the crossbow, he handled his handgun and piece very well. ... He descended of a good honest parentage, being born at Penrhyn in Cornwall.

And yet notwithstanding in this Rebellion an Archcaptain, and a principal doer: he was charged with three principal crimes. The first was that he did not only persuade the people to the contemning of the reformed religion according to the king's proceedings and to keep and observe the Romish and popish religion, but also did erect, keep and use the same in his parish Church; secondarily, he was a Captain and a principal dealer in the cause of the Rebellion which was chiefly directed by his order and advice; thirdly, he caused one Kingwell, a Tinner [miner] of Tavistock and servant to Mr John Charles of Tavistock to be hanged, because secretly he had conveyed letters between my Lord [Russell] and his master, who was earnest in the reformed religion which was then termed the king's proceedings and an enemy of the popish state, and being a sharp inveigher against the one and earnest defender of t'other it procured unto him great hatred and malice. When the Rebellion was begun he sought by all the means he could how to escape away, but he was so narrowly watched that he could never have any opportunity so to do. They used all the devices they could to recover him to their opinion, sometimes fair words, sometimes with threatenings and sometimes with imprisonment; but still he inveighed against them, calling them Rebels and Traitors both against God and the King and fore-prophesying unto them that destruction and confusion would be the end and reward of their doings. Thus when they could not reclaim him to their disposition, then by the order and judgment of this vicar Welsh he was fetched out of the prison and forthwith brought before Caiaphas and Pilate and condemned to be hanged: which was executed upon him forthwith and he was brought to an elm tree in Exe-lond without the west gate of the city before the house of one Nicholas Cove and there hanged.

The like cruelty or rather tyranny was done at Sampford Courtenay, where when a certain franklin or gentleman named William Hellions, who coming to Sampford to have some communication with them for the stay of their rebellion and for the pacifying them in their due obedience was at the town's end taken prisoner and carried to the Church house, where he so earnestly reproved them of their rebellion, and so sharply threatened them of an evil success, that they all fell in a rage with him – and not only with evil words reviled him, but also as he was going out of the Church house and going down the stairs, one of them named Lithbridge with a bill struck him in the neck, and immediately notwithstanding his pitiful requests and lamentations, a number of the rest fell upon him and slew him and cut him in small pieces; and notwithstanding they counted him for a heretic, yet they buried him in the churchyard there.

These things being called to remembrance and objected against this Vicar, although some men in respect of his virtues and good gifts did pity and lament his cause and would have gladly been suitors for his pardon, yet, the greatness of his lewdness [ignorance] and follies considered, they left him unto his deserts, and so he was by the martial law condemned to death.

And yet this one thing by the way I must speak in his commendation. There was among the Rebels a stranger and Alien who was a very skilful gunner, and could handle his piece very well and did much harm to the City, and among others slew one Smith standing at a door in North Gate Street with a great shot from St David's Hill; this fellow took upon him that he would set the whole City on fire and it should be clean burned within four hours, do what they could. This his offer was so well liked that the day and time was appointed when this should be done. This Vicar hearing hereof assembleth unto him as many men as he could make and have, and came to this company when this fire should be kindled, and was so hot and earnest against their attempts that he would nowise suffer so lewd an act and wicked a thing to be done. For, saith he, do you what you can by policy, force, or dint of sword to take the City, and I will join with you, and do my best. But to burn a City which shall be hurtful to all men and good to no man, I will never consent thereunto, but will here stand with all my power against you. And so stout he was in this matter that he stopped them of their further enterprise of so wicked a fact.

But to the matter. The execution of this man was committed to Barnard Duffield, who being nothing slack to follow his commission caused a pair of gallows to be made and to be set up upon the top of the Tower of the said vicar's parish Church of St Thomas. And all things being ready and the stage perfected for this Tragedy, the Vicar was brought to the place, and by a rope about his middle drawn up to the top of the Tower and there in chains hanged in his popish apparel and having a holy water bucket, a sprinkle, a sacring bell, a pair of beads and such other like popish trash hanged about him; and there with the same about him remained a long time. He made a very small or no confession but very patiently took his death. He had been a good member in his commonwealth had not the weeds overgrown the good corn and his foul vices overcome his virtues.

'The Behaviour of Dr Ridley and Master Latimer, at the Time of their Death, which was the 16th of October 1555', from John Foxe (1516–1587), 'Book of Martyrs'

John Foxe took refuge in Protestant Europe when the Catholic Queen Mary succeeded her brother Edward VI, and began compiling his history of Protestant persecution, the 'Book of Martyrs', eventually published in 1563 as Actes and Monuments, *following his return to England on Elizabeth's accession. He was ordained in 1560. By order of Convocation in 1571, copies were chained alongside the Great Bible in cathedrals and several churches, as an instrument of affirming the new Anglican order.*

*Nicholas Ridley (1500–1555), one-time chaplain to Archbishop Cranmer and Henry VIII, a reforming Bishop of London, who aided Cranmer in drawing up the 39 Articles, was in his fifties. He was imprisoned after supporting Lady Jane Grey's cause to succeed Edward VI. Hugh Latimer (*c. *1487–1555), a former Bishop of Worcester and a noted doctrinal reformer, was about seventy.*

Upon the north-side of the town, in the ditch over against Balliol-college, the place of execution was appointed: and for fear of any tumult that might arise, to let the burning of them, the lord Williams was commanded, by the queen's letters, and the householders of the city, to be there assistant, sufficiently appointed. And when everything was in a readiness, the prisoners were brought forth by the mayor and the bailiffs.

Master Ridley had a fair black gown furred, and faced with foins, such as he was wont to wear being bishop, and a tippet of velvet furred likewise about his neck, a velvet night-cap upon his head, and a corner cap upon the same, going in a pair of slippers to the stake, and going between the mayor and an alderman, etc.

After him came master Latimer in a poor Bristol frieze frock all worn, with his buttoned cap, and a kerchief on his head, all ready to the fire, a new long shroud hanging over his hose, down to the feet: which at the first sight stirred men's hearts to rue upon them, beholding on the one side, the honour they sometime had, and on the other, the calamity whereunto they were fallen.

Master doctor Ridley, as he passed toward Bocardo [the town prison], looked up where master Cranmer did lie, hoping belike to have seen him at the glass-window, and to have spoken unto him. But then master Cranmer was busy with friar Soto and his fellows, disputing together, so Ridley, looking back, espied master Latimer coming after, unto whom he said, 'Oh, be ye there?' 'Yea,' said master Latimer, 'have after as fast as I can follow.' So he, following a pretty way off, at length they came both to the stake, the one after the other, where first Dr. Ridley entering the place, marvellous earnestly holding up both his hands, looked towards heaven. Then shortly after espying master Latimer, with a wonderous cheerful look he ran to him, embraced, and kissed him; and, as they that stood near reported, comforted him, saying, 'Be of good heart, brother, for God will either assuage the fury of the flame, or else strengthen us to abide it.'

With that went he to the stake, kneeled down by it, kissed it, and most effectuously prayed, and behind him master Latimer kneeled, as earnestly calling upon God as he. After they arose, the one talked with the other a little while, till they which were appointed to see the execution, removed themselves out of the sun. What they said I can learn of no man.

Then Dr. Smith, of whose recantation in king Edward's time ye heard before, began his sermon to them upon this text of St. Paul, 'If I yield my body to the fire to be burnt, and have not charity, I shall gain nothing thereby.' Wherein he alleged that the goodness of the cause, and not the order of death, maketh the holiness of the reason. ...

Dr. Ridley said to master Latimer, 'Will you begin to answer the sermon, or shall I?' Master Latimer said, 'Begin you first, I pray you.' 'I will,' said master Ridley.

Then, the wicked sermon being ended, Dr. Ridley and master Latimer kneeled down upon their knees towards my lord Williams of Thame, the vice-chancellor of Oxford, and divers other commissioners appointed for that purpose, who sat upon a form thereby; unto whom master Ridley said, 'I beseech you, my lord, even for Christ's sake, that I may speak but two or three words.' And whilst my lord bent his head to the mayor and vice-chancellor, to know (as it appeared) whether he might give him leave to speak, the bailiffs and Dr. Marshall, vice-chancellor, ran hastily unto him, and with their hands stopped his mouth, and said, 'Master Ridley, if you will revoke your erroneous opinions, and recant the same, you shall not only have liberty so to do, but also the benefit of a subject; that is, have your life.' 'Not otherwise?' said master Ridley. 'No,' quoth Dr. Marshal. 'Therefore if you will not so do, then there is no remedy but you must suffer for your deserts.' 'Well,' quoth master Ridley, 'so long as the breath is in my body, I will never deny my Lord Christ, and his known truth: God's will be done in me!' And with that he rose up, and said with a loud voice, 'Well then, I commit our cause to Almighty

God, which shall indifferently judge all.' To whose saying, master Latimer added his old posy, 'Well! there is nothing hid but it shall be opened.' And he said, he could answer Smith well enough, if he might be suffered.

Incontinently they were commanded to make them ready, which they with all meekness obeyed. Master Ridley took his gown and his tippet, and gave it to his brother-in-law master Shipside, who all his time of imprisonment, although he might not be suffered to come to him, lay there at his own charges to provide him necessaries, which from time to time he sent him by the serjeant that kept him. Some other of his apparel that was little worth, he gave away; other the bailiffs took.

He gave away besides, divers other small things to gentlemen standing by, and divers of them pitifully weeping, as to sir Henry Lea he gave a new groat; and to divers of my lord Williams's gentlemen some napkins, some nutmegs, and rases of ginger; his dial, and such other things as he had about him, to every one that stood next him. Some plucked the points off his hose. Happy was he that might get any rag of him.

Master Latimer gave nothing, but very quietly suffered his keeper to pull off his hose, and his other array, which to look unto was very simple: and being stripped into his shroud, he seemed as comely a person to them that were there present, as one should lightly see; and whereas in his clothes he appeared a withered and crooked silly old man, he now stood bolt upright, as comely a father as one might lightly behold.

Then master Ridley, standing as yet in his truss, said to his brother, 'It were best for me to go in my truss still.' 'No,' quoth his brother, 'it will put you to more pain: and the truss will do a poor man good.' Whereunto master Ridley said, 'Be it, in the name of God;' and so unlaced himself. Then, being in his shirt, he stood upon the foresaid stone, and held up his hand and said, 'O heavenly Father, I give unto thee most hearty thanks, for that thou hast called me to be a professor of thee, even unto death. I beseech thee, Lord God, take mercy upon this realm of England, and deliver the same from all her enemies.'

Then the smith took a chain of iron, and brought the same about both Dr. Ridley's, and master Latimer's middles: and, as he was knocking in a staple, Dr. Ridley took the chain in his hand, and shaked the same, for it did gird in his belly, and looking aside to the smith, said, 'Good fellow, knock it in hard, for the flesh will have his course.' Then his brother did bring him gunpowder in a bag, and would have tied the same about his neck. Master Ridley asked, what it was. His brother said, 'Gunpowder.' 'Then,' said he, 'I take it to be sent of God; therefore I will receive it as sent of him. And have you any,' said he, 'for my brother'; meaning master Latimer. 'Yea sir, that I have,' quoth his brother. 'Then give it unto him,' said he, 'betime; lest ye come too late.' So his brother went, and carried of the same gunpowder unto master Latimer.

In the mean time Dr. Ridley spake unto my lord Williams, and said, 'My lord, I must be a suitor unto your lordship in the behalf of divers poor men, and especially in the cause of my poor sister: I have made a supplication to the queen's majesty in their behalfs. I beseech your lordship for Christ's sake, to be a mean to her grace for them. My brother here hath the supplication, and will resort to your lordship to certify you hereof. There is nothing in all the world that troubleth my conscience, I praise God, this only excepted. Whilst I was in the see of London, divers poor men took leases of me, and agreed with me for the same. Now I hear say the bishop that now occupieth the same room, will not allow my grants unto them made. but contrary unto all law and conscience, hath taken from them their livings, and will not suffer them to enjoy the same. I beseech you, my lord, be a mean for them: you shall do a good deed, and God will reward you.'

Then they brought a faggot, kindled with fire, and laid the same down at Dr. Ridley's feet. To whom master Latimer spake in this manner: 'Be of good comfort, master Ridley, and play the man. We shall this day light such a candle, by God's grace, in England, as I trust shall never be put out.'

And so the fire being given unto them, when Dr. Ridley saw the fire flaming up towards him, he cried with a wonderful loud voice, 'In manus tuas, Domine, commendo spiritum meum: Domine recipe spiritum meum.' And after, repeated this latter part often in English, 'Lord, Lord, receive my spirit;' master Latimer crying as vehemently on the other side, 'O Father of heaven, receive my soul!' who received the flame as it were embracing of it. After that he had stroked his face with his hands, and as it were bathed them a little in the fire, he soon died (as it appeareth) with very little pain or none. And thus much concerning the end of this old and blessed servant of God, master Latimer, for whose laborious travails, fruitful life, and constant death, the whole realm hath cause to give great thanks to Almighty God.

But master Ridley, by reason of the evil making of the fire unto him, because the wooden faggots were laid about the gorse, and over high built, the fire burned first beneath, being kept down by the wood; which when he felt he desired them for Christ's sake to let the fire come unto him. Which when his brother-in-law heard, but not well understood, intending to rid him out of his pain (for the which cause he gave attendance), as one in such sorrow not well advised what he did, heaped faggots upon him, so that he clean covered him, which made the fire more vehement beneath, that it burned clean all his nether parts, before it once touched the upper; and that made him leap up and down under the faggots, and often desire them to let the fire come unto him, saying, 'I cannot burn.' Which indeed appeared well; for, after his legs were consumed by reason of his struggling through the pain (whereof he had no release, but only his contentation in God), he showed that side toward us clean, shirt all untouched with flame. Yet in all this torment he forgot not to call unto God still, having in his mouth, 'Lord have mercy upon me,' intermingling his cry, 'Let the fire come unto me, I cannot burn.' In which pangs he laboured till one of the standers by with his bill pulled off the faggots above, and where he saw the fire flame up, he wrested himself unto that side. And when the flame touched the gunpowder, he was seen to stir no more, but burned on the other side, falling down at master Latimer's feet; which, some said, happened by reason that the chain loosed; others said, that he fell over the chain by reason of the poise of his body, and the weakness of the nether limbs.

Some said, that before he was like to fall from the stake, he desired them to hold him to it with their bills. However it was, surely it moved hundreds to tears, in beholding the horrible sight; for I think there was none that had not clean exiled all humanity and mercy, which would not have lamented to behold the fury of the fire so to rage upon their bodies.

Why his family had moved to New England, from Benjamin Franklin (1706–1790), autobiography

In 1755 Benjamin Franklin visited the ironstone village of Ecton, near Northampton, and found out from the church register that he was 'the youngest Son of the youngest Son for 5 Generations back'. He began putting together his 'little anecdotes' in 1771, addressing them to his 'Dear Son', during the time that he was in England campaigning for colonial representation in parliament. Though continued later in Paris and Philadelphia, his autobiography remained uncompleted.

This simple piece of family legend from Tudor Mary's reign, followed by Franklin's outline of the pilgrimage that lay ahead of one ordinary family, must represent countless other, untold stories of religious persecution and exile.

'Conventicles' were assemblies of religious Dissenters; any gathering of more than five people (apart from family) was prohibited by an Act of 1664, in an attempt to enforce adherence to the Church of England. It was repealed in 1689.

This obscure family of ours was early in the Reformation, and continu'd Protestants thro' the Reign of Queen Mary, when they were sometimes in Danger of Trouble on Account of their Zeal against Popery. They had got an English Bible, and to conceal and secure it, it was fastned open with Tapes under and within the Frame of a Joint Stool. When my Great Great Grandfather read in it to his Family, he turn'd up the Joint Stool upon his Knees, turning over the Leaves then under the Tapes. One of the Children stood at the Door to give Notice if he saw the Apparitor coming, who was an Officer of the Spiritual Court. In that Case the Stool was turn'd down again upon its feet, when the Bible remain'd conceal'd under it as before. This Anecdote I had from my Uncle Benjamin. – The Family continu'd all of the Church of England till about the End of Charles the 2nds Reign, when some of the Ministers that had been outed for Nonconformity, holding Conventicles in Northamptonshire, Benjamin and Josiah adher'd to them, and so continu'd all their Lives. The rest of the Family remain'd with the Episcopal Church.

Josiah, my Father, married young, and carried his Wife with three Children unto New England, about 1682. The Conventicles having been forbidden by Law, and frequently disturbed, induced some considerable Men of his Acquaintance to remove to that Country, and he was prevail'd with to accompany them thither, where they expected to enjoy their Mode of Religion with Freedom. – By the same Wife he had 4 Children more born there, and by a second Wife ten more, in all 17, of which I remember 13 sitting at one time at his Table, who all grew up to be Men and Women.

William Kethe (d. 1594), 'The Old Hundredth'

Kethe published his hymn version of Psalm 100 in 1561. During his time abroad as a refugee from persecution (as a follower of John Knox), he contributed to the Geneva Bible and other translations. For his last thirty years he was back in Elizabeth's England as a Dorset village parish priest. The tune of the 'Old 100th' was composed by the French Protestant Louis Bourgeois (d. 1561), mainly known now for his settings of the Calvinist Psalter, the novelty of which did not go down well with some of his stricter fellow Genevans.

All people that on earth do dwell,
Sing to the Lord with cheerful voice;

Him serve with fear, his praise forth tell,
Come ye before him, and rejoice.

The Lord, ye know, is God indeed;
Without our aid he did us make;
We are his folk, he doth us feed,
And for his sheep he doth us take.

O enter then his gates with praise,
Approach with joy his courts unto;
Praise, laud, and bless his name always,
For it is seemly so to do.

For why? The Lord our God is good;
His mercy is forever sure;
His truth at all times firmly stood,
And shall from age to age endure.

The Church of England under Queen Elizabeth takes shape, from William Harrison (1534–1593), *The Description of England* (1577)

Harrison's work was published as part of Holinshed's Chronicles. *His description of the England that was settling into the Elizabethan Age is an important contemporary source. The parishes in which he himself served as priest were both in Essex; but as chaplain too to Lord Cobham he gained plenty of insight into the worlds of the court and political power.*

A few parish churches still display Elizabeth's coats of arms, e.g. Ludham and Preston in Suffolk and Tivetshall in Norfolk.

And thus do we spend the Sabbath day in good and godly exercises, all done in our vulgar tongue that each one present may hear and understand the same, which also in cathedral and collegiate churches is so ordered that the psalms only are sung by note, the rest being read (as in common parish churches) by the minister with a loud voice, saving that in the administration of the communion the choir singeth the answers, the creed, and sundry other things appointed, but in so plain, I say, and distinct manner that each one present may understand what they sing, every word having but one note, though the whole harmony consist of many parts, and those very cunningly set by the skilful in that science.

Certes this translation of the service of the church into the vulgar tongue hath not a little offended the pope almost in every age, as a thing very often attempted by divers princes, but never generally obtained, for fear lest the consenting thereunto might breed the overthrow (as it would indeed) of all his religion and hierarchy.

As for our churches themselves, bells and times of morning and evening prayer remain as in times past, saving that all images, shrines, tabernacles, rood-lofts, and monuments of idolatry are removed, taken down, and defaced, only the stories in glass windows excepted, which for want of sufficient store of new stuff, and by reason of extreme charge that should grow by the alteration of the same into white panes throughout the realm, are not altogether abolished in most places at once, but by little and little suffered to decay, that white glass may be provided and set up in their rooms. Finally, whereas there was wont to be a great partition between the choir and the body of the church, now it is either very small or none at all, and (to say the truth) altogether needless, sith the minister saith his service commonly in the body of the church, with his face toward the people, in a little tabernacle of wainscot provided for the purpose, by which means the ignorant do not only learn divers of the psalms and usual prayers by heart, but also such as can read do pray together with him, so that the whole congregation at one instant pour out their petitions unto the living God for the whole estate of His church in most earnest and fervent manner. Our holy and festival days are very well reduced also unto a less number; for whereas (not long since) we had under the pope four score and fifteen, called festival, and thirty *profesti*, beside the Sundays, they are all brought unto seven and twenty, and, with them, the superfluous numbers of idle wakes, guilds, fraternities, church-ales, help-ales, and soul-ales, called also dirge-ales, with the heathenish rioting at bride-ales, are well diminished and laid aside. And no great matter were it if the feasts of all our apostles, evangelists, and martyrs, with that of all saints, were brought to the holy days that follow Christmas, Easter, and Whitsuntide, and those of the Virgin Mary, with the rest, utterly removed from the calendars, as neither necessary nor commendable in a reformed church.

The apparel in like sort of our clergymen is comely, and, in truth, more decent than ever it was in the popish church, before the universities bound their graduates unto a stable attire, afterward usurped also even by the blind Sir Johns. For, if you peruse well my Chronology ensuing, you shall find that they went either in divers colours like players, or in garments of light hue, as yellow, red, green, etc. with their shoes piked, their hair crisped, their girdles armed with silver, their shoes, spurs, bridles, etc. buckled with like metal, their apparel (for the most part) of silk, and richly furred, their caps laced and buttoned with gold, so that to meet a priest in those days was to behold a peacock that spreadeth his tail when he danceth before the hen, which now (I say) is well reformed. Touching hospitality, there was never any greater used in England, sith by reason that marriage is permitted to him that will choose that kind of life, their meat and drink is more orderly and frugally dressed, their furniture of household more convenient and better looked unto, and the poor oftener fed generally than heretofore they have been, when only a few bishops and double or treble beneficed men did make good cheer at Christmas only, or otherwise kept great houses for the entertainment of the rich, which did often see and visit them. It is thought much peradventure that some bishops, etc. in our time do come short of the ancient gluttony and prodigality of their predecessors; but to such as do consider of the curtailing of their livings, or excessive prices whereunto things are grown, and how their course is limited by law, and estate looked into on every side, the cause of their so doing is well enough perceived. This also offended many, that they should, after their deaths, leave their substances to their wives and children, whereas they consider not that in old time such as had no lemans nor bastards (very few were there, God wot, of this sort) did leave their goods and possessions to their brethren and kinsfolks, whereby (as I can shew by good record) many houses of gentility have grown and been erected. If in any age some one of them did found a college, almshouse, or school, if you look unto these our times, you shall see no fewer deeds of charity done, nor better grounded upon the right stub of piety than before. If you say that their wives be fond, after the decease of their husbands, and bestow themselves not so advisedly as their calling requireth (which, God knoweth, these curious surveyors make small account of truth, further than thereby to gather matter of reprehension), I beseech you then to look into all states of the laity, and tell me whether some duchesses, countesses, barons' or knights' wives, do not fully so often offend in the like as they? For Eve will be Eve, though Adam would say nay. Not a few also find fault with our threadbare gowns, as if not our patrons but our wives were causes of woe.

An account of Ailgnia (England), from Philip Stubbes (*c.* 1555–1610), *The Anatomy of Abuses* (1583)

According to Antony à Wood, Stubbes 'was mostly educated at Cambridge, but having a restless and hot head, left that University, rambled thro' several parts of the nation, and settled for a time in Oxon ... [He] was a most rigid Calvinist, a bitter enemy to Popery, and a great corrector of the vices and abuses of his time.'

The Anatomy of Abuses, *dedicated to the Earl of Arundel, takes the form of a dialogue between Master Philoponus, who has just returned from seven winters abroad in 'Ailgnia' (England), and Spudeus, 'a country man rude and unlearned'. 'Ailgnia is a pleasant and famous island, immured about with the sea, as it were with a wall, wherein the air is temperate, the ground fertile, the earth aboundyng with all thinges, either necessarie for men, or needfull for beast.' The 'strong kind of people' are 'audacious, bolde, puissant, and heroicall, of great magnanimitie, valiauncie, and prowess, of an incomparable feature, of an excellent complexion, and in all humanitie inferiour to none under the sunne.' Yet 'notwithstandyng that the Lord hath blessed that land with the knowledge of his truth above all other landes in the worlde, ... there is not a people more corrupt, wicked, or perverse livyng upon the face of the earth.'*

The catalogue of abuses follows, from pride of heart, mouth, and especially of apparel, through the 'horrible vices' of adultery, gluttony, covetousness and so on, to the 'manner of sanctifying the Sabbaoth in Ailgnia'.

PHILO. The Sabboth daie of some is well observed, in hearing the blessed worde of God read, preached, and interpreted; in private and publique praiers; in singing of godly psalmes; in celebrating the sacraments; and in collecting for the poore and indigent, which are the true uses and endes whereto the Sabbaoth was ordained. But other some spende the Sabbaoth day (for the most parte) in frequenting of baudy stage plaies and enterludes, in maintayning lordes of misrule (for so they call a certaine kinde of plaie which they use in Maie games), church ales, feastes, and wakesses, in pyping, dauncing, dicyng, carding, bowlynge, tenniss playing; in beare baytyng, cocke fightyng, hawkyng, hunting, and such like; in keeping of fayres and markettes on the Sabbaoth; in keepyng of courtes and leetes; in foote ball playing, and such other develish pastymes; in readyng of lascivious and wanton bookes, and an infinite nomber of such like practises and prophane exercises used upon that day, whereby the Lorde God is dishonoured, his Sabaoth violated, his word neglected, his sacramentes contemned, and his people mervailously corrupted, and carried away from true vertue and godlines.

Lordes of Misrule in Ailgnia

SPUD. Of what sorte be the other kinde of players, whiche you call Lordes of Misrule? For me think the very name it self importeth some evill.

PHILO. The name indeede is odious both to God and good men, and suche as the very heathen people would have blushed at once to have named amongst them. And, if the name importeth some evill, then what maie the thyng it self bee, judge you? But, because you desire to knowe the maner of them, I will shewe you as I have seen them practised by myself.

Firste, all the wilde heades of the parishe, conventyng together, chuse them a ground capitaine (of mischeef), whom they innoble with the title of my Lorde of Misserule, and hym they crown with great solemnitie, and adopt for their kyng. This kyng anoynted, chuseth for the twentie, fourtie, three score, or a hundred lustie guttes like to hymself to wait uppon his lordely majestie, and to guarde his noble persone. Then every one of these his menne he investeth with his liveries of greene, yellowe, or some other light wanton colour. And as though they were not (baudie) gaudy enough, I should saie, they bedecke themselves with scarffes, ribons, and laces, hanged all over with golde rynges, precious stones, and other jewelles; this done, they tye about either legge twentie or fourtie belles, with riche hande-kercheefes in their handes, and somtymes laied across over their shoulders and neckes, borrowed for the moste parte of their prety mopsies and lovyng bessies, for bussyng them in the darcke.

Thus all thinges sette in order, then have they their hobbie horses, dragons, and other antiques, together with their baudie pipers and thunderyng drommers, to strike up the devilles daunce withall; then marche these heathen companie towardes the churche and churche-yarde, their pipers pipyng, their drommers thonderyng, their stumppes dauncyng, their belles jynglyng, their handkerchefes swyngyng about their heades like madmen, their hobbie horses and other monsters skirmishyng amongest the throng; and in this sorte they goe to the churche (though the minister bee at praier or preachyng), dauncyng and swingyng their handkercheefes over their heades, in the churche, like devilles incarnate, with suche a confused noise, that no man can heare his owne voice. Then the foolish people they looke, they stare, they laugh, they fleere, and mount upon formes and pewes, to see these goodly pageaunts, solemnized in this sort. Then after this, about the churche they goe againe and againe, and so forthe into the churche-yarde, where they have commonly their sommer halles, their bowers, arbours, and banquetyng houses set up, wherein they feaste, banquet, and daunce all that daie, and (peradventure) all that night too. And thus these terrestrial furies spend the Sabbaoth daie!

Then, for the further innoblyng of this honorable lurdane [idler] (lorde, I should saye), they have also certaine papers, wherein is paynted some babblerie or othere, of imagerie worke; and these they call my Lord of Misrule's badges; these they give to every one that will give money for them, to maintaine them in this their heathenrie, divelrie, whoredome, dronkennesse, pride, and what not. And who will not shewe himself buxome to them, and give them money for these devilles cognizaunces, they shall be mocked and flouted at shamefully.

Some cases from the Archdeacon of Essex's Ecclesiastical Court, 1586–91

The Archdeacon presided over the ecclesiastical court that administered canon law. It was not unknown for the better-off accused to buy their way out of public humiliation.

7 November 1586 A young man of Romford was brought into the court on the charge of 'playing at stool-ball on Holy Thursday last in service time, and gave cruel words to the churchwardens for demanding 12 pence of him for his absence from church.' He admitted that he had been at stool-ball that afternoon, but asserted that he had been at Evening Prayer. He was sentenced to pay 12 pence to the poor, plus court and summoner's fees.

16 December 1590 A young woman of Bradwell-on-Sea was ordered 'upon Saturday next to come into Malden town, where she shall be placed openly upon some scaffold, about XI of the clock of the forenoon of the same day, and shall there stand until one of the clock in the afternoon of the same day, in a white sheet, and a white wand in her hand; and the next Sunday following she shall come into the church of Bradwell, at the beginning of the first lesson for morning prayer, attired in a white sheet, and shall there in penitent manner continue until the service and sermon be ended.'

17 June 1591 The sentence of a Burnham-on-Crouch parishioner: 'He shall upon the next Sabbath, or upon Sunday come sevennight, at the beginning of morning prayer, come into the church of Burnham, apparelled in a white sheet, and white wand in his hand, and there shall be place in some convenient place, near the minister and in sight of the congregation there assembled, and to stand until such time as the minister in time of sermon (or of reading of an homily) shall call for him, and then he shall confess and acknowledge that, whereas he hath been called before the judge of this court for suspicion of evil life, and by denying thereof hath had the benefit of law to purge himself (if he so could), wherein he hath failed, and is therefore found by law and pronounced guilty of the fact, he doth therefore acknowledge that he hath grievously offended the majesty of God in his wicked life and adulterous living; for which his most wicked and adulterous life, he shall ask mercy at the hands of almighty God and desire him in his mercy to pardon him his former ill life, and desire the congregation present also to forgive him, and to pray with him that he may be forgiven his wickedness at God's hands; and promise amendment of his former wickedness; and shall then say some prayer after the minister, at the minister's direction.'

Before a court of 'Interrogatories' concerning Sir Walter Raleigh (*c.* 1552–1618) at Cerne Abbas, Dorset, 1594

The court was set up to examine witnesses and take down depositions from members of Sir Walter Raleigh's circle and their servants, seeking evidence of their atheism. A Jesuit pamphlet accusing Sir Walter of leading a 'school of atheism' gave ammunition to his enemies for this enquiry, at a time when he had already been in trouble with Queen Elizabeth for his affair with Bessie Throckmorton. Allen of Portland Castle was one of his West Country friends. Under James I Raleigh was a prisoner in the Tower from 1603 to 1616, only released for his second Orinoco expedition, that was to end in failure. He was executed in 1618.

Grace Brewer of Sherborne sworn & examined the day and year last aforesaid before the said Sir Raulfe Horsey, Knight, & ffraunces James, Chancellor &c.

Who sayeth that about Michaelmas last coming from Lillington in the afternoon from a sermon, being accompanied with Mistress Whetcome and one Oliver, servant unto Mr Allen of Portland Castle, this deponent said, That they were happy that had so good a minister. Whereunto Oliver replied, That he said many things but might have made it shorter. Unto which Mistress

Whetcome answered, If you love to hear the word of God you cannot be weary with hearing it. Whereunto Oliver answered, I believe in Jesus Christ and that Jesus Christ is God, but if a man believes all that is in the scriptures he must believe that Moses has 52 concubines, or whores, but whether concubines or whores this deponent doth not well remember, but she well remembereth that she willed him to go home & sleep, for she did well perceive he was gone with drink. And more to the Interrogatories she cannot depose.

A pickpocket in the City of London, from Robert Greene (1558–1592), *The Second Part of Coney-Catching* (1591)

Greene was a prolific author and 'university wit', and the denigrator of Shakespeare as an 'upstart crow'. He evidently experienced London's underworld at first hand. 'Foists' were pickpockets, and considered themselves superior to 'nips' (cutpurses). 'Paul's men', like Ben Jonson's 'Captain' Bobadill, prided themselves on their style and swagger, and evidently found rich pickings among visitors who hung about in the City.

While I was writing this discovery of foisting and was desirous of any intelligence that might be given me, a Gentleman friend of mine reported unto me this pleasant tale of a Foist, and as I well remember, it grew to this effect.

There walked in the middle walk a plain country farmer, a man of good wealth, and that had a well-lined purse only barely tucked up in a loose smock, which a crew of Foists having perceived, their hearts were set on fire to have it, and every one had a fling at him, but all in vain; for he kept his hand close in his pocket, and his purse fast in his fist like a subtle churl that either had been forewarned of Paul's, or else had aforetime smoked some of that faculty: well, whatever, it was impossible to do any good with him, he was so wary.

The Foists, spying this, strained their wits to the highest string how to compass this bung, yet could not for all their politic conceits fetch the farmer over, for jostle him, chat with him, offer to shake him by the hand, all would not serve to get his hand out of his pocket.

At last one of the crew that for his skill might have been Doctorate in his mystery, amongst them all chose out a good Foist, one of a nimble hand and great agility, and said to the rest thus: 'Masters, it shall not be said such a base peasant shall slip away from such a crew of Gentlemen Foists as we are, and not have his pocket picked, and therefore this time I'll play the stall myself, and if I hit him not home, count me for a bungler forever.' And so he left them and went to the farmer and walked directly before him and next to him three or four turns. At last standing still, he cried, 'Alas, honest man, help me, I am not well,' and with that sank down suddenly in a swoon.

The poor Farmer, seeing a proper young gentleman (as he thought) fall dead afore him, stepped to him, held him in his arms, rubbed him and chafed him. At this there gathered a great multitude of people about him, and in the mean time the Foist drew out the Farmer's purse, and away.

When the other thought the feat was done, he began to come something to himself again, and so half staggering, stumbled out of Paul's, and went after the crew where they had appointed to meet, and there boasted of his wit and experience.

The Farmer, little suspecting this villainy, thrust his hand into his pocket and missed his purse, searched for it, but lining and case and all was gone, which made the country man in a great maze, that he stood still in a dump so long, that a gentleman perceiving it asked what he ailed.

'What ail I, sir?' quoth he. 'Truly, I am thinking how men may have longings as well as women.'

'Why dost thou conjecture that, honest man?' quoth he.

'Marry, sir,' answers the Farmer, 'the gentleman even now that swooned here I warrant he breeds his wife's child, and her longing was the cause of his falling down dead of a sudden qualm.'

The gentleman demanded how he knew that.

'Well enough, sir,' quoth he, 'and he has his longing too, for the poor man longed for my purse, and thanks be to God he has it with him.' At this, all the hearers laughed, but not so merrily as the Foist and his fellows that were then sharing out his money.

William Alabaster (1568–1640): the disputation between Catholic and Protestant brothers

The poem celebrates the case of two brothers, John Reynolds (c. 1549–1607) and William Reynolds (c. 1544–1594), one of whom was Protestant, the other Catholic, who then converted to each other's persuasion. Written in Latin, it was very popular. This translation is by Peter Heylyn (1682).

In points of Faith some undetermin'd jars
Betwixt two Brothers kindled Civil Wars.
One for the Church's Reformation stood;
The other thought no Reformation good.
The points propos'd, they traversed the field
With equal skill, and both together yield.
As they desir'd, his Brother each subdues;
Yet such their Fate, that each his Faith did lose,
Both Captives, none the prisoners thence do guide;
The Victor flying to the Vanquisht side.
Both joyn'd in being Conquer'd (strange to say),
And yet both mourn'd because both won the day.

Samuel Taylor Coleridge commented on the case in his essay 'Tolerance and Intolerance' in The Friend *(1818):*

> The former being a Papist, and the latter a Protestant, they met and disputed, with a purpose to confute, and to convert each other. And so they did: for those arguments, which were used, prevailed fully against their adversary, and yet did not prevail with themselves. The Papist turned Protestant, and the Protestant became a Papist, and so remained to their dying day... Of which some ingenious person gave a most handsome account in the following excellent Epigram.

William Shakespeare (1564–1616): 'Winter's song', from *Love's Labour's Lost*, early 1590s

The play closes with a performance of songs of Spring and Winter, which, though supposedly composed by 'the two learned men' Holofernes, schoolmaster and pedant, and his equally ridiculous sidekick, the parish curate Sir Nathaniel, are unmistakably youthful Shakespeare. (The parson's 'saw' is his sermonizing; 'crabs' are crab-apples.)

When icicles hang by the wall,
   And Dick the shepherd blows his nail,
And Tom bears logs into the hall,
   And milk comes frozen home in pail,
When blood is nipped, and ways be foul,
Then nightly sings the staring owl,
      Tu-whit,
Tu-who, a merry note,
While greasy Joan doth keel the pot.

When all aloud the wind doth blow,
   And coughing drowns the parson's saw,
And birds sit brooding in the snow,
   And Marian's nose looks red and raw,
When roasted crabs hiss in the bowl,
Then nightly sings the staring owl,
      Tu-whit,
Tu-who, a merry note,
While greasy Joan doth keel the pot.

Varieties of religion and women, from John Donne (1572–1631), Satyre III, 'Of Religion' (probably 1590s)

Donne's mother came from a Catholic family that claimed kinship with Sir Thomas More. His younger brother Henry was arrested with William Harrington, a Catholic priest he had been sheltering, broke down under torture, but died in prison of the plague before he came to trial. Harrington was hanged, drawn and quartered in 1594. Donne's mother went into exile in 1595. His satires date from the period when he was studying Law at Lincoln's Inn, womanising, starting to make a name for himself as a poet, and searching for ways to enter public life.

Seeke true religion. O where? Mirreus
Thinking her unhous'd here, and fled from us,
Seekes her at Rome, there, because hee doth know
That shee was there a thousand years agoe,

He loves her rags so, as wee here obey
The statecloth where the Prince sate yesterday.
Crantz to such brave Loves will not be inthrall'd,
But loves her onely, who at Geneva is call'd
Religion, plaine, simple, sullen, yong,
Contemptuous, yet unhandsome; As among
Lecherous humors, there is one that judges
No wenches wholesome, but coarse country drudges.
Graius stayes still at home here, and because
Some Preachers, vile ambitious bauds, and lawes
Still new like fashions, bid him thinke that shee
Which dwels with us, is onely perfect, hee
Imbraceth her, whom his Godfathers will
Tender to him, being tender, as Wards still
Take such wives as their Guardians offer, or
Pay valewes. Carelesse Phrygius doth abhorre
All, because all cannot be good, as one
Knowing some women whores, dares marry none.
Graccus loves all as one, and thinks that so
As women do in divers countries goe
In divers habits, yet are still one kinde,
So doth, so is Religion; and this blind-
Nesse too much light breeds; but unmoved thou
Of force must one, and forc'd but one allow;
And the right; aske thy father which is shee,
Let him aske his; though truth and falsehood bee
Neare twins, yet truth a little elder is;
Be busie to seeke her, believe mee this,
Hee's not of none, nor worst, that seekes the best.
To adore, or scorne an image, or protest,
May all be bad; doubt wisely; in strange way
To stand inquiring right, is not to stray;
To sleep, or runne wrong , is. On a huge hill,
Cragged, and steep, Truth stands, and he that will
Reach her, about must, and about must goe;
And what the hills suddennes resists, winne so;
Yet strive so, that before age, deaths twilight,
Thy Soule rest, for none can worke in that night.

'Of Superstition', from Francis Bacon (1561–1626), *Essays*

This essay comes from Bacon's 1612 expansion of his first group, published in 1597. The complete Essays or Counsels, Civil and Moral *were assembled after his fall from office as Lord Chancellor in 1621. He regarded them as a 'recreational' part of his philosophical writing.*

The Council of Trent met three times between 1545 and 1563 to fix Catholic dogma in the face of the rise of Protestantism.

It were better to have no opinion of God at all than such an opinion as is unworthy of Him; for the one is unbelief, the other is contumely. ... And as the contumely is greater towards God, so the danger is greater towards men. Atheism leaves a man to sense, to philosophy, to natural piety, to laws, to reputation; all which may be guides to an outward moral virtue, though religion were not; but superstition dismounts all these, and erecteth an absolute monarchy in the minds of men. Therefore, atheism did never perturb States; for it makes men wary of themselves, as looking no further. And we see the times inclined to atheism, as the time of Augustus Caesar were civil times. But superstition hath been the confusion of many States, and bringeth in a new *primum mobile* that ravisheth all the spheres of government.

The master of superstition is the people, and in all superstition wise men follow fools, and arguments are fitted to practise in a reverse order. It was gravely said by some of the prelates in the Council of Trent, where the doctrine of the schoolmen bear great sway, 'That the schoolmen were like astronomers, which did feign eccentrics and epicycles, and such engines of orbs, to save the phenomena, though they knew there were no such things.' And, in like manner, that the schoolmen had framed a number of subtile and intricate axioms and theorems to save the practice of the Church.

The causes of superstition are: Pleasing and sensual rites and ceremonies; excess of outward and pharisaical holiness; over-great reverence of traditions, which cannot but load the Church; the stratagems of prelates for their own ambition and lucre; the favouring too much of good intentions, which openeth the gate to conceits and novelties; the taking an aim at divine matters by human, which cannot but breed mixture of imaginations; and lastly, barbarous times, especially joined with calamities and disasters. Superstition, without a veil, is a deformed thing; for as it addeth deformity to an ape to be so like a man, so the similitude of superstition to religion makes it the more deformed. And as wholesome meat corrupteth to little worms, so good forms and orders corrupt into a number of petty observances.

There is a superstition in avoiding superstition, when men think to do best if they go furthest from the superstition formerly received. Therefore care would be had that, as it fareth in ill purgings, the good be not taken away with the bad, which commonly is done when the people is the reformer.

Lancelot Andrewes and the good fat alderman, from John Aubrey (1626–1697), *Brief Lives*

Aubrey was a Fellow of the fledgling Royal Society. His sociability and love of a good story made him an engaging recorder of his age. His Brief Lives *(over four hundred of them) were first drawn together from the mass of manuscripts Aubrey left behind by the Rev. Andrew Clark in 1898.*

Lancelot Andrewes (1555–1626) was one of the great churchmen of his time. Chaplain to Queen Elizabeth, he was appointed to several bishoprics under James I, and his learning and powerful presence were said to have been sufficient to 'restrain King James from that unseemly levity in which he was rather prone to indulge'. He had skills in fifteen languages, and had a leading role in producing the Authorized Version of the Bible (1611).

Lancelot Andrewes, Lord Bishop of Winton, was borne in London; went to Schoole at Merchant Taylors schoole. Mr. Mulcaster was his schoolemaster, whose picture he hung in his Studie.

Old Mr. Sutton, a very learned man in those dayes, of Blandford St. Maries, Dorset, was his school fellow, and sayd that Lancelot Andrewes was a great long boy of 18 yeares old at least before he went to the University.

The Puritan faction did begin to increase in those dayes, and especially at Emanuel College. This party had a great mind to drawe in this learned young man, whom (if they could make theirs) they knew would be a great honour to them. They carried themselves outwardly with great sanctity and strictnesse. They preached up very strict keeping and observing the Lord's day: made, upon the matter, damnation to breake it, and that 'twas less Sin to kill a man. Yet these Hypocrites did bowle in a private green at their colledge every Sunday after Sermon; and one of the Colledge (a loving friend to Mr. L. Andrewes) to satisfie him, one time lent him the Key of a Private back dore to the bowling green, on a Sunday evening, which he opening, discovered these zealous Preachers with their Gownes off, earnest at play. But they were strangely surprised to see the entrey of one that was not of the Brotherhood.

There was then at Cambridge a good fatt Alderman that was wont to sleep at Church, which the Alderman endeavoured to prevent but could not. Well! this was preached against as a signe of Reprobation. The good man was exceedingly troubled at it, and went to Andrewes his Chamber to be satisfied in point of Conscience. Mr. Andrewes told him, that it was an ill habit of Body, not Mind, and that it was against his Will; advised him on Sundays to make a more sparing meale, and to mend it at Supper. The Alderman did so, but Sleepe comes on again for all that, and was preached at; comes againe to be resolved with Teares in his eies. Andrewes then told him he would have him make a good heartie meal as he was wont to doe, and presently [at once] take out his full sleep. He did so, came to St. Maries, where the Preacher was prepared with a Sermon to damne all who slept at Sermon, a certain signe of Reprobation. The good Alderman, having taken his full nap before, lookes on the Preacher all Sermon time, and and spoyled the design. But I should have sayd that Andrewes was most extremely spoken against and preached against for offering to assoil [absolve]or excuse a sleeper in sermon time. But he had learning and witt enough to defend himselfe.

His good learning quickly made him known in the University, and also to King James, who much valued him for it, and advanced him, and at last made him Bishop of Winchester.

Three pieces from Nicholas Breton (*c.* 1545–1626), *Fantastickes* (1626)

Breton, poet, pastoralist and satirist, composed Fantastickes *as a calendar of the months, seasons and festivals of the Jacobean year.*

Christmas Day

It is now Christmas, and not a Cup of drinke must passe without a Caroll, the Beasts, Fowle and Fish come to a general execution, and the Corne is ground to dust for the Bakehouse, and the Pastry: Cards and Dice purge many a purse, and the Youth show their agility in shoeing of the wild mare [exacting forfeits from the unwary]: now good cheere and welcome, and God be with you, and I thanke you: and against the new yeere, provide for the presents: the Lord of Mis-rule is no meane man for his time, and the guests of the high Table must lack no Wine: the lusty bloods must looke about them like men, and piping and dauncing puts away much melancholy: stolen Venison is sweet, and a fat Coney is worth money: Pit-falles are now set for small Birdes, and a Woodcocke hangs himselfe in a gynne: a good fire heats all the house, and a full Alms-basket makes the Beggars' Prayers: the Maskers and Mummers make the merry sport: but if they lose their money, their Drumme goes dead: Swearers and Swaggerers are sent away to the Ale-house, and unruly Wenches goe in danger of Judgement: Musicians now make their Instruments speak out, and a good song is worth the hearing. In summe, it is a holy time, a duty in Christians, for the remembrance of Christ, and custome among friends, for the maintenance of good fellowship: In briefe, I thus conclude it: I hold it a memory of the Heavens Love, and the worlds peace, the mirth of the honest, and the meeting of the friendly. *Farewell.*

Good Friday

It is now Good Friday, and a general Fast must be kept among all Christians, in remembrance of Christs Passion: Flesh and Fish must be vanished all stomackes, strong or weake: Now beginnes the Farewell to thin fare, and the Fishmongers may shut up their shops till the Holy-dayes be past: the Butchers now must wash their Boords, make cleane their Aprons, sharpen their knives, and sort their prickers [skewers], and cut out their meat for Easter Eve market: Now must the Poulters make ready their Rabbets and their Fowle, the Cookes have their Ovens cleane, and all for Pies and Tarts against the merry Feast: Now the Maids bestir them about their houses, the Launders about their Linen, the Taylors about Apparell, and all for this holy time: Now young Lambs, young Rabbets and young Chickens dye for fine appetites, and now the Minstrell tunes his Instruments, to have them ready for the young people: but with the aged and the religious, there is nothing but sorrow and mourning, confession, contrition, and absolution, and I know not what: few that are merry, but children that breake up schoole, and wenches that are upon the mariage. In summe, it is such an odde day by it selfe, that I will only make this conclusion of it: It is the Bridle of Nature, and the Examiner of Reason. *Farewell.*

Easter Day

It is now Easter, and Jacke of Lent [a puppet thrown at during Lent] is turned out of doores: the Fishermen now hang up their nets to dry, while the Calfe and the Lambe walke toward the Kitchin and the Pastry: the velvet heads of the Forrests fall at the loose of the Crosse-bow: the Samman Trowt playes with the Fly, and the March Rabbit runs dead into the dish: the Indian

Commodities pay the Merchants' adventure: and Barbary Sugar puts Honey out of countenance: the holy feast is kept for the faithfull, and a knowne Jew hath no place among Christians: the Earth now beginnes to paint her upper garmen and the trees put out their young buds, the little Kids chew their Cuds, and the Swallow feeds on the Flyes in the Ayre: the Storke clenseth the Brookes of the Frogges, and the Sparhawke prepares her wing for the Partridge: the little Fawne is stolne from the Doe, and the male Deere begin to herd: the spirit of Youth is inclined to mirth, and the conscionable Scholler will not breake a holy-day: the Minstrell calls the Maid from her dinner, and the Lovers' eyes doe troule [roll] like Tennis balls. There is mirth and joy, when there is health and liberty; and he that hath money will be no mean man in his mansion: the Ayre is wholsome, and the Skye comfortable, the Flowers odoriferous, and the Fruits pleasant: I conclude, it is a day of much delightfulnesse: the Sunne's dancing day, and the Earth's Holy-day. *Farewell.*

Declaration by James I to his subjects 'concerning lawful sports to be used', 24 May 1618

Whereas upon Our return, the last year out of Scotland, We did publish Our Pleasure touching the recreations of Our people in those parts, under Our hand: for some causes Us thereunto moving, We have thought good to command these Our Directions, then given in Lancashire, with a few words thereunto added and most applicable to these parts of Our Realms, to be published to all Our subjects.

Whereas We did justly, in Our progress through Lancashire, rebuke some Puritans and precise people, and took order that the like unlawful carriage should not be used by any of them hereafter, in the prohibiting and unlawful punishment of Our good people for using their lawful recreations and honest exercises upon Sundays and other Holy Days, after the afternoon Sermon or Service; We now find, that two sorts of people wherewith that country is much infested (We mean Papists and Puritans) have maliciously traduced and calumniated those Our just and honourable proceedings. And therefore lest Our reputations might, upon the one side, though innocently, have some aspersion laid upon it; and that, upon the other part, Our good people in that country be misled by the mistaking and misinterpretation of Our meaning: We have therefore thought good hereby to clear and make Our Pleasure to be manifested to all Our good people in those parts. ...

[The report of growing amendment amongst them] made Us the more sorry, when, with Our own ears, We heard the general complaint of Our people, that they were barred from all lawful recreation and exercise upon the Sunday's afternoon, after the ending of all Divine Service. Which cannot but produce two evils. The one, hindering of the conversion of many whom their priests will take occasion hereby to vex; persuading them that 'no honest mirth or recreation is lawful or tolerable in Our Religion!' which cannot but breed a great discontentment in Our people's hearts; especially of such as are, peradventure, upon the point of turning. The other inconvenience is, that this prohibition barreth the common and meaner sort of people from using such exercises as may make their bodies more able for war, when We, or our Successors shall have occasion to use them: and in place thereof sets up filthy tiplings and drunkenness, and breeds a number of idle and discontented speeches in their alehouses. For when shall the common people have leave to exercise, if not upon the Sundays and Holy Days? Seeing they must apply their labour, and win their living in all working days!

Our express pleasure therefore is, That the Laws of Our Kingdom, and Canons of Our Church be as well observed in that County, as in all other places of this Our Kingdom. ...

And as for Our good people's lawful recreation; Our Pleasure likewise is, That after the end of Divine Service, Our good people be not disturbed, letted, or discouraged from any lawful recreation, such as Dancing (either men or women), Archery for men, Leaping, Vaulting, or any other such harmless recreations; nor from having of May Games, Whitsun Ales, and Morris Dances; and the setting up of May Poles, and other sports therewith used: so as the same be had in due and convenient time, without impediment or neglect of Divine Service. And, That women shall have leave to carry rushes to the church for the decoring of it, according to their old custom.

But withal, We do here account still as prohibited, all unlawful games, to be used on Sundays only; as Bear and Bull baitings, Interludes: and, at all times, in the meaner sort of people by Law prohibited, Bowling.

And, likewise, We bar from this benefit and liberty, all such known Recusants, either men or women, as will abstain from coming to Church or Divine Service: being, therefore, unworthy of any lawful recreation after the said Service, that will not first come to the Church, and serve GOD.

From the sermon at Whitehall by John Donne on the first Friday in Lent, 8 March 1622

Donne took holy orders, after years of exhortation (for his earlier character see his Satyre, *above, p. 111), in January 1615, was a chaplain to James I, and eventually grew into 'Doctor Donne', the Dean of St Paul's, where Nicholas Stone's funerary sculpture of him in a shroud – the only monument to survive the Great Fire of 1666 – may be seen.*

We die every day, and we die all the day long. And because we are not absolutely dead we call that eternity, an eternity of dying. And is there comfort in that state? Why, that is the state of Hell itself: eternal dying, and not dead.

[Death] comes equally to us all, and makes us all equal when it comes. The ashes of an oak in the chimney are no epitaph of that oak, to tell me how high or large that was. It tells me not what flocks it sheltered while it stood, nor what men it hurt when it fell. The dust of great persons' graves is speechless too: it says nothing, it distinguishes nothing. As soon the dust of a wretch whom thou wouldest not, as of a prince whom thou couldest not look upon, will trouble thine eyes if the wind blow it thither. And when a whirlwind hath blown the dust of the churchyard into the church, and the man sweeps out the dust of the church into the churchyard, who will undertake to sift those dusts again and to pronounce, This is the patrician, this is the noble flower, and this the yeomanly, this the plebeian bran?

'When he and I meet, we are up by the ears': Mistress Ann Prideaux on John Trevelyan in 1628, from the *Trevelyan Papers*

John Trevelyan, of a Cornish branch of the family (St Cleder), was a man of 'a bold and active spirit' and a recusant who, when forced to attend the parish church on Sundays or pay the fine, used to call out to the clergyman as he walked out before the sermon, 'When thou hast said what thou hast to say, come and dine with me.' There was a standing quarrel with his neighbour Mistress Prideaux of Trevorder: 'When he and I meet, we are up by the ears, he for the Papists and I for the Protestants.' She was unable to resist telling the Bishop of Exeter's chaplain some outrageous things he had said to her, and after these reached the Bishop's ears she found herself undergoing an examination at Bodmin before Lord Lambert, Sir John Trelawny and Sir Richard Buller (11 October 1628).

In his deposition the chaplain, Martin Nansog, declared that he said to Mistress Prideaux: 'I wonder with what patience you and your husband could heare these words, but if I had heard these words I should have cutte his throate; praye let me have some inke and paper for I will noate downe these words'. 'Nay,' said Mrs Prideaux, 'Pray doe not soe, let him alone, he is too lowe, he is almost sunke in his estate.'

The said examinant, being sworne, sayeth, that she heard Mr. John Trevillyan of St. Cleder, in the countye of Cornwall, Esq., say (about three weekes sythence [*sic*]) that, being talking about matters of religion, that, after the reading of a chapiter, they of the Church of England did sing a Geneva gygg, meaning one of the Psalms, and that Mr. Trevillyan sayed unto her that Queene Tibb (interpreting himself and meaning Queene Elizabeth) was as arrant a whore as ever breathed, and that she was kept by Essex and Leicester, and others, or words to the like effect; and she further sayeth she heard the said Trevillyan say that there was knaverye in our Byble; and she further sayeth she heard, by one Marshe of Padstow, that one Mr. Burlace of Newlynd tooke the Byble out of the Viccar of Meryan's hand, one Smalrudge, and spurned at yt with his foote; and she further sayeth that Mr. Trevillyan tould her that yf it weere not for Images wee shalbe all atheists. And Mr. Trevillyan tould her that yf shee were a Papist shee would be a good woman, and hee did hope she would turne before shee dyed, and yf shee would not be a Papist, shee should dye before shee was willing, and have but a monethes warning, or words to that effect.

'Now love is his business and aim', from George Herbert (1593–1633), *The Country Parson, His Character, and Rule of Holy Life*

Until 1627 George Herbert, already Public Orator at Cambridge University, seemed set for a public life as glittering as those of his brothers Edward and Henry. Some of his poetry offers clues to elements of a crisis. It is on this body of devotional poems that his literary reputation rests. As he was dying, he asked for his 'little book' that contained them to be taken to his 'dear brother' Nicholas Ferrar, the founder of the religious community at Little Gidding (celebrated three centuries later by T. S. Eliot: see p. 356), who had them published as The Temple. *Several of them have become familiar as hymns.*

He spent the last three years of his life as the devoted rector of Bemerton and Fugglestone, between Salisbury and Wilton, the seat of the senior branch of the Herbert family. He put together The Country Parson, His Character, and Rule of Holy Life, *eventually published in 1652 as* A Priest to the Temple.

The Parson's Condescending

The Country Parson is a Lover of Old Customs, if they be good and harmless; and the rather, because Country people are much addicted to them, so that to favour them therein is to win their hearts, and to oppose them therein is to deject them. If there be any ill in the custom, that may be severed from the good, he pares the apple and gives them the clean to feed on. Particularly he loves procession, and maintains it, because there are contained therein four manifest advantages: First, a blessing of God for the fruits of the field: Secondly, Justice in the Preservation of bounds: Thirdly, Charity in loving walking, and neighbourly accompanying one another, with reconciling of differences at that time, if there be any: Fourthly, Mercy in relieving the poor by a liberal distribution and largess, which at that time is, or ought to be used. Wherefore he exacts of all to be present at the perambulation, and those that withdraw, and sever themselves from it, he mislikes, and reproves as uncharitable and unneighbourly; and if they will not reform, presents them. Nay, he is so far from condemning such assemblies, that he rather procures them to be often, as knowing that absence breeds strangeness, but presence love. Now love is his business and aim; wherefore he likes well, that his Parish at good times invite one another to their houses, and he urgeth them to it: and sometimes, where he knows there hath been or is a little difference, he takes one of the parties, and goes with him to the other, and all dine or sup together. There is much preaching in this friendliness. Another old Custom there is of saying, when light is brought in, God sends us the light of heaven; And the Parson likes this very well: neither is he afraid of praising, or praying to God at all times, but is rather glad of catching opportunities to do them. Light is a great Blessing, and as great as food, for which we give thanks; and those that think this superstitious, neither know superstition nor themselves. As for those that are ashamed to use this form as being old, and obsolete, and not the fashion, he reforms and teaches them, that at Baptism they professed not to be ashamed of Christ's Cross, or for any shame to leave that which is good. He that is ashamed in small things, will extend his pusillanimity to greater. Rather should a Christian Soldier take such occasions to harden himself and to further his exercises of Mortification.

'Thus she had a child for every day of the year, and one over', from Thomas Fuller (1608–1661), *Worthies of England* (1662)

The son of a Northamptonshire rector, Fuller joined Charles I's court at Oxford and became chaplain to the Royalist army. On the Royalist defeat, he lost all preferments, but he was appointed chaplain to Charles II on the restoration in 1660. His writings earned him his living and much esteem besides. Mary Honywood's monument with kneeling figure was moved to nearby Great Coggeshall when Markshall Church was demolished in 1932.

Mary Waters was born at Lenham in this county, and how abundantly entitled to memorability, the ensuing epitaph in Markeshall church in Essex will sufficiently discover.

'Here lieth the body of Mary Waters, the daughter and co-heir of Robert Waters of Lenham in Kent, esquire, wife of Robert Honeywood of Charing in Kent, esquire, her only husband, who had at her decease lawfully descended from her, three hundred sixty-seven children; sixteen of her own body, one hundred and fourteen grandchildren, two hundred twenty-eight in the third generation, and nine in the fourth. She lived a most pious life, and in a Christian manner died here at Markeshall, in the ninety-third year of her age, and in the forty-fourth year of her widowhood, the eleventh of May, 1620.'

Thus she had a child for every day in the (though Leap) year, and one over. Here we may observe, that (generally) the highest in honour, do not spread the broadest in posterity. For time was, when all the earls in England (and those then seventeen in number) had not, put together, so many sons and daughters, as one of them had, viz. Edward Somerset, earl of Worcester. And yet of both sexes he never had but thirteen. But to return to Mistress Waters, she since hath been much outstripped in point of fruitfulness, by one still surviving; and therefore this worthy matron (in my mind) is more memorable on another account, viz. for patient weathering out the tempest of a troubled conscience, whereon a remarkable story dependeth: being much afflicted in mind, many ministers repaired to her, and amongst the rest, Reverend Mr John Fox, than whom no more happy an instrument to set the joints of a broken spirit. All his counsels proved ineffectual, insomuch that in the agony of her soul, having a Venice glass in her hand, she brake forth into this expression, 'I am as surely damned as this glass is broken,' which she immediately threw with violence to the ground.

Here happened a wonder, the glass rebounded again, and was taken up whole and entire. I confess it is possible, though that juncture of time it seemed little less than miraculous.

However the gentlewoman took no comfort thereat (as some have reported, and more have believed) but continued a great time after (short is long to people in pain) in her former disconsolate condition without any amendment. Until at last, God, the great clock-keeper of time, who findeth out the fittest minutes for his own mercies, suddenly shot comfort like lightning into her soul; which once entered, ever remained therein (God does not palliate cures; what he heals, it holds); so that she led the remainder of her life in spiritual gladness. This she herself told to the reverend father Thomas Morton bishop of Durham, from whose mouth I have received this relation.

In the days of queen Mary she used to visit the prisons, and to comfort and relieve the confessors therein. She was present at the burning of Mr Bradford in Smithfield, and resolved to see the end of his suffering, though so great the press of people, that her shoes were trodden off, and she forced thereby to go barefoot from Smithfield to St Martin's, before she could furnish herself with a new pair for her money. Her dissolution happened as is aforesaid, in 1620.

John Milton (1608–1674)

These two poems were written in the early 1630s. Milton's Puritan scrivener father was an organist and amateur composer, and evidently encouraged his young son's interest in music as well as supporting his freedom to study and write. Milton's collaborations with the composer Henry Lawes on 'Arcades' and 'Comus' belong to this period too. His career as public controversialist and Secretary of Foreign Tongues to the Council of State under the Commonwealth belonged to the 1640s–50s. After the Restoration of 1660 it took the payment of a large fine to free him from prison for a life of retirement and the completion of Paradise Lost.

At a Solemn Musick

Blest pair of *Sirens,* pledges of Heav'ns joy,
Sphear-born harmonious Sisters, Voice, and Vers,
Wed your divine sounds, and mixt power employ
Dead things with inbreath'd sense able to pierce,
And to our high-rais'd phantasie present,

That undisturbed song of pure concent,
Ay sung before the saphire-colour'd throne
To him that sits theron
With Saintly shout, and solemn Jubily,
Where the bright Seraphim in burning row
Their loud up-lifted Angel trumpets blow,
And the Cherubick host in thousand quires
Touch their immortal Harps of golden wires,
With those just Spirits that wear victorious Palms,
Hymns devout and holy Psalms
Singing everlastingly;
That we on Earth with undiscording voice
May rightly answer that melodious noise;
As once we did, till disproportion'd sin
Jarr'd against natures chime, and with harsh din
Broke the fair musick that all creatures made
To their great Lord, whose love their motion sway'd
In perfect Diapason, whilst they stood
In first obedience, and their state of good.
O may we soon again renew that Song,
And keep in tune with heav'n, till God ere long
To his celestial consort us unite,
To live with him, and sing in endles morn of light.

From *Il Penseroso*

But let my due feet never fail,
To walk the studious Cloysters pale,
And love the high embowed Roof,
With antick Pillars massy proof,
And storied Windows richly dight,
Casting a dimm religious light.
There let the pealing Organ blow,
To the full voic'd Quire below,
In Service high, and Anthems cleer,
As may with sweetnes, through mine ear,
Dissolve me into extasies,
And bring all Heav'n before mine eyes.

And may at last my weary age
Find out the peacefull hermitage,
The Hairy Gown and Mossy Cell
Where I may sit and rightly spell
Of every Star that Heav'n doth shew,
And every Herb that sips the dew;
Till old experience do attain
To something like Prophetic strain.
These pleasures *Melancholy* give,
And I with thee will choose to live.

Alehouses, from Donald Lupton (d. 1676), *London and the Countrey Carbonadoed and Quartred into Severall Characters* (1632)

After a period as an army chaplain Lupton failed to find preferment and subsisted by work as a hack author. London and the Country *was written in ten days. He eventually became vicar of Sunbury, Middlesex, in 1663, after the Restoration.*

If these houses have a box bush, or an old post, it is enough to show their profession. But if they be graced with a sign complete, it's a sign of good custom. In these houses you shall see the history of Judith, Susanna, Daniel in the lions' den, or Dives and Lazarus painted upon the wall. It may be reckoned a wonder to see or find the house empty, for either the parson, churchwarden, or clerk, or all, are doing some church or court business usually in this place. They thrive best where there are fewest.

It is the host's chiefest pride to be speaking of such a gentleman or such a gallant that was here, and will be again ere long. Hot weather and thunder and want of company are the hostess's grief, for then her ale sours. Your drink usually is very young, two days old. Her chiefest wealth is seen if she can have one brewing under another. If either the hostess, or her daughter, or maid will kiss handsomely at parting, it is a good shoeing-horn or bird-lime to draw the company thither again the sooner. She must be courteous to all, though not by nature, yet by her profession; for she must entertain all, good and bad, tag, and rag, cut, and long tail. She suspects tinkers and poor soldiers most, not that they will not drink soundly, but that they will not pay lustily. She must keep touch with three sorts of men, that is: the malt man, the baker, and the justice's clerks.

She is merry, and half made upon Shrove Tuesday, May days, feast days, and Morris dances. A good ring of bells in the parish helps her to many a tester [sixpence]. She prays that the parson may not be a puritan. A bagpiper and a puppet play bring her in birds that are flush. She defies a wine tavern as an upstart, outlandish fellow, and suspects the wine to be poisoned. Her ales, if new, looks like a misty morning, all thick. Well, if her ale be strong, her reckoning right, her house clean, her fire good, her face fair, and the town great or rich, she shall seldom or never sit without chirping birds to bear her company, and at the next churching or christening, she is sure to be rid of two or three dozen of cakes and ale by gossiping neighbours.

Dirge, by James Shirley (1596–1666), concluding his play *The Contention of Ajax and Ulysses for the Armour of Achilles* (c. 1654–58)

Briefly in holy orders, following spells at both Oxford and Cambridge, Shirley converted to Catholicism. He fought with the Royalists in the Civil War. Both he and his wife appear to have died in the aftermath of the Great Fire of London (1666).

We are told that 'Oliver Cromwell is said, on the recital of the dirge, to have been seized with great terror, and agitation of mind.' And Charles II, it is also claimed, used to have this dirge sung to him. It forms the conclusion of a play first published in 1659.

Death the Leveller

The glories of our blood and state
Are shadows, not substantial things;
There is no armour against fate;
Death lays his icy hand on kings:
Sceptre and crown
Must tumble down,
And in the dust be equal made
With the poor crooked scythe and spade.

Some men with swords may reap the field,
And plant fresh laurels where they kill:
But their strong nerves at last must yield;
They tame but one another still:

Early or late
They stoop to fate,
And must give up their murmuring breath
When they, pale captives, creep to death.

The garlands wither on your brow;
Then boast no more your mighty deeds;
Upon Death's purple altar now
See, where the victor-victim bleeds.
Your heads must come
To the cold tomb;
Only the actions of the just
Smell sweet, and blossom in their dust.

Monuments to such 'glories' are a feature of numerous parish churches, e.g. Bottesford, Castle Frome and Framlingham. A sardonic retort is occasionally to be found, as at Kingsbridge in Devon:

Here I lie, at the chancel door,
Here I lie, because I'm poor:
The farther in, the more you pay,
Here I lie as warm as they.

Puritan iconoclasts at work, from the *Journal* of William Dowsing (1596–1668)

Dowsing, a Puritan soldier, was appointed 'Commissioner for the destruction of monuments of idolatry and superstition' in 1643.

January 6th 1643. 1. At HAVERHILL. We broke down about an hundred superstitious Pictures; and seven Fryars hugging a Nunn; and the Picture of God and Christ; and diverse others very superstitious; and 200 had been broke down before I came. We took away two popish Inscriptions with *ora pro nobis*; and we beat down a great stoneing Cross on the top of the Church.

2. At CLARE, Jan. the 6th. We brake down 1000 Pictures superstitious; I brake down 200; 3 of God the Father, and 3 of Christ, and the Holy Lamb, and 3 of the Holy Ghost like a Dove with Wings; and the 12 Apostles were

carved in Wood, on the top of the Roof, which we gave order to take down; and 20 Cherubims to be taken down; and the Sun and Moon in the East Window, by the King's Arms, to be taken down.

26. UFFORD, Jan. the 27th. We brake down 30 superstitious Pictures; and gave direction to take down 37 more; and 40 Cherubims to be taken down of Wood; and the chancel levelled. There was a Picture of Christ on the Cross, and God the Father above it; and left 37 superstitious Pictures to be taken down; and took up 6 superstitious Inscriptions in Brass.

124. UFFORD, Aug. 31st. See No. 26, where is set down what we did, Jan. the 27th. '30 superstitious Pictures; and left 37 more to brake down', and some of them we brake down now. In the Chancel, we brake down an Angel; 3 *orate pro anima* in the Glass; and the Trinity in a Triangle; and 12 Cherubims on the Roof of the Chancel; nigh a 100 JESUS – MARIA, in Capital Letters; and the Steps to be levelled. And we brake down the Organ Cases, and gave them to the Poor. – In the Church, there was on the Roof, above 100 JESUS and MARY, in great Capital Letters; and a Crosier Staff to be broke down, in Glass; and above 20 Stars on the Roof. There is a glorious Cover over the Font, like a Pope's Tripple Crown, with a Pelican on the Top, picking its Breast, all gilt over with Gold. And we were kept out of the Church above 2 hours, and neither Churchwardens, *William Brown*, nor *Roger Small*, that were enjoined these things above three months afore, had not done them in May, and I sent one of them to see it done, and they would not let him have the key. And now, neither the Churchwardens, nor *William Brown*, nor the Constable *James Tokelove*, and *William Gardener* the Sexton, would not let us have the key in 2 hours time. New Churchwardens, *Thomas Stanard*, *Thomas Stroud*. And *Samuel Canham*, of the same Town, said, 'I sent men to rifle the Church;' – and *Will. Brown*, old Churchwarden, said, 'I went about to pull down the Church, and had carried away part of the Church.'

The Ufford font cover is indeed 'glorious', reaching right up to the roof, and thanks to the sturdy delaying tactics by the locals is still there to be seen.

The 'Diggers' on George Hill appeal for justice, from Gerrard Winstanley (1609–1676), 'To the Ministers of both Universities and the Lawyers of Every Inns-A-Court from A fellow commoner of England, and true friend of Freedom' (1650)

In 1650 Gerrard Winstanley and his band of 'True Levellers' created a settlement on George Hill, near Cobham in Surrey, exercising their belief that, following the Parliamentary defeat of the King and the House of Lords, 'the work of digging upon the Commons is not only warranted by Scripture, but by the Law of the Commonwealth of England likewise. ... Let not sottish covetousness in the Gentry deny the poor or younger Brethren their just Freedom to build and plant Corn upon the common waste Land: nor let slavish fear possess the hearts of the poor, to stand in awe of the Norman yoke [i.e. the monarchy] any longer, seeing it is broke.'

When the local landowners invaded the settlement, on 9 April he published the appeal of which this is an extract.

The week before Easter, Parson Plat, Minister of Horsley, being the Lord of the Manor of Cobham, where the Diggers were at work, and Thomas Sutton, the impropriator of Cobham [holder of its advowson], came in person, and brought divers men, whom they hired to pull down a poor man's house, that was built upon the Commons, and kicked and struck the poor man's wife, so that she miscarried of her Child, and by the blows and abuses they gave her she kept her bed a week.

And at this time I went to Mr. Plat, and spoke with him, about our freedom in the commons, he answered me that if I could make it good by the Scriptures, he would never trouble us more, but let us build and plant: Nay he said, he would cast in all his estate, and become one with the diggers.

The next week after I carried him this writing afore printed, being Monday in Easter week, and upon our discourse, he seemed to consent to many things, and was very moderate, and promised me to read it over, and to give me an Answer: moreover he promised me, that if the diggers would not cut the wood upon the Common, he would not pull down their houses: And the diggers resolved for peace sake, to let the wood alone till people did understand their freedom a little more.

And upon Friday in Easter week, he came and brought his answer, which was this. He came accompanied with about 50 men, and had hired 4 or 5 of them, to fire down the diggers' houses: some that stood by said, do not fire them, the wood will do some good; his answer was, no, no, fire them to the ground, that these Heathens, who know not God, may not build them again; for if you let the wood alone, they will build again.

Thereupon at the Command of this Parson Plat, they set fire to six houses, and burned them down, and burned likewise some of their householdstuff, and wearing Clothes , throwing their beds, stools, and householdstuff, up and down the Common, not pitying the cries of many little Children, and their frighted Mothers, which are Parishioners born in the Parish. And yet some of these hired men lives not in the Parish, and some are strangers newly come into the Parish: and so were bewitched by the covetous make-bate Priests, to do this heathenish Turkish act.

The poor diggers being thus suddenly cast out of their houses by fire, both they, their wives and Children were forced to lie upon the open Common all night: yet the rage of Parson Plat and his Company rested not here, but in the night time, some of them came again upon the Commons, while the diggers were quiet, and some of them in bed, and said, we have Authority from our Master, that is Mr. Plat, to kill you, and burn the rest of your goods, if you will not be gone: thereupon Sir Anthony Vincent's Servant, called Davy, struck at one, and cut some of their Chairs and other Goods to pieces, frighting the women and Children again. And some of the Diggers asked them, why they would do thus cruelly by them, they answered, because you do not know God, nor will come to the Church.

Surely if the God of these men, by their going to Church, teach both their preacher and they, to do such cruel deeds, we will neither come to Church, nor serve their God. Mr. Plat in his Sermons can say, *live in peace with all men, and love your Enemies*; therefore if the Diggers were enemies, he ought to love them in action; but it is a true badge of an hypocrite, to say, and not to do.

Let every Man's actions be tried, and see who serves God, They or the Diggers. Mr. Plat and the Gentlemen (so would be called) that were with him, were full of rage, and gnashed their tongues with vexation; but the Diggers are patient, cheerful, quiet in spirit, loving to those that have burned their houses.

Therefore the poor diggers have got the Crown, and wear it, and the Priests and Gentry have lost their Crown ...

A young Puritan sets out on a preaching career, from the memoir of John Shaw (1608–1672)

The memoir that Shaw wrote for his son provides a vivid account of the life and career of a Nonconformist minister at this period.

After three years as a 'lecturer' in Brampton, Derbyshire, he received his licence to preach from Bishop Morton. With a growing reputation he was invited to London, and at a 'solemn feast' of Devonshire merchants and tradesmen there he so impressed them that they pitched on him for 'a baren place, viz. Chimleigh, a market town in Devonshire'. After a repeat performance a year later, 'some of them followed me from the church to my lodging, and there told me their pious intentions, the great barrenness and need of a ministry in their county, and that their custom was to maintain a minister at their own charge for three years at one place; and if his ministry so far prevailed upon that people's hearts as that they of themselves would afterwards maintain him there, he should stil continue there, if not, the merchants would maintain him stil, but remove him to another place.' And so he went, bringing his wife and first two infants the 200 miles from Ecclesfield the following April to join him.

I was born at Sicke-house ['sike' being dialect for a small stream] in the chapelry of Bradfield and parish of Ecclesfield, in the West-riding of the county of Yorke, on June 23, 1608, in the sixth yeare of King James, which house and land thereto belonging, I intend (if God wil), to leave to you, and which my father left to me, and therefore I desire that you will not sell that inheritance of your fathers. …

From a child I had a great mind and earnest desire of learning, but thro' the great want of good schoolmasters in that country at those times, I was tossed from one school to another without that benefit which I might have obtained.

My parents having no other child but me, and some competent estate to leave me, were very loath to have me depart from them; but desired that I would take up some calling, which I might follow in that country near to them; but they observing my eager desire (when so young) after knowledge and learning, my good God so overruled their hearts as to incline them (at my desire, and seeing me to have no genius at anything but learning) to send me to Cambridge, where I was (at the age of betwixt fourteen and fifteen years) admitted pensioner into Christ's colledge; under the tuition of Mr. William Chappell (who was a very acute learned man, and a most painful and vigilant tutor, and was (tho' long after) provost of Dublin and dean of Cashell, and bishop of Cork, in Ireland; and with some difficulty he escaped out of Ireland with his life, in the late rebellion there).

When I first came to Cambridge, I had not so great a desire after learning, but I had as little desire after religion, in the power and practice of the truth and life thereof; yet, the only wise and good God so ordered it, that I was put into a chamber (called Lancashire), where I had some good chamber-fellows, which was a means to keep me from that sad plague and ruin of young schollers, viz. bad company. When I was about two years standing, it pleased God that Mr. Weld (then minister of Haveril, but afterwards went over into New England, and put forth an usefull book of the rise, growth, and ruin of the errors of New England, and after that returned to Old England, and was preacher at Newcastle in the North, and there I think he died), this Mr. Weld (I say) then preached one Lord's day, at a church three miles from Cambridge; some of my chamber-fellows resolved to walk on foot to hear him, and I (as sometime Austin to hear Ambrose, more for company and novelty than conscience) went along with them, and it pleased God in mercy to set on his sermon with much power and no small terrour on my heart (for which I bless that great prophet and soul bishop, the Lord Jesus). I yet very well remember his texts (in the morning he preached on Luke xiii.24, and in the afternoon on Mark xvi.16), and some of his sermons, and tho' many of the words I forget, yet I felt much heat and power, and from that time forth more and more change in heart, affections, speeches, practises, etc., so that I was much taken notice of in the colledge and much opposed for a Puritane; yet, I continued still in that coll., and under the tutour aforesaid I commenced bachelor and afterwards master of arts.

Dr. Butts, master of Bennett coll., was vice-chancellor of Cambridge, when I commenced M.A., who not long after upon his study door (which was lower than himself) did, in that colledge, upon an Easter day in the fore-noon, hang himself in his head-kerchief; at which time he might from that place have seen down into the colledge chapel where the Lord's Supper was then administering, and where he ought to have been. ...

The pestilence was very sore in Cambridge, when I commenced master of arts, anno 1630, so that whereas commencements usually are the first Tuesday in July, we were scattered abroad, and I (with others) commenced in October following. That contagious infection was one occasion to make me leave the university (wherein I much delighted) the sooner, but especially my very eager desire to the office and work of the ministry, to which I was fully perswaded God had called me (though yet I entered upon it with much reverence and fear, out of the sense of my own weakness).

The Presbyterian knight, from Samuel Butler (1613–1680), *Hudibras* (1662)

The popularity of Part I of this satire on Puritanism and the Roundheads earned Butler a state pension in 1663, and two further parts followed. Sir Hudibras is a Quixotic figure of comic-grotesque proportions.

For his *Religion* it was fit
To match his learning and his Wit:
'Twas Presbyterian true Blue,
For he was of that stubborn Crew
Of Errant Saints, whom all men grant
To be the true Church *Militant*:
Such as do build their Faith upon
The holy Text of *Pike* and *Gun*;
Decide all Controversies by
Infallible *Artillery*;
And prove their Doctrine Orthodox
By Apostolick *Blows* and *Knocks*:
Call Fire, and Sword, and Desolation,
A godly thorough Reformation,
Which always must be carry'd on,
And still be doing, never done:
As if Religion were intended
For nothing else but to be mended,
A Sect whose chief Devotion lies
In odd perverse Antipathies:
In falling out with that or this,
And finding somewhat still amiss:
More peevish, cross, and splenetick,
Than Dog distract, or Monkey sick.
That with more care keep Holy-day
The wrong, than others the right way:
Compound for Sins they are inclin'd to,
By damning those they have no mind to.
Still so perverse and opposite,
As if they worship'd God for spight.
The self-same thing they will abhor

One way, and long another for.
Free-will they one way disavow,
Another, nothing else allow.
All Piety consists therein
In them, in other Men all Sin.
Rather than fail, they will defy
That which they love most tenderly:
Quarrel with Minc'd-pies, and disparage
Their best and dearest Friend *Plum-porridge*;
Fat *Pig* and *Goose* itself oppose,
And blaspheme *Custard* thro' the *Nose.*
Th' Apostles of this fierce Religion,
Like *Mahomet's*, were Ass and Widgeon,
To whom our Knight, by fast Instinct
Of Wit and Temper, was so linkt.
As if Hypocrisy and Nonsense
Had got the' Advowson of his Conscience.

A young preacher and a hypocrite, from John Earle (*c.* 1601–1665), *Microcosmographie, or, A Piece of the World Discovered in Essays and Characters* (1628)

Initially anonymous, the book quickly won the young cleric fame. It features a number of characters – expanded to seventy-eight in early reprints. Patronage brought him a Wiltshire living, but it wasn't long before Charles I made him tutor to the future Charles II, whose exile and Restoration he shared. He fought against the persecution of the Nonconformists, and in his last few years was appointed Bishop first of Worcester, then of Salisbury. The historian and statesman Clarendon described Earle's conversation as 'so pleasant and delightful, so very innocent, and so very facetious, that no man's company was more desired and more loved'.

II *A young raw preacher*

Is a bird not yet fledged, that hath hopped out of his nest to be chirping on a hedge, and will be straggling abroad at what peril soever. His backwardness in the university hath set him thus forward; for had he not truanted there, he had not been so hasty a divine. His small standing, and time, hath made him a proficient only in boldness, out of which, with his table-book, he is furnished for a preacher. His collections of study are the notes of sermons, which, taken up at St. Mary's [the university church], he utters in the country: and if he write brachigraphy, his stock is so much the better. His writing is more than his reading, for he reads only what he gets without book. Thus accomplished he comes down to his friends, and his first salutation is grace and peace out of the pulpit. His prayer is conceited, and no man remembers his college more at large. The pace of his sermon is a full career, and he runs wildly over hill and dale, till the clock stop him. The labour of it is chiefly in his lungs; and the only thing he hath made in it himself, is the faces. He takes on against the pope without mercy, and has a jest still in lavender for Bellarmine: yet he preaches heresy, if it comes in his way, though with a mind, I must needs say, very orthodox. His action is all passion, and his speech interjections. He has an excellent faculty in bemoaning the people, and spits with a very good grace. He will not draw his handkercher out of his place, nor blow his nose without discretion. His commendation is, that he never looks upon book; and indeed he never was used to it. He preaches but once a year, though twice on Sunday; for the stuff is still the same, only the dressing a little altered: he has more tricks with a sermon, than a taylor with an old cloak, to turn it, and piece it, and at last quite disguise it with a new preface. If he have waded farther in his profession, and would shew reading of his own, his authors are postils, and his school-divinity a catechism. His fashion and demure habit gets him in with some town-precisian, and makes him a guest on Friday nights. You shall know him by his narrow velvet cape, and serge facing; and his ruff, next his hair, the shortest thing about him. The companion of his walk is some zealous tradesman, whom he astonishes with strange points, which they both understand alike. His friends and much painfulness may prefer him to thirty pounds a year, and this means to a chambermaid; with whom we leave him now in the bonds of wedlock: – next Sunday you shall have him again.

XXXIV *A she-precise hypocrite*

Is one in whom good women suffer, and have their truth misinterpreted by her folly. She is one, she knows not what her self if you ask her, but she is indeed one that has taken a toy at the fashion of religion, and is enamoured of the new fangle. She is non-conformist in a close stomacher and ruff of Geneva print, and her purity consists much in her linnen. She has heard of the rag of Rome, and thinks it a very sluttish religion, and rails at the whore of Babylon for a very naughty woman. She has left her virginity as a relick of popery, and marries in her tribe without a ring. Her devotion at the church is much in turning up of her eye; and turning down the leaf in her book, when she hears named chapter and verse. When she comes home, she commends the sermon for the scripture, and two hours. She loves preaching better than praying, and of preachers, lecturers; and thinks the weekday's exercise far more edifying than the Sunday's. Her oftest gossipings are sabbath-day's journeys, where, (though an enemy to superstition,) she will go in pilgrimage five mile to a silenced minister, when there is a better sermon in her own parish. She doubts of the virgin Mary's salvation, and dares not saint her, but knows her own place in heaven as perfectly as the pew she has a key to. She is so taken up with faith she has no room for charity, and understands no good works but what are wrought on the sampler. She accounts nothing vices but superstition and an oath, and thinks adultery a less sin than to swear *by my truly*. She rails at other women by the names of Jezebel and Dalilah; and calls her own daughters Rebecca and Abigail, and not Ann but Hannah. She suffers them not to learn on the virginals, because of their affinity with organs, but is reconciled to the bells for the chimes sake, since they were reformed to the tune of a psalm. She overflows so with the bible, that she spills it upon every occasion, and will not cudgel her maids without scripture. It is a question whether she is more trouble with the Devil, or the Devil with her: She is always challenging and daring him, and her weapon is the Practice of Piety. Nothing angers her so much as that women cannot preach, and in this point only thinks the Brownist [a dissenter from the Church of England] erroneous; but what she cannot at the church she does at the table, where she prattles more than any against sense and Antichrist, 'till a capon's wing silence her. She expounds the priests of Baal, reading ministers, and thinks the salvation of that parish as desperate as the Turks. She is a main derider to her capacity of those that are not her preachers, and censures all sermons but bad ones. If her husband be a tradesman, she helps him to customers, howsoever to good cheer, and they are a most faithful couple at these meetings, for they never fail. Her conscience is like others' lust, never satisfied, and you might better answer Scotus [Duns Scotus (*c.* 1265–1308), internationally celebrated 'subtle doctor', whose name has degenerated into 'dunce'] than her scruples. She is one that thinks she performs all her duties to God in hearing, and shows the fruits of it in talking. She is more fiery against the may-pole than her husband, and thinks she might do a Phineas' act to break the pate of the fiddler. [In the Book of Numbers, Phineas was the grandson of the priest Aaron; he took a spear and killed a fellow Israelite and his Midianite woman, so ending a plague sent by God as a punishment for cohabitation in which 24,000 people had died.] She is an everlasting argument, but I am weary of her.

Iconoclasm and the Civil War reach Worcestershire in 1642, from *Reliquiae Baxterianae, or Mr. Richard Baxter's Narrative of the Most Memorable Passages of his Life and Times*

The Rev. Richard Baxter (1615–1691) managed his own remarkable course through his turbulent age. Intense, severe, and 'sparingly facetious, but never light or frothy', he was unafraid of courting controversy with anyone, including Protector Cromwell. He was not a republican, and as a moderate Nonconformist preached and wrote to avoid sectarian splits. Although made a chaplain to Charles II after the Restoration, he refused a bishopric. In 1685 he found himself before Judge Jeffreys on a charge of libelling the Church, and it was eighteen months before he was released from prison. Reliquiae *was published in 1696, after his death. There is a statue of him outside the Kidderminster church where he served, on and off, for nineteen years.*

The following event took place in Kidderminster, where the young Baxter had only recently begun his reforming ministry.

About that time the parliament sent down an order for the demolishing of all statues and images of any of the three Persons in the Blessed Trinity, or of the Virgin Mary, which should be found in churches, or on the crosses in churchyards. My judgment was for the obeying of this order, thinking it came from just authority; but I meddled not in it, but left the churchwarden to do what he thought good. The churchwarden (an honest, sober, quiet man), seeing a crucifix upon the cross in the churchyard, set up a ladder to have reached it, but it proved too short; whilst he was gone to seek another, a crew of the drunken riotous party of the town (poor journeymen and servants) took the alarm, and run altogether with weapons to defend the crucifix and the church images (of which there were divers left since the time of Popery). The report was among them that I was the actor, and it was me they sought; but I was walking almost a mile out of the town, or else I suppose I had there ended my days; when they missed me and the churchwarden both, they went raving about the streets to seek us. Two neighbours that dwelt in other parishes, hearing that they sought my life, ran in among them to see whether I were there, and they knocked them both down in the streets, and both of them are since dead and I think never perfectly recovered that hurt. When they had foamed about half an hour, and met with none of us, and were newly housed, I came in from my walk, and hearing the people cursing at me in their doors, I wondered what the matter was, but quickly found out how fairly I had scaped. The next Lord's-day I dealt plainly with them, and laid open to them the quality of that action, and told them, seeing they so requited me as to seek my blood, I was willing to leave them, and save them from that guilt. But the poor sots were so amazed and ashamed, that they took on sorrily and were loth to part with me.

Advised to withdraw a while, Baxter took refuge in Gloucester for a month, but returned to Kidderminster when his old neighbours came and told him that 'if I stayed any longer the people would interpret it either that I was afraid upon some guilt, or that I was against the king.'

As the Parliamentarian army under the Earl of Essex began to confront the Royalists, there was an early cavalry skirmish outside Worcester that Baxter experienced – 'I had a great mind to go see them, having never seen any part of an army' – and before long he became attached to them as a preacher. But the first major battle of the Civil War, at Edgehill, came first, on 23 October.

The king's army was upon the march from Shrewsbury towards Oxford. Their way lying through Wolverhampton, some of their scouts appeared on the top of Kinver Edge, three miles from Kidderminster. The brigades in Kidderminster, not knowing but all the king's army might come that way, marched off to Worcester, and in haste left a carriage or two with arms behind. Some of the inhabitants hasted to the king's soldiers and told them all, which made them come into the town and take those arms.

The fury of our own rabble and of the king's soldiers was such that I saw no safety in staying at home. The civility of the Earl of Essex's army was such that among them there was no danger (though none of them knew me). And there was such excellent preaching among them at Worcester that I stayed among them a few days, till the marching of the king's army occasioned their remove.

Upon the Lord's-day following I preached at Alcester for my reverend friend Mr. Samuel Clark. As I was preaching, the people heard the cannon play, and perceived that the armies were engaged; when sermon was done (in the afternoon) the report was more audible, which made us all long to hear of the success. About sun-setting many troops fled through the town, and told us that all was lost on the parliament side, and the carriage taken and waggons plundered before they came away; and none that followed brought any other news. The townsmen sent a messenger to Stratford-upon-Avon to know the certain truth.

John Evelyn (1620–1706), from his *Diary* for 1653

As a Royalist, Evelyn had left England after Charles I's execution in 1649. He returned in 1652, and at Sayes Court, Deptford, began work on a great scheme of gardens that soon became famous. Evelyn was an early fellow of the Royal Society. His Sylva, Or, a Discourse of Forest Trees *made a significant contribution to the young science of arboriculture.*

On the 11th of October, at half past ten at night, my son, John Stansfield Evelyn, was born, being my second child. On the 17th we christened him by the name of my mother's father, that name being now quite extinct. The ceremony was performed in my library at Sayes Court by Mr Owen.

The 7th of November, my wife was churched by Mr Owen, whom I always made use of on these occasions, for the parish minister durst not, or perhaps would not, have officiated according to the form and usage of the Church of England, to which I always adhered.

December the 4th. Till now I had met with no fanatical preachers but, going this day to church, I was surprised to see a tradesman step up. I resolved yet to stay and see what he would make of his text, which was II Samuel, xxiii, 20: 'And Benaiah the son of Jehoiada, the son of a valiant man, of Kabzeel, who had done many acts, he slew two lionlike men of Moab: he went down also and slew a lion in the midst of a pit in time of snow'. He inferred that no danger was to be thought difficult when God called for shedding of blood, and that the saints are called to destroy temporal governments. And this was truculent, anabaptistical stuff, so dangerous a crisis were things grown to.

Christmas Day. There being no churches to attend, nor any public assembly, I was obliged to pass the devotions of this blessed day with my family at home.

Samuel Pepys (1633–1703), from his *Diary* for 1664

The deciphering of Pepys's diary, which he kept in code between 1 January 1660 and 31 May 1669, began in the early 1800s and was only completed in 1983, culminating in an eleven-volume edition. Along with the historical value of his detailed and colourful accounts of the first years of the Restoration from his official positions in the Naval Office, the candour of his personal confidences sheds its own inimitable light on the age in which he lived.

His admiration for Frances Butler was mentioned on earlier Sunday viewings, on 23 June and 11 August 1661.

2 October 1664 – Lord's Day

I walked through the City, putting in at several churches. And so over Moorfields, and thence to Clerkenwell church; and there, as I wished, sat next pew to the fair Butler, who indeed is a most perfect beauty still, and one I do very much admire myself for my choice of her as a beauty, she having the best lower part of her face that ever I saw all days of my life. After church I walked to my Lady Sandwich's, and dined with her. So away back to Clerkenwell Church, thinking to have got sight of la belle Boteler again, but failed, and so after church walked all over the fields home, and there my wife was angry with me for not coming home, and for gadding abroad to look after beauties, she told me plainly; so I made all peace, and to supper. This evening came Mrs. Lane (now Martin) with her husband to desire my help about a place for him.

The country gentleman of the seventeenth century, from Thomas Babington Macaulay (1800–1859), *History of England* (1848)

Essayist, poet and Whig politician whose five-volume history of the years 1685–1702 was an immediate success.

Many lords of manors had received an education differing little from that of their menial servants. The heir of an estate often passed his boyhood and youth at the seat of his family with no better tutors than grooms and gamekeepers, and scarce attained learning enough to sign his name to a Mittimus. If he went to school and to college, he generally returned before he was twenty to the seclusion of the old hall, and there, unless his mind were very happily constituted by nature, soon forgot his academical pursuits in rural business and pleasures. His chief serious employment was the care of his property. He examined samples of grain, handled pigs, and, on market days, made bargains over a tankard with drovers and hop merchants. His chief pleasures were commonly derived from field sports and from an unrefined sensuality. His language and pronunciation were such as we should now expect to hear only from the most ignorant clowns. His oaths, coarse jests, and scurrilous terms of abuse, were uttered with the broadest accent of his province. It was very easy to discern, from the first words which he spoke, whether he came from Somersetshire or Yorkshire. He troubled himself little about decorating his abode, and, if he attempted decoration, seldom produced anything but deformity. ...

It was very seldom that the country gentleman caught glimpses of the great world; and what he saw of it tended rather to confuse than to enlighten his understanding. His opinions respecting religion, government, foreign countries and former times, having been derived, not from study, from observation, or from conversation with enlightened companions, but from such traditions as were current in his own small circle, were the opinions of a child. He adhered to them, however, with the obstinacy which is generally found in ignorant men accustomed to be fed with flattery. His animosities were numerous and bitter. He hated Frenchmen and Italians, Scotchmen and Irishmen, Papists and Presbyterians, Independents and Baptists, Quakers and Jews. Towards London and Londoners he felt an aversion which more than once produced important political effects. His wife and daughter were in tastes and acquirements below a housekeeper or a stillroom maid of the present day. They stitched and spun, brewed gooseberry wine, cured marigolds, and made the crust for the venison pasty.

From this description it might be supposed that the English esquire of the seventeenth century did not materially differ from a rustic miller or alehouse keeper of our time. There are, however, some important parts of his character still to be noted, which will greatly modify this estimate. Unlettered as he was and unpolished, he was still in some most important points a gentleman. He was a member of a proud and powerful aristocracy, and was distinguished by many both of the good and of the bad qualities which belong to aristocrats. ...

There was one institution, and one only, which [country gentlemen] prized even more than hereditary monarchy; and that institution was the Church of England. Their love of the Church was not, indeed, the effect of study or meditation. Few among them could have given any reason, drawn from Scripture or ecclesiastical history, for adhering to her doctrines, her ritual, and her polity; nor were they, as a class, by any means strict observers of that code of morality which is common to all Christian sects. But the experience of many ages proves that men may be ready to fight to the death, and to persecute without pity, for a religion whose creed they do not understand, and whose precepts they habitually disobey.

John Bunyan (1628–1688), from *The Pilgrim's Progress,* Part II (1684)

Bunyan returned in 1647 from service in the Parliamentary army to his father's trade as a tinker in Bedfordshire, and the following years of his spiritual crisis were the substance of his first book, Grace Abounding to the Chief of Sinners. *The freedom he enjoyed as a Nonconformist preacher of widening celebrity came to an end with the 1660 Restoration, and he spent most of the next twelve years in prison, studying and writing. The Declaration of Indulgence brought release in 1672, but it was during another spell in prison in 1677 that the first part of* The Pilgrim's Progress from This World to That Which is to Come *was finished. This extract comes from Part II, published in 1684.*

The fame of Christian's journey to the Celestial City has at last moved his wife Christiana and four sons to undertake the same pilgrimage. Great-Heart has joined them as their guide and bodyguard. Now nearing their goal, they have encountered Valiant-for-Truth, sword in hand, who has for three hours been fighting off three assailants, Wild-Head, Inconsiderate and Pragmatick, with his 'right Jerusalem blade'.

GREAT-HEART ... Were your father and mother willing that you should become a pilgrim?

VALIANT-FOR-TRUTH O no; they used all means imaginable to persuade me to stay at home.

GREAT-HEART Why, what could they say against it?

VALIANT-FOR-TRUTH They said it was an idle life; and if I myself were not inclined to sloth and laziness, I would never countenance a pilgrim's condition.

GREAT-HEART And what did they say else?

VALIANT-FOR-TRUTH Why, they told me that it was a dangerous way; yea, the most dangerous way in the world, said they, is that which the pilgrims go.

GREAT-HEART Did they show you wherein this way is so dangerous?

VALIANT-FOR-TRUTH Yes, and that in many particulars.

GREAT-HEART Name some of them.

VALIANT-FOR-TRUTH They told me of the Slough of Despond, where Christian was well nigh smothered. They told me that there were archers standing ready in Beelzebub-Castle to shoot them who should knock at the Wicket-Gate for entrance. They told me also of the wood and dark mountains; of the hill Difficulty; of the lions; and also of the three giants, Bloody-Man, Maul, and Slay-Good. They said, moreover, that there was a foul fiend haunted the Valley of Humiliation; and that Christian was by him almost bereft of life. Besides, said they, you must go over the Valley of the Shadow of Death, where the hobgoblins are, where the light is darkness, where the way is full of snares, pits, traps, and gins. They told me also of Giant Despair, of Doubting-Castle, and of the ruin that the pilgrims met with there. Further, they said I must go over the Enchanted Ground, which was dangerous; and that after all this I should find a river, over which there was no bridge; and that that river did lie betwixt me and the Celestial Country.

GREAT-HEART And was this all?

VALIANT-FOR-TRUTH No. They also told me that this way was full of deceivers, and of persons that lay in wait there to turn good men out of the path.

GREAT-HEART But how did they make that out?

VALIANT-FOR-TRUTH They told me that Mr. Worldly-Wiseman did lie there in wait to deceive. They said also, that there were Formality and Hypocrisy continually on the road. They said also, that By-Ends, Talkative, or Demas, would go near to gather me up; that the Flatterer would catch me in his net; or that, with green-headed Ignorance, I would presume to go on to the gate, from whence he was sent back to the hole that was in the side of the hill, and made to go the by-way to hell.

GREAT-HEART I promise you this was enough to discourage you; but did they make an end here?

VALIANT-FOR-TRUTH No, stay. They told me also of many that had tried that way of old, and that had gone a great way therein, to see if they could find something of the glory there that so many had so much talked of from time to time, and how they came back again, and befooled themselves for setting a foot out of doors in that path, to the satisfaction of the country. And they named several that did so, as Obstinate and Pliable, Mistrust and Timorous, Turn-Away, and old Atheist, with several more; who, they said, had some of them gone far to see what they could find, but not one of them had found so much advantage by going as amounted to the weight of a feather.

GREAT-HEART Said they anything more to discourage you?

VALIANT-FOR-TRUTH Yes. They told me of one Mr. Fearing, who was a pilgrim, and how he found his way so solitary that he never had a comfortable hour therein; also, that Mr. Despondency had like to have been starved therein: yea, and also (which I had almost forgot), that Christian himself, about whom there has been such a noise, after all his adventures for a Celestial Crown, was certainly drowned in the Black River, and never went a foot further; however, it was smothered up.

GREAT-HEART And did none of these things discourage you?

VALIANT-FOR-TRUTH No; they seemed but as so many nothings to me.

GREAT-HEART How came that about?

VALIANT-FOR-TRUTH Why, I still believed what Mr. Tell-True had said; and that carried me beyond them all.

GREAT-HEART Then this was your victory, even your faith.

VALIANT-FOR-TRUTH It was so. I believed, and therefore came out, got into the way, fought all that set themselves against me, and, by believing, am come to this place.

The Pilgrim's Song

Who would true valor see,
Let him come hither;
One here will constant be,
Come wind, come weather;
There's no discouragement
Shall make him once relent
His first avow'd intent
To be a pilgrim.

Whoso beset him round
With dismal stories,
Do but themselves confound;
His strength the more is.
No lion can him fright,
He'll with a giant fight,
But he will have a right
To be a pilgrim.

Hobgoblin nor foul fiend
  Can daunt his spirit;
He knows he at the end
  Shall life inherit.
Then fancies fly away,
He'll not fear what men say;
He'll labour night and day
  To be a pilgrim.

By this time they were got to the Enchanted Ground, where the air naturally tended to make one drowsy. And that place was all grown over with briers and thorns, excepting here and there, where was an enchanted arbor, upon which if a man sits, or in which if a man sleeps, it is a question, some say, whether ever he shall rise or wake again in this world. Over this forest, therefore, they went both one and another, and Mr. Great-Heart went before, for that he was the guide; and Mr. Valiant-for-Truth came behind, being rear-guard, for fear lest peradventure some fiend, or dragon, or giant or thief, should fall upon their rear, and so do mischief. They went on here, each man with his sword drawn in his hand; for they knew it was a dangerous place. Also they cheered up one another as well as they could. Feeble-Mind, Mr. Great-Heart commanded, should come up after him, and Mr. Despondency was under the eye of Mr. Valiant.

Now they had not gone far, but a great mist and darkness fell upon them all; so they could scarce, for a great while, the one see the other; wherefore they were forced, for some time, to feel for one another by words; for they walked not by sight. But anyone must think, that here was but sorry going for the best of them all; but how much worse for the women and children, who both of feet and heart were but tender! Yet so it was, that through the encouraging words of him that led in the front, and of him that brought them up behind, they made a pretty good shift to wag along.

The way was also here very wearisome, through dirt and slabbiness. Nor was there, on all this ground, so much as one inn or victualling-house wherein to refresh the feebler sort. Here, therefore, was nothing but grunting, and puffing, and sighing, while one tumbleth over a bush, another sticks fast in the dirt, and the children, some of them, lost their shoes in the mire; while one cries out, I am down; and another, Ho, where are you? and a third, The bushes have got such fast hold on me I think I cannot get away from them.

Then they came at an arbor, warm, and promising much refreshing to the pilgrims; for it was finely wrought above head, beautified with greens, furnished with benches and settles. It also had in it a soft couch, whereon the weary might lean. This, you must think, all things considered, was tempting.

John Dryden (1631–1700), 'Harvest Home' from *King Arthur: or, The British Worthy* (1691)

The first official poet laureate, Dryden wrote two long poems addressing the religious issues of his time, A Layman's Faith *(1682) and* The Hind and the Panther *(1687), by which time he had converted to Roman Catholicism (the 'milk-white Hind' is the Catholic Church, arguing and bandying satire and fable with the more aggressive Anglican Panther). His new adherence lost him the Laureateship in 1688.*

Dryden's words in King Arthur *were the libretto to music by Henry Purcell. This rumbustious 'Harvest Home' with country dance is followed by Venus's more idealised vision of Britain, at the climax of the final act, as 'Fairest isle, all other isles excelling, Seat of pleasure and of love'.*

Enter Comus with peasants

COMUS Your hay, it is mow'd and your corn is reap'd,
Your barns will be full and your hovels heap'd.
Come, boys, come, Come, boys, come,
And merrily roar out our harvest home!

PEASANTS Harvest home, harvest home,
And merrily roar out our harvest home!

COMUS We've cheated the parson, we'll cheat him again,
For why shou'd a blockhead have one in ten?
One in ten, One in ten,
For why shou'd a blockhead have one in ten?

PEASANTS One in ten, One in ten,
For why shou'd a blockhead have one in ten?

COMUS For prating so long, like a book-learn'd sot,
Till pudding and dumpling are burnt to the pot:
Burnt to pot, Burnt to pot,
Till pudding and dumpling are burnt to the pot.

PEASANTS Burnt to pot, Burnt to pot,
Till pudding and dumpling are burnt to the pot.

COMUS We'll toss off our ale till we cannot stand,
And heigh for the honour of old England;
Old England, Old England,
And heigh for the honour of old England!

PEASANTS Old England, Old England,
And heigh for the honour of old England!

Church membership voluntary, from John Locke (1632–1704), *Letters Concerning Toleration* (1689–92)

The philosopher Locke claimed that in 'the commonwealth of learning' of his time it was 'ambition enough to be employed as an under-labourer in clearing the ground a little, and removing some of the rubbish that lies in the way to knowledge'. His Letters *were an early argument, in an age when it was much needed, for religious toleration and against a ruling power's right to coerce people into its idea of 'true religion'.*

This is from the contemporary translation of Locke's Latin by William Popple.

A church, then, I take to be a voluntary society of men, joining themselves together of their own accord.

The only business of the church is the salvation of souls; and it no ways concerns the commonwealth, or any member of it, that this or the other ceremony be there made use of. Neither the use, nor the omission of any ceremonies in those religious assemblies, does either advantage or prejudice the life, liberty, or estate of any man. For example: Let it be granted, that the washing of an infant with water is in itself an indifferent thing. Let it be granted also, that if the magistrate understand such washing to be profitable to the curing or preventing of any disease that children are subject unto, and esteem the matter weighty enough to be taken care of by a law, in that case he may order it to be done. But will anyone therefore say, that the magistrate has the same right to ordain by law, that all children shall be baptised by priests in the sacred font, in order to the purification of their souls? The extreme difference of these two cases is visible to everyone at first sight. Or let us apply the last case to the child of a jew, and the thing will speak itself.

For what hinders but a christian magistrate may have subjects that are jews? Now if we acknowledge that such an injury may not be done unto a jew, as to compel him, against his own opinion, to practise in his religion a thing that is in its nature indifferent, how can we maintain that anything of this kind may be done to a christian?

The Vicar of Bray

George Orwell wrote in a 1946 essay in Tribune*: 'The Vicar of Bray, though he was well-equipped to be a leader-writer on* The Times*, could hardly be described as an admirable character. Yet, after this lapse of time, all that is left of him is a comic song and a beautiful [yew] tree which has rested the eyes of generation after generation and must surely have outweighed any bad effects which he produced by his political quislingism.'*

Several cases have been made for who the original 'trimming parson' might have been, none conclusively. Similarly, various authors have been suggested, including a dragoon in George I's reign.

In good King Charles's golden day,
When loyalty no harm meant;
A zealous High-Church man I was,
And so I gained Preferment.
Unto my Flock I daily Preach'd,
Kings are by God appointed,
And Damn'd are those who dare resist,
Or touch the Lord's Anointed.
And this is Law, I will maintain
Unto my Dying Day, Sir,
That whatsoever King may reign,
I will be the Vicar of Bray, Sir!

When Royal James possest the crown,
And popery grew in fashion;
The Penal Law I shouted down,
And read the Declaration:
The Church of Rome I found would fit
Full well my Constitution,

And I had been a Jesuit
But for the Revolution.
  And this is Law, etc. ...

When William our Deliverer came
To heal the Nation's Grievance,
I turn'd the Cat in Pan again,
And swore to him Allegiance:
Old Principles I did revoke,
Set conscience at a distance,
Passive Obedience is a Joke,
A Pish on non-resistance.
  And this is Law, etc. ...

When Royal Anne became our Queen,
Then Church of England's Glory,
Another face of things was seen,
And I became a Tory.
Occasional Conformists base
I Damn'd, and Moderation,
And thought the Church in danger was,
From such Prevarication.
  And this is Law, etc. ...

When George in Pudding time came o'er,
And Moderate men looked big, Sir,
My Principles I chang'd once more,
And so became a Whig, Sir.
And thus Preferment I procur'd
From our Faith's great Defender,
And almost every day abjur'd
The Pope, and the Pretender.
  And this is Law, etc. ...

The Illustrious House of Hanover,
And Protestant succession,
To these I lustily will swear,
Whilst they can keep possession:
For in my Faith, and Loyalty,
I never once will faulter,

But George my lawful King shall be,
Except the Times should alter.
And this is Law, etc. ...

The story of one pew in the church at Myddle, from Richard Gough (1635–1723), *The History of Myddle* (1701)

Richard Gough was of Shropshire yeoman stock, and in addition to his grammar-school education picked up considerable legal knowledge in his employment as clerk to a leading county family and steward of one of their manors. He inherited a tenement of his own as well, and evidently grew into a man of local standing.

The local history he was compiling followed the well-worn pattern of antiquities and accounts of land-ownership and parish dues and local disputes and customs and so on, until in 1701 the idea came to him of a new frame through which to view his parish. He drew up a seating-plan of the church with all the family names attached, and wrote his 'Observations concerning the Seates in Myddle and the familyes to which they belong'. The man who had been churchwarden and a leading parish figure had devised a highly informative scheme for arranging his perspective on his whole community.

I hope noe man will blame mee for not nameing every person according to that which hee conceives is his right and superiority in the seats in Church, because it is a thing impossible for any man to know; and therefore I have not endeavoured to doe it, but have written the names according as they came to my memory; but if any one bee minded to give a guess in this matter, lett him first take notice of every man's church leawan [a church rate payable for renting a pew], and then look over what I have written concerning the descent and pedigree of all, or most of the familyes in this side of the parish, and then hee may give some probable conjecture in this matter. If any man shall blame mee for that I have declared the viciouse lives or actions of theire Ancestors, let him take care to avoid such evil courses, that hee leave not a blemish on his name when he is dead, and let him know that I have written nothing out of malice. ...

The Fourth Peiw [*sic*] on the South side of the North Isle

This peiw belongs to Richard Groom's tenement in Marton, this leawan is 2s. 8d. – to Mr Mather's tenement in Balderton, the leawan is 2s. 0d. – to Billmarsh farme the leawan is 1s. 4d., and to Mr Hayward's land in Newtown whose leawan is 1s. I know not who ought to have the cheife seat in this peiw, for I have seene Richard Groome's Mother-in-law, and after her decease, his wife, sit uppermost in this seate – I have seene Mr Mather doe the like – I have seene Mrs Alice Hayward sit uppermost in their seate, and I have seene widow Reve of Billmarsh doe the like. Butt I have placed theire names here (but not in the platforme of the seates) according to their leawans, and in that order will speake of theire familys and predecessors.

Richard Groome's tenement or farme in Marton, is the lands of the Earle of Bridgewater; it was formerly held by the family of the Elkses, the last of which family (if I mistake not his name) was Hugh Elks, but whatever his name was, hee was an ill man – for hee, knowing that a neighbour of his who lived in Eyton had a considerable sum of money in the house, this Elks and some other of his companions came to Eyton on the Lords day att time of morning service, and, haveing visors on theire faces, they came into the house and found there onely one servant maid who was makeing of a cheese, and this Elks stooping downe to binde her shee saw under his visor, and said, 'Good uncle Elks, do mee noe harme,' and upon that hee pulled out his knife and cutt her throat. His companions beeing terrifyed at the act fled away to Baschurch Church, and Elkes seeing his companions were gon fled likewise and tooke noe money, and for haste shut the doore after him and left his dogge in the house, and came to Marton, but stayd not there, but ran to Petton to Church whither hee came sweating exceedingly a little before the end of the service. *Qui crimen gestat in pectore, idem nemesin in tergo gestare solet.* [He who carries a crime in his breast, the same man usually carries nemesis on his back.]

When people came from Church to Eyton, they found the girl dead, and Elks his dogge in the house almost bursted with eating the cheese. They followed the dogge, who brought them to Elks his house, and upon this, Elks was apprehended upon suspicion. The next day the Coroner summoned his inquest, and Elks still denyed the fact, alledging that hee was at Petton Church that morning; but a servant maid of John Ralphe's of Marton witnessed, that she heard the town-feild gate at Marton clapp, and lookeing through a window out of her master's house, shee saw Elks comeing from that gate about the mydle of service time. But Elks pretended that it was impossible to see the town-feild gate through any window in that house; and thereupon the whoale Jury came from Eyton to Marton, and then the mayd shewed them through the window the town-feild gate, and thereupon the Jury found him guilty of the murder. Hee was after found guilty upon his tryall att Shrewsbury, and was hanged. Thus ended the family of the Elkses in this parish, and this was one of the first escheats, or forfeitures, which happened to the Lord Keeper Egerton, after his new purchases in this Country. …

But to returne to Marton. When Elks his tenement there was forfeited to the Lord of the Manor, one Clowes tooke a lease of it, and had a daughter who was marryed to Richard Groome, of Sleape Hall, brother by a second venter [womb] to my grandmother, (on my mother's side). This Richard Groome had no son by Clowes his daughter, but had 5 daughters.

'The Poor Vicar's Complaint in a Letter to a Member of Parliament', from a pamphlet published in 1705

A charity board in St Giles, Bredon, in Worcestershire, shows an 'Extract from the Will of William Hancocke Esq.', dated 1718: 'And my desire is such boys intended to be educated in the said school, shall constantly attend divine service in the said Church every Sunday, at least both morning and evening: and such who shall neglect or refuse, or shall be detain'd from coming by their Parents or relations shall be taken and esteemed not deserving of such Charity, and shall be removed, and put out of the said school, and be wholly incapable of any benefit of this my intent and Charity.'

The other Course that many a poor *Clergyman* is compell'd to take for his better Support, is, his *Teaching a School*, which must necessarily divert him from those Studies that do more immediately relate to his *Sacred Office*; whereby the People committed to his Charge, must receive some Prejudice as to their Spiritual Edification. For tho' such a one may be able to compose a Sermon Weekly, suitable to the Wants of his Auditory, yet he has not time to afford many Visits to his Parishioners, nor Lungs to spare (having spent 'em before in his *School*) to discourse with *Heterodox People*, that they might not persist in those Errors which oppose that *Form of sound Words deliver'd of old unto the Saints*. Neither has he time for other private Admonitions and Reproofs, which every Clergyman knows to be his Duty to perform, but can't many of 'em for want of a sufficient Maintenance from Tithes, being forced to take up with a *small school* to add to as *small tithes*, for a decent Subsistence.

That which also adds to his Misery, is, the great Fatiegue of Disciplining Boys, in Conjunction with his Spiritual Imployment; *so great*, that not only unspeakable Perplexity of Mind, but great Waste of the *Spirits*, in dictating to, and instructing Boys, even of the quickest *Parts*, is a necessary Consequence of this Profession. It may be positively affirm'd, that scarce any mean *Trade* assaults the Constitution of Body so violently, as does the close pursuing the Business of a *School-Master*. How fatal then is it like to prove to *the Man of God*, when such a laborious Profession must be follow'd with his Sacred Function, otherwise he must want *even Necessaries* for one in his Post! This Consideration alone methinks, shou'd move the Bowels of all good Men (that are in a Capacity) to contrive some way to augment the *Income* of the *poorer Clergy*, that none of 'em may be under a Compulsion to undergo so great a Fatiegue (as *Teaching a School* is) for their necessary Support in the Ministry.

Sir Roger de Coverley at church: Joseph Addison (1672–1719) in *The Spectator*, July 1712

Joseph Addison was son of the Dean of Lichfield. His literary and journalistic life did not fully get under way until after the Whig government collapsed in 1710, and with it his further political prospects. In The Spectator, *the periodical that he and his old friend Richard Steele created, Sir Roger de Coverley, the mildly comic yet somehow endearing old Tory squire, became one of the most familiar features.*

I am always very well pleased with a Country *Sunday*; and think, if keeping holy the Seventh Day were only a human Institution, it would be the best Method that could have been thought of for the polishing and civilizing of Mankind. It is certain the Country-People would soon degenerate into a kind of Savages and Barbarians, were there not such frequent Returns of a stated Time, in which the whole Village meet together with their best Faces, and in their cleanest Habits, to converse with one another upon indifferent Subjects, hear their Duties explained to them, and join together in Adoration of the Supreme Being. *Sunday* clears away the Rust of the whole Week, not only as it refreshes in their Minds the Notions of Religion, but as it puts both the Sexes upon appearing in their most agreeable Forms, and exerting all such Qualities as are apt to give them a Figure in the Eye of the Village. A Country-Fellow distinguishes himself as much in the *Churchyard*, as a Citizen does upon the *[Ex]Change*; the whole Parish-Politicks being generally discuss'd in that Place after Sermon or before the Bell rings.

My Friend Sir ROGER being a good Churchman, has beautified the Inside of his Church with several Texts of his own Chusing: He has likewise given a handsome Pulpit-Cloth, and railed in the Communion-Table at his own Expence. He has often told me, that at his coming to his Estate he found his Parishioners very irregular; and that in order to make them kneel and join in the Responses, he gave every one of them a Hassock and a Common-prayer Book: and at the same Time employed an itinerant Singing-Master, who goes about the Country for that Purpose, to instruct them rightly in the Tunes of the Psalms; upon which they now very much value themselves, and indeed out-do most of the Country Churches that I have ever heard.

As Sir ROGER is Landlord to the whole Congregation, he keeps them in very good Order, and will suffer no Body to sleep in it besides himself; for if by Chance he has been surprized into a short Nap at Sermon, upon recovering out of it he stands up and looks about him, and if he sees any Body else nodding, either wakes them himself, or sends his Servants to them. Several other of the old Knight's Particularities break out upon these Occasions: sometimes he will be lengthening out a Verse in the Singing-Psalms, half a Minute after the rest of the Congregation have done with it; sometimes, when he is pleased with the Matter of his Devotion, he pronounces *Amen* three or four times to the same Prayer; and sometimes stands up when every Body else is upon their Knees, to count the Congregation, or see if any of his Tenants are missing.

I was yesterday very much surprized to hear my old Friend, in the Midst of the Service, calling out to one *John Matthews* to mind what he was about, and not disturb the Congregation. This *John Matthews* it seems is remarkable for being an idle Fellow, and at that Time was kicking his Heels for his Diversion. This Authority of the Knight, though exerted in that odd Manner which accompanies him in all Circumstances of Life, has a very good Effect upon the Parish, who are not polite enough to see anything ridiculous in his Behaviour; besides that, the general good Sense and Worthiness of his Character, make his friends observe these little Singularities as Foils that rather set off than blemish his good Qualities.

As soon as the Sermon is finished, no Body presumes to stir till Sir ROGER is gone out of the Church. The Knight walks down from his seat in the Chancel between a double Row of his Tenants, that stand bowing to him on each Side; and every now and then enquires how such an one's Wife, or Mother, or Son, or Father do whom he does not see at Church; which is understood as a secret Reprimand to the Person that is absent.

The Chaplain has often told me, that upon a Catechizing-day, when Sir ROGER has been pleased with a Boy that answers well, he has ordered a Bible to be given him next Day for his Encouragement; and sometimes accompanies it with a Flitch of Bacon to his Mother. Sir ROGER has likewise added five Pounds a Year to the Clerk's Place; and that he may encourage the young Fellows to make themselves perfect in the Church-Service, has promised upon the Death of the present Incumbent, who is very old, to bestow it according to Merit.

The fair Understanding between Sir ROGER and his Chaplain, and their mutual Concurrence in doing Good, is the more remarkable, because the very next Village is famous for the Differences and Contentions that rise between the Parson and the 'Squire, who live in a perpetual State of War. The Parson is always preaching at the 'Squire, and the 'Squire to be revenged on the Parson never comes to Church. The 'Squire has made all his Tenants Atheists and Tithe-Stealers; while the Parson instructs them every *Sunday* in the Dignity of his Order, and insinuates to them in almost every Sermon, that he is a better Man than his Patron. In short, Matters are come to such an Extremity, that the 'Squire has not said his Prayers either in publick or private this half Year; and that the Parson threatens him, if he does not mend his Manners, to pray for him in the Face of the whole Congregation.

Feuds of this Nature, though too frequent in the Country, are very fatal to the ordinary People; who are so used to be dazled with Riches, that they pay as much Deference to the Understanding of a Man of an Estate, as of a Man of Learning; and are very hardly brought to regard any Truth, how important soever it may be, that is preached to them, when they know there are several Men of five hundred a Year who do not believe it.

Just and unjust impediments to courtship: Richard Steele (1672–1729) in *The Spectator*, January 1712

Steele's career included two years in the Life Guards, the theatre, politics as a Whig, and essay-writing. He started The Tatler *in 1709, and then* The Spectator *with Addison in 1711.*

MR SPECTATOR　　　　Jan. the 14th, 1712

I am a young woman, and have my fortune to make; for which reason I come constantly to church to hear divine service, and make conquests: but one great hinderance in this my design, is, that our clerk, who was once a gardener, has this Christmas so overdecked the church with greens, that he has quite spoiled my prospect; insomuch that I have scarce seen the young baronet that I dress at, these three weeks, though we have both been very constant at our devotions, and do not sit above three pews off. The church as it is now equipped, looks more like a greenhouse than a place of worship. The middle aisle is a very pretty shady walk, and the pews look like so many arbours on each side of it. The pulpit itself has such clusters of ivy, holly, and rosemary about it, that a light fellow in our pew took occasion to say, that the congregation heard the word out of a bush, like Moses. Sir Anthony Love's pew in particular is so well hedged, that all my batteries have no effect. I am obliged to shoot at random among the boughs, without taking any manner of aim. Mr Spectator, unless you give orders for removing these greens, I shall grow a very awkward creature at church, and soon have little else to do there but to say my prayers. I am in haste, Dear Sir,

Your most obedient servant,
Jenny Simper.

The following issue has the Parish Clerk's reply:

MR SPECTATOR, Jan. 24, 1712

I am clerk of the parish from whence Mrs Simper sends her complaint, in your Spectator of Wednesday last. I must beg of you to publish this as a public admonition to the aforesaid Mrs Simper, otherwise all my honest care in the disposition of the greens in the church will have no effect: I shall therefore with your leave lay before you the whole matter. I was formally, as she charges me, for several years a gardener in the county of Kent: but I must absolutely deny that it is out of any affection I retain for my old employment that I have placed my greens so liberally about the church, but out of particular spleen I conceived against Mrs Simper (and others of the same sisterhood) some time ago. As to herself, I had one day set the hundredth Psalm, and was singing the first line in order to put the congregation into the tune: she was all the while curtsying to Sir Anthony, in so affected and indecent a manner, that the indignation I conceived at it made me forget myself so far, as from the tune of that psalm to wander into Southwell tune, and from thence into Windsor tune, still unable to recover myself, till I had with the utmost confusion set a new one. Nay, I have often seen her rise up and smile, and curtsy to one at the lower end of the church in the midst of a Gloria Patri; and when I have spoken the assent to a prayer with a long Amen, uttered with decent gravity, she has been rolling her eyes around about in such a manner, as plainly shewed, however he was moved, it was not towards an heavenly object. In fine, she extended her conquests so far over the males, and raised such envy in the females, that what between love of those, and jealousy of these, I was almost the only person that looked in a prayer-book all church time. I had several projects in my head to put a stop to this growing mischief; but as I have long lived in Kent, and there often heard how the Kentish men evaded the Conqueror, by carrying green boughs over their heads, it put me in mind of practicing this device against Mrs Simper. I find I have preserved many a young man from her eye-shot by this means; therefore humbly pray the boughs may be fixed, till she shall give security for her peaceful intentions.

Your humble servant,
Francis Sternhold.

'This miserable age is so sunk between animosities of party and those of religion': Alexander Pope (1688–1744), letter to John Caryll, 1 May 1714

The brilliance of his first major poems made Pope famous in his early twenties but not financially secure, and like all Catholics he was barred from public employment by the Test Act of 1673 (which was not repealed until 1828). John Caryll and Edward Blount came from leading Catholic families, and it was the former who had suggested the topic of 'The Rape of the Lock' to Pope to heal the rift in their social world caused by Lord Petre's snipping off a lock of Arabella Fermor's hair. Charles Jervas was a society painter who took lessons from Sir Godfrey Kneller.

Dear Sir, – Your letter found me at Binfield, very busy in my grand undertaking, to which I must wholly give myself up for some time, unless when I snatch an hour to please myself with a distant conversation with you and one or two more, by writing a line or two.

His 'grand undertaking' was to complete a verse translation of Homer's Iliad, *subscriptions for which were to bring him the financial independence that authors at the time found hard to win.*

... I have also encountered much malignity on the score of religion, some calling me a papist and a tory, the latter because the heads of the party have been distinguishingly favourable to me; but why the former I cannot imagine, but that Mr Caryll and Mr E. Blount have laboured to serve me. Others have styled me a whig, because I have been honoured with Mr Addison's good word, and Mr Jervas's good deeds, and of late with my Lord Halifax's patronage. How much more natural a conclusion would it be to any good-natured man to think a person who has been favoured by all sides has been inoffensive to all. This miserable age is so sunk between animosities of party and those of religion, that I begin to fear most men have politics enough to make the best scheme of government a bad one, through their extremity of violence, and faith enough to hinder their salvation. I hope, for my own part, never to have more of either than is consistent with common justice and charity, and always so much as becomes a christian and honest man – that is, just as much as you. Though I find it an unfortunate thing to be bred a papist, when one is obnoxious to four parts in five as being too much, and to the fifth part for being so too little, I shall yet be easy under both their mistakes, and be what I more than seem to be, for I suffer for it. God is my witness, that I no more envy the protestants their places and possessions than I do our priests their charity or learning. I am ambitious of nothing but the good opinion of all good men of all sides, for I know that one virtue of a free spirit is more worth than all the virtues put together of all the narrow-souled people in the world. If they promise me all the good offices they ever did, or could do, I would not change for them all one kind word of yours. I am entirely, dear sir, your obliged and faithful friend and servant.

Jonathan Swift (1667–1745)

'A Whig in politics and a Tory in religion', Swift joined the coffee-house network of leading literary and political figures in London, and had hopes of consolidating his career there as a man of letters via the route of preferments in the Anglican Church. But his supposedly anonymous 1704 satire A Tale of a Tub *seems to have spoilt his prospects, and from 1713 – apart from visits to old friends – his life was back in Ireland, where he had been brought up and educated, as Dean of St Patrick's in Dublin.* Gulliver's Travels *was published anonymously in 1726.*

• From 'AN ARGUMENT to prove that the Abolishing of CHRISTIANITY IN ENGLAND, may as Things now stand, be attended with some Inconveniences, and perhaps not produce those many good Effects proposed thereby' (1708)

Another Advantage proposed by the Abolishing of Christianity, is the clear Gain of one Day in Seven, which is now entirely lost, and consequently the Kingdom one Seventh less considerable in Trade, Business, and Pleasure; beside the Loss to the Publick of so many Stately Structures now in the Hands of the Clergy, which might be converted into Play-houses, Exchanges, Market-houses, common Dormitories, and other Publick Edifices.

I hope I shall be forgiven a hard Word if I call this a perfect Cavil. I readily own there hath been an old Custom time out of mind, for People to assemble in the Churches every *Sunday*, and that shops are still frequently shut, in order as it is conceived, to preserve the Memory of that antient Practice; but how this can prove a hindrance to Business or Pleasure, is hard to imagine. What if the Men of Pleasure are forced one Day in the Week to Game at Home instead of the *Chocolate-House*. Are not the *Taverns* and *Coffee-Houses* open? Can there be a more convenient Season for taking a Dose of Physick? Are fewer Claps got upon *Sundays* than other Days? Is not the chief Day for Traders to Sum up the Accounts of the Week, and for Lawyers to prepare their Briefs? But I would fain know how it can be pretended that the Churches are misapplied. Where are more Appointments and Rendevouzes of Gallantry? Where more Care to appear in the foremost Box with greater Advantage of Dress? Where more Meetings for Business? Where more Bargains driven of all sorts? And where so many Conveniences or Incitements to Sleep?

There is one Advantage greater than any of the foregoing, proposed by the Abolishing of Christianity, that it will utterly extinguish Parties among us, by removing those Factious Distinctions of High and Low Church, of *Whig* and *Tory*, *Presbyterian* and *Church of England*, which are now so many mutual Clogs upon Publick Proceedings, and are apt to prefer the gratifying themselves or depressing their Adversaries, before the most important Interest of the State.

I confess, if it were certain that so great an Advantage would redound to the Nation by this Expedient, I would submit and be silent: But, will any Man say that if the Words, *Whoring, Drinking, Cheating, Lying, Stealing,* were by Act of Parliament ejected out of the *English* Tongue and Dictionaries, We should all Awake next Morning Chaste and Temperate, Honest and Just, and Lovers of Truth? Is this a fair Consequence? Or if the Physicians would forbid us to pronounce the Words *Pox, Gout, Rhumatism* and *Stone*, would that Expedient serve like so many *Talismans* to destroy the Diseases themselves? Are Party and Faction rooted in Mens Hearts no deeper than Phrases borrowed from Religion, or founded upon no firmer Principles? And is our Language so poor that we cannot find other Terms to express them?

• From *Gulliver's Travels*, Part I, *A Voyage to Lilliput*: 'The most obstinate war between the two great empires of Lilliput and Blefuscu'

Standing in the palm of the hand of the 'man mountain' Gulliver so that he can reach his ear, the Principal Secretary of Lilliput addresses him on the background to the current threat of invasion, which Gulliver's strength and valour will be required to resist.

It began upon the following Occasion. It is allowed on all Hands, that the primitive Way of breaking Eggs before we eat them, was upon the larger End: But his present Majesty's Grand-father, while he was a Boy, going to eat an Egg, and breaking it according to the ancient Practice, happened to cut one of his Fingers. Whereupon the Emperor his Father, published an Edict, commanding all his Subjects, upon great Penalties, to break the smaller End of their Eggs. The People so highly resented this Law, that our Histories tell us, there have been six Rebellions raised on that Account; wherein one Emperor lost his Life, and another his Crown. These civil Commotions were constantly fomented by the Monarchs of *Blefuscu*; and when they were quelled, the Exiles always fled for Refuge to that Empire. It is computed, that eleven Thousand Person have, at several Times, suffered Death, rather than submit to break their Eggs at the smaller End. Many hundred large Volumes have been published upon this Controversy: But the Books of the *Big-Endians* have been long forbidden, and the whole Party rendered incapable by Law of holding Employments. During the Course of these Troubles, the Emperors of *Blefuscu* did frequently expostulate by their Ambassadors, accusing us of making a Schism in Religion, by offending against a fundamental Doctrine of our great Prophet *Lustrog*, in the fifty-fourth Chapter of the *Brundrecal*, (which is their *Alcoran*).This, however, is thought to be a meer Strain upon the Text: For the Words are these; *That all true Believers shall break their Eggs at the convenient End*: and which is the convenient End, seems, in my humble Opinion, to be left to every Man's Conscience, or at least in the Power of the chief Magistrate to determine.

Daniel Defoe (*c.* 1660–1731)

The first of these extracts, an early product of what would become a vast and extraordinarily versatile output, won Defoe the favour of William III, but the following year he was pilloried for three days and put in prison for his attack on religious extremism, which had caused serious affront to both High Anglican Tories and leading Dissenters. Defoe's own Dissenting spirit led to a committed career as a leading political journalist and pamphleteer; it was only when he was nearly sixty that his novel-writing began.

• From 'The True-Born Englishman' (1701)

Defoe's verse satire mocks the Englishman's pride in the 'Englishness' of his blood, when the truth is he is a 'heterogeneous thing' from 'a mongrel half-bred race'. And as for his claim of piety –

Wherever God erects a house of prayer,
The Devil always builds a chapel there:
And 'twill be found, upon examination,
The latter has the biggest congregation:
For ever since he first debauch'd the mind
He made a perfect conquest of mankind.

• From *A Tour through the Whole Island of Great Britain*, Letter IV

Defoe's Tour was published in three volumes in the 1720s, the fruit of 'seventeen very large circuits, or journeys ... taken through divers parts separately, and three general tours over almost the whole English part of the island'. As a description of 'the most flourishing and opulent country in the world', his 'earnest concern for its usefulness' focused on the people's employments, trades, commerce and industries, although he was aware it could not be 'what we call a finished account, as no clothes can be made to fit a growing child'.

Biddiford is a pleasant, clean, well-built town; the more ancient street which lies next the river is very pleasant, where is the bridge, a very noble quay, and the custom-house; this part also is very well built and populous, and fronts the river for above three-quarters of a mile: but besides this, there is a new spacious street, which runs N and S, or rather NW and SE a great length, broad as the high-street of Excester, well-built and, which is more than all, well inhabited, with considerable and wealthy merchants, who trade to most parts of the trading world.

Here, as is to be seen in almost all the market towns of Devonshire, is a very large, well-built, and well-finished meeting-house, and, by the multitude of people which I saw come out of it, and the appearance of them, I thought all the town had gone thither, and began to enquire for the church. But when I came to the church, I found that also large, spacious, and well filled too, and that with people of the best fashion. The person who officiates at the meeting-house in this town, I happened to have some conversation with, and found him to be not only a learned man, and master of good reading, but a most acceptable gentlemanly person, and one who, contrary to our received opinion of these people, had not only good learning, and good sense, but abundance of good manners, and good humour; nothing sour, cynical, or morose in him, and, in a word, a very valuable man: and as such a character always recommends a man to men of sense and good breeding, so I found this gentleman was very well received in the place, even by those he differed from in matters of religion, and those differences did not, as is usual, make any breach in their conversing with him: his name, as I remember, was Bartlet. But this is a digression: I wish I could say the like of all the rest of his brethren.

The trade of this town being very much in fish, as it is also of all the towns on this coast, I observed here, that several ships were employed to go to Leverpool, and up the river Mersey to Warrington, to fetch the rock salt, which is found in that county, (and of which I shall say more in my remarks on those parts) which rock salt they bring to Biddiford and Barnstable, and here they dissolve it into brine in the sea water, joining the strength of two bodies into one, and then boil it up again into a new salt, as the Dutch do by the French and Portuguese salt: this is justly called salt upon salt, and with this they cure their herrings; and as this is a trade which can be but of a few years' standing, because the rock itself has not been discovered in England much above twenty years; so the difference in curing the fish has been such, and it has so recommended their herrings in foreign markets, that the demand for them has considerably increased, and consequently the trade.

Voltaire (1694–1778): 'An *Englishman*, as one to whom liberty is natural, may go to heaven his own way', from 'Letter V, on the Church of England', in *Letters concerning the English Nation* (1726, English translation 1733)

Voltaire was thirty-one when he chose exile in England to avoid the Bastille. The thirty months or so he spent between 1726 and 1728 among English men of letters and the comparative freedom of English society made a great impression on him.

England is properly the country of sectarists. *Multae sunt mansiones in domo patris mei* [In my father's house are many mansions].

Nevertheless, tho' every one is permitted to serve God in whatever mode of fashion he thinks proper, yet their true religion, that in which a man makes his fortune, is the sect of Episcoparians or Churchmen, call'd the Church of *England*, or simply the Church, by way of eminence. No person can possess an employment either in *England* or *Ireland*, unless he be rank'd among the faithful, that is, professes himself a member of the Church of *England*. This reason (which carries mathematical reason with it) has converted such numbers of dissenters of all persuasions, that not a twentieth part of the nation is out of the pale of the establish'd church. The *English* clergy have retain'd a great number of the Romish ceremonies, and especially that of receiving, with a most scrupulous attention, their tithes. They also have the pious ambition to aim at superiority.

Moreover, they inspire very religiously their flock with a holy zeal against Dissenters of all denominations. This zeal was pretty violent under the Tories, in the four last years of queen *Anne*; but was productive of no greater mischief than the breaking of windows of some meeting-houses, and the demolishing of a few of them. For religious rage ceas'd in *England* with the civil wars; and was no more under queen *Anne*, than the hollow noise of a sea whose billows still heav'd, tho' so long after the storm, when the Whigs and Tories laid waste their native country, in the same manner as the Guelphs and Gibelins formerly did theirs. ...

With regard to the morals of the *English* clergy, they are more regular than those of *France*, and for this reason. All the clergy (a very few excepted) are educated in the universities of *Oxford* or *Cambridge*, far from the depravity and corruption which reign in the capital. They are not call'd to dignities till very late, in an Age when men are sensible of no other passion but avarice, that is, when their ambition craves a supply. Employments are here bestow'd both in the church and the army, as a reward for long services; and we never see youngsters made bishops or colonels immediately upon laying aside the academical gown; and besides, most of the clergy are married. The stiff and awkward air contracted by them at the university, and the little familiarity the men of this country have with the ladies, commonly oblige a bishop to confine himself to, and rest contented with his own. Clergymen sometimes take a glass at the tavern, custom giving them a sanction on this occasion; and if they fuddle themselves 'tis in a very serious manner, and without giving the least scandal.

'A plain Love-Letter, a Specimen', from *The Gentleman's Magazine*, February 1732

The Gentleman's Magazine, or Monthly Intelligencer *ran from 1731 till 1914. Its founder, Edward Cave, was an enterprising and outgoing printer who, in the guise of 'Sylvanus Urban, Gent.', assembled a popular periodical of news, reviews, and social and political information from a variety of sources.*

Madam,

When I see you upon your Gravity-Looks, I conclude you to be a suitable Wife for me; my last Wife, when I first saw her, told me that she intended to marry, being weary of Boarding, she would have a House and Table of her own; and if you should be sick, none so tender over you as a Husband; my last Wife had 700 l. [£700] of ready Money; she brought me a Silver Tankard cost 8 l. and 10 Silver Spoons, and as many Suits of Grave Silks as cost about 40 l. laced with Silver and Gold Lace up to the Pocket; her best of which I keep for you.

My Father gave me about 1200 l. besides my Education; I have been a good Husband, and have settled my Family; my eldest Son hath a Living of about 120 l. a Year, a Minister, and so is my second Son, who has two Places besides teaching a School; they have been above 10 Years for themselves; my third Son is married, a Confectioner and Grocer, sells also Tea and Chocolate, and Coffee, which he roasts himself, had 200 Pounds with his Wife, and now 80 Pounds a Year fallen to him lately by the Death of her Brother; I have two Daughters at Home with me at present, the Youngest as tall as your self; they have their portions set out, my Eldest Son is to pay them out of my perpetual Advowson I have settled on him after my Decease; my Eldest Daughter has lived twice with her Brother the Confectioner, and intends to go again as soon as I marry you; then I have but one Daughter who waits upon me and you, and one Maid you shall chuse; my Brewing an old Servant does it, and I hire a Washer-woman, a Baker and a Butcher, both which we have in Town near us; so that you and I may enjoy our selves with all the exquisite Pleasure of Matrimony so long as God shall send us Health. I shall keep a Calash [a light vehicle with low wheels and a folding hood] to take the Air; I can walk three Miles in the Middle of Winter, dry one Way; and a Wood within a Furlong, in *May* full of Lillies of the Valley, and all Variety of Herbs; I understand Physick: My first Wife died in Childbed, and the last would take nothing of Physick to stope a Looseness, when I cured divers of it; her Fever seized her Vitals; she was not sick till the two last Days. I had four eminent Physicians, but she would not take what they prescribed; but said she was burnt up and scorched within, and that their Cordials were too hot for her.

Madam, I hope you have had the Letter I left for you at the *George*; the Bearer was an Exciseman, and can inform you there is 40 Fir Trees, Gold and Silver Hollies, with many Yew Trees, and all green, to entertain you with; fine Gardens, and a new-built House lately. You know where to direct to me.

I beg an Answer,

Edward – – –

I am sorry I can't acquaint the Publick with the Success of this Letter upon the Lady it is addressed to, but if I may be allowed to guess, I think it could not fail, for however the Author might be wrong in point of Form and Ceremony, I assure you I have heard several sensible Women declare that in the main he talk'd very much to the Purpose.

A very curious adventure, from Henry Fielding (1707–1754), *The Adventures of Joseph Andrews* (1742)

Fielding was a dramatist, lawyer, political satirist, and novelist. Joseph Andrews *was his first, a 'comic essay in prose', as he called it.*

Joseph has quit service in London and is now on the road with his equally virtuous lover Fanny, and the guileless Parson Adams as their worthy companion. An appeal to the charity of the coarse local clergyman Parson Trulliber has just been rebuffed, and they are now virtually penniless.

A very curious adventure, in which Mr. Adams gave a much greater instance of the honest simplicity of his heart, than of his experience in the ways of this world.

Our travellers had walked about two miles from that inn, which they had more reason to have mistaken for a castle than Don Quixotte ever had any of those in which he sojourned, seeing they had met with such difficulty in escaping out of its walls, when they came to a parish, and beheld a sign of invitation hanging out. A gentleman sat smoking a pipe at the door, of whom Adams inquired the road, and received so courteous and obliging an answer, accompanied with so smiling a countenance, that the good parson, whose heart was naturally disposed to love and affection, began to ask several other questions; particularly the name of the parish, and who was the owner of a large house whose front they then had in prospect. The gentleman answered as obligingly as before; and as to the house, acquainted him it was his own. He then proceeded in the following manner: 'Sir, I presume by your habit you are a clergyman; and as you are travelling on foot I suppose a glass of good beer will not be disagreeable to you; and I can recommend my landlord's within, as some of the best in all this country. What say you, will you halt a little and let us take a pipe together? There is no better tobacco in the kingdom.'

This proposal was not displeasing to Adams, who had allayed his thirst that day with no better liquor than what Mrs. Trulliber's cellar had produced; and which was indeed little superior, either in richness or flavour to that which distilled from those grains her generous husband bestowed on his hogs. Having therefore abundantly thanked the gentleman for his kind invitation, and bid Joseph and Fanny follow him, he entered the alehouse, where a large loaf and cheese and a pitcher of beer, which truly answered the character given of it, being set before them, the three travellers fell to eating, with appetites infinitely more voracious than are to be found at the most exquisite eating-houses in the parish of St. James's.

The gentleman expressed great delight in the hearty and cheerful behaviour of Adams; and particularly in the familiarity with which he conversed with Joseph and Fanny, whom he often called his children; a term he explained to mean no more than his parishioners; saying, 'He looked on all those whom God had entrusted to his cure to stand to him in that relation.' The gentleman, shaking him by the hand, highly applauded these sentiments. 'They are indeed,' says he, 'the true principles of a Christian divine; and I heartily wish they were universal; but, on the contrary, I am sorry to say the parson of our parish, instead of esteeming his poor parishioners as a part of his family, seems rather to consider them as not of the same species with himself. He seldom speaks to any, unless some few of the richest of us; nay, indeed, he will not move his hat to the others. I often laugh when I behold him on Sundays strutting along the church-yard like a turkey-cock through rows of his parishioners, who bow to him with as much submission, and are as unregarded, as a set of servile courtiers by the proudest prince in Christendom. But if such temporal pride is ridiculous, surely the spiritual is odious and detestable; if such a puffed-up empty human bladder, strutting in princely robes, justly moves one's derision, surely in the habit of a priest it must raise our scorn.'

'Doubtless,' answered Adams, 'your opinion is right; but I hope such examples are rare. The clergy whom I have the honour to know maintain a different behaviour; and you will allow me, sir, that the readiness which too many of the laity show to contemn the order may be one reason of their avoiding too much humility.'

'Very true, indeed,' says the gentleman; 'I find, sir, you are a man of excellent sense, and am happy in this opportunity of knowing you; perhaps our accidental meeting may not be disadvantageous to you neither. At present I shall only say to you that the incumbent of this living is old and infirm, and that it is in my gift. Doctor, give me your hand; and assure yourself of it at his decease.'

Adams told him 'He was never more confounded in his life than at his utter incapacity to make any return to such noble and unmerited generosity.'

'A mere trifle, sir,' cries the gentleman, 'scarce worth your acceptance; a little more than three hundred a-year. I wish it was double the value for your sake.' Adams bowed, and cried from the emotion of his gratitude; when the other asked him, 'If he was married, or had any children, besides those in the spiritual sense he had mentioned.' 'Sir,' replied the parson, 'I have a wife and six at your service.' 'That is unlucky,' says the gentleman, 'for I would otherwise have taken you into my own house as my chaplain; however, I have another in the parish (for the parsonage-house is not good enough), which I will furnish for you. Pray, does your wife understand a dairy?' 'I can't profess she does,' says Adams. 'I am sorry for it,' quoth the gentleman; 'I would have given you half a dozen cows, and very good grounds to have maintained them.' 'Sir,' said Adams, in an ecstacy, 'you are too liberal; indeed you are.' 'Not at all,' cries the gentleman: 'I esteem riches only as they give me an opportunity of doing good; and I never saw one whom I had a greater inclination to serve.'

At which words he shook him heartily by the hand, and told him he had sufficient room in his house to entertain him and his friends. Adams begged he might give him no such trouble; that they could be very well accommodated in the house where they were; forgetting they had not a sixpenny piece among them. The gentleman would not be denied; and, informing himself how far they were travelling, he said it was too long a journey to take on foot, and begged that they would favour him by suffering him to lend them a servant and horses; adding, withal, that, if they would do him the pleasure of their company only two days, he would furnish them with his coach and six.

Adams, turning to Joseph, said, 'How lucky is this gentleman's goodness to you, who I am afraid would be scarce able to hold out on your lame leg!' and then, addressing the person who had made him these liberal promises, after much bowing, he cried out, 'Blessed be the hour which first introduced me to a man of your charity! You are indeed a Christian of the true primitive kind, and an honour to the country wherein you live. I would willingly have taken a pilgrimage to the Holy Land to have beheld you; for the advantages that we draw from your goodness give me little pleasure, in comparison of what I enjoy for your own sake when I consider the treasures you are by these means laying up for yourself in a country that passeth not away. We will therefore, most generous sir, accept your goodness, as well the entertainment you have so kindly offered us at your house this evening as the accommodation of your horses to-morrow morning.'

He then began to search for his hat, as did Joseph for his; and both they and Fanny were in order of departure, when the old gentleman, stopping short, and seeming to meditate by himself for the space of about a minute, exclaimed thus: 'Sure was never anything so unlucky; I had forgot that my housekeeper was gone abroad, and hath locked up all my rooms; indeed, I would break them open for you, but shall not be able to furnish you with a bed; for she has likewise put away all my linen. I am glad that it entered into my head before I had given you the trouble of walking there; besides, I believe you will find better accommodations here than you expected. – Landlord, you can provide good beds for these people, can't you?' 'Yes, and please your worship,' cries the host, 'and such as no lord or justice of the peace in the kingdom need be ashamed to lie in.' 'I am heartily sorry for this disappointment. I am resolved I will never suffer her to carry away the keys again.' 'Pray, sir, let it not make you uneasy,' cries Adams; 'we shall do very well here; and the loan of your horses is a favour we shall be incapable of making any return to.' 'Ay,' said the squire, 'the horses shall attend you here at what hour in the morning you please,' and now, after many civilities too tedious to enumerate, many squeezes by the hand, with most affectionate looks and smiles at each other, and after appointing the horses at seven the next morning, the gentleman took his leave of them, and departed to his own house. Adams and his companions returned to the table, where the parson smoked another pipe, and then they all retired to rest.

When no horses appear the next morning and it becomes clear that Adams has been the victim of a cruel joke, it is the kindly publican who bails them out.

Missions from Wiltshire to Northumberland, from the *Journal* of John Wesley (1703–1791), January–March 1747

Wesley's equestrian statue outside his New Room headquarters in Bristol commemorates his immense stamina and evangelical influence, journeying into his old age over 280,000 miles, it has been calculated, and delivering over 40,000 sermons. He had followed his father into holy orders, but the zeal of his mission alarmed conventional Anglicanism into making him unwelcome; he discovered a new voice in open-air meetings, and founded a whole new church – the Presbyterian 'Methodists'.

Saturday, January 3, 1747. I called upon poor Mr. C., who once largely 'tasted of the good word, and the powers of the world to come.' I found him very loving, and very drunk; as he commonly is, day and night. But I could fix nothing upon him. 'He may fall foully, but not finally!'

Sun. 11. In the evening I rode to Brentford; the next day to Newbury; and, *Tuesday, 13,* to the Devizes. The town was in an uproar from end to end, as if the French were just entering; and abundance of swelling words we heard, oaths, curses, and threatenings. The most active man in stirring up the people, we were informed, was Mr. J., the C. [Mr. Innys, the curate]. He had been indefatigable in the work, going all the day from house to house. He had also been at the pains of setting up an advertisement in the most public places of the town of 'An Obnubilative Pantomime Entertainment, to be exhibited at Mr. Clark's' (where I was to preach); the latter part of it contained a kind of *double entendre,* which a modest person cannot well repeat. I began preaching at seven, on 'the grace of our Lord Jesus Christ'. Many of the mob came in, listened a little, and stood still. No one opened his mouth, but attention sat on the face of every hearer.

Wed. 14. I rode on to Bristol, and spent a week in great peace.
Thursday, 22. About half-hour after twelve I took horse for Wick, where I had appointed to preach at three. I was riding by the wall through St. Nicholas-gate (my horse having been brought to the house where I dined) just as a cart turned short from St. Nicholas-street, and came swiftly down the hill. There was just room to pass between the wheel of it and the wall; but that space was taken up by the carman. I called to him to go back, or I must ride over him; but the man, as if deaf, walked straight forward. This obliged me to hold back my horse. In the mean time the shaft of the cart came full against his shoulder with such a shock as beat him to the ground. He shot me forward over his head as an arrow out of the bow, where I lay, with my arms and legs, I know not how, stretched out in a line close to the wall. The wheel ran by, close to my side, but only dirtied my clothes. I found no flutter of spirit, but the same composure as if I had been sitting in my study. When the cart was gone, I rose. Abundance of people gathered round, till a gentleman desired me to step into his shop. After cleaning myself a little, I took horse again, and was at Wick by the time appointed.

I returned to Bristol (where the report of my being killed had spread far and wide) time enough to praise God in the great congregation, and to preach on, 'Thou, Lord, shalt save both man and beast.' My shoulders, and hands, and side, and both my legs, were a little bruised; my knees something more; my right thigh the most, which made it a little difficult for me to walk; but some warm treacle took away all the pain in an hour, and the lameness in a day or two …
Monday, February 16. I was wondering, the day before, at the mildness of the weather; such as seldom attends me in my journeys. But my wonder now ceased: The wind was turned full north, and blew so exceeding hard and keen, that when we came to Hatfield, neither my companions nor I had much use of our hands or feet. After resting an hour, we bore up again, through the wind and snow, which drove full in our faces. But this was only a squall. In Baldock-field the storm began in earnest. The large hail drove so vehemently in our faces, that we could not see, nor hardly breathe. However, before two o'clock we reached Baldock, where one met and conducted us safe to Potten. About six I preached to a serious congregation.
By March he has reached Newcastle.
Sun. 8. I preached at Gateshead, and declared the loving-kindness of the Lord. In the evening, observing abundance of strangers at the Room, I changed my voice, and applied those terrible words, 'I have overthrown some of you as I

overthrew Sodom and Gomorrah, and the rest of you were as brands plucked out of the burning; yet have ye not turned unto me, saith the Lord.'

Thomas Gray (1716–1771), 'Elegy written in a Country Churchyard' (1751)

As a man of letters, Gray spent much of his life in Cambridge, and was Regius Professor of Modern History; as a poet, he turned down the laureateship in 1757. The country churchyard was in Stoke Poges, Buckinghamshire (where he was later buried alongside his mother). Gray sent the verses to his old friend Horace Walpole in 1750, and they were published the following year.

The Curfew tolls the knell of parting day,
  The lowing herd wind slowly o'er the lea,
The plowman homeward plods his weary way,
  And leaves the world to darkness and to me.

Now fades the glimmering landscape on the sight,
  And all the air a solemn stillness holds,
Save where the beetle wheels his droning flight,
  And drowsy tinklings lull the distant folds:

Save that from yonder ivy-mantled tow'r
  The mopeing owl does to the moon complain
Of such as, wand'ring near her secret bow'r,
  Molest her ancient solitary reign.

Beneath those rugged elms, that yew-tree's shade,
  Where heaves the turf in many a mould'ring heap,
Each in his narrow cell for ever laid,
  The rude Forefathers of the hamlet sleep.

The breezy call of incense-breathing Morn,
  The swallow twitt'ring from the straw-built shed,
The cock's shrill clarion, or the echoing horn,
  No voice shall rouse them from their lowly bed.

For them no more the blazing hearth shall burn,
  Or busy housewife ply her evening care:

No children run to lisp their sire's return,
   Or climb his knee the envied kiss to share.

Oft did the harvest to their sickle yield,
   Their furrow oft the stubborn glebe has broke:
How jocund did they drive their team afield!
   How bow'd the woods beneath their sturdy stroke!

Let not Ambition mock their useful toil,
   Their homely joys, and destiny obscure;
Nor Grandeur hear with a disdainful smile
   The short and simple annals of the poor.

The boast of heraldry, the pomp of pow'r,
   And all that beauty, all that wealth e'er gave,
Awaits alike th'inevitable hour.
   The paths of glory lead but to the grave.

Nor you, ye Proud, impute to These the fault,
   If Mem'ry o'er their Tomb no Trophies raise,
Where through the long-drawn aisle and fretted vault
   The pealing anthem swells the note of praise.

Can storied urn or animated bust
   Back to its mansion call the fleeting breath?
Can Honour's voice provoke the silent dust,
   Or Flatt'ry soothe the dull cold ear of death?

Perhaps in this neglected spot is laid
   Some heart once pregnant with celestial fire;
Hands, that the rod of empire might have sway'd,
   Or wak'd to extasy the living lyre.

But Knowledge to their eyes her ample page
   Rich with the spoils of time did ne'er unroll;
Chill Penury repress'd their noble rage,
   And froze the genial current of the soul.

Full many a gem of purest ray serene,
   The dark unfathom'd caves of ocean bear:
Full many a flower is born to blush unseen,
   And waste its sweetness on the desert air.

Some village-Hampden, that with dauntless breast
  The little Tyrant of his fields withstood,
Some mute inglorious Milton here may rest,
  Some Cromwell guiltless of his country's blood.

Th'applause of list'ning senates to command,
  The threats of pain and ruin to despise,
To scatter plenty o'er a smiling land,
  And read their hist'ry in a nation's eyes,

Their lot forbad: nor circumscrib'd alone
  Their growing virtues, but their crimes confin'd;
Forbad to wade through slaughter to a throne,
  And shut the gates of mercy on mankind,

The struggling pangs of conscious truth to hide,
  To quench the blushes of ingenuous shame,
Or heap the shrine of Luxury and Pride
  With incense kindled at the Muse's flame

Far from the madding crowd's ignoble strife,
  Their sober wishes never learn'd to stray;
Along the cool sequester'd vale of life
  They kept the noiseless tenor of their way.

Yet ev'n these bones from insult to protect
  Some frail memorial still erected nigh,
With uncouth rhimes and shapeless sculpture deck'd,
  Implores the passing tribute of a sigh.

Their name, their years, spelt by th'unletter'd muse,
  The place of fame and elegy supply:
And many a holy text around she strews,
  That teach the rustic moralist to die.

For who to dumb Forgetfulness a prey,
  This pleasing anxious being e'er resign'd,
Left the warm precincts of the cheerful day,
  Nor cast one longing, ling'ring look behind?

On some fond breast the parting soul relies,
  Some pious drops the closing eye requires;

E'en from the tomb the voice of Nature cries,
  E'en in our Ashes live their wonted Fires.

For thee, who mindful of th'unhonour'd Dead,
  Dost in these lines their artless tale relate;
If chance, by lonely contemplation led,
  Some kindred spirit shall inquire thy fate, –

Haply some hoary-headed Swain may say,
  'Oft have we seen him at the peep of dawn
Brushing with hasty steps the dews away
  To meet the sun upon the upland lawn.

'There at the foot of yonder nodding beech,
  That wreathes its old fantastic roots so high,
His listless length at noontide would he stretch,
  And pore upon the brook that babbles by.

'Hard by yon wood, now smiling as in scorn,
  Mutt'ring his wayward fancies he would rove,
Now drooping, woeful-wan, like one forlorn,
  Or craz'd with care, or cross'd in hopeless love.

'One morn I miss'd him on the custom'd hill,
  Along the heath, and near his fav'rite tree;
Another came; nor yet beside the rill,
  Nor up the lawn, nor at the wood was he:

'The next, with dirges due in sad array
  Slow thro' the church-way path we saw him borne. –
Approach and read (for thou can'st read) the lay,
  Grav'd on the stone beneath yon aged thorn.'

The Epitaph

Here rests his head upon the lap of Earth
  A Youth, to Fortune and to Fame unknown,
Fair Science frown'd not on his humble birth,
  And Melancholy mark'd him for her own.

Large was his bounty, and his soul sincere,
  Heav'n did a recompense as largely send:

He gave to Mis'ry all he had, a tear,
He gain'd from Heav'n ('twas all he wish'd) a friend.

No farther seek his merits to disclose,
Or draw his frailties from their dread abode,
(There they alike in trembling hope repose,)
The bosom of his Father and his God.

'A Genuine Letter from a Noble Lord to a Right Reverend Prelate June 15, 1754', from *The Gentleman's Magazine*, January 1769

For The Gentleman's Magazine *see 'A plain Love-Letter' above (p. 164).*

My Lord,

I was yesterday informed that your lordship had laid your commands upon Mr. ****, the vicar of this parish, to repair to his living; your lordship it seems, being no longer disposed to dispense with his non-residence. The vicar and his friends give out, that this order is occasioned by a vote the vicar gave at a late election contrary to your lordship's judgment.

I do not pay the least regard to this representation, nor have I any suspicion that your lordship was determined in this matter by any other consideration than a pious concern for the good of the parishioners. And on that account, I make myself sure your lordship will no longer insist upon Mr. ****'s residence with us, after your lordship is informed that it is likely to have a contrary effect.

In short, my lord, the parishioners of **** desire to see no more of their present vicar than they usually do, which is for about a fortnight or three weeks annually in partridge time. They are a serious good sort of people, and the diligence, sobriety, good sense, and humanity of their present curate, are highly acceptable and edifying to them. This worthy man must of course be dismissed if the vicar comes to reside, and the people think they shall be no gainers by the exchange.

We acknowledge, my lord, that Mr. **** has his accomplishments. He is a polite gentleman, plays a good fiddle, dances gracefully, knows whist perfectly, is no contemptible marksman at a partridge or a woodcock, of an excellent taste, and exquisite judgment on the merit of claret and port, and by the strength of his head, is able to carry off his full share of either, always with decency, and not seldom with glory. But the misfortune is, that the poor people of his parish, have no opportunities of sitting under his ministry, when and where he is displaying these admirable talents; and when it comes to their turn to profit by his pastoral gifts, it is an universal complaint, that their attention cannot keep pace with his expedition, in reading the lessons and prayers, and that their capacities cannot fathom the depth of his dissertations on the idea of deity, eternal relations, or the dignity of the church; which last point he always contrives to touch upon either in the exordium or peroration of his discourse.

When the vicar is with us, the curate migrates to his master's other living, above fifty miles off, (though certified, by the bye, to be only thirty) and whatever occasional duties are wanted in the interval, the parishioners are for the most part obliged to have recourse to a neighbouring clergyman to perform, as the vicar's engagements are not to be broken by such trifling avocations.

Some time before your lordship's promotion to the episcopal bench, a motion was made in our house for a bill to compel the incumbents of benefices yielding 150 l. [£150] per ann. or upwards, clear of reprisals, to constant residence. The bench were in general against the motion, on account of the discouragement this would be to learning, (as the motion was in effect designed to exclude pluralities) and the hardship it would be on men of superior parts, to be confined to the performance of the ordinary parochial duty, which might be discharged by curates of much inferior qualifications; and to these were added an argument taken from the obligation there was upon the state to protect the church in her rights and privileges.

I did not, I own, comprehend the force of this reasoning, but however, I struck in the party against the motion, upon a plainer and more intelligible argument of my own, taken from the inconvenience of confining numbers of the more opulent and fashionable clergy, to their respective cures; with their intriguing, ambitious, secular and sensual spirit about them. I thought then, and I continue still to think, that they would be very bad examples to the people, and do more harm by their practice, than they would do good by their instructions. I expressed my opinion, that where a man's conscience would not dispose him to take the care of his parish personally upon himself, he must have some very unclerical qualities, which it would not be expedient for his people to imitate. I have known resident clerks, and so perhaps has your lordship, who have greatly contributed to corrupt their parishioners, by their unedifying conversation, and the influence their superior fortune gave them. It is true, a curate may be vicious and disorderly as well as a rector or vicar: but their bad example seldom does any very extensive mischief. Their scanty stipend and subordination to their principal, prevents their rising to any great degree of estimation, except what they purchase by a virtuous conduct and an attention to their duty; and a poor scoundrel may always lay his account with being contemptible. But this is a subject which, being of so clear illustration from facts, there is no occasion to enlarge upon. And I have now only to request your lordship to consider me as the amanuensis of my well-meaning neighbours, save only, that being interested in the success of their application as a parishioner, I most heartily join in their request; and am, my Lord, your Lordship's most obedient servant,

****.

Mr William Grimshaw of Haworth, from *The Life of Charlotte Brontë* by Mrs Gaskell (1810–1865)

Elizabeth Gaskell was married to a Unitarian minister who was a professor at Manchester New College. Her own writing career had started before she met Charlotte Brontë in 1850; the factual and sympathetic Life *of her friend was published in 1857, two years after Charlotte died. Northern life and society was the province of her own writing, and here she is sketching in the background of the Pennine parish where the Brontës grew up.*

The people of Haworth were not less strong and full of character than their neighbours on either side of the hills. The village lies embedded in the moors, between the two counties, on the old road between Keithley and Colne. About the middle of the last century, it became famous in the religious world as the scene of the ministrations of the Rev. William Grimshaw [1708–1763], curate of Haworth for twenty years. Before this time, it is probable that the curates were of this same order as one Mr. Nicholls, a Yorkshire clergyman, in the days immediately succeeding the Reformation, who was 'much addicted to drinking and company-keeping,' and used to say to his companions, 'You must not heed me but when I am got three feet above the earth,' that was, into the pulpit.

Mr. Grimshaw's life was written by Newton, Cowper's friend; and from it may be gathered some curious particulars of the manner in which a rough population were swayed and governed by a man of deep convictions, and strong earnestness of purpose. It seems that he had not been in any way remarkable for religious zeal, though he had led a moral life, and been conscientious in fulfilling his parochial duties, until a certain Sunday in September, 1744, when the servant, rising at five, found her master already engaged in prayer; she stated that, after remaining in his chamber for some time, he went to engage in religious exercises in the house of a parishioner, then home again to pray; thence, still fasting, to the church, where, as he was reaching the second lesson, he fell down, and on his partial recovery, had to be led from the church. As he went out, he spoke to the congregation, and told them not to disperse, as he had something to say to them, and would return presently. He was taken to the clerk's house, and again became insensible. His servant rubbed him, to restore the circulation; and when he was brought to himself 'he seemed in a great rapture,' and the first words he uttered were, 'I have had a glorious vision from the third heaven.' He did not say what he had seen, but returned into the church, and began the service again, at two in the afternoon, and went on until seven.

From this time he devoted himself, with the fervour of a Wesley, and something of the fanaticism of a Whitfield [Wesley's fellow open-air evangelist], to calling out a religious life among his parishioners. They had been in the habit of playing foot-ball on Sunday, using stones for this purpose; and giving and receiving challenges from other parishes. There were horse-races held on the moors just above the village, which were periodical sources of drunkenness and profligacy. Scarcely a wedding took place without the rough amusement of foot-races, where the half-naked runners were a scandal to all decent strangers. The old custom of 'arvills,' or funeral feasts, led to frequent pitched battles between the drunken mourners. Such customs were the outward signs of the kind of people with whom Mr. Grimshaw had to deal. But, by various means, some of the most practical kind, he wrought a great change in his parish. In his preaching he was occasionally assisted by Wesley and Whitfield, and at such times the little church proved much too small to hold the throng that poured in from distant villages, or lonely moorland hamlets; and frequently they were obliged to meet in the open air; indeed, there was not room enough in the church even for the communicants. Mr. Whitfield was once preaching in Haworth, and made use of some such expression, as that he hoped there was no need to say much to this congregation, as they had sat under so pious and godly a minister for so many years; 'whereupon Mr. Grimshaw stood up in his place, and said with a loud voice, "Oh, sir! for God's sake do not flatter them. I fear the greater part of them are going to hell with their eyes open."' But if they were so bound, it was not for want of exertion on Mr. Grimshaw's part to prevent them. He used to preach twenty or thirty times a week in private houses. If he perceived any one inattentive to his prayers, he would stop and rebuke the offender, and not go on till he saw every one on their knees. He was very earnest in enforcing the strict observance of Sunday; and would not allow his parishioners to walk in the fields between services. He sometimes gave out a very long Psalm (tradition says the 119th), and while it was being sung, he left the reading-desk, and taking a horse-whip went into the public-houses, and flogged the loiterers into church. They were swift who could escape the lash of the parson by sneaking out the back way. He had strong health and an active body, and rode far and wide over the hills, 'awakening' those who had previously had no sense of religion. To save time, and be no charge to the families at whose houses he held his prayer-meetings, he carried his provisions with him; all the food he took in a day on such occasions consisting simply of a piece of bread and butter, or dry bread and a raw onion.

The horse-races were justly objectionable to Mr. Grimshaw; they attracted numbers of profligate people to Haworth, and brought a match to the combustible materials of the place, only too ready to blaze out into wickedness. The story is, that he tried all means of persuasion, and even intimidation, to have the races discontinued, but in vain. At length, in despair, he prayed with such fervour of earnestness that the rain came down in torrents, and deluged the ground, so that there was no footing for man or beast, even if the multitude had been willing to stand such a flood let down from above. And so Haworth races were stopped, and have never been resumed to this day. Even now the memory of this good man is held in reverence, and his faithful ministrations and real virtues are one of the boasts of the parish.

From the diary of a village shopkeeper, Thomas Turner (1729–1793)

Thomas Turner ran a draper's shop in the village of East Hoathly, Sussex, and kept a diary from 1754 to 1765, running in total to 111 volumes in manuscript. In the selections published, Turner's preoccupations, and his eye on his fellow villagers, come vividly alive. He enjoyed reading and moralising as well as eating and socialising, and was evidently a kindly and conscientious, if anxious, man. When he remarried after the death of his temperamental and invalid first wife, his diary stops.

Jeremiah French was the largest tenant farmer in the village, twenty years older than Turner, and a dominant, noisy character. The Rev. Thomas Porter was the Cambridge-educated rector, keen on parties and acquiring land.

Saturday, 18th February 1758. ... A remarkable cold day, but no frost. I begin to find trade once more to grow very dull and that it is almost next to impossible to get in any money due on book.
Tuesday 21st. ... Tho. Davy at our house in the even for me to instruct him in gauging and the use of the sliding rule.
Wednesday 22nd. About 1.10 Mr French sent his servant with a horse for my wife, who accordingly went with him and dined at Mr French's. Myself and family dined on the remains of Wednesday's supper and a dish of cheap soup. Tho. Davy dined with us in order to taste our soup. About 6.40 I walked down to Whyly, where we played at brag the first part of the even; myself and wife won 1s. 2d. About 10.20 we went to supper on 4 boiled chickens, 4 boiled ducks, some minced veal, sausages, cold roast goose, cold chicken pasty, cold ham, damson and gooseberry tarts, marmelade, and raspberry puffs. Our company was Mr and Mrs Porter, Mr and Mrs Coates, Mrs Atkins, Mrs Hicks, Mr Piper and his wife, Joseph Fuller and his wife, Tho. Fuller and his wife, Dame Durrant, myself and wife and Mr French's family. After supper our behaviour was far from that of serious, harmless mirth, for it was downright obstreperous mirth mixed with a great deal of folly and stupidity. Our diversion was dancing (or jumping about) without a violin or any music, singing of foolish and bawdy healths and more such-like stupidity, and drinking all the time as fast as could be well poured down; and the parson of the parish was one amongst the mixed multitude all the time, so doubtless in point of sound divinity it was all harmless. But if conscience dictates right from wrong, as doubtless it sometimes does, mine is one that we may say is soon offended. For I must say I am always very uneasy at such behaviour, thinking it is not like the behaviour of the primitive Christians, which I imagine was most in conformity to our Saviour's gospel. Nor would I on the other hand be thought to be either a cynic or a stoic, but let improving discourse pass around the company. But, however, about 3.30, finding myself to have as much liquor as would do me good, I slipped away unobserved, leaving my wife to make my excuse; for sure it was rude, but still ill-manners are preferable to drunken-ness (though I was far from being sober). However, I came home, thank God, very safe and well without ever tumbling or other misfortune, and Mr French's servant brought my wife home about 5.10 ...
Thursday 23rd. This morn about 6 o'clock, just as my wife was gladly got to bed and had laid herself down to rest, we was awakened by Mrs Porter, who pretended she wanted some cream of tartar. But as soon as my wife got out of bed, she vowed she should come down, which she complied with and

found she, Mr Porter, Mr Fuller and his wife with a lighted candle, part of a bottle of wine and a glass. Then the next thing in course must be to have me downstairs, which I being apprised of, fastened my door. But, however, upstairs they came and threatened as also attempted to break open my door, which I found they would do; so I therefore ordered the boys to open it. But as soon as ever it was open, they poured into my room, and as modesty forbid me to get out of my bed in the presence of women, so I refrained. But their immodesty permitted them to draw me out of bed (as the common phrase is) tipsy turvy. But, however, at the intercession of Mr Porter they permitted me to put on my breeches (though it was no more than to cast a veil over what undoubtedly they had before that time discovered); as also, instead of my clothes, they gave me time to put on my wife's petticoat. In this manner they made me dance with them without shoes or stockings until they had emptied their bottle of wine and also a bottle of my beer. They then contented themselves with sitting down to breakfast on a dish of coffee etc. They then obliged my wife to accompany them to Joseph Durrant's, where they again breakfasted on tea etc. They then all adjourned to Mr Fuller's, where they again breakfasted on tea, and there they also stayed and dined; and about 3.30 they all found their ways to their respective homes, beginning by that time to be a little serious, and in my opinion ashamed of their stupid enterprise, or drunken perambulation. Now let anyone but call in reason to his assistance and seriously reflect on what I have before recited, and they must I think join with me in thinking that the precepts delivered from the pulpit on Sundays by Mr Porter, though delivered with the greatest ardour, must lose a great deal of their efficacy by such examples. Myself and family at home dined on the remains of yesterday's dinner. Mr Jordan called on me but did not stay. Mr Elless and Joseph Fuller in the evening called in to ask me how I did after my fatigue and stayed and smoked a pipe with me. And so this ends the silliest frolic as I think I ever knew, and one that must cast an odium on Mr and Mrs P. and Mrs F. so long as it shall be remembered.

Friday 24th. ... Sadly indisposed.

Saturday 25th. ... At home all day except going down to Mr Porter's with two salt fish, whom, when I went into the parlour, I found a-drinking coffee, though he had not generosity or goodness enough to ask me to drink a dish with him. So one may see that the most profusest from home (that is, freest at other people's houses) are the most abstemious at home, nay even as is now the case, to a degree of mean-spiritedness, or if there can be a worse name found it deserves that. ...

Sunday, March 5th. In the morn myself, Philip and servant at church; the text in Proverbs 18.21: 'Death and life are in the power of the tongue', from which words we had as good a sermon as I ever heard Mr Porter preach, it being against swearing ...

Laurence Sterne (1713–1768), letter to his friend John Wodehouse

Sterne was the great-grandson of an archbishop. He went into the church after Cambridge, and eventually held three livings near York: first, Sutton-on-the-Forest, then Stillingfleet, and lastly, in 1760, Coxwold. By this time the first volumes of his highly original The Life and Opinions of Tristram Shandy *('a civil, nonsensical, good-humoured book' as he called it) had brought him considerable celebrity in London. His love of female company put strains on his marriage, and extended travels abroad (1762–64) ended in his wife and only child, Lydia, remaining in France.*

Coxwould, Friday, August 23 1765

At this moment I am sitting in my summer house with my head and heart full, not of my uncle Toby's amours with the widow Wadman, but my sermons – and your letter has drawn me out of a pensive mood – the spirit of it *pleaseth me* – but in this solitude, what can I tell or write to you but about myself – I am glad you are in love – 'twill cure you (at least) of the spleen, which has a bad effect on both man and woman – I myself must ever have some Dulcinea in my head – it harmonises the soul – and in those cases I first endeavour to make the lady believe so, or rather I begin first to make myself believe that I am in love – but I carry on my affairs quite in the French way, sentimentally – '*l'amour*' (they say) '*n'est rien sans sentiment*' – Now notwithstanding they make such a pother about the *word*, they have no precise idea annex'd to it – And so much for the subject called love – I must tell you how I have just treated a French gentleman of fortune in France, who took a liking to my daughter – Without any ceremony (having got my direction from my wife's banker) he wrote me word that he was in love with my daughter, and desired to know what *fortune* I would give her at present, and how much at my *death* – by the bye I think there was very little *sentiment* on *his side* – My answer was 'Sir, I shall give her ten thousand pounds the day of her marriage – my calculation is as follows – she is not eighteen, you are sixty-two – there goes five thousand pounds – then Sir, you at least think her not ugly – she has many accomplishments, speaks Italian, French, plays upon the guittar, and as I fear you play upon no instrument whatever, I think you will be happy to take her at my terms, for here finishes the account of the ten thousand pounds' – I do not suppose but that he will take this as I mean, that is – a flat refusal.

What follows in the letter relates to an event reported in the York Courant *of August 6: 'Last Thursday ... in the afternoon, the end of the parsonage house of Sutton in the Forest, next the church, was discovered to be on fire: but by timely assistance, it was extinguished without much damage, and some men sat up all night to watch it. Next day every thing was thought to be safe, but in the afternoon the other end of the house was found to be on fire, which burnt so furiously, that its progress could not be stopp'd, and the whole building was consum'd, but the greater part of the furniture was saved. How these fires happened is not known.' Sterne's curate was Marmaduke Callis, who had been asking for release so he could take up a position at Walsby and Wellow, at a higher salary. It would appear that his and his wife's patience had run out.*

– I have had a parsonage house burnt down by the carelessness of my curate's wife – as soon as I can I must rebuild it, I trow – but I lack the means at present – yet I am never happier than when I have not a shilling in my pocket – for when I have I can never call it my own. Adieu my dear friend – may you enjoy better health than me, tho' not better spirits, for that is impossible.

Yours sincerely,

L. Sterne

The Vicar of Wakefield regulates his 'little republic': Oliver Goldsmith (?1728–1774)

From an Irish clerical background, Goldsmith was turned down for the ministry himself, travelled abroad, studied but gave up on medicine, and eventually made his living and literary reputation in London. Dr Johnson admired his writing, and arranged for the publishing of The Vicar of Wakefield *(1766) that rescued the author at a very bad time. The book went on to enjoy an enduring popularity.*

By Chapter IV, the first of many misfortunes that will beset Dr Primrose and his family has occurred, and they have had to leave their comfortable and congenial old parish to face a more straitened existence in less favoured country.

The place of our retreat was in a little neighbourhood consisting of farmers, who tilled their own grounds, and were equal strangers to opulence and poverty. As they had almost all the conveniences of life within themselves, they seldom visited towns or cities in search of superfluity. Remote from the polite, they still retained the primeval simplicity of manners; and, frugal by habit, they scarce knew that temperance was a virtue. They wrought with cheerfulness on days of labour, but observed festivals as intervals of idleness and pleasure. They kept up the Christmas carol, sent true love-knots on Valentine morning, ate pancakes on Shrovetide, showed their wit on the first of April, and religiously cracked nuts on Michaelmas eve. Being apprised of our approach, the whole neighbourhood came out to meet their minister, dressed in their fine clothes, and preceded by a pipe and tabor. A feast also was provided for our reception, at which we sat cheerfully down; and what the conversation wanted in wit was made up in laughter.

Our little habitation was situated at the foot of a sloping hill, sheltered with a beautiful underwood behind, and a prattling river before; on the one side a meadow, on the other a green. My farm consisted of about twenty acres of excellent land, having given an hundred pound for my predecessor's good-will. Nothing could exceed the neatness of my little enclosures, the elms and hedgerows appearing with inexpressible beauty. My house consisted of but one storey, and was covered with thatch, which gave it an air of snugness; the walls on the inside were nicely whitewashed, and my daughters undertook to adorn them with pictures of their own designing. Though the same room served us for parlour and kitchen, that only made it the warmer. Besides, as it was kept with the utmost neatness – the dishes, plates, and coppers being well scoured, and all disposed in bright rows on the shelves – the eye was agreeably relieved, and did not want richer furniture. There were three other apartments; one for my wife and me, another for our two daughters within our own, and the third, with two beds, for the rest of the children.

The little republic to which I gave laws was regulated in the following manner:– By sunrise we all assembled in our common apartment, the fire being previously kindled by the servant. After we had saluted each other with proper ceremony – for I always thought fit to keep up some mechanical forms of breeding, without which freedom ever destroys friendship – we all bent in gratitude to that Being who gave us another day. This duty being performed, my son and I went to pursue our usual industry abroad, while my wife and daughters employed themselves in providing breakfast, which was always ready at a certain time. I allowed half an hour for this meal, and an hour for dinner, which time was taken up in innocent mirth between my wife and daughters, and in philosophical arguments between my son and me.

As we rose with the sun, so we never pursued our labours after it was gone down, but returned home to the expecting family, where smiling looks, a neat hearth, and pleasant fire were prepared for our reception. Nor were we without guests: sometimes Farmer Flamborough, our talkative neighbour, and often the blind piper, would pay us a visit, and taste our gooseberry wine, for the making of which we had lost neither the receipt nor the reputation. These harmless people had several ways of being good company; while one played, the other would sing some soothing ballad – Johnny Armstrong's Last Good-night, or the cruelty of Barbara Allen. The night was concluded in the manner we began the morning, my youngest boys being appointed to read the lessons of the day; and he that read loudest, distinctest, and best was to have an halfpenny on Sunday to put into the poor's box.

When Sunday came, it was indeed a day of finery, which all my sumptuary edicts could not restrain. How well soever I fancied my lectures against pride had conquered the vanity of my daughters, yet I still found them secretly attached to all their former finery; they still loved laces, ribbons, bugles, and catgut; my wife herself retained a passion for her crimson paduasoy [a fashionable corded silk fabric], because I formerly happened to say it became her.

The first Sunday, in particular, their behaviour served to mortify me. I had desired my girls the preceding night to be dressed early the next day; for I always loved to be at church a good while before the rest of the congregation. They punctually obeyed my directions; but when we were to assemble in the morning at breakfast, down came my wife and daughters dressed out in all their former splendour; their hair plastered up with pomatum, their faces patched to taste, their trains bundled up into a heap behind, and rustling at every motion. I could not help smiling at their vanity, particularly that of my wife, from whom I expected more discretion. In this exigence, therefore, my only resource was to order my son, with an important air, to call our coach. The girls were amazed at the command; but I repeated it with more solemnity than before. 'Surely, my dear, you jest,' cried my wife; 'we can walk it perfectly well; we want no coach to carry us now.' – 'You mistake, child,' returned I, 'we do want a coach; for if we walk to church in this trim, the very children in the parish will hoot after us.' – 'Indeed,' replied my wife; 'I always imagined that my Charles was fond of seeing his children neat and handsome about him.' – 'You may be as neat as you please,' interrupted I, 'and I shall love you the better for it; but all this is not neatness, but frippery. These rufflings, and pinkings and patchings will only make us hated by all the wives of our neighbours. No, my children,' continued I more gravely, 'those gowns may be altered into something of a plainer cut; for finery is very unbecoming in us who want the means of decency. I do not know whether such flouncing and shredding is becoming even in the rich, if we consider, upon a moderate calculation, that the nakedness of the indigent world may be clothed from the trimmings of the vain.'

This remonstration had the proper effect. They went with great composure, that very instant, to change their dress; and the next day I had the satisfaction of finding my daughters, at their own request, employed in cutting up their trains into Sunday waistcoats for Dick and Bill, the two little ones, and what was still more satisfactory, the gowns seemed improved by this curtailing.

Country superstitions, from Gilbert White (1720–1793), *The Natural History of Selborne* (1789)

In 1758 the naturalist-parson returned to the village where he had been born, holding several curacies in the vicinity, and stayed there the rest of his life. Gilbert White's letters to fellow naturalists Pennant and Barrington were brought together as The Natural History of Selborne, *and the charm of his close observations has seen them through over two hundred editions since. He is commemorated in the church with a window depicting St Francis surrounded by White's beloved fauna and flora.*

To Daines Barrington — Selborne, January 9th, 1776

DEAR SIR,–It is the hardest thing in the world to shake off superstitious prejudices: they are sucked in, as it were, with our mother's milk; and, growing up with us at a time when they take the fastest hold and make the most lasting impressions, become so interwoven into our very constitutions, that the strongest good sense is required to disengage ourselves from them. No wonder, therefore, that the lower people retain them their whole lives through, since their minds are not invigorated by a liberal education, and therefore not enabled to make any efforts adequate to the situation.

Such a preamble seems to be necessary before we enter on the superstitions of this district, lest we should be suspected of exaggeration in a recital of practices too gross for this enlightened age.

But the people of Tring, in Hertfordshire, would do well to remember, that no longer ago than the year 1751, and within twenty miles of the capital, they seized on two superannuated wretches, crazed with age, and overwhelmed with infirmities, on a suspicion of witchcraft; and, by trying experiments, drowned them in a horse-pond.

In a farm-yard near the middle of this village stands, at this day, a row of pollard-ashes, which, by the seams and long cicatrices down their sides, manifestly show that, in former times, they have been cleft asunder. These trees, when young and flexible, were severed and held open by wedges, while ruptured children, stripped naked, were pushed through the apertures, under a persuasion that, by such a process, the poor babes would be cured of their infirmity. As soon as the operation was over, the tree, in the suffering part, was plastered with loam, and carefully swathed up. If the parts coalesced and soldered together, as usually fell out, where the feat was performed with any adroitness at all, the party was cured; but, where the cleft continued to gape, the operation, it was supposed, would prove ineffectual. Having occasion to enlarge my garden not long since, I cut down two or three such trees, one of which did not grow together.

We have several persons now living in the village, who, in their childhood, were supposed to be healed by this superstitious ceremony, derived down perhaps from our Saxon ancestors, who practised it before their conversion to Christianity.

At the fourth corner of the Plestor, or area, near the church, there stood, about twenty years ago, a very grotesque hollow pollard-ash, which for ages had been looked on with no small veneration as a shrew-ash. Now a shrew-ash is an ash whose twigs or branches, when gently applied to the limbs of cattle, will immediately relieve the pains which a beast suffers from the running of a shrew-mouse over the part affected; for it is supposed that a shew-mouse is of so baneful and deleterious a nature, that wherever it creeps over a beast, be it horse, cow, or sheep, the suffering animal is afflicted with cruel anguish, and threatened with the loss of the use of the limb. Against this accident, tow which they were continually liable, our provident forefather always kept a shrew-ash at hand, which, when once medicated, would maintain its virtue for ever. A shrew-ash was made thus: – Into the body of the tree a deep hole was bored with an auger, and a poor devoted shrew-mouse was thrust in alive, and plugged in, no doubt, with several quaint incantations long since forgotten. As the ceremonies necessary for such a consecration are no longer understood, all succession is at an end, and no such tree is known to subsist in the manor, or hundred.

As to that on the Plestor, 'The late Vicar* stubb'd and burnt it,' when he was way-warden, regardless of the remonstrances of the bystanders, who interceded in vain for its preservation, urging its power and efficacy, and alleging that it had been

'Religione partum multos servata per annos.'†

I am, etc.

* *Dr Duncombe Bristowe, parson from 1740 to 1758.*
† *'Preserved for many years through the reverence of the fathers': Virgil,* Aeneid *II, l. 715.*

James Boswell (1740–1795), from *The Life of Samuel Johnson, LL.D.* (1791)

Boswell began keeping records of their conversations and activities after first meeting Dr Johnson (1709–1784) in a London bookshop in 1763.

1772: Johnson supports the expulsion of Methodist students from Oxford
I talked of the recent expulsion of six students from the University of Oxford, who were methodists, and would not desist from publickly praying and exhorting. JOHNSON. 'Sir, that expulsion was extremely just and proper. What have they to do at an University, who are not willing to be taught, but will presume to teach? Where is religion to be learnt, but at an University? Sir, they were examined, and found to be mighty ignorant fellows.' BOSWELL. 'But, was it not hard, Sir, to expel them, for I am told they were good beings?' JOHNSON. 'I believe they might be good beings, but they are not fit to be in the University of Oxford . A cow is a very good animal in the field; but we turn her out of a garden.' Lord Elibank used to repeat this as an illustration uncommonly happy.

1776: Johnson visits Dr Taylor, the vicar and 'King of Ashbourne'
On Tuesday, March 26, there came for us an equipage properly suited to a wealthy, well-beneficed clergyman: Dr. Taylor's large, roomy post-chaise, drawn by four stout plump horses, and driven by two steady jolly postillions, which conveyed us to Ashbourne; Where I found my friend's schoolfellow

living upon an establishment perfectly corresponding with his substantial creditable equipage: his house, garden, pleasure grounds, table, in short every thing good, and no scantiness appearing. Every man should form such a plan of living as he can execute completely. Let him not draw an outline wider than he can fill up. I have seen many skeletons of shew and magnificence which excite at once ridicule and pity. Dr. Taylor had a good estate of his own, and good preferment in the church, being a prebendary of Westminster, and rector of Bosworth. He was a diligent justice of the peace, and presided over the town of Ashbourne, to the inhabitants of which I was told he was very liberal; and as a proof of this it was mentioned to me, he had the preceding winter distributed two hundred pounds among such of them as stood in need of his assistance. He has consequently a considerable political interest in the county of Derby, which he employed to support the Devonshire family; for though the schoolfellow and friend of Johnson, he was a Whig. I could not perceive in his character much congeniality of any sort with that of Johnson, who, however, said to me, 'Sir, he has a very strong understanding.' His size, and figure, and countenance, and manner, were that of a hearty English 'Squire, with the parson super-induced: and I took particular notice of his upper-servant, Mr. Peters, a decent grave man, in purple clothes, and a large white wig, like the butler or *major domo* of a bishop.

Dr. Johnson and Dr. Taylor met with great cordiality; and Johnson soon gave him the same sad account of their schoolfellow, Congreve, that he had given to Mr. Hector; adding a remark of such moment to the rational conduct of a man in the decline of life, that deserves to be imprinted upon every mind: 'There is nothing against which an old man should be so much upon his guard as putting himself to nurse.' Innumerable have been the melancholy instances of men once distinguished for firmness, resolution, and spirit, who in their latter days have been governed like children, by interested female artifice.

The severity of the early Church Fathers, from Edward Gibbon (1737–1794), *The History of the Decline and Fall of the Roman Empire*

Gibbon wrote in his Autobiography *(3 February 1779): 'Had I believed that the majority of English readers were so fondly attached even to the name and shadow of Christianity; had I foreseen that the pious, the timid and the prudent would feel or affect to feel with such exquisite sensibility; I might perhaps have softened the two invidious Chapters [XV & XVI], which would create many enemies, and conciliate few friends. But the shaft was shot ...'*

From Chapter XV, The primitive Christians condemn pleasure and luxury

The acquisition of knowledge, the exercise of our reason or fancy, and the cheerful flow of unguarded conversation, may employ the leisure of a liberal mind. Such amusements, however, were rejected with abhorrence, or admitted with the utmost caution, by the severity of the fathers, who despised all knowledge that was not useful to salvation, and who considered all levity of discourse as a criminal abuse of the gift of speech. In our present state of existence, the body is so inseparably connected with the soul, that it seems to be our interest to taste, with innocence and moderation, the enjoyments of which that faithful companion is susceptible. Very different was the reasoning of our devout predecessors; vainly aspiring to imitate the perfection of angels, they disdained, or they affected to disdain, every earthly and corporeal delight. Some of our senses indeed are necessary for our preservation, others for our subsistence, and others again for our information, and thus far it was impossible to reject the use of them. The first sensation of pleasure was marked as the first moment of their abuse. The unfeeling candidate for Heaven was instructed, not only to resist the grosser allurements of the taste or smell, but even to shut his ears against the profane harmony of sounds, and to view with indifference the most finished productions of human art. Gay apparel, magnificent houses, and elegant furniture, were supposed to unite the double guilt of pride and sensuality: a simple and mortified appearance was more suitable to the Christian who was certain of his sins and doubtful of his salvation. In their censures of luxury, the fathers are extremely minute and circumstantial; and among the various articles which excite their pious indignation, we may enumerate false hair, garments of any colour except white, instruments of music, vases of gold or silver, downy pillows (as Jacob reposed his head on a stone), white bread, foreign wines, public salutations, the use of warm baths, and the practice of shaving the beard, which, according to the expression of Tertullian, is a lie against our own faces, and an impious attempt to improve the works of the Creator. When Christianity was introduced among the rich and the polite, the observation of these singular laws was left, as it would be at present, to the few who were ambitious of superior sanctity. But it is always easy, as well as agreeable, for the inferior ranks of mankind to claim a merit from the contempt of that pomp and pleasure, which fortune has placed beyond their reach. The virtue of the primitive Christians, like that of the first Romans, was very frequently guarded by poverty and ignorance.

The chaste severity of the fathers, in whatever related to the commerce of the two sexes, flowed from the same principle; their abhorrence of every enjoyment, which might gratify the sensual, and degrade the spiritual, nature of man. It was their favourite opinion, that if Adam had preserved his obedience to the Creator, he would have lived forever in a state of virgin purity, and that some harmless mode of vegetation might have peopled paradise with a race of innocent and immortal beings. The use of marriage was permitted only to his fallen posterity, as a necessary expedient to continue the human species, and as a restraint, however imperfect, on the natural licentiousness of desire. The hesitation of the orthodox casuists on this interesting subject, betrays the perplexity of man, unwilling to approve an institution, which they were compelled to tolerate. The enumeration of the very whimsical laws, which they most circumspectly imposed on the marriage-bed, would force a smile from the young, and a blush from the fair. It was their unanimous sentiment, that a first marriage was adequate to all the purposes of nature and of society. The sensual connexion was refined into a resemblance of the mystic union of Christ with his church, and was pronounced to be indissoluble either by divorce or by death. The practice of second nuptials was branded with the name of a legal adultery; and the persons who were guilty of so scandalous an offence against Christian purity, were soon excluded from the honours, and even from the alms, of the church. Since desire was imputed as a crime, and marriage was tolerated as a defect, it was consistent with the same principles to consider a state of celibacy as the nearest approach to the Divine perfection. It was with the utmost difficulty that ancient Rome could support the institution of six vestals; but the primitive church was filled with a great number of persons of either sex, who had devoted themselves to the profession of perpetual chastity. A few of these, among whom we may reckon the learned Origen, judged it the most prudent to disarm the tempter. Some were insensible and some were invincible against the assaults of the flesh. Disdaining an ignominious flight, the virgins of the warm climate of Africa encountered the enemy in the closest engagement; they permitted priests and deacons to share their bed, and gloried amidst the flames in their unsullied purity. But insulted Nature sometimes vindicated her rights, and this new species of martyrdom served only to introduce a new scandal into the church. Among the Christian ascetics, however (a name which they soon acquired from their painful exercise), many, as they were less presumptuous, were probably more successful. The loss of sensual pleasure was supplied and compensated by spiritual pride. Even the multitude of Pagans were inclined to estimate the merit of the sacrifice by its apparent difficulty; and it was in the praise of these chaste spouses of Christ that the fathers have poured forth the troubled stream of their eloquence. Such are the early traces of monastic principles and institutions, which, in a subsequent age, have counterbalanced all the temporal advantages of Christianity.

A German tourist experiences the English Sunday, from Karl Philip Moritz (1756–1793), *Travels, chiefly on foot, through Several Parts of England, in 1782* (English translation 1795)

From an impoverished background Moritz eventually found the education he longed for, and became a preacher and teacher. On later travels in Italy he met Goethe, with whose encouragement he made an academic life in Berlin. Here he is on his travels in his mid-twenties exploring England. After being rejected at Oxfordshire inns from Henley onward, he arrives in Nettlebed.

Everything seemed to be all alive in this little village; there was a party of militia soldiers who were dancing, singing, and making merry. Immediately on my entrance into the village, the first house that I saw lying on my left was an inn, from which, as usual in England, a large beam extended across the street to the opposite house, from which hung dangling an astonishingly large sign, with the name of the proprietor.

'May I stay here to night?' I asked with eagerness: 'Why, yes, you may;' an answer which, however cold and surly, made me exceedingly happy.

They shewed me into the kitchen, and set me down to sup at the same table with some soldiers and servants. I now, for the first time, found myself in one of those kitchens which I had so often read of in Fielding's fine novels; and which certainly give one, on the whole, a very accurate idea of English manners.

The chimney in this kitchen, where they were roasting and boiling, seemed to be taken off from the rest of the room and enclosed by a wooden partition: the rest of the apartment was made use of as a sitting and eating room. All round on the sides were shelves with pewter dishes and plates, and the ceiling was well stored with provisions of various kinds, such as sugar-loaves, black-puddings, hams, sausages, flitches of bacon, &c.

While I was eating, a post-chaise drove up: and in a moment both the folding-doors were thrown open, and the whole house set in motion, in order to receive, with all due respect, these guests, who, no doubt, were supposed to be persons of consequence. The gentlemen alighted however only for a moment, and called for nothing but a couple of pots of beer; and then drove away again. Notwithstanding, the people of the house behaved to them with all possible attention, for they came in a post-chaise.

Though this was only an ordinary village, and they certainly did not take me for a person of consequence, they yet gave me a carpeted bed-room, and a very good bed.

The next morning I put on clean linen, which I had along with me, and dressed myself as well as I could. And now, when I thus made my appearance, they did not, as they had the evening before, shew me into the kitchen, but into the parlour; a room that seemed to be allotted for strangers, on the ground-floor. I was also now addressed by the most respectful term, *Sir*; whereas, the evening before I had been called only *Master*; by this latter appellation, I believe, it is usual to address only farmers, and quite common people.

This was Sunday; and all the family were in their Sunday-cloaths. I now began to be much pleased with this village, and so I resolved to stop at it for the day, and attend divine-service. For this purpose I borrowed a prayer-book of my host. Mr. *Illing* was his name, which struck me the more, perhaps, because it is a very common name in Germany. During my breakfast, I read over several parts of the English liturgy, and could not help being struck at the circumstance that every word in the whole service seems to be prescribed and dictated to the clergyman. They do not visit the sick but by a prescribed form: as, for instance, they must begin by saying, 'Peace be to this house,' &c.

Its being called a *prayer-book* rather than, like ours, an *hymn-book*, arises from the nature of the English service, which is composed very little of singing; and almost entirely of praying. The psalms of David, however, are here translated into English verse; and are generally printed at the end of English prayer-books.

The prayer-book, which my landlord lent me, was quite a family-piece; for all his children's births and names, and also his own wedding-day, were very carefully set down in it. Even on this account alone the book would not have been uninteresting to me.

At half-past nine, the service began. Directly opposite to our house, the boys of the village were all drawn up, as if they had been recruits, to be drilled; all well-looking, healthy lads, neat and decently dressed, and with their hair cut short and combed on the forehead, according to the English fashion. Their bosoms were open, and the white frills of their shirts turned back on each side. They seemed to be drawn up here at the entrance of the village, merely to wait the arrival of the clergyman.

I walked a little way out of the village; where, at some distance, I saw several people coming from another village, to attend divine-service here at Nettlebed.

At length came the parson on horseback. The boys pulled off their hats, and all made him very low bows. He appeared to be rather an elderly man, and wore his own hair round and decently dressed; or rather curling naturally.

The bell now rung in, and so I too, with a sort of secret proud sensation, as if I also had been an Englishman, went with my prayer-book under my arm to church, along with the rest of the congregation; and when I got into the church, the clerk very civilly seated me close to the pulpit.

Nothing can possibly be more simple, apt, and becoming than the few decorations of this church.

Directly over the altar, on two tables, in large letters, the ten commandments were written. There surely is much wisdom and propriety in this placing, full in the view of the people, the sum and substance of all morality.

Under the pulpit, near the steps that led up to it, was a desk, from which the clergyman read the liturgy. The responses were all regularly made by the clerk; the whole congregation joining occasionally, though but in a low voice: As for instance, the minister said, 'Lord have mercy upon us!' the clerk and the congregation immediately subjoin, 'and forgive us all our sins.' In general, when the clergyman offers up a prayer, the clerk, and the whole congregation answer only, *Amen!*

The English service must needs be exceedingly fatiguing to the officiating minister, inasmuch as, besides a sermon, the greatest part of the liturgy falls to his share to read, besides the psalms, and two lessons. The joining of the whole congregation in prayer has something exceedingly solemn and affecting in it. Two soldiers, who sat near me in the church, and who had probably been in London, seemed to wish to pass for philosophers, and wits; for they did not join in the prayers of the church.

The service was now pretty well advanced, when I observed some little stir in the desk: the clerk was busy, and they seemed to be preparing for something new and solemn; and I also perceived several musical instruments. The clergyman now stopped and the clerk then said, in a loud voice, 'Let us sing to the praise and glory of God, the forty-seventh psalm.'

I cannot well express how affecting and edifying it seemed to me, to hear this whole, orderly, and decent congregation, in this small country church, joining together, with vocal and instrumental music, in the praise of their Maker. It was the more grateful, as having been performed not by mercenary musicians, but by the peaceful and pious inhabitants, of this sweet village. I can hardly figure to myself any offering more likely to be grateful to God.

The congregation sang and prayed alternately several times; and the tunes of the psalms were particularly lively and cheerful, though at the same time sufficiently grave, and uncommonly interesting. I am a warm admirer of all sacred music; and I cannot but add, that that of the church of England is particularly calculated to raise the heart in devotion. I own it often affected me even to tears.

The clergyman now stood up and made a short, but very proper discourse on this text, 'Not all they who say, Lord, Lord! Shall enter the kingdom of heaven.' His language was particularly plain, though forcible; his arguments were no less plain, convincing, and earnest; but contained nothing that was particularly striking. I do not think the sermon lasted more than half an hour.

The clergyman had not perhaps a very prepossessing appearance; I thought him also a little distant and reserved; and I did not quite like his returning the bows of the farmers with a very formal nod.

I staid till the service was quite over; and then went out of the church with the congregation, and amused myself with reading the inscriptions of the tomb-stones in the church-yard; which, in general, are simpler, more pathetic, and better written that ours.

There were some of them which, to be sure, were ludicrous and laughable enough. Among these is one on the tomb of a smith which, on account of its singularity, I here copy and send you.

> My sledge and anvil lie declin'd,
> My bellows too have lost their wind;
> My fire's extinct, my forge decay'd,*
> My coals are spent, my iron's gone,
> My nails are drove; my work is done.

... All the farmers whom I saw here were dressed, not as ours are, in coarse frocks, but with some taste, in fine good cloth; and they were to be distinguished from the people of the town, not so much by their dress, as by the greater simplicity and modesty of their behaviour.

I staid here to dinner. In the afternoon there was no service; the young people, however, went to church, and there sang some few psalms. Others of the congregation were also present. This was conducted with so much decorum, that I could hardly help considering it as, actually, a kind of church-service. I staid, with great pleasure, till this meeting also was over.

I seemed indeed to be enchanted, and as if I could not leave this village. Three times did I get off, in order to go on farther, and as often returned, more than half resolved to spend a week, or more, in my favourite Nettlebed.

* *From the several versions of this blacksmith's epitaph to be found, it looks as if Moritz missed out a fourth line: 'And in the dust my vice is laid.'*

Beating the Bounds, and Tithe Audit Day, from *Diary of a Country Parson* by Parson Woodforde (1740–1803)

James Woodforde was a parsonage son himself. He recorded forty-four years of a largely unremarkable bachelor life in outstanding everyday detail, and his Diary *is uniquely interesting, his first editor observed, just because his life was so tranquil and obscure. From 1776 he was parson of Weston Longville in Norfolk, one of the richer livings of his old college – New College, Oxford.*

May 3, 1780. I breakfasted, dined, supped and slept again at home. About ½ past 9 o'clock this morning my Squire called on me, and I took my Mare and went with him to the Hart just by the Church where most of the Parish were assembled to go the Bounds of the Parish, and at 10 we all set of for the same about 30 in number. Went towards Ringland first; then to the breaks near Mr. Townshend's Clumps, from thence to Attertons on France Green, where the People had some Liquor, and which I paid, being usual for the Rector – 0. 4. 6 [4 shillings and 6 pence]. Mr. Press Custance was with us also. From France Green we went away to Mr. Dades, from thence towards Risings, from thence down to Mr. Gallands, then to the old Hall of my Squire's, thence to the old Bridge at Lenewade, then close to the River till we came near Morton, then by Mr. Le Grisse's Clumps, then by Bakers and so back till we came to the place where we first set off. Mr. Custance Senr then called the six following old men (that is) Richd. Bates, Thos. Cary, Thos. Dicker, Richd. Buck, Thos. Cushion and Thos. Carr, and gave each of them half a guinea – To George Wharton, who carried a Hook and marked the Trees, my Squire gave also five shillings. To Robin Hubbard also who carried a Spade he gave

5 shillings, and sent all the rest of the People to the Hart to eat and drink as much as they would at his expense. The Squire behaved most generously on the occasion. He asked me to go home and dine with him but I begged to be excused being tired, as I walked most of the way. Our Bounds are supposed to be about 12 miles round. We were going of them full five hours. We set off at 10 in the morning and got back a little after 3 in the afternoon. Nancy was got to dinner when I returned. Ben, Will and Jack all went the Bounds. Ben's Father Wm. Legate in crossing the River on horseback was thrown off and was over head and ears in the River. My Squire's man John was likely to have had a very bad accident in leading the Squire's horse over a boggy place, both horses were stuck fast up to their Bellies, and by plunging threw him off in the mire and was very near being hurt by the horses plunging to get out, but by great and providential means escaped free from any mischief. The horses also were not injured at all. The man had his new suit of Livery on and new hat, which were made very dirty. Where there were no trees to mark, Holes were made and Stones cast in.

Tuesday, Dec. 6, 1791. This being my Tithe Audit Day the following People waited on me, paid me their respective dues and dined and spent the remaining part of the day with me, they left me about 12 o'clock at night, well pleased with their entertainment. Mr. Girling and Son, Mr. Peachman, Mr. Howlett, John Baker, Jonas Silvey, Henry Case, Js. Pegg, Robt. Emeris, Stephen Andrews, Hugh Bush, Willm. Bidewell, John Buck, John Norton, Thos. Reynolds Junr., John Culley, Charles Hardy, Henry Rising, Thos. Cary, and John Heavers. Widow Pratts Son James came soon after dinner and paid me for his Mother. He came quite drunk and behaved very impudently. Stephen Andrews and Billy Bidewell rather full. Billy Bidewell paid me for a Calf which he is to have of me in a few days, 0. 10. 6. Recd. For Tithe to day about 285. 0. 0 [£285]. I gave them for Dinner a Sirloin of Beef rosted, Sliff-Marrow-Bone of Beef boiled, a boiled Leg of Mutton and Caper-Sauce, a Couple of Rabbits and Onion Sauce, Some salt Fish boiled and Parsnips, and Egg Sauce with plenty of plumb-Puddings and plain ditto. They spoke highly in favour of my strong Beer, they never drank any better they said. Paid Stephen Andrews for Carriage of Coal, 0. 15. 0. Paid Ditto, for 1½ d [1½ pence] Rate to the Church 0. 2. 0. Recd. Of Ditto, my last Visitation Fee, 0. 2. 6. Mr. Howlett was very dull and dejected. There was drank, six Bottles of Rum which made three Bowls of Punch, four Bottles of Port Wine, besides strong-Beer. No Punch or Wine suffered in Kitchen. Mr. Girling who had been to Norwich this Morning brought us News of Lord Orfords Death a Man universally respected and will be universally lamented as he was one of the Most Charitable, human Men, as has been known many a day. His Death is supposed to be entirely owing to the Loss of his most intimate Friend, Mrs. Park, who lived with him and had many Years. She had been a particular Friend to him.

William Cowper (1731–1800), 'The Yearly Distress, or Tithing Time at Stock, in Essex', 1779

'Verses addressed to a country Clergyman complaining of the disagreeableness of the day annually appointed for receiving the dues at the parsonage' – written to his young friend William Unwin, the son of his long-term companion Mary Unwin, and now a parson faced with the annual ordeal of extracting his tithe income from parishioners. Cowper was a vicarage child himself, who, during the unstable periods of his life, suffered from considerable religious torment. His memorial is to be seen in Dereham Church, Norfolk, but his creative years were mostly spent in Olney, Bedfordshire, where he wrote 'God moves in a mysterious way' (1773).

Come, ponder well, for 'tis no jest,
To laugh it would be wrong,
The troubles of a worthy priest,
The burthen of my song.

This priest he merry is and blithe
Three quarters of a year,
But oh! It cuts him like a scythe
When tithing time draws near.

He then is full of fright and fears,
As one at point to die,
And long before the day appears
He heaves up many a sigh.

For then the farmers come, jog, jog,
Along the miry road,
Each heart as heavy as a log,
To make their payments good.

In sooth, the sorrow of such days
Is not to be expressed,

When he that takes and he that pays
  Are both alike distressed.

Now all unwelcome at his gates
  The clumsy swains alight,
With rueful faces and bald pates; –
  He trembles at the sight.

And well he may, for well he knows
  Each bumpkin of the clan,
Instead of paying what he owes,
  Will cheat him if he can.

So in they come – each makes his leg,
  And flings his head before,
And looks as if he came to beg,
  And not to quit a score.

'And how does miss and madam do,
  The little boy and all?'
'All tight and well. And how do you,
  Good Mr. What-d'ye call?'

The dinner comes, and down they sit;
  Were e'er such hungry folk?
There's little talking and no wit;
  It is no time to joke.

One wipes his nose upon his sleeve,
  One spits upon the floor,
Yet not to give offence or grieve,
  Holds up the cloth before,

The punch goes round, and they are dull
  And lumpish still as ever;
Like barrels with their bellies full,
  They only way the heavier.

At length the busy time begins.
  'Come, neighbours, we must wag – '
The money chinks, down drop their chins,
  Each lugging out his bag.

One talks of mildew and of frost,
And one of storms of hail,
And one of pigs that he has lost
By maggots at the tail.

Quoth one, 'A rarer man than you
In pulpit none shall hear;
But yet, methinks, to tell you true,
You sell it plaguy dear.'

O why were farmers made so coarse,
Or clergy made so fine?
A kick that scarce would move a horse,
May kill a sound divine.

Then let the boobies stay at home;
'Twould cost him, I dare say,
Less trouble taking twice the sum,
Without the clowns that pay.

A Ferry Fable, from Cornwall

A bumpkin came to the river's side
With a sow from his master's store,
And strict command to cross the tide –
A task which vexed him sore.

For though the boat was waiting there,
And the skipper watched the shore –
And the tide was high and the wind was fair,
For sail or labouring oar –

There still remained a task more stern
Than ruling wind or tide;
For the sow would neither walk nor turn
Towards the vessel's side.

The bumpkin screamed – enticed and gored –
And cursed with might and main;

But still to get the sow on board
His efforts were in vain.

At length a parson hurried down,
With chidings oft and long,
Upon the language of the clown,
Because it was so strong.

'Now cease your oaths,' said Clerico,
'For naught can they avail;
But slyly give a poke or so,
Till in the way you want to go
You find the lady turning – ho!
Then pull her by the tail!'

The clown obeyed – and, quick as thought,
The victim was on board.
Though hard to learn, yet quickly taught,
Are lessons rightly stored.

The bumpkin stared aghast to know
How 'twas that priests so learned grow;
The skipper stood amazed –
And had it been some years ago,
The parson then and there, I trow,
'Midst faggots would have blazed.

Now if you wish to reason how
The parson learnt his plan,
'Tis simply this you have to know –
He was a married man!

William Blake (1757–1827)

Blake's poetry found little recognition in his own lifetime, when his reputation and income derived from his painting, illustrating and engraving. His passionate and original perceptions of the human spirit and its corruption, fed by the cross-currents of the London of his times, are best known now from his Songs of Innocence and Experience, *'Shewing the Two Contrary States of the Human Soul'.*

• From his Notebook (1793)

An Answer to the Parson

'Why of the sheep do you not learn peace?'
'Because I don't want you to shear my fleece.'

• From *Songs of Experience* (1793)

The Garden of Love

I went to the Garden of Love,
And saw what I never had seen:
A Chapel was built in the midst,
Where I used to play on the green.

And the gates of this Chapel were shut,
And 'Thou shalt not' writ over the door;
So I turn'd to the Garden of Love
That so many sweet flowers bore;

And I saw it filled with graves,
And tomb-stones where flowers should be;
And Priests in black gowns were walking their rounds,
And binding with briars my joys & desires.

The following was omitted from the first printed edition of 1839 as too subversive of authority

The Little Vagabond

Dear Mother, dear Mother, the Church is cold,
But the Ale-house is healthy & pleasant & warm;
Besides I can tell where I am used well,
Such usage in heaven will never do well.

But if at the Church they would give us some Ale,
And a pleasant fire our souls to regale,
We'd sing and we'd pray all the live-long day,
Nor ever once wish from the Church to stray.

Then the Parson might preach, & drink, & sing,
And we'd be as happy as birds in the spring;
And modest dame Lurch, who is always at Church,
Would not have bandy children, nor fasting, nor birch.

And God, like a father rejoicing to see
His children as pleasant and happy as he,
Would have no more quarrel with the Devil or the Barrel,
But kiss him, & give him both drink and apparel.

'A Dialogue … addressed to all the mechanics, journeymen, and labourers in Great Britain', from Hannah More (1745–1833), *Village Politics* (1792)

Hannah More was a member of Elizabeth Montagu's 'blue-stocking' society and wrote plays that Garrick produced. Her strong Evangelical bent took her into the field of didactic writing that sold in hundreds of thousands, and the Religious Tract Society was founded to continue her work. As a philanthropist she founded schools and was an early associate of Wilberforce and the Abolitionists opposing slavery. In the alarm caused by the French Revolution and the revolutionary appeal of Thomas Paine's Rights of Man *she was asked to write a pamphlet in plain English 'for the lower orders', which resulted in* Village Politics, *supposedly by 'Will Chip, a Country Carpenter': 'A Dialogue Between Jack Anvil, the Blacksmith, and Tom Hod, the Mason, addressed to all the mechanics, journeymen, and labourers in Great Britain'.*

Tom. What is it to be an enlightened people ?

Jack. To put out the light of the Gospel, confound right and wrong, and grope about in pitch darkness.

Tom. What is *philosophy,* that Tim Standish talks so much about?

Jack. To believe that there's neither God, nor devil, nor heaven, nor hell: to dig up a wicked old fellow [Voltaire]'s rotten bones, whose books, Sir John says, have been the ruin of thousands, and to set his figure up in a church and worship him.

Tom. And what is a *patriot* according to the new school?

Jack. A man who loves every other country better than his own, and France best of all.

Tom. And what is benevolence ?

Jack. Why, in the new-fangled language, it means contempt of religion, aversion to justice, overturning of law, doting on all mankind in general, and hating every body in particular.

Tom. And what mean the other hard words that Tim talks about, – *organisation*, and *function*, and *civism*, and *incivism*, and *equalisation*, and *inviolability*, and *imprescriptible*, and *fraternisation*?

Jack. Nonsense, gibberish, downright hocus-pocus. I know 'tis not English; Sir John says 'tis not Latin; and his valet de sham says 'tis not French neither.

Tom. And yet Tim says he never shall be happy till all these fine things are brought over to England.

Jack. What! Into this Christian country, Tom? Why, dost know they have no *Sabbath* in France? Their mob parliament meets on a Sunday to do their wicked work, as naturally as we do to go to church. They have renounced God's word and God's day, and they don't even date in the year of our Lord. Why dost turn pale, man? And the rogues are always making such a noise, Tom, in the midst of their parliament-house, that their speaker rings a bell, like our penny-postman, because he can't keep them in order.

Tom. And dost thou believe they are as cruel as some folks pretend?

Jack. I am sure they are, and I think I know the reason. We Christians set a high value on life, because we know that every fellow-creature has an immortal soul; a soul to be saved or lost, Tom. Whoever believes that, is a little cautious how he sends a soul unprepared to his grand account. But he who believes a man is no better than a dog will make no more scruple of killing one than the other.

Tom. And dost thou think our Rights of Man will lead to all this wickedness?

Jack. A sure as eggs are eggs.

Tom. I begin to think we're better off as we are.

'The cold charities of man to man', from George Crabbe (1755–1832), *The Village* (1783)

Doctor, botanist, clergyman, and poet of social and psychological insight, Crabbe is best known for his Aldeburgh-based work (e.g. Peter Grimes*).* The Village *is a poem in two books, depicting the life of the countryside 'As Truth will paint it, and as Bards will not'. When he was training to be a doctor Crabbe treated the sick in the poorhouse in Aldeburgh.*

Such is that room which one rude beam divides,
And naked rafters form the sloping sides;
Where the vile bands that bind the thatch are seen,
And lath and mud are all that lie between;
Save one dull pane, that, coarsely patch'd, gives way
To the rude tempest, yet excludes the day:
Here, on a matted flock, with dust o'erspread,
The drooping wretch reclines his languid head;
For him no hand the cordial cup applies,
Or wipes the tear that stagnates in his eyes;
No friends with soft discourse his pain beguile,
Or promise hope till sickness wears a smile.
But soon a loud and hasty summons calls,
Shakes the thin roof, and echoes round the walls;
Anon a figure enters, quaintly neat,
All pride and business, bustle and conceit;
With looks unalter'd by these scenes of woe,
With speed that, entering, speaks his haste to go
He bids the gazing throng around him fly,
And carries fate and physic in his eye;
A potent quack, long versed in human ills,
Who first insults the victim whom he kills;
Whose murd'rous hand a drowsy Bench protect,
And whose most tender mercy is neglect.
Paid by the parish for attendance here,
He wears contempt upon his sapient sneer;
In haste he seeks the bed where Misery lies,
Impatience mark'd in his averted eyes;
And, some habitual queries hurried o'er,
Without reply, he rushes on the door:
His drooping patient, long inured to pain,
And long unheeded, knows remonstrance vain;
He ceases now the feeble help to crave
Of man; and silent sinks into the grave.
But ere his death some pious doubts arise,
Some simple fears, which 'bold bad' men despise;
Fain would he ask the parish-priest to prove
His title certain to the joys above:

For this he sends the murmuring nurse, who calls
The holy stranger to these dismal walls:
And doth not he, the pious man, appear,
He, 'passing rich with forty pounds a year'?
Ah! no; a shepherd of a different stock,
And far unlike him, feeds this little flock:
A jovial youth, who thinks his Sunday's task
As much as God or man can fairly ask;
The rest he gives to loves and labours light,
To fields the morning, and to feasts the night;
None better skill'd the noisy pack to guide,
To urge their chase, to cheer them or to chide;
A sportsman keen, he shoots through half the day,
And, skill'd at whist, devotes the night to play:
Then, while such honours bloom around his head,
Shall he sit sadly by the sick man's bed,
To raise the hope he feels not, or with zeal
To combat fears that e'en the pious feel?
Now once again the gloomy scene explore,
Less gloomy now; the bitter hour is o'er,
The man of many sorrows sighs no more. –
Up yonder hill, behold how sadly slow
The bier moves winding from the vale below;
There lie the happy dead, from trouble free,
And the glad parish pays the frugal fee:
No more, O Death! thy victim starts to hear
Churchwarden stern, or kingly overseer;
No more the farmer claims his humble bow,
Thou art his lord, the best of tyrants thou!
Now to the church behold the mourners come,
Sedately torpid and devoutly dumb;
The village children now their games suspend,
To see the bier that bears their ancient friend;
For he was one in all their idle sport,
And like a monarch ruled their little court.
The pliant bow he form'd, the flying ball,
The bat, the wicket, were his labours all;
Him now they follow to his grave, and stand

Silent and sad, and gazing, hand in hand;
While bending low, their eager eyes explore
The mingled relics of the parish poor:
The bell tolls late, the moping owl flies round,
Fear marks the flight and magnifies the sound;
The busy priest, detain'd by weightier care,
Defers his duty till the day of prayer;
And, waiting long, the crowd retire distress'd,
To think a poor man's bones should lie unbless'd.

'But why are you to be a clergyman?', from Jane Austen (1775–1817), *Mansfield Park* (1814)

Jane Austen grew up in Steventon rectory, and apart from a few years in Bath after her father retired spent the rest of her life back in provincial Hampshire.

Mansfield Park *was her fourth novel. The Bertram family, in company with their charming and witty new acquaintances from London, Mary Crawford and her brother Henry, have been invited to visit nearby Sotherton Court; its owner, Mr. Rushworth, a wealthy if 'heavy young man', is intent on some fashionable 'improvements' to the grounds. Fanny Price is a poor relation who Sir Thomas Bertram took into Mansfield Park as a ward when she was a young girl; she is now eighteen. 'Creepmouse' Fanny eventually emerges from the goings-on at Mansfield Park as the unlikely heroine.*

'This is insufferably hot,' said Miss Crawford when they had taken one turn on the terrace, and were drawing a second time to the door in the middle which opened to the wilderness. 'Shall any of us object to being comfortable? Here is a nice little wood, if one can but get into it. What happiness if the door should not be locked! – but of course it is, for in these great places, the gardeners are the only people who can go where they like.'

The door, however, proved not to be locked, and they were all agreed in turning joyfully through it, and leaving the unmitigated glare of day behind. A considerable flight of steps landed them in the wilderness, which was a planted wood of about two acres, and though chiefly of larch and laurel, and beech cut down, and though laid out with too much regularity, was darkness and shade, and natural beauty, compared with the bowling-green and the terrace. They all felt the refreshment of it, and for some time could only walk and admire. At length, after a short pause, Miss Crawford began with, 'So you are to be a clergyman, Mr. Bertram. This is rather a surprise to me.'

'Why should it surprise you? You must suppose me designed for some profession, and might perceive that I am neither a lawyer, nor a soldier, nor a sailor.'

'Very true; but, in short, it had not occurred to me. And you know there is generally an uncle or a grandfather to leave a fortune to the second son.'

'A very praiseworthy practice,' said Edmund, 'but not quite universal. I am one of the exceptions, and *being* one, must do something for myself.'

'But why are you to be a clergyman? I thought *that* was always the lot of the youngest, where there were many to choose before him.'

'Do you think the church itself never chosen then?'

'*Never* is a black word. But yes, in the *never* of conversation which means *not very often*, I do think it. For what is to be done in the church? Men love to distinguish themselves, and in either of the other lines, distinction may be gained, but not in the church. A clergyman is nothing.'

'The *nothing* of conversation has its gradations, I hope, as well as the *never*. A clergyman cannot be high in state or fashion. He must not head mobs, or set the tone in dress. But I cannot call that situation nothing, which has the charge of all that is of the first importance to mankind, individually or collectively considered, temporally and eternally – which has the guardianship of religion and morals, and consequently of the manners which result from their influence. No one here can call the *office* nothing. If the man who holds it is so, it is by the neglect of his duty, by forgoing its just importance, and stepping out of his place to appear what he ought not to appear.'

'*You* assign greater consequence to the clergyman than one has been used to hear given, or that I can quite comprehend. One does not see much of this influence and importance in society, and how can it be acquired where they are so seldom seen themselves? How can two sermons a week, even supposing them worth hearing, supposing the preacher to have the sense to prefer Blair's to his own [Blair was an eighteenth-century Scottish preacher who published five volumes of sermons], do all that you speak of? govern the conduct and fashion the manners of a large congregation for the rest of the week? One scarcely sees a clergyman out of his pulpit.'

'*You* are speaking of London, I am speaking of the nation at large.'

'The metropolis, I imagine, is a pretty fair sample of the rest.'

'Not, I should hope, of the proportion of virtue to vice throughout the kingdom. We do not look to great cities for our best morality. It is not there, that respectable people of any denomination can do most good; and it certainly is not there, that the influence of the clergy can be most felt. A fine preacher is followed and admired; but it is not in fine preaching only that a good clergyman will be useful in his parish and his neighbourhood, where the parish and neighbourhood are of a size capable of knowing his private character, and observing his general conduct, which in London can rarely be the case. The clergy there are lost in the crowds of their parishioners. They are known to the largest part only as preachers. And with regard to their influencing public manners, Miss Crawford must not misunderstand me, or suppose that I mean to call them the arbiters of good breeding, the regulators of refinement and courtesy, the masters of the ceremonies of life. The *manners* I speak of, might rather be called *conduct*, perhaps, the result of good principles; the effect, in short, of those doctrines which it is their duty to teach and recommend; and it will, I believe, be every where found, that as the clergy are, or are not what they ought to be, so are the rest of the nation.'

'Certainly,' said Fanny with quiet earnestness.

'There,' cried Miss Crawford, 'you have quite convinced Miss Price already.'

'I wish I could convince Miss Crawford too.'

'On the Causes of Methodism', from William Hazlitt (1778–1830), *The Round Table* (1817)

The son of a Unitarian minister, after his own training for the ministry Hazlitt developed an 'extreme distaste' for the religious life, and forged a prominent career as a journalist, essayist and lecturer.

The first Methodist on record was David. He was the first person we read of, who made a regular compromise between religion and morality, between faith and good works. After any trifling peccadillo in point of conduct, as a murder, adultery, perjury, or the like, he ascended with his harp into some high tower of his palace; and having chaunted, in a solemn strain of poetical inspiration, the praises of piety and virtue, made his peace with heaven and his own conscience. This extraordinary genius, in the midst of his personal errors, retained the same lofty abstract enthusiasm for the favourite objects of his contemplation; the character of the poet and the prophet remained unimpaired by the vices of the man – 'Pure in the last recesses of the mind;' – and the best test of the soundness of his principles and the elevation of his sentiments, is, that they were proof against his practice. The Gnostics afterwards maintained, that it was no matter what a man's actions were, so that his understanding was not debauched by them – so that his opinions continue uncontaminated, and *his heart,* as the phrase is, *right towards God.* Strictly speaking, this sect (whatever name it might go by) is as old as human nature itself; for it has existed ever since there was a contradiction between the passions and the understanding – between what we are, and what we desire to be. The principle of Methodism is nearly allied to hypocrisy, and almost unavoidably slides into it: yet it is not the same thing; for we can hardly call anyone a hypocrite, however much at variance his professions and his actions, who really wishes to be what he would be thought.

The Jewish bard, whom we have placed at the head of this class of devotees, was of a sanguine and robust temperament. Whether he chose to 'sinner it or saint it,' he did both royally, with a fulness of gusto, and carried off his penances and his *faux pas* in a style of oriental grandeur. This is by no means the character of his followers among ourselves, who are a most pitiful set. They may rather be considered as a collection of religious invalids; as the refuse of all that is weak and unsound in body and mind. To speak of them as they deserve, they are not well in the flesh, and therefore they take refuge in the spirit; they are not comfortable here, and they seek for the life to come; they are deficient in steadiness of moral principles, and they trust to grace to make up the deficiency; they are dull and gross in apprehension, and therefore they are glad to substitute faith for reason, and to plunge in the dark, under the supposed sanction of superior wisdom, into every species of mystery and jargon. This is the history of Methodism, which may be defined to be religion with its slabbering-bib and go-cart. It is a bastard kind of Popery, stripped of its painted pomp and outward ornaments, and reduced to a state of pauperism. 'The whole need not a physician.' Popery owed its success to its constant appeal to the senses and to the weakness of mankind. The Church of England deprives the Methodists of the pride and pomp of the Romish Church: but it has left open to them the appeal to the indolence, the ignorance, and the vices of the people; and the secret of the success of the Catholic faith and evangelical preaching is the same – both are a religion by proxy. What the one did by auricular confessions, absolution, penance, pictures, and crucifixes, the other does, even more compendiously, by grace, election, faith without works, and words without meaning.

In the first place, the same reason makes a man a religious enthusiast that makes a man an enthusiast in any other way, an uncomfortable mind in an uncomfortable body. Poets, authors, and artists in general, have been ridiculed for a pining, puritanical, poverty-struck appearance, which has been attributed to their real poverty. But it would perhaps be nearer the truth to say, that their being poets, artists, &c. has been owing to their original poverty of spirit and weakness of constitution. As a general rule, those who are dissatisfied with themselves, will seek to go out of themselves into an ideal world. Persons in strong health and spirits, who take plenty of air and exercise, who are 'in favour with their stars,' and have a thorough relish of the good things of this life, seldom devote themselves in despair to religion or the Muses. Sedentary, nervous, hypochondriacal people, on the contrary, are forced, for want of an appetite for the real and substantial, to look out for a more airy food and speculative comforts. If you live near a chapel or tabernacle in London, you may almost always tell, from physiognomical signs, which of the passengers will turn the corner to go there. We were once staying in a remote place in the country, where a chapel of this sort had been erected by the force of missionary zeal: and in the morning, we perceived a long procession of people coming from the next town to the consecration of this same chapel. Never was there such a set of scarecrows. Melancholy tailors, consumptive hair-dressers, squinting coblers, women with child or in the ague, made up the forlorn hope of the pious cavalcade. The pastor of this half-starved flock, we confess, came riding after, with a more goodly aspect, as if he had 'with sound of bell been knelled to church, and sat at good men's feasts.' He had in truth lately married a thriving widow, and been pampered with hot suppers, to strengthen the flesh and the spirit. We have seen several of these 'round fat oily men of God, That shone all glittering with ungodly dew' [quoting James Thomson's 1748 poem *The Castle of Indolence*]. They grow sleek and corpulent by getting into better pasture, but they do not appear healthy. They retain the original sin of their constitution, an atrabilious taint in their complexion, and do not put a right-down, hearty, honest, good-looking face upon the matter, like the regular clergy.

Again, Methodism, by its leading doctrines, has a peculiar charm for all these, who have an equal facility in sinning and repenting, – in whom the spirit is willing, but the flesh is weak, – who have neither fortitude to withstand temptation, nor to silence the admonitions of conscience, – who like the theory of religion better than the practice, – and are willing to indulge in all the raptures of speculative devotion, without being tied down to the dull, literal performance of its duties. There is a general propensity in the human mind (even in the most vicious) to pay virtue a distant homage; and this desire is only checked, by the fear of condemning ourselves by our own acknowledgments. What an admirable expedient then in 'that burning and shining light,' Whitefield [the tireless evangelist who gripped crowds of thousands in America as well as Britain], and his associates, to make this very disposition to admire and extol the highest patterns of goodness, a substitute for, instead of an obligation to, the practice of virtue, to allow us to be quit for 'the vice that most easily besets us,' by canting lamentations over the depravity of human nature, and loud hosannahs to the Son of David! How comfortably this doctrine must sit on all those who are loth to give up old habits of vice, or are just tasting the sweets of new ones; on the withered hag who looks back on a life of dissipation, or the young devotee who looks forward to a life of pleasure: the knavish tradesman retiring from business, or entering on it; the battered rake; the sneaking politician, who trims between his place and his conscience, wriggling between heaven and earth, a miserable two-legged creature, with sanctified face and fawning gestures; the maudling sentimentalist, the religious prostitute, the disinterested poet-laureat, the humane war-contractor, or the Society for the Suppression of Vice! This scheme happily turns morality into a sinecure, takes all the practical drudgery and trouble off your hands, 'and sweet religion makes a rhapsody of words.' Its proselytes besiege the gates of heaven, like sturdy beggars about the doors of the great, lie and bask in the sunshine of divine grace, sigh and groan and bawl out for mercy, expose their sores and blotches to excite commiseration, and cover the deformities of their nature with a garb of borrowed righteousness!

The jargon and nonsense that are so studiously inculcated in the system, are another powerful recommendation of it to the vulgar. It does not impose any tax upon the understanding. Its essence is to be unintelligible. It is a *carte blanche* for ignorance and folly! Those 'numbers without number,' who are either unable or unwilling to think connectedly or rationally on any subject, are at once released from every obligation of the kind, by being told that faith and reason are opposed to one another, and the greater the impossibility, the greater the merit of the faith. A set of phrases which, without conveying any distinct idea, excite our wonder, our fear, our curiosity and desires, which let loose the imagination of the gaping multitude, and confound and baffle common sense, are the common stock-in-trade of the conventicle. They never stop for the distinctions of the understanding, and have thus got the start of other sects, who are so hemmed in with the necessity of giving reasons for their opinions, that they cannot get on at all. 'Vital Christianity' is no other than an attempt to lower all religion to the level of the capacities of the lowest of the people. One of their favourite places of worship combines the noise and turbulence of a drunken brawl at an ale-house, with the indecencies of a bagnio. They strive to gain a vertigo by abandoning their reason, and give themselves up to the intoxications of a distempered zeal, that

'Dissolves them into ecstasies
And brings all heaven before their eyes.'

Religion, without superstition, will not answer the purposes of fanaticism, and we may safely say, that almost every sect of Christianity is a perversion of its essence, to accommodate it to the prejudices of the world. The Methodists have greased the boots of the Presbyterians, and they have done well. While the latter are weighing their doubts and scruples to the division of a hair, and shivering on the narrow brink that divides philosophy from religion, the former plunge without remorse into hell-flames, – soar on the wings of divine love, – are carried away with the motions of the spirit, – are lost in the unfathomable mysteries, election, reprobation, predestination, – and revel in a sea of boundless nonsense. It is a gulf that swallows up every thing. The cold, the calculating, and the dry, are not to the taste of the many; religion is an anticipation of the preternatural world, and it in general requires preternatural excitements to keep it alive. If it takes a definite consistent form, it loses its interest: to produce its effect, it must come in the shape of an apparition. Our quacks treat grown people as nurses do the children: – terrify them with what they have no idea of, or take them to a puppet show.

'I begin to hate Parsons': John Keats (1795–1821) in a letter to his brother George and sister-in-law Georgiana, 14 February 1819

From a long letter that Keats compiled for his brother George and his sister-in-law (who had emigrated to America in June 1818). Only a few weeks earlier he had nursed their brother Tom, just nineteen years old, to his death from tuberculosis, and was taking a badly needed break with his friend Brown in Chichester.

The owner of Stansted Park had turned a former hunting lodge into a chapel of delicate Regency Gothic, and on 25 January Keats had attended its long consecration – a great local event. (The owner, Lewis Way, had come into a fortune, given up the law, and been ordained in 1817. He spent his money generously but did not always meet with gratitude.) Keats's 'annus mirabilis' as a poet began to unfold the following April.

I have not gone on with Hyperion – for to tell the truth I have not been in great cue for writing lately – I must wait for the spring to rouse me up a little – The only time I went out from Bedhampton was to see a Chapel consecrated – Brown, I and John Snook the boy went in a chaise behind a leaden horse, Brown drove, but the horse did not mind him – This Chapel is built by a Mr. Way, a great Jew converter – who in that line has spent one hundred thousand Pounds. He maintains a great number of poor Jews. … The Chapel is built in Mr. Way's park – The Consecration was – not amusing – there were numbers of carriages, and his house was crammed with Clergy – they sanctified the Chapel – and it being a wet day consecrated the burial ground through the vestry window. I begin to hate Parsons – they did not make me love them that day – when I saw them in their proper colours – A Parson is a Lamb in a drawing room and a lion in a vestry. The notions of Society will not permit a Parson to give way to his temper in any shape – so he festers in himself – his features get a peculiar diabolical self-sufficient iron stupid expression. He is continually acting. His mind is against every Man and every Mans mind is against him. He is an Hippocrite to the Believer and a Coward to the unbeliever – He must be either a Knave or an Ideot. And there is no Man so much to be pitied as an ideot parson. The Soldier who is cheated into an esprit du corps – by a red coat, a Band and Colours for the purpose of nothing – is not half so pitiable as the Parson who is led by the nose by the Bench of Bishops – and is smothered in absurdities – a poor necessary subaltern of the Church …

'I am in fact a pig driver', from the *Diary* of the Rev. John Skinner (1772–1839)

Skinner was vicar of Claverton, Somerset, and an amateur archaeologist with an obsessive bent. His personal and parochial trials and tribulations are revealingly evident from the three trunks of papers left behind after he shot himself. Virginia Woolf wrote a sympathetic short account of his life and world in her essay 'Two Parsons' (the other was Woodforde).

June 10th, 1822

I went into the field where they were tithing Day's rye grass. Smallcombe and Heal, who were appointed to take up the tithe, I had heard were dissatisfied because I did not allow them beer, and on enquiring for Smallcombe learnt he was gone to the Red Post public house, thinking if he took the opportunity of my dinner hour I should not discover it. I took the direction of the Red Post, and found him seated very comfortably with his beer before him. However, his enjoyment was not of long duration, since I took him by the collar of his jacket and soon showed him the way to the door. He begged to go back to drink his beer, but this I would not permit him to do. Having seen him into the field I arrived when dinner was over, but I was so warm both internally and externally I had little inclination to eat anything.

June 11th

On making enquiries what had been done as to tithing the evening before, and understanding that Smallcombe had left the field at six o'clock, although Day continue hauling till ten (consequently all the tithing was done by his people), I went to Smallcombe, and, after upbraiding him with his great ingratitude and insolence, dismissed him.

This man I have attended and relieved in sickness, employed him when he could not get employment elsewhere during the dead part of the year, and now because work is plenty he behaves in this manner. When I said he would doubtless suffer for his conduct before the next winter was over, and probably groan again on a bed of sickness without a friend to relieve him as I had done in his distress, instead of being called to any grateful recollection by this apostrophe he replied, many a parson might groan in hell, which was still worse. As Smallcombe took a scythe, pickaxe and shovel with him from the Glebe House, which I had no opportunity of examining, I walked down to his cottage to endeavour to ascertain whether they were his own. Mrs. Smallcombe was in the house, and immediately began by asking what business I had on her premises: that I had turned her husband off mine, and I should not come on hers. I replied I had business to visit any place in my parish; that when her husband had been so ill, and I frequently called to see and relieve him, neither she nor her husband then found fault with me for coming on the premises. She replied, if I did come then she did not send for me and never should again, nor should I ever again enter her garden. The insolence of this woman increased and her fury became so violent and her countenance so distorted she resembled one of the witches in the painting of Sir Joshua Reynolds. 'You are a parson, a shepherd of the flock, to come here,' she vociferated, 'and insult a poor woman like me (because I called her 'beldame'). You will smart for this, I assure you, I assure you.' Tyler's wife, a very rank Methodist, who was in the house, then began to join in the contest and asked whether I was not ashamed of myself to call such names: that I might talk about canting Methodists, but there never was a Churchman like me in a house but the Devil was there also. I then said, 'Woman, such expressions I might make you answer for in the Ecclesiastical Court, if you were not infinitely beneath my notice.' Her husband then came in and compelled her to go back to his own home, but not before she had retorted in the greatest rage, 'Why, you called Mrs. Smallcombe worse; you said she was a "Beldame."' I asked her what she supposed was meant by that? And when I explained that it meant a scold, both she and Smallcombe's wife became more tranquil, and said they had supposed it meant something much worse.

I particularise these absurd scenes, not only because they are worth recording as curiosities but, in another point of view, they are indices of the malignity of these sectarists. Both Smallcombe and this Tyler's wife gave the same pious expressions towards the clergy: the one that parsons would howl in hell, and the other that where there was a Churchman like me in a house there was the Devil. I am heartily sick of the flock over which I am nominated and placed: instead of being a shepherd, as I told the methodistical beldame when she twitted me with the name, I am in fact a pig driver; I despise myself most thoroughly for suffering irritation from such vermin. Leaving these scenes of discord, I endeavoured to tranquilise my mind by visiting those more softened by sickness and sorrow, and to converse with those who do indeed need assistance.

On returning home to dinner I found an invitation from Mr. Johnson to join the party at Timsbury House in the evening. As my mind needed some change of idea, I determined on accepting it. I mounted my horse about six, on my arrival at Mr. Palmer's found a large party was expected: Mr. and Mrs. Barter, Colonel and Mrs. Scobel, Captain Savage, Mr. James [Deputy Lieutenant for the county] and family, etc. After tea, they stood up to dance, one of the ladies playing upon the piano. I danced two sets with Mrs. Scobel, formerly Mrs. James, with whom I used to dance in former times at Bath and Weymouth; sed tempora mutantur [but times are changed]. As the evening was dark Mrs. Palmer invited me to take my bed at her house. I was glad to accept the offer, and reposed very comfortably in the Ancient Mansion of the Sambournes, without being interrupted by ghosts or goblins.

June 12th (Timsbury House)

I walked about the premises before breakfast, and am pretty well assured there was a fortified post on the hill on which the Mansion is built. As my obliging entertainers did everything to render my stay with them agreeable, and I knew it would be tout au contraire if I returned to my Tithemakers in the Hayfield I came to the resolution of enjoying for a day longer the lively conversation of the better part of our species, and lounged away the morning in their society, and I may add, the evening too, as I took an interesting walk on a charitable errand after dinner under the direction of Miss Palmer and Mr. Johnson, who conducted me to visit a poor girl, who had both her legs broken by a wagon passing over them, and has supported her sufferings with exemplary patience.

I occupied my apartment in the old Mansion, having despatched a person to Camerton, to inform my housekeeper of my intention, and to procure me some linen.

William Cobbett (1763–1835), from *Rural rides in the counties of Surrey, Kent, Sussex, etc.* (1830)

Self-educated and fearless radical and activist, both in America and back in England, Cobbett constantly aimed his pen at 'the vermin-breeding system'. He eventually became an MP in the parliament (1832) he had fought so hard to reform.

Sunday, August 30th 1823
I got to Goudhurst to breakfast, and as I heard that the Dean of Rochester was to preach a sermon on behalf of the *National Schools*, I stopped to hear him. In waiting for his reverence I went to the Methodist Meeting-house, where I found the Sunday school boys and girls assembled, to the almost filling of the place, which was about thirty feet long and eighteen wide. The 'minister' was not come, and the schoolmaster was reading to the children out of a *tract-book*, and shaking the brimstone bag at them most furiously. This schoolmaster was a sleek-looking young fellow, his skin perfectly tight: well fed, I'll warrant him: and he has discovered the way of living, without work, on the labour of those that do work. There were 36 little fellows in smock-frocks, and about as many girls listening to him; and I dare say he eats as much meat as any ten of them.

By this time the *dean*, I thought, would be coming on; and, therefore, to the church I went; but to my great disappointment, I found that the parson was operating *preparatory* to the appearance of the dean, who was to come on in the afternoon, when I, agreeably to my plan, must be off. … In his sermon he called upon them to subscribe with all their hearts; but alas! How little of *persuasive power* was there in what he said! No effort to make them see *the use of the schools*. No inducement *proved* to exist. No argument, in short, nor anything to move. No appeal to the *reason* or to the *feeling*. All was general, commonplace, cold observation; and that, too, in language which the far greater part of the hearers could not understand.

This church is about 110 feet long and 70 feet wide in the clear. It would hold *three thousand people*, and it had in it 214, besides 53 Sunday School or National School boys; and these sat together, in a sort of lodge, up in a corner, 16 feet long and 10 feet wide. Now, will any Parson Malthus, or anybody else, have the impudence to tell me that this church was built for the use of a population not much more numerous than the present? … The Methodists cannot take away above four or five hundred; and what, then, was this great church built *for*, if there were no more people, in those days, at Goudhurst, than there are now? It is very true that the *labouring* people have, in great measure, ceased to go to church. There were scarcely any of that class at this great country church to-day. I do not believe there were *ten*. I can remember when they were so numerous that the parson could not attempt to begin till the rattling of their nailed shoes ceased. I have seen, I am sure, five hundred boys and men in smock-frocks coming out of church at one time. To-day has been a fine day: there would have been many at church to-day, if ever there are; and here I have another to add to the many things that convince me that the labouring classes have, in great part, ceased to go to church; that their way of thinking and feeling with regard to both church and clergy are totally changed; and that there is now very little *moral hold* which the latter possess. …

Coming through the village of Benenden, I heard a man at my right talking very loud about *houses! houses! houses!* It was a Methodist parson, in a house close by the road side. I pulled up, and stood still, in the middle of the road, but looking, in silent soberness, into the window (which was open) of the room in which the preacher was at work. I believe my stopping rather disconcerted him, for he got into shocking *repetition*. 'Do you *know*,' said he, laying great stress on the word *know*: 'do you *know*, that you have ready for you houses, houses, I say; I say do you know; do you know that you have houses in the heavens not made with hands? Do you know this from *experience?* Has the blessed Jesus *told you so?*' And on he went to say that, if Jesus had told them so, they would be saved, and that if he had not, they would be damned. Some girls whom I saw in the room, plump and rosy as could be, did not seem at all daunted by these menaces; and indeed, they appeared to me to be thinking much more about getting houses for themselves *in this world first; just to see a little* before they entered, or endeavoured to enter, or even thought much about, those '*houses*' of which the parson was speaking: houses with pig-styes and little snug gardens attached to them, together with all the other domestic and conjugal circumstances these girls seemed to me to be preparing themselves for. The truth is, these fellows have no power on the minds of any but the miserable.

A passion for the chase, from E. W. L. Davies (1812–1894), *A Memoir of the Rev. John Russell and his out-of-door Life* (1878)

Jack Russell (1795–1883) was ordained after Oxford, and began his parochial and celebrated hunting life in Devon. Davies wrote his Memoir *a few years before the legend's death.*

If hunting in itself be no sin, then it is an innocent pastime; and if so, why, if their sacred duties be duly fulfilled, should clergymen be denied its enjoyment? Is it not an act of tyranny and asceticism to say to them, 'You are free to boat, shoot, fish, play cricket or lawn-tennis, and ride – but not with hounds; no, that is a recreation you shall not share with your fellow-men'?

But the French proverb, which says, *Qui s'excuse s'accuse*, must not be forgotten; and Russell himself would be the last to admit the need of apology on such a point. He would say what an old country clergyman, who had been scurrilously attacked for his love of the chase, said before him: 'I only wish my hours of recreation had all been spent as happily and as innocently as in the hunting-field; but point out to me the moral turpitude of hunting, and I'll never follow a hound again.'

To be planted as a curate on £60 a year at George Nympton, and to vegetate like a cabbage among a scanty population, engaged chiefly in agricultural labour; to pass his days without one out-of-door occupation beyond that of paying an occasional visit to a suffering cottager or a busy farmer; to endure the solitude of an Eremite, compared with the lively, social scene he had so recently quitted, was a state of existence so little in accordance with the stirring aspirations of Russell's mind, that the want of 'something to do' became almost a torture to him.

Against books requiring close study his whole nature rebelled; they had too long been his bane both at school and at college; and rather than be forced to read, he would almost have endured the pains of purgatory.

The God of Nature would surely never have given him that innate love for a sylvan life which possessed him even on entering the world; nor would He have blessed him with those eagle wings which have enabled him so long to enjoy it, if he had been intended for a recluse or a mere book-worm; for, as well might the spots of the bearded pard be expunged, as that instinct blotted out from Russell's nature. ...

He had been but a short time in harness at George Nympton, when he was required by his rector, who was also curate of South Molton, to undertake the weekly duty of that parish besides that of his own. With this request he readily complied; and settling at South Molton, that being a convenient centre for his double work, he fulfilled the duties of both parishes for a considerable period; and this, too, with no little amount of additional labour, but without additional pay.

Nevertheless, had the sphere of his duty been quadrupled, the parochial work alone would still have been utterly insufficient to supply a man of Russell's powers with full occupation of body and mind. The early habits of his life, his wondrous energy, his muscular frame, the strength and endurance of which no fatigue seemed capable of subduing; and, above all, that innate fire – his love, or, to call it by its right name, his passion for the chase – combined irresistibly to suggest a stronger exercise than any he could find from the due fulfilment of parochial labour, however great that might be. So to hounds he turned – the summit to him of earthly enjoyment and manly recreation.

'December', from John Clare (1793–1864), *The Shepherd's Calendar* (1827)

The Northamptonshire farm labourer's Poems Descriptive of Rural Life *(1820) caused a small stir in the literary world with the freshness and truth of their evocations. But changing fashion denied him the recognition he has today for his eye and feeling for the human and the natural. Editors struggle now, as then, with the mess of his manuscripts and their alterations, and with how far to 'correct' the language natural to him. As Clare himself complained in a letter of 1825, 'Editors are troubled with nice amendings & if Doctors were as fond of amputation as they are of altering & correcting the world would have nothing but cripples.'*

Christmass is come and every hearth
Makes room to give him welcome now
Een want will dry its tears in mirth
And crown him wi a holly bough
Tho tramping neath a winters sky
Oer snow track paths and ryhmey [*sic*] stiles
The huswife sets her spinning bye
And bids him welcome wi her smiles

Each house is swept the day before
And windows stuck wi evergreens
The snow is beesomd [swept] from the door
And comfort crowns the cottage scenes
Gilt holly wi its thorny pricks
And yew and box wi berrys small
These deck the unusd candlesticks
And pictures hanging by the wall

Neighbours resume their annual cheer
Wishing wi smiles and spirits high
Glad christmass and a happy year
To every morning passer bye
Milk maids their christmass journeys go
Accompanyd wi favourd swain
And children pace the crumping snow
To taste their grannys cake again ...

Old customs O I love the sound
However simple they may be
What ere wi time has sanction found
Is welcome and is dear to me
Pride grows above simplicity
And spurns it from her haughty mind
And soon the poets song will be
The only refuge they can find.

The shepherd now no more afraid
Since custom doth the chance bestow
Starts up to kiss the giggling maid
Beneath the branch of mizzletoe

That neath each cottage beam is seen
Wi pearl-like berrys shining gay
The shadow still of what hath been
Which fashion yearly fades away

And singers too a merry throng
At early morn wi simple skill
Yet imitate the angels song
And chant their christmass ditty still
And mid the storm that dies and swells
By fits – in humings softly steals
The music of the village bells
Ringing round their merry peals

And when its past a merry crew
Bedeckt in masks and ribbons gay
The 'Morrice danse' their sports renew
And act their winter evening play
The clown-turnd-kings for penny praise
Storm wi the actors strut and swell
And harlequin a laugh to raise
Wears his hump back and tinkling bell.

And oft for pence and spicy ale
Wi winter nosgays pind before
The wassail singer tells her tale
And drawls her christmass carrols oer
The prentice boy wi ruddy face
And rhyme bepowderd dancing locks
From door to door wi happy pace
Runs round to claim his 'christmass box' …

While snows the window panes bedim
The fire curls up a sunny charm
Where creaming oer the pitchers rim
The flowering ale is set to warm
Mirth full of joy as summers bees
Sits there its pleasure to impart
While children tween their parents knees
Sing scraps of carrols oer by heart

And some to view the winter weathers
Climb up the window seat wi glee
Likening the snow to falling feathers
In fancys infant extacy
Laughing wi superstitious love
Oer visions wild that youth supplyes
Of people pulling geese above
And keeping christmass in the skyes ...

Thou day of happy sound and mirth
That long wi childish memory stays
How blest around the cottage hearth
I met thee in my boyish days
Harping wi raptures dreaming joys
On presents that thy coming found
The welcome sight of little toys
The christmass gifts of comers round

The wooden horse wi arching head
Drawn upon wheels around the room
The gilded coach of ginger bread
And many colord sugar plumb
Gilt coverd books for pictures sought
Or storys childhood loves to tell
Wi many a urgent promise bought
To get tomorrows lesson well ...

Around the glowing hearth at night
The harmless laugh and winter tale
Goes round – while parting friends delight
To toast each other oer their ale
The cotter oft wi quiet zeal
Will musing oer his bible lean
While in the dark the lovers steal
To kiss and toy behind the screen

The yule cake dotted thick wi plumbs
Is on each supper table found
And cats look up for falling crumbs
Which greedy children litter round

And huswifes sage stuffed seasond chine
Long hung in chimney nook to drye
And boiling eldern berry wine
To drink the christmas eves 'good bye'

'Advice to Parishioners' by Sydney Smith (1771–1845), from the *Memoir* (1855) written by his daughter, Lady Holland

Parson, wit, one of the founders of the Edinburgh Review *(1802), Smith was a popular preacher, lecturer and society guest in London, and a conscientious minister during his years in Yorkshire and Somerset. Here, he mock-plays the Justice of the Peace.*

If you begin stealing a little, you will go on from little to much, and soon become a regular thief; and then you will be hanged, or sent over seas to Botany Bay. And give me leave to tell you, transportation is no joke. Up at five in the morning, dressed in a jacket half blue, half yellow, chained on to another person like two dogs, a man standing over you with a great stick, weak porridge for breakfast, bread and water for dinner, boiled beans for supper, straw to lie upon; and all this for thirty years; and then you are hanged there by order of the government, without judge or jury. All this is very disagreeable, and you had far better avoid it by making a solemn resolution to take nothing which does not belong to you.

Never sit in wet clothes. Off with them as soon as you can: no constitution can stand it. Look at Jackson, who lives next door to the blacksmith; he was the strongest man in the parish. Twenty different times I warned him of his folly in wearing wet clothes. He pulled off his hat and smiled, and was very civil, but clearly seemed to think it all old woman's nonsense. He is now, as you see, bent double with rheumatism, is living upon parish allowance, and scarcely able to crawl from pillar to post.

Off with your hat when you meet a gentleman. What does it cost? Gentlemen notice these things, are offended if the civility is not paid, and pleased if it is; and what harm does it do you? When first I came to this parish, Squire Tempest wanted a postillion, John Barton was a good, civil fellow; and in thinking over the names of the village, the Squire thought of Barton, remembered his constant civility, sent for one of his sons, made him postillion, then coachman, then bailiff, and he now holds a farm under the Squire of £500 per annum. Such things are constantly happening. ...

I must positively forbid all poaching; it is absolute ruin to yourself and your family. In the end you are sure to be detected – a hare in one pocket and a pheasant in the other. How are you to pay ten pounds? You have not tenpence beforehand in the world. Daniel's breeches are unpaid for; you have a hole in your hat, and want a new one; your wife, an excellent woman, is about to lie in – and you are, all of a sudden, called upon by the Justice to pay ten pounds. I shall never forget the sight of poor Cranford, hurried to Taunton Jail; a wife and three daughters on their knees to the Justice, who was compelled to do his duty, and commit him. The next day, beds, chairs, and clothes sold, to get the father out of jail. Out of jail he came; but the poor fellow could not bear the sight of his naked cottage, and to see his family pinched with hunger. You know how he ended his days. Was there a dry eye in the church-yard when he was buried? It was a lesson to poachers. It is indeed a desperate and foolish trade. Observe, I am not defending the game-laws, but I am advising you, as long as the game-laws exist, to fear them, and to take care that you and your family are not crushed by them. And then, smart, stout young men hate the game-keeper, and make it a point of courage and spirit to oppose him. Why? The game-keeper is paid to protect the game, and he would be a very dishonest man if he did not do his duty. What right have you to bear malice against him for this? After all, the game in justice belongs to the land-owners, who feed it; and not to you, who have no land at all, and can feed nothing.

I don't like that red nose, and those blear eyes, and that stupid, downcast look. You are a drunkard. Another pint, and one pint more; a glass of gin and water, rum and milk, cider and pepper, a glass of peppermint, and all the beastly fluids which drunkards pour down their throats. It is very possible to conquer it, if you will but be resolute. ...

It is all nonsense about not being able to work without ale, and gin, and cider, and fermented liquors. Do lions and cart-horses drink ale? It is mere habit. If you have good nourishing food, you can do very well without ale. Nobody works harder than the Yorkshire people, and for years together there are many Yorkshire labourers who never taste ale. I have no objection, you will observe, to a moderate use of ale, or any other liquor you can afford to purchase. My objection is, that you cannot afford it; that every penny you spend at the ale-house comes out of the stomachs of the poor children, and strips off the clothes of the wife.

My dear little Nanny, don't believe a word he says. He merely means to ruin and deceive you. You have a plain answer to give: 'When I am axed in the church, and the parson has read the service, and all about it is written in the book, then I will listen to your nonsense, and not before.' Am not I a Justice of the Peace, and have not I had a hundred foolish girls brought before me, who have all come with the same story? 'Please your worship, he is a false man; he promised me marriage over and over again.' I confess I have often wished for the power of hanging these rural lovers. But what use is my wishing? All that can be done with the villain is to make him pay half a crown a week, and you are handed over to the poor-house, and to infamy. Will no example teach you? Look to Mary Willet – three years ago the handsomest and best girl in the village, now a slattern in the poor-house! Look at Harriet Dobson, who trusted in the promises of James Harefield's son, and, after being abandoned by him, went away in despair with a party of soldiers! How can you be such a fool as to surrender your character to the stupid flattery of a ploughboy? If the evening is pleasant, and birds sing, and flowers bloom, is that any reason why you are to forget God's Word, the happiness of your family, and your own character? A profligate carpenter, or a debauched watch-maker, may gain business from their skill; but how is a profligate woman to gain her bread? Who will receive *her*?

Hartley Coleridge (1796–1849), from *On Parish Clerks, and Parish Vestries*

Hartley Coleridge, the eldest son of Samuel Taylor Coleridge, was an essayist and poet.

The interests of the Church imperiously demand that the duties of the clerk should always be performed, not, indeed, by a clergyman, but by a person of respectability and education. The place is too often conferred, I fear, from motives of favour or mistaken charity, or more mistaken economy; with little regard to character and none at all to acquirement, beyond the simple capacity to read, write, and set a psalm, on individuals who have no better claims than having been an old servant, or having large families, or being like to be burdensome to the parish. How often, in town and country, do we hear and see our divine Liturgy rendered absolutely ludicrous by all imaginable tones, twangs, drawls, mouthings, wheezings, gruntings, snuffles, and quid-rollings, by all diversity of dialects, cacologies, and cacophonies, by twistings, and contortions, and consolidations of visage, squintings, and blinkings, and upcastings of eyes, which remind one more of Punch than of any animated comedian; and where the schoolmaster has been abroad, we are not seldom nauseated by conceited airs and prim grimaces, and pronouncing dictionary affectations, that make us heartily wish for the old grotesques again. Then, too, the discretion assumed by these Hogarthic studies, of selecting the tunes and the verses to be sung, makes the Psalmody, instead of an integral and affecting portion of the Service, as distracting and irrelevant an episode as the jigs and country-dances scraped between the acts of a tragedy. These selections of four stanzas out of a long psalm, cut off from all connection and signification, are, at best, unmeaning; but they very frequently are made to allude slily to the politics of the day or the scandal of the village, and so, if they do not produce a universal titter, or a downright commotion, give rise to infinite shuffling, whispering, knowing looks, smiles, and frowns, and a train of thoughts and feelings very unfit for the place and occasion.

'John Ashford – In Sickness and Poverty', from G. W. Fulcher (1795–1855), *The Village Paupers* (1834)

Fulcher was a printer in Sudbury, Suffolk, where he was also a magistrate, four times mayor, and governor of the Court of Guardians. He was said to have known the work of Crabbe and Cowper 'almost by rote', and also produced a biography of Gainsborough. This is his loud and informed protest against the new 1834 Poor Law.

John Ashford has been a strong farmworker, skilful enough to have won the local ploughing competition. But now, struck down by illness, he and his well-brought-up family are faced by ruin. When their last possessions have been sold for bread, his only hope lies in applying for temporary poor relief. The Board of Guardians is sympathetic, but the regulations of the new Poor Law prevent this: they can only offer to take two of his children into the workhouse. Parents and children cannot face this prospect. John returns to work before he has fully recovered, becoming so ill again that starvation forces the whole family into the workhouse – but it is too late for John.

When sickness takes the Peasant's strength away,
Who has not seen him struggling day by day,
With honest poverty and manly pride
For his dear children vainly to provide?

– Who has not seen the nerveless arm sink down,
When the high spirit still would urge it on?
– Who has not seen this fruitless struggle end
In ruin so complete – death seemed a friend?
Oh! many a prayer John Ashford offered up,
That God would spare him that last bitter cup;
That he might earn his independent bread,
Nor ever be by parish bounty fed.

Vain was the wish, for lingering sickness came,
Shook like a reed the strong man's iron frame,
And all his little earnings soon were spent
In food and medicine, and arrears of rent; –
True he had friends; but want, day after day,
Like drops on stones, wears charity away.
He has for years a monthly payment made
To a small club, formed it was said to aid
The industrious poor and kindly to assuage
The ills that wait on sickness and old age;
Defective rules: it was dissolved of course,
And on its fraudful ruins one was raised
From which the sick and aged were erased,
Whose payments made in poverty and woe,

Amidst privations such as few can know,
Were squandered all: – this left him quite forlorn:
Then one by one his goods were placed in pawn;
The 'cuckoo-clock', to all the household dear,
Which told of Spring throughout the changeful year;
Oft gathering round, they with mute wonder heard
It strike the hour, and imitate the bird: –
The old oak-chest his aged Mother gave,
Her last bequest when sinking to the grave,
So long preserved, in memory of the dead,
Was bartered now, to find his Children bread.
The time-worn Bible yet alone remained
Of all their household wreck, it has sustained
His sinking soul through trials, doubts, and fears,
And many a leaf was blistered with his tears:

Sad was the Sunday, when, the service done,
He took his sobbing children one by one
Upon his knees, that they might once more look
At the large prints that graced the Holy Book.
Precept and promise marked with pious care
By the loved dead, in faded lines were there,
Appealing records of the faith HE gave
Their trusting souls in prospect of the grave,
And as he turned its sacred pages o'er,
So full of comfort to the suffering poor,
The clouds of unbelief awhile would part,
And gleams of sunshine cheer his fainting heart.
Sharp was the struggle, but the daily cry
'Bread, Father, bread,' and the half-smothered sigh
Which from his patient partner's withered breast
Whispered of misery louder than the rest,
Its fate decided: – 'twas his last resource,
Yet self-reproach and undeserved remorse
Haunted his homeward steps, and every day
Disturbed his troubled mind when he knelt down to pray.

Frances Trollope (1780–1863), from *The Vicar of Wrexhill* (1837)

The mother of Anthony Trollope, she was the daughter of a Hampshire parson. She became an author in a constant struggle to keep on top of the family finances. She denied that she based her portrait of Cartwright here on the evangelical vicar of Harrow, who had leased the fine new house on which her husband had overspent.

The intelligent reader will not be surprised to hear that Mr Cartwright did not suffer himself to be long expected in vain on the following morning. Fanny, however, was already in the garden when he arrived; and as it so happened that he saw her as she was hovering near the shrubbery gate, he turned from the carriage-road and approached her.

'How sweetly does youth, when blessed with such a cheek and eye as yours, Miss Fanny, accord with the fresh morning of such a day as this! – I feel,' he added, taking her hand and looking in her blushing face, 'that my soul never offers adoration more worthy of my Maker than when inspired by intercourse with such a being as you!'

'Oh! Mr Cartwright!' cried Fanny, avoiding his glance by fixing her beautiful eyes upon the ground.

'My dearest child! Fear not to look at me – fear not to meet the eye of a friend, who would watch over you, Fanny, as the minister of God should watch over that which is best and fairest, to make and keep it holy to the Lord! Let me have that innocent heart in my keeping, my dearest child, and all that is idle, light, and vain shall be banished thence, while heavenward thoughts and holy musings shall take its place. Have you essayed to hymn the praises of your Saviour and your God, Fanny, since we parted yesterday?'

This question was accompanied by an encouraging pat upon her glowing cheek; and Fanny, her heart beating with vanity, shyness, hope, fear, and sundry other feelings, drew the MS containing a fairly-written transcript of her yesterday's labour from her bosom, and placed it in his hand.

Mr Cartwright pressed it with a sort of pious fervour to his lips, and enclosing it for greater security in a letter which he drew from his pocket, he laid it carefully within his waistcoat, on the left side of his person, and as near as possible to that part of it appropriated for the residence of the heart.

'This must be examined in private, my beloved child,' said he solemnly. 'The first attempt to raise such a spirit as yours to God the Saviour in holy song, has to my feelings something as awful in it as the first glad moment of a seraph's wing! ... Where is your mother, Fanny?'

'She is in the library.'

'Alone?'

'Oh, yes! – at least I should think so, for I am sure she is expecting you.'

'Farewell, then, my dear young friend! – Pursue your solitary musing walk; and remember, Fanny, that as by your talents you are marked and set apart, as it were, from the great mass of human souls, so will you be looked upon the more fixedly by the searching eye of God. It is from him you received this talent – keep it sacred to his use, as David did, and great shall be your reward! – Shall I startle your good mother, Fanny, if I enter by the library window?'

'Oh, no! Mr Cartwright – I am sure mamma would be quite vexed if you always went round that long way up to the door, especially in summer, you know, when the windows are always open.'

'Once more, farewell, then!'

Fanny's hand was again tenderly pressed, and they parted.

It would be a needless lengthening of my tale, were I to record all that passed at this and three or four subsequent interviews which took place between the vicar and Mrs Mowbray on the subject of proving the will.

Together with the kindest and most soothing demonstrations of rapidly increasing friendship and esteem, Mr Cartwright conveyed to her very sound legal information respecting what it was necessary for her to do.

Cambridge 1828–31, from Charles Darwin (1809–1882), *Autobiography*

In his late sixties the natural historian was asked by a German editor for 'an account of the development of my mind and character with some sketch of my autobiography', and he thought the attempt would amuse him and possibly interest his family.

After having spent two sessions in Edinburgh, my Father perceived or he heard from my sisters that I did not like the thought of being a physician, so he proposed that I should become a clergyman. He was very properly vehement against my turning an idle sporting man, which then seemed my probable destination. I asked for some time to consider, as from what little I had heard and thought on the subject I had scruples about declaring my belief in all the dogmas of the Church of England; though otherwise I liked the thought of being a country clergyman. Accordingly I read with care Pearson on the Creeds and a few other books on divinity; and as I did not then in the least doubt the strict and literal truth of every word in the Bible, I soon persuaded myself that our Creed must be fully accepted. It never struck me how illogical it was to say that I believed in what I could not understand and what is in fact unintelligible. I might have said with entire truth that I had no wish to dispute any dogma; but I never was such a fool as to feel and say 'credo quia incredibile' [I believe because it is unbelievable].

Considering how fiercely I have been attacked by the orthodox, it seems ludicrous that I once intended to be a clergyman. Nor was this intention and my Father's wish ever formally given up, but died a natural death when on leaving Cambridge I joined the Beagle as Naturalist. If the phrenologists are to be trusted, I was well fitted in one respect to be a clergyman. A few years ago the Secretaries of a German psychological Society asked me earnestly by letter for a photograph of myself; and sometime afterwards I received the Proceedings of one of the meetings, in which it seemed that the shape of my head had been the subject of a public discussion, and one of the speakers declared that I had the bump of Reverence developed enough for ten Priests.

As it was decided that I should be a clergyman, it was necessary that I should go to one of the English Universities and take a degree; but as I had never opened a classical book since leaving school, I found to my dismay that in the two intervening years I had actually forgotten, incredible as it may appear, almost everything which I had learnt even to some few of the Greek letters. I did not therefore proceed to Cambridge at the usual time in October, but worked with a private tutor in Shrewsbury and went to Cambridge after the Christmas vacation, early in 1828. I soon recovered my school standard of knowledge, and could translate easy Greek books, such as Homer and the Greek Testament, with moderate facility.

During the three years which I spent at Cambridge my time was wasted, as far as the academical studies were concerned, as completely as at Edinburgh and at school. I attempted mathematicks, and even went during the summer of 1828 with a private tutor (a very dull man) to Barmouth, but I got on very slowly. The work was repugnant to me, chiefly from my not being able to see any meaning in the early steps in algebra. This impatience was very foolish, and in after years I have deeply regretted that I did not proceed far enough at least to understand something of the great leading principles of mathematicks; for men thus endowed seem to have an extra sense. But I do not believe that I should ever have succeeded beyond a very low grade. With respect to classics I did nothing except attend a few compulsory college lectures, and the attendance was almost nominal. In my second year I had to work for a month or two to pass the Little Go, which I did easily. Again in my last year I worked with some earnestness for my final degree of B.A., and brushed up my Classics together with a little algebra and Euclid, which latter gave me much pleasure as it did whilst at school. In order to pass the B.A. examination it was, also, necessary to get up Paley's Evidences of Christianity and his Moral Philosophy.* This was done in a thorough manner, and I am convinced that I could have written out the whole of the Evidences with perfect correctness, but not of course in the clear language of Paley. The logic of this book, and as I may add of his Natural Theology gave me as much delight as did Euclid. The careful study of these works, without attempting to learn any part by rote, was the only part of the Academical Course which as I then felt and as I still believe, was of the least use to me in the education of my mind. I did not at that time trouble myself about Paley's premises; and taking these on trust I was charmed and convinced by the long line of argumentation. By answering well the examination questions in Paley, by doing Euclid well, and by not failing miserably in Classics, I gained a good place amongst the *hoi polloi*, or crowd of men who do not go in for honours. Oddly enough I cannot remember how high I stood, and my memory fluctuates between the fifth, tenth or twelfth name on the list.

Public lectures on several branches were given in the University, attendance being quite voluntary; but I was so sickened with lectures at Edinburgh that I did not even attend Sedgwick's eloquent and interesting lectures. Had I done so I should probably have become a geologist earlier than I did. I attended, however, Henslow's lectures on Botany, and I liked them much for their extreme clearness, and the admirable illustrations; but I did not study botany. Henslow used to take his pupils, including several of the older members of the University, [on] field excursions, on foot, or in coaches to distant places, or in a barge down the river, and lectured on the rarer plants or animals which were observed. These excursions were delightful.

Although as we shall presently see there were some redeeming features in my life at Cambridge, my time was sadly wasted there and worse than wasted. From my passion for shooting and for hunting and when this failed for riding cross-country I got into a sporting set, including some dissipated, low-minded young men. We used often to dine together in the evening, though these dinners often included men of a higher stamp, and we sometimes drank too much, with jolly singing and playing at cards afterwards. I know that I ought to feel ashamed of days and evenings thus spent, but as some of my friends were very pleasant, and we were all in the highest spirits, I cannot help looking back to these times with much pleasure.

But I am glad to think that I had many other friends of a widely different nature. …

* *The Rev. William Paley's* A View of the Evidences of Christianity *(1794) and* Natural Theology *(1802) remained on the Cambridge syllabus until 1920.*

'Our Parish', from Charles Dickens (1812–1870), *Sketches by Boz* (1836)

Sketches by Boz, *a collection of pieces that he wrote for periodicals while still working as a parliamentary reporter, was the first fruit of Dickens's lifelong absorption with London life and also his first published book.*

The parish beadle is one of the most, perhaps *the* most, important member of the local administration. He is not so well off as the churchwardens, certainly, nor is he so learned as the vestry clerk, nor does he order things quite so much his own way as either of them. But his power is very great, notwithstanding; and the dignity of his office is never impaired by the absence of efforts on his part to maintain it. The beadle of our parish is a splendid fellow. It is quite delightful to hear him, as he explains the state of the existing poor-laws to the deaf old women in the board-room passage on business nights; and to hear what he said to the senior churchwarden, and what the senior churchwarden said to him; and what 'we' (the beadle and the other gentlemen) came to the determination of doing. A miserable-looking woman is called into the board-room, and represents a case of extreme destitution, affecting herself – a widow, with six small children. 'Where do you live?' inquires one of the overseers. 'I rents a two-pair back, gentlemen, at Mrs. Brown's, Number 3, Little King William's Alley, which has lived there this fifteen year, and knows me to be very hard-working and industrious, and when my poor husband was alive, gentlemen, as died in the hospital – ' 'Well, well,' interrupts the overseer, taking a note of the address, 'I'll send Simmons, the beadle, to-morrow morning, to ascertain whether your story is correct; and, if so, I suppose you must have an order into the House. Simmons, go to this woman's the first thing to-morrow morning, will you?' Simmons bows assent, and ushers the woman out. Her previous admiration of 'the board' (who all sit behind great books, and with their hats on) fades into nothing before her respect for her lace-trimmed conductor; and her account of what has passed inside increases – if that be possible – the marks of respect shown by the assembled crowd to that solemn functionary. As to taking out a summons, it's quite a hopeless case if Simmons attends it on behalf of the parish. He knows all the titles of the Lord Mayor by heart; states the case without a single stammer; and it is even reported that on one occasion he ventured to make a joke, which the Lord Mayor's head footman (who happened to be present) afterwards told an intimate friend, confidentially, was almost equal to one of Mr. Hobler's.

See him, again, on Sunday in his state coat and cocked hat, with a large-headed staff for show in his left hand, and a small cane for use in his right. How pompously he marshals the children into their places! and how demurely the little urchins look at him askance as he surveys them, when they are all seated, with a glare of the eye peculiar to beadles! The churchwardens and overseers being duly installed in their curtained pews, he seats himself on a mahogany bracket, erected expressly for him at the top of the aisle, and divides his attention between his Prayer-book and the boys. Suddenly, just at the commencement of the communion service, when the whole congregation is hushed into a profound silence, broken only by the voice of the officiating clergyman, a penny is heard to ring on the stone floor of the aisle with astounding clearness. Observe the generalship of the beadle. His involuntary look of horror is instantly changed into one of perfect indifference, as if he were the only person present who had not heard the noise. The artifice succeeds. After putting forth his right leg now and then, as a feeler, the victim who dropped the money ventures to make one or two distinct dives after it; and the beadle, gliding softly round, salutes his little round head, when it again appears above the seat, with divers double knocks, administered with the can before noticed, to the intense delight of three young men in an adjacent pew, who cough violently at intervals until the conclusion of the sermon. ...

The personages next in importance to the beadle are the master of the workhouse and the parish schoolmaster. The vestry clerk, as everybody knows, is a short, pudgy little man in black, with a thick gold watch-chain of considerable length, terminating in two large seals and a key. He is an attorney, and generally in a bustle; at no time more so than when he is hurrying to some parochial meeting, with his gloves crumpled up in one hand, and a large red book under the other arm. As to the churchwardens and overseers, we exclude them altogether, because all we know of them is, that they are usually respectable tradesmen, who wear hats with brims inclined to flatness, and who occasionally testify in gilt letters on a blue ground, in some conspicuous part of the church, to the important fact of a gallery having been enlarged and beautified, or an organ rebuilt.

Warwickshire in the 1830s, from Joseph Arch (1826–1919), *The Story of his Life, Told by Himself* (1898)

The story of the hardships of rural life in the nineteenth century is a long one, and Joseph Arch played a 'village-Hampden' part in it. From scaring crows away from the crops as a lad, he found work further afield as a young man, experiencing how widespread poor conditions were. After he returned to his home village of Barford he became a Primitive Methodist preacher, and his serious self-education began. His fellow farmworkers turned to him in 1872 when yet again the lack of a living wage was causing a widespread rural crisis. He very soon found himself at the head of thousands of men looking for a leader, and became the first president of the National Agricultural Labourers' Union.

In 1885 Arch was the first labourer to become an MP (Liberal), and he served a Norfolk constituency for most of the next decade.

There is one thing, however, for which I shall always be thankful, and the thought of it is like a bright spot in that dark, black time. I am glad to say that, even when things were at their very worst with us, my father was never obliged to go out and steal food. We grew carrots and turnips in our garden, and we had not to pay anything out for rent. There was always some money coming in. There was my father's wage, which varied from eight to ten shillings a week, and during those eighteen weeks, when he was without work, my mother, as I have already said, turned to and managed to earn sufficient to keep our heads above water – above ground rather! ...

Numbers of people used to go to the rectory for soup, but not a drop of it did we touch. I have stood at our door with my mother, and I have seen her face look sad as she watched the little children toddle past, carrying the tin cans, and their toes coming out of their boots. 'Ah, my boy,' she once said, 'you shall never, never do that. I will work these fingers to the bone before you have to do it!' She was as good as her word – *I never went to the rectory for soup.*

My mother, as might be expected, was not in favour at the rectory from the first. She did not order herself lowly and reverently towards her betters according to the Church Catechism. She had no betters for the matter of that, – not in Barford. She would not duck down to the rector's wife just because she happened to be the rector's wife, and she was not properly and humbly thankful for coals and soup. She showed plainly that she put a value on herself as a free and independent woman, and she would not stoop to beg favours of any one, let it be squire or parson or rich farmer. Threatening and bullying would not make her budge an inch – just the contrary. She had a good sound head on her shoulders, and when once she had thought a thing out and made up her mind about it she would stick to her opinion through thick and thin. The lady-despot at the rectory did not want to have anything to do with a woman of that kind; a woman with grit, and a good stiff backbone, had no business to be in the village at all, she thought. That a labourer's wife should ever have dared to stand up against her sacred authority was gall and wormwood to her.

Of course, if my mother had been a strong church-woman, and a regular churchgoer, things would have been all the other way. If she had been ready to conform to the Church as by law established, the rector and his wife would have put up with a good deal of independence, and would have overlooked a lot of plain-speaking about other matters. But she was not appealed to by the Church service, and she did not hold with the Church teaching. It was not that she was an irreligious woman – very far from it; but there seemed very little practical religion in the Church in those days, and it was quite enough for her if preaching and practice did not go together. All men are equal in the sight of God, but if the parson preached that doctrine he did not act up to it in God's House. In the parish church the poor man and his wife were shown pretty plainly where they came among their fellow-creatures and fellow-worshippers – men and women of the same flesh and blood, and of like passions with themselves, however superior they might seem to be in the eyes of the world because they were rich and high-placed. In the parish church the poor were apportioned their lowly places, and taught that they must sit in them Sunday after Sunday all their lives long. They must sit meekly and never dare to mingle with their betters in the social scale. It was an object lesson repeated week after week, one which no one could mistake, and it sank deep into my mind.

I remember a thing which made my mother very angry. The parson's wife issued a decree, that the labourers should sit on one side of the church and their wives on the other. When my mother heard of it she said, 'No, "those whom God hath joined together let no man put asunder," and certainly no woman shall!'

I can also remember the time when the parson's wife used to sit in state in her pew in the chancel, and the poor women used to walk up the church and make a curtsey to her before taking the seats set apart for them. They were taught in this way that they had to pay homage and respect to those 'put in authority over them,' and made to understand that they must 'honour the powers that be,' as represented in the rector's wife. You may be pretty certain that many of these women did not relish the curtsey-scraping and other humiliations they had to put up with, but they were afraid to speak out. They had their families to think of, children to feed and clothe somehow; and when so many could not earn a living wage, but only a half-starving one, when very often a labouring man was out of work for weeks at a stretch, – why, the wives and mothers learned to take thankfully whatever was doled out to them at the parsonage or elsewhere, and drop the curtsey expected of them, without making a wry face. A smooth face and a smooth tongue was what their benefactors required of them, and they got both. It was only human nature that the poor 'had-nots' should look up to the 'hads' and be obedient to their wishes; especially when the 'hads' gave to the 'had-nots' out of their abundance, dropped a few pence into the wife's hand when the husband's pocket was empty, or sent the family enough for a bite and a sup when the cottage cupboard was as bare as Mother Hubbard's.

With bowed head and bended knee the poor learned to receive from the rich what was only their due, had they but known it. Years of poverty had ground the spirit of independence right out of them; these wives and mothers were tamed by poverty, they were cowed by it, as their parents had been before them in many cases, and the spirit of servitude was bred in their very bones. And the worst of it was the mischief did not stop at the women – it never does. They set an example of spiritless submission, which their children were only too inclined to follow. Follow it too many of them did and they and their children are reaping the consequences and paying the price of it to-day.

I can remember when the squire and the other local magnates used to sit in state in the centre of the aisle. They did not, if you please, like the look of the agricultural labourers. Hodge sat too near them, and even in his Sunday best he was an offence to their eyes. They also objected to Hodge looking at them, so they had curtains put up to hide them from the vulgar gaze. And yet, while all this was going on, while the poor had to bear with such high-handed dealings, people wondered why the Church had lost its hold, and continued to lose its hold, on the labourers in the country districts! It never had any hold on me – in that, I was my mother's son also. I never took the Communion in the parish church in my life. When I was seven years old I saw something which prevented me once for all. One Sunday my father was going to stop to take the Communion, and I, being a boy, had of course to go out before it began. I may here mention that the church door opened then in a direct line with the chancel and the main aisle, so that anybody looking through the keyhole could easily see what was going on inside. The door is now more to the side of the church, and out of direct line with the chancel. I was a little bit of a fellow, and curious. I said to myself, 'What does father stop behind for? What is it they do? I'll see.' So I went out of church, closed the door, placed my eye at the keyhole and peeped through, and what I saw will be engraved on my mind until the last day of my life. That sight caused a wound which has never been healed. My proud little spirit smarted and burned when I saw what happened at that Communion service.

First, up walked the squire to the communion rails; the farmers went up next; then up went the tradesmen, the shopkeepers, the wheelwright, and the blacksmith; and then, the very last of all, went the poor agricultural labourers in their smock frocks. They walked up by themselves; nobody else knelt with them; it was as if they were unclean – and at that sight the iron entered straight into my poor little heart and remained fast embedded there. I said to myself, 'If that's what goes on – never for me!' I ran home and told my mother what I had seen, and I wanted to know why my father was not as good in the eyes of God as the squire, and why the poor should be forced to come up last of all to the table of the Lord. My mother gloried in my spirit.

Thomas Carlyle (1795–1881), from *Past and Present* (1843)

The historian and essayist wrote his attack on the lack of real leadership from the 'aristocracies' of his day, compared with the quality of leadership given by a medieval monk like Jocelin de Brakelond (see p. 38) whose Chronicle *had recently come to light. At least something of these qualities persists in the humblest church.*

More touching still, there is not a hamlet where poor peasants congregate, but, by one means and another, a Church-Apparatus has been got together, – roofed edifice, with revenues and belfries; pulpit, reading-desk, with Books and Methods: possibility, in short, and strict prescription, that a man stand there and speak of spiritual things to men. It is beautiful; – even in its great obscuration and decadence, it is among the beautifulest, most touching objects one sees on the Earth. This Speaking Man has indeed, in these times, wandered terribly from the point; has, alas, as it were, totally lost sight of the point: yet, at bottom, whom have we to compare with him?

'The religion of England is part of good-breeding', from Ralph Waldo Emerson (1803–1882), *English Traits* (1856)

Emerson's father, a Unitarian minister in Boston, Massachusetts, died when the boy was not quite eight. He became a pastor himself in 1829, but the increasingly controversial nature of his views soon led to his resignation and to a new career giving lectures in which he developed his ideas on natural philosophy and spiritual individualism. Volumes of essays and poetry followed.

His first visit to Europe was in 1833, when he sought out both Wordsworth and Coleridge; Thomas Carlyle was to become a lifelong friend and correspondent.

On his second lecture tour, in 1847–48, there was a breakfast meeting with young Mary Ann Evans (George Eliot: see p. 274).

In English Traits *Emerson enjoys bringing his new-world freedom of thought to bear on the old-world 'Saxon' culture.*

The English church has many certificates to show of humble effective service in humanizing the people, in cheering and refining men, feeding, healing and educating. It has the seal of martyrs and confessors; the noblest books; a sublime architecture; a ritual marked by the same secular merits, nothing cheap or purchasable.

From this slow-grown church important reactions proceed; much for culture, much for giving a direction to the nation's affection and will to-day. The carved and pictured chapel, – its entire surface animated with image and emblem, – made the parish-church a sort of book and Bible to the people's eye.

Then, when the Saxon instinct had secured a service in the vernacular tongue, it was the tutor and university of the people. In York minster, on the day of the enthronization of the new archbishop, I heard the service of evening prayer read and chanted in the choir. It was strange to hear the pretty pastoral of the betrothal of Rebecca and Isaac, in the morning of the world, read with circumstantiality in York minster, on the 13th January, 1848, to the decorous English audience, just fresh from the Times newspaper and their wine, and listening with all the devotion of national pride. That was binding old and new to some purpose. The reverence for the Scriptures is an element of civilization, for thus has the history of the world been preserved and is preserved. Here in England every day a chapter of Genesis, and a leader in the Times.

ii

But the age of the Wicliffes, Cobhams, Arundels, Beckets; of the Latimers, Mores, Cranmers; of the Taylors, Leightons, Herberts; of the Sherlocks and Butlers, is gone. Silent revolutions in opinion have made it impossible that men like these should return, or find a place in their once sacred stalls. The spirit that dwelt in this church has glided away to animate other activities, and they who come to the old shrines find apes and players rustling the old garments.

The religion of England is part of good-breeding. When you see on the continent the well-dressed Englishman come into his ambassador's chapel and put his face for silent prayer into his smooth-brushed hat, you cannot help feeling how much national pride prays with him, and the religion of a gentleman. So far is he from attaching any meaning to the words, that he believes himself to have done almost the generous thing, and that it is very condescending in him to pray to God.

iii

But you must pay for conformity. All goes well as long as you run with the conformists. But you, who are an honest man in other particulars, know that there is alive somewhere a man whose honesty reaches to this point also that he shall not kneel to false gods, and the day when you meet him, you sink into the class of counterfeits. Besides, this succumbing has grave penalties. If you take in a lie, you take in all that belongs to it. England accepts this ornamental national church, and it glazes the eye, bloats the flesh, gives the voice a stertorous clang, and clouds the understanding of the receivers.

The English church, undermined by German criticism, had nothing left but tradition; and was led logically back to Romanism. But that was an element which only hot heads could breathe: in the view of the educated classes, generally, it was not a fact to front the sun; and the alienation of such men from the church became complete.

iv

The church at this moment is much to be pitied. She has nothing left but possession. If a bishop meets an intelligent gentleman and reads fatal interrogations in his eyes, he has no resource but to take wine with him. False position introduces cant, perjury, simony and ever a lower class of mind and character into the clergy: and, when the hierarchy is afraid of science and education, afraid of piety, afraid of tradition and afraid of theology, there is nothing left but to quit a church which is no longer one.

Snobs and good clerics, from William Makepeace Thackeray (1811–1863), *The Book of Snobs*

Thackeray's 'Snobs' appeared weekly in Punch *in 1846–47, characterising the divisions and posturings of his Early Victorian society with an energy of amusement and understanding that left his readers clamouring for more. Over the next two years his astute eye for class consciousness was to find new scope in the publication of* Vanity Fair *in monthly instalments.*

... I have seen many examples of the clergy falling away. When, for instance, Tom Sniffle first went into the country as Curate for Mr. Fuddleston (Sir Huddleston Fuddleston's brother), who resided on some other living, there could not be a more kind, hard-working, and excellent creature than Tom. He had his aunt to live with him. His conduct to his poor was admirable. He wrote annually reams of the best-intentioned and most vapid sermons. When Lord Brandyball's family first came down into the country, and invited him to dine at Brandyball Park, Sniffle was so agitated that he almost forgot how to say grace, and upset a bowl of currant-jelly sauce in Lady Fanny Toffy's lap.

What was the consequence of his intimacy with that noble family? He quarrelled with his aunt for dining out every night. The wretch forgot his poor altogether, and killed his old nag by always riding over to Brandyball; where he revelled in the maddest passion for Lady Fanny. He ordered the neatest new clothes and ecclesiastical waistcoats from London; he appeared with corazza-shirts, lackered boots, and perfumery; he bought a blood-horse from Bob Toffy: was seen at archery meetings, public breakfasts, – actually at cover; and, I blush to say, that I saw him in a stall at the Opera; and afterwards riding by Lady Fanny's side in Rotten Row. He *double-barrelled* his name (as many poor Snobs do), and instead of T. Sniffle, as formerly, came out, in a porcelain card, as Rev. T. D'Arcy Sniffle, Burlington Hotel.

The end of all this may be imagined: when the Earl of Brandyball was made acquainted with the curate's love for Lady Fanny, he had that fit of the gout which so nearly carried him off (to the inexpressible grief of his son, Lord Alicompayne), and uttered that remarkable speech to Sniffle, which disposed of the claims of the latter: 'If I didn't respect the Church, Sir,' his Lordship said, 'by Jove, I'd kick you downstairs:' his Lordship then fell back into the fit aforesaid; and Lady Fanny, as we all know, married General Podager.

As for poor Tom, he was over head and ears in debt as well as in love: his creditors came down upon him. Mr. Hemp, of Portugal Street, proclaimed his name lately as a reverend outlaw; and he has been seen at various foreign watering-places; sometimes doing duty; sometimes 'coaching' a stray gentleman's son at Carlsruhe or Kissingen; sometimes – must we say it? – lurking about the roulette-tables with a tuft to his chin.

If temptation had not come upon this unhappy fellow in the shape of a Lord Brandyball, he might still have been following his profession, humbly and worthily. He might have married his cousin with four thousand pounds, the wine-merchant's daughter (the old gentleman quarrelled with his nephew for not soliciting wine-orders from Lord B. for him): he might have had seven children, and taken private pupils, and eked out his income, and lived and died a country parson.

And 'the many good ones'

... And I know this, that if there are some Clerics who do wrong, there are straightway a thousand newspapers to haul up those unfortunates, and cry, 'Fie upon them, fie upon them!' while, though the press is always ready to yell and bellow excommunication against these stray delinquent parsons, it somehow takes very little count of the many good ones – of the tens of thousands of honest men, who lead Christian lives, who give to the poor generously, who deny themselves rigidly, and live and die in their duty, without ever a newspaper paragraph in their favour. My beloved friend and reader, I wish you and I could do the same: and let me whisper my belief, *entre nous*, that of those eminent philosophers who cry out against parsons the loudest, there are not many who have got their knowledge of the church by going thither often.

But you who have ever listened to village bells, or have walked to church as children on sunny Sabbath mornings; you who have ever seen the parson's wife tending the poor man's bedside; or the town clergyman threading the dirty stairs of noxious alleys upon his sacred business; – do not raise a shout when one of these falls away, or yell with the mob that howls after him.

Every man can do that. When old Father Noah was overtaken in his cups, there was only one of his sons that dared to make merry at his disaster, and he was not the most virtuous of the family. Let us too turn away silently, nor huzzah like a parcel of school-boys, because some big young rebel suddenly starts up and whops the schoolmaster.

The Brontës

The lives of the children of the Rev. Patrick Brontë offer particular insight into provincial vicarage life and the prospects facing its young, and the Haworth Parsonage Museum is now their shrine. The eventual revelation of Charlotte as the author of the sensationally successful Jane Eyre *(1847) brought her freedom from life as a governess. Her younger sisters'* Wuthering Heights *and* Agnes Grey *were only published 'on terms somewhat impoverishing for the two authors', and it was a matter of months after their failed artist brother Bronwen died, an alcoholic, that Emily died of tuberculosis, and Anne the summer after.*

On 14 July 1840 **Charlotte (1816–1855)** *wrote to her friend Ellen Nussey about their father's new curate, William Weightman, a handsome and clever young Durham graduate, and the flutterings he caused. (In October 1842 Patrick Brontë was to give his funeral sermon after his death from cholera.)*

I am very glad you continue so heart-whole I rather feared our mutual nonsense might have made a deeper impression on you than was safe. Mr Weightman – left Haworth this morning, we do not expect him back again for some weeks – I am fully convinced, Ellen, that he is a thorough male-flirt his sighs are deeper than ever – and his treading on toes more assiduous – I find he has scattered his impressions far and wide – Keighley has yielded him a fruitful field of conquest, Sarah Sugden is quite smitten so is Caroline Dury – She however has left – and his Reverence has not yet ceased to idolize her memory – I find he is perfectly conscious of his irresistibleness & is as vain as a peacock on the subject – I am not at all surprised at all this – it is perfectly natural – a handsome – clever – prepossessing – good-humoured young man – will never want troops of victims amongst young ladies – So long as you are not among the number it is alright

On 31 July 1845 **Anne (1820–1849)** *and Emily (1818–1848) took stock of their lives on the occasion of Emily's birthday. This is from Anne's diary papers:*

Yesterday was Emily's birthday and the time when we should have opened our 1841 paper but by mistake we opened it to day instead – How many things have happened since it was written – some pleasant some far otherwise – Yet I was then at Thorp Green and now I am only just escaped from it – I was wishing to leave it then and if I had known that I had four years longer to stay how wretched I should have been during my stay I have had some very unpleasant and undreamt of experience of human nature – Others have seen more changes Charlotte has left Mr White's and been twice to Brussels where she stayed each time nearly a year – Emily has been there too and stayed nearly a year – Branwell has left Luddenden Foot and been a Tutor at Thorpe Green and had much tribulation and ill health he was very ill on Tuesday but he went with John Brown to Liverpool where he now is I suppose and I hope he will be better and do better in future – This is a dismal cloudy wet evening we have had so far a very cold wet summer – Charlotte has lately been to Hathersage in Derbyshire on a visit of three weeks to Ellen Nussey – she is now sitting sewing in the Dining-Room Emily is ironing upstairs I am sitting in the Dining-Room in the Rocking chair before the fire with my feet on the fender Papa is in the parlour Tabby and Martha are I think in the Kitchen Keeper and Flossy are I do not know where little Dick is hopping in his cage – When the last paper was written we were thinking of setting up a School – the scheem has been dropt and long after taken up again and dropt again because we could not get pupils – Charlotte is thinking about getting another situation – she wishes to go to Paris – will she go? she has let Flossy in by the bye and he is now lying on the sopha – Emily is engaged in writing the Emperor Julius's life She has read some of it and I want very much to hear the rest – She is writing some poetry too I wonder what it is about – I have begun the third volume of passages in the life of an Individual, I wish I had finished it – This afternoon I began to set about making my grey figured silk frock that was dyed at Keighley – What sort of a hand shall I make of it? E. and I have a great deal of work to do – when shall we sensibly diminish it? I want to get a habit of early rising shall I succeed? We have not yet finished our Gondal chronicles that we began three years and a half ago when will they be done? – The Gondals are at present in a sad state the Republicans are uppermost but the Royalists are not quite overcome – the young sovereigns with their brothers and sisters are still at the palace of Instruction – the Unique Society above half a year ago were wrecked on a dezart Island as they were returning from Gaaldin – they are still there but we have not played at them much yet – The Gondals in general are not in first rate playing condition – will they improve?

I wonder how we shall all be and where and how situated on the thirtyeth of July 1848 when if we are all alive Emily will be just 30 I shall be in my 29th year Charlotte in her 33rd and Branwell in his 32nd and what changes shall we have seen and known and shall we be much changed ourselves? I hope not – for the worse at least – I for my part cannot well be *flatter* or older in mind than I am now – Hoping for the best I conclude

Anne Brontë

John Ruskin (1819–1900), from 'The Lamp of Sacrifice' in *The Seven Lamps of Architecture* (1849)

During the period of the Gothic Revival, Ruskin's Seven Lamps *was the young critic's first significant venture into architectural theory. The seven principles to which he thought buildings should answer were Beauty, Truth, Sacrifice, Power, Life, Obedience, and Memory.*

It has been said – it ought always to be said, for it is true, – that a better and more honourable offering is made to our Master in ministry to the poor, in extending the knowledge of His name, in the practice of the virtues by which that name is hallowed, than in material presents to His temple. Assuredly it is so: woe to all who think that any other kind or manner of offering may in any wise take the place of these! Do the people need place to pray, and calls to hear His word? Then it is no time for smoothing pillars or carving pulpits; let us have enough first of walls and roofs. Do the people need teaching from house to house, and bread from day to day? Then they are deacons and ministers we want, not architects. I insist on this, I plead for this; but let us examine ourselves, and see if this be indeed the reason for our backwardness in the lesser work. The question is not between God's house and His poor: it is not between God's house and His Gospel. It is between God's house and ours. Have we no tessellated colours on our floors? no frescoed fancies on our roofs? no niched statuary in our corridors? no gilded furniture in our chambers? no costly stones in our cabinets? Has even the tithe of these been offered? They are, or they ought to be, the signs that enough has been devoted to the great purposes of human stewardship, and that there remains to us what we can spend in luxury; but there is a great and prouder luxury than this selfish one – that of bringing a portion of such things as these into sacred service, and presenting them for a memorial that our pleasure as well as our toil has been hallowed by the remembrance of Him who gave both the strength and the reward. And until this has been done, I do not see how such possessions can be retained in happiness. I do not understand the feeling which would arch our own gates and pave our own thresholds and leave the church with its narrow door and foot-worn sill; the feeling which enriches our own chambers with all manner of costliness, and endures the bare wall and mean compass of the temple. There is seldom even so severe a choice to be made, seldom so much self-denial to be exercised. There are isolated cases, in which men's happiness and mental activity depend upon a certain degree of luxury in their houses; but then this is true luxury, felt and tasted, and profited by. In the plurality of instances nothing of the kind is attempted, or can be enjoyed; men's average resources cannot reach it; and that which they *can* reach, gives them no pleasure, and might be spared. It will be seen, in the course of the following chapters, that I am no advocate for meanness of private habitation. I would fain introduce into it all magnificence, care, and beauty, where they are possible; but I would not have that useless expense in unnoticed fineries or formalities; cornicing of ceilings and graining of doors, and fringing of curtains, and thousands such; things which have become foolishly and apathetically habitual ... – things on whose common appliance hang whole trades, to which there never yet belonged the blessing of giving one ray of real pleasure, or becoming of the remotest or most contemptible use – things which cause half the expense of life, and destroy more than half its comfort, manliness, respectability, freshness, and facility. I speak from experience: I know what it is to live in a cottage with a deal floor and roof, and a hearth of mica slate; and I know it to be in many respects healthier and happier than living between a Turkey carpet and gilded ceiling, beside a steel grate and polished fender. ... I do not say that such things have not their place and propriety; but I say this, emphatically, that the tenth part of the expense which is sacrificed in domestic vanities, if not absolutely and meaninglessly lost in domestic discomforts, and incumbrances, would, if collectively offered and wisely employed, build a marble church for every town in England; such a church as it should be a joy and a blessing even to pass near in our daily ways and walks, and as it would bring the light into the eyes to see from afar, lifting its fair height above the purple crowd of humble roofs.

I have said for every town: I do not want a marble church for every village; nay, I do not want marble churches at all for their own sake, but for the sake of the spirit that would build them. The church has no need of any visible splendours; her power is independent of them, her purity is in some degree opposed to them. The simplicity of a pastoral sanctuary is lovelier than the majesty of an urban temple; and it may be more than questioned whether, to the people, such majesty has ever been the source of any increase of effective piety; but to the builders it has been, and ever must be. It is not the church we want, but the sacrifice; not the emotion of admiration, but the act of adoration; not the gift, but the giving.

From the Appendix

The greatest service which can at present be rendered to architecture, is the careful delineation of its details from the beginning of the twelfth to the close of the fourteenth century, by means of photography. I would particularly desire to direct the attention of amateur photographers to this task; earnestly requesting them to bear in mind that while a photograph of landscape is merely an amusing toy, one of early architecture is a precious historical document; and that this architecture should be taken, not merely when it presents itself under picturesque general forms, but stone by stone, and sculpture by sculpture; seizing every opportunity afforded by scaffolding to approach it closely, and putting the camera in any position that will command the sculpture, wholly without regard to the resultant distortions of the vertical lines; such distortion can always be allowed for, if once the details are completely obtained.

Letter to the Editor of the *Suffolk Chronicle*, 14 August 1850

The letter is ostensibly from 'Cosmopolite', a visitor to Southwold, and registers his pleasure at the removal of the old pews and their replacement with 'open benches', and his shock at hearing about the minister's quarrelsome crusade against the change. He ends with this point for the parson. (The handwriting of a surviving draft of the letter reveals that 'Cosmopolite' was in fact the Town Clerk, Jonathan Gooding.)

There is one other point with regard to the manner in which the service is performed at Southwold Church, which, methinks, it would be well if the minister would give his attention to it, I mean the pompous, irreverent and sententious manner in which the Parish Clerk reads the responses, he, poor, vain and foolish man, thinks no doubt he performs in the most approved and orthodox manner, and it would be a matter for much fun and drollery, was not the subject of too grave a nature. And then as to his singing – for so I suppose he calls it, why it is true he has a strong voice, so has a bull, but it is so ill managed and ill timed that I consider it quite as much his misfortune as that of the congregation that he could be heard: Just fancy, Mr Editor, a tall statured gawky looking fellow with a prodigious stiff white neckcloth round his throat – so stiff that if by any accident he dropped a leaf from his book – he could not, to save his soul alive, bend down within his elegant desk to pick it up. However there is one thing I will say of him and his coadjutors, the men and boys in the gallery, what they wanted in skill they made up in loudness and variety, every one has frequently his own time and the result of all I heard was like the choosing of parliament men, where everyone endeavours to cry loudest.

'The longer my cousin talked, the less I trusted him', from Charles Kingsley (1819–1875), *Alton Locke, Tailor and Poet* (1850)

A clergyman's son, Kingsley was for thirty-five years rector of Eversley in Hampshire, and the author of immensely popular fiction. He became professor of Modern History at Cambridge in the 1860s, and also chaplain to Queen Victoria. As a leading figure in F. D. Maurice's Christian Socialism movement he founded the Working Men's College with him in 1854.

Alton Locke *traces the struggles of its central character in trying to break through the social barriers of his time. In a later Preface for the work Kingsley wrote: 'I have tried to express in this book, what I know were, twenty years ago, the feelings of clever working men, looking upon the superior educational advantages of our clas. ... Does not the increased civilization and education of the working classes call on the Universities to consider whether they may not now try to become, what certainly they were meant to be, places of teaching and training for genius of every rank, and not merely for that of young gentlemen?'*

The University Tests Act, abolishing the requirement of subscribing to the 39 Articles of the Anglican Church, was finally passed in 1871, at last permitting Catholics, Nonconformists and non-Christians to attend Oxford and Cambridge.

In Chapter XIII, Alton Locke has come to visit his better-off cousin, an undergraduate at Cambridge. They are both from Dissenting stock, their fathers in trade. Alton's natural gifts have already shown themselves in his poetry, but his frustrations in breaking through the social barriers of his time have led him into some dangerous liaisons with Chartist groups.

Then came the question, 'What had brought me to Cambridge?' I told him all, and he seemed honestly to sympathize with my misfortunes.

'Never mind; we'll make it all right somehow. Those poems of yours – you must let me have them and look over them; and I dare say I shall persuade the governor to do something with them. After all, it's no loss for you; you couldn't have got on tailoring – much too sharp a fellow for that; – you ought to be at college, if one could only get you there. These sizarships, now, were meant for – just such cases as yours – clever fellows who could not afford to educate themselves; if we could only help you to one of them, now – '

'You forget that in that case,' said I, with something like a sigh, 'I should have to become a member of the Church of England.'

'Why, no; not exactly. Though, of course, if you want to get all out of the university which you ought to get, you must do so at last.'

'And pretend to believe what I do not; for the sake of deserting my own class, and pandering to the very aristocrats, whom – '

'Hullo!' and he jumped with a hoarse laugh. 'Stop that till I see whether the door is sported. Why, you silly fellow, what harm have the aristocrats, as you call them, ever done you? Are they not doing you good at this moment? Are you not, by virtue of their aristocratic institutions, nearer having your poems published, your genius recognized, &c. &c., than ever you were before?'

'Aristocrats? Then you call yourself one?'

'No, Alton, my boy; not yet,' said he quietly and knowingly. 'Not yet: but I have chosen the right road, and shall end at the road's end; and I advise you – for really, as my cousin, I wish you all success, even for the mere credit of the family, to choose the same road likewise.'

'What road?'

'Come up to Cambridge, by hook or by crook, and then take orders.'

I laughed scornfully.

'My good cousin, it is the only method yet discovered for turning a snob (as I am, or was) into a gentleman; except putting him into a heavy cavalry regiment. My brother, who has no brains, preferred the latter method. I, who flatter myself that I have some, have taken the former.' The thought was new and astonishing to me, and I looked at him in silence while he ran on –

'If you are once a parson, all is safe. Be you who you may before, from that moment you are a gentleman. No one will offer an insult. You are good enough for any man's society. You can dine at any nobleman's table. You can be friend, confidant, father confessor, if you like, to the highest women in the land; and if you have person, manners, and common sense, marry one of them into the bargain, Alton, my boy.'

'And it is for that that you will sell your soul – to become a hanger-on of the upper classes, in sloth and luxury?'

'Sloth and luxury? Stuff and nonsense! I tell you that after I have taken orders, I shall have years and years of hard work before me; continual drudgery of serving tables, managing charities, visiting, preaching, from morning till night, and after that often from night to morning again. Enough to wear out any but a tough constitution, as I trust mine is. Work, Alton, and hard work, is the only way now-a-days to rise in the Church, as in other professions. My father can buy me a living some day: but he can't buy me success, notoriety, social position, power – ' and he stopped suddenly, as if he had been on the point of saying something more which should not have been said.

'And this,' I said, 'is your idea of a vocation for the sacred ministry? It is for this, that you, brought up a Dissenter, have gone over to the Church of England?'

'And how do you know' – and his whole tone of voice changed instantly into what was meant, I suppose, for a gentle seriousness and reverent suavity – 'that I am not a sincere member of the Church of England? How do you know that I may not have loftier plans and ideas, though I may not choose to parade them to everyone, and give that which is holy to the dogs?'

'I am the dog, then?' I asked, half amused, for I was too curious about his state of mind to be angry.

'Not at all, my dear fellow. But those great men to whom we (or at least I) owe our conversion to the true Church, always tell us (and you will feel yourself how right they are) not to parade religious feelings; to look upon them as sacred things, to be treated with that due reserve which springs from real reverence. You know, as well as I, whether that is the fashion of the body in which we were, alas, brought up. You know as well as I, whether the religious conversation of that body has heightened your respect for sacred things.'

'I do, too well.' And I thought of Mr. Wigginton and my mother's tea parties.

'I dare say the vulgarity of that school has, ere now, shaken your faith in all that was holy?'

I was very near confessing that it had: but a feeling came over me, I knew not why, that my cousin would have been glad to get me into his power, and would therefore have welcomed a confession of infidelity. So I held my tongue.

'I can confess,' he said, in the most confidential tone, 'that it had for a time that effect on me. I have confessed it, ere now, and shall again and again, I trust. But I shudder to think of what I might have been believing or disbelieving now, if I had not in a happy hour fallen in with Mr. Newman's sermons [John Henry Newman, leader of the High Church Oxford Movement], and learnt from them, and from his disciples, what the Church of England really was; not Protestant, no; but Catholic in the deepest and highest sense.'

'So you are one of these new Tractarians? You do not seem to have adopted yet the ascetic mode of life, which I hear they praise up so highly.'

'My dear Alton, if you have read, as you have, your Bible, you will recollect a text which tells you not to appear to men to fast. What I do or do not do in the way of self-denial, unless I were actually profligate, which I give you my sacred honour I am not, must be a matter between Heaven and myself.'

There was no denying that truth; but the longer my cousin talked the less I trusted in him – I had almost said, the less I believed him. Ever since the tone of his voice had changed so suddenly, I liked him less than when he was honestly blurting out his coarse and selfish ambition. I do not think he was a hypocrite. I think he believed what he said, as strongly as he could believe anything. He proved afterwards that he did so, as far as man can judge man, by severe and diligent parish work: but I cannot help doubting at times, if that man ever knew what believing meant. God forgive him! In that, he is no worse than hundreds more who have never felt the burning and shining flame of intense conviction, of some truth rooted in the inmost recesses of the soul, by which a man must live, for which he would not fear to die.

Alfred, Lord Tennyson (1809–1892), from *In Memoriam* (1850)

Tennyson grew up in a Lincolnshire vicarage. His father died in 1831 after a mental breakdown, and Tennyson left Cambridge without taking his degree. His close friend, the gifted Arthur Henry Hallam, who had visited the vicarage several times and become engaged to Tennyson's younger sister, died suddenly of a stroke in 1833 aged twenty-two. What commenced in 1834 as an expression of personal grief was finally assembled as a poem of 132 sections, conveying his 'conviction that fear, doubts and suffering will find answer and relief only through Faith in a God of Love'. Queen Victoria's remark to Tennyson that 'Next to the Bible In Memoriam *is my comfort' is an indication of the bardic mantle his age came to expect him to wear.*

Ring out, wild bells, to the wild sky,
The flying cloud, the frosty light:
The year is dying in the night;
Ring out, wild bells, and let him die.

Ring out the old, ring in the new,
Ring, happy bells, across the snow:
The year is going, let him go;
Ring out the false, ring in the true.

Ring out the grief that saps the mind,
For those that here we see no more;
Ring out the feud of rich and poor,
Ring in redress to all mankind.

Ring out a slowly dying cause,
   And ancient forms of party strife;
   Ring in the nobler modes of life,
With sweeter manners, purer laws.

Ring out the want, the care, the sin,
   The faithless coldness of the times;
   Ring out, ring out my mournful rhymes,
And ring the fuller minstrel in.

Ring out false pride in place and blood,
   The civic slander and the spite;
   Ring in the love of truth and right,
Ring in the common love of good.

Ring out old shapes of foul disease;
   Ring out the narrowing lust of gold;
   Ring out the thousand wars of old,
Ring in the thousand years of peace.

Ring in the valiant man and free,
   The larger heart, the kindlier hand;
   Ring out the darkness of the land,
Ring in the Christ that is to be. ...

'With what purpose are you come a wolf among these sheep?', from J. A. Froude (1818–1894), *The Nemesis of Faith* (1848)

James Froude and his older brother Richard were clergy sons who came under the influence of John Henry Newman at Oxford, Richard collaborating (until his early death) over the Tracts for the Times *that forged the 'Tractarian' Oxford Movement. James resigned his fellowship over the scandal caused by his novel* The Nemesis of Faith. *He wrote to his friend A. H. Clough on 28 February 1849: 'Oxford grows too hot for me. I have resigned. I was preached against Sunday in Chapel, denounced in Hall, and yesterday burnt publicly (by Sewell) before two Lectures.'*

Eventually he made a name for himself as a man of letters and historian and lecturer, ending up back at Oxford in 1892 holding the Regius Chair of Modern History. He was close to Carlyle and Clough, and brother-in-law of Charles

Kingsley. Of this novel, he said that he had written a Tragedy, the tragedy of a man whose spiritual constitution was too shocked by his struggle of conscience to enable him to face successfully the trials of life: his faith became his 'nemesis'. The novel is written in letters from the Rev. Markham Sutherland to his friend Arthur.

Well, never mind, I must tell my story. About a fortnight ago I was asked to dine with the Hickmans. They are one of the few families that I really like here. Miss Hickman and I often meet in the dark staircases and the back alleys; and, though the least trifle in the world given to cant, they have enough good sense and active conscience about them to be saved from any serious harm from it. I had often been there before, and yet I felt a strange reluctance on this unhappy evening. I think there is a spiritual scent in us which feels mischief coming, as they say birds scent storms. I felt somewhat assured on entering the drawing-room. I was the last; and of the six or seven people present, there was only one I did not know at all, and one more with whom I was not intimate – this last, a young lady, a Miss Lennox, a niece of Mrs Hickman, who had for some weeks been staying with them. The other was the newly-arrived rector of a parish in the neighbourhood, who, I understood, had brought with him a reputation for cleverness, and was shortly to be married to the young lady. No one was coming in the evening; alas! who could have guessed from the plain unthreatening surface of that quiet little assembly, what a cunning mine had been run below it, – that I had been brought there to be dragged into an argumentary examination in which this new-found chymist was to analyse me, to expose my structure for his betrothed's spiritual pleasure, his own vanity, and the parish scandal. Well, unsuspecting, I went on tolerably well for some time: I rather liked the fellow. He was acute, not unwitty, and with a *savoir faire* about him which made his talk a pleasing variety to me. Once or twice the ladies made serious remarks; but he, as well as I, appeared to shrink from mixing more religion with our dinner than the grace which went before and which succeeded it; and in the half-hour we were left together after the ladies were gone, there was nothing to make me change my mind about him, except that I felt I could never be his friend; he knew too much and felt too little.

In the evening the conversation turned on a projected meeting of the Bible Society, where they were all going. There was much talk – what such talk is you know. Nothing at first was addressed to me, so I took no part in it. The good rector came out with some tolerably eloquent discoursing; and the poor ladies drank up his words; oh, you should have seen them. I fancy the fair *fiancée* drank a little too much of them, and got rather spiritually intoxicated – at least I hope she did – as some excuse for her. As he went rolling on for an hour or more, he described the world as grinding between the nether millstone of Popery and the upper millstone of Infidelity, and yet a universal millennium was very near indeed through this Bible activity. At the end he turned sharp upon me. Of course Mr. Sutherland would feel it his duty to take the chair on so truly blessed an occasion?

Now, conceive societies, with chairmen, dragging at the poor world from between two such millstones!!

'I believe you need not ask Mr. Sutherland,' the young lady said, in a tone of satiric melancholy; 'he never preaches the Bible.'

I didn't laugh. I was very near it; but I luckily looked first at Mrs. Hickman, and saw her looking so bitterly distressed – and distressed, too, (how much a look can say!) from her partly sharing her niece's feeling, that I gathered up as much gravity as I could command. 'I believe I read it to you twice every day,' I said, 'and my sermons are a great deal better than my own practice, perhaps than the practice of most of us.' She coloured, because she thinks daily service formal and superstitious. I do not know what indignation would not have bubbled out of her lips, when the rector heroically flew in to the rescue, and with a sufficient tact only noticed her with a smile, and repeated his own question.

'I fear not,' I said. 'I shrink from meetings where a number of people are brought together, not to learn something which they are themselves to do, but to give money to help others in a remote employment. There is a great deal of talking and excitement, and they go away home fancying they have been doing great things, when they have, in fact, only been stirring up some unprofitable feeling, and giving away a few shillings or pounds, when all their active feeling and all the money they can spare is far more profitably required at home. Charity is from person to person; and it loses half, more than half, its moral value when the giver is not brought into personal relation with those to whom he gives.'

'Mr. Sutherland is general enough, and perhaps vague enough,' was the answer. 'Permit me to keep to my subject. The Bible Society in the course of each year disperses over the world hundreds of thousands of Bibles in many different languages. The Word of God is sent into lands of Egyptian darkness, and souls at least may come to saving knowledge who else were lost without hope.'

I said coldly, I was sorry. I found my own duties far beyond my powers both of mind and money. I had only expressed my own feelings to explain my own conduct. I passed no opinion about others.

'I fear you cannot defend yourself on so general a ground without reflecting upon others, M. Sutherland,' he said. 'I could understand you, in a manner sympathize with you, if you took the ground of objection so many good churchmen take, in declining to act with a mixed body; but in this case I fear, pardon me, I think you have some other reason. I do not fancy the objects of the society can entirely meet your approbation, or you would not have spoken so coldly.'

Miss Lennox was looking infinitely disagreeable; the Hickmans as much concerned. The vulgar impertinence of such offensive personality disgusted me out of temper. Partly, too, I was annoyed at feeling he had heard, or she had been cunning enough to see, I had some particular feeling on the point beyond what I had spoken out.

'Yes,' I said, 'it is true I have particular feelings; I dislike societies generally; I would join in none of them. For your society in particular, as you insist on my telling you, I think it is the very worst, with the establishment of which I have been acquainted. Considering all the heresies, the enormous crimes, the wickednesses, the astounding follies which the Bible has been made to justify, and which its indiscriminate reading has suggested; considering it has been, indeed, the sword which our Lord said that he was sending; that not the Devil himself could have invented an implement more potent to fill the hated world with lies, and blood, and fury; I think, certainly, that to send hawkers over the world loaded with copies of this book, scattering it in all places among all persons – not teaching them to understand it; not standing, like Moses, between that heavenly light and them; but cramming it into their own hands as God's book, which He wrote, and they are to read, each for himself, and learn what they can for themselves – is the most culpable folly of which it is possible for man to be guilty.'

I had hardly spoken before I felt how wrong, how foolish, I had been; and that a mere vulgar charlatan, as I felt the man was, should have had the power to provoke me so! I had said nothing which was not perfectly true, in fact; but I ought to have known it was not true to the ignorant women who were listening with eyes fixed and ears quivering, as if the earth was to open and swallow a blasphemer – What did they know of the world's melancholy history?

I saw Mr. – – 's sparkle as he felt the triumph I was giving him, and his next word showed me it was a preconcerted plan.

'It is as I told you,' he said, turning away from me; 'the enemy is among us.' The ladies gathered together for mutual protection in a corner.

'What do you mean, Sir?' I said; 'this is most unwarrantable language. With what purpose did you come here?'

'Language! Sir,' he sighed, 'unwarrantable! – I might ask you, Sir, what you mean – with what purpose you are come a wolf among these sheep? They know you now, Mr. Sutherland. I knew what you were before, but your disguise had been too cunning for their eyes.'

Mrs. Hickman looked the picture of despair; quite wretched enough to disarm any anger I might feel at her. 'Really, Madam,' I said, rising, 'if you have connived at this scene, you must be sufficiently punished at its results. I will not add to your pain by continuing my presence.' The miserable young lady was flushed with exultation; the rector had smoothed himself into an expression of meek triumph in a successful exorcism. I had been too much in the wrong myself to enable me to say *then* what might have to be said. I would wait till the next morning, which I supposed must bring my hostess's apology, and so bowed coldly and departed. The whole thing was so very insufferably bad that I could not even let myself think of what I was to do till I had considered it coolly. I went home and went to bed. The next morning came, but no note, and the day passed without any; and I began to feel, as a clergyman, in a most embarrassing position indeed. As a man, it was far too contemptible to affect me; but as I thought it over, I saw that it was a seriously concerted design, whether from dislike or suspicion – what I do not know – to attack my position, and I had not heard the end of it. I called once or twice at the Hickmans, but they were not at home to me; long faces began to show about the parish. It was evident tongues had been busy, and last Sunday the church was half empty. I was at a loss what to resolve upon, and had been thinking over various plans, when something came this evening which is likely to resolve it all for me and save me the trouble. My folly has bred its consequence; the word flies out and has a life of its own, and goes its own way and does its own work. Just now a note was brought me, a very kind one, from the Bishop, requesting me to take an early opportunity of calling on him: if I were not engaged, fixing tomorrow morning. The sooner down the better with all nasty medicine, from the first magnesia draught to the death finish. I shall present myself at the first moment. I can have no doubt of the occasion.

Arthur Hugh Clough (1819–1861)

Among Clough's Oxford friends in that Tractarian period were Matthew Arnold and J. A. Froude (see above). His failure to subscribe to the 39 Articles cost him his fellowship at Oriel College, and his stint as principal of University Hall in London was brief. Thanks to his friendship with Ralph Waldo Emerson (see p. 239) he was given a position at Harvard. On his return in 1853 he held posts in the Education Office in London until his early death in 1861. Much of his poetic output is still relatively unfamiliar.

The Spirit's Song

'There is no God,' the wicked saith,
  'And truly it's a blessing,
For what He might have done with us
  It's better only guessing.'

'There is no God,' a youngster thinks,
  'Or really, if there may be,
He surely didn't mean a man
  Always to be a baby.'

'There is no God, or if there is,'
  The tradesman thinks, ''twere funny
If He should take it ill of me
  To make a little money.'

'Whether there be,' the rich man says,
  'It matters very little,
'For I and mine, thank somebody,
  Are not in want of victual.'

Some others, also, to themselves,
  Who scarce so much as doubt it,
Think there is none, when they are well,
  And do not think about it.

But country folks who live beneath
  The shadow of the steeple;
The parson and the parson's wife,
  And mostly married people;

Youths green and happy in first love,
So thankful for illusion,
And men caught out in what the world
Calls guilt, in first confusion;

And almost everyone when age,
Disease, or sorrows strike him,
Inclines to think there is a God,
Or something very like Him.

The Latest Decalogue

Thou shalt have one God only; who
Would be at the expense of two?
No graven images may be
Worshipped, except the currency:
Swear not at all; for, by thy curse
Thine enemy is none the worse:
At church on Sunday to attend
Will serve to keep the world thy friend:
Honour thy parents; that is, all
From whom advancement may befall;
Thou shalt not kill; but need'st not strive
Officiously to keep alive:
Do not adultery commit;
Advantage rarely comes of it:
Thou shalt not steal; an empty feat,
When it's so lucrative to cheat:
Bear not false witness; let the lie
Have time on its own wings to fly:
Thou shalt not covet, but tradition
Approves all forms of competition.

Matthew Arnold (1822–1888)

Son of the Rev. Dr Thomas Arnold, the reforming Headmaster of Rugby School, Arnold was one of the leading writers of his time in the fields of education and culture. Despite becoming Professor of Poetry at Oxford in 1857, he produced only one subsequent volume of poems (1867). It included 'Dover Beach', completed after he and his wife stayed in Dover on the last night of their honeymoon in 1851.

Dover Beach

The sea is calm to-night.
The tide is full, the moon lies fair
Upon the straits; – on the French coast the light
Gleams and is gone; the cliffs of England stand,
Glimmering and vast, out in the tranquil bay.
Come to the window, sweet is the night-air!
Only, from the long line of spray
Where the sea meets the moon-blanch'd land,
Listen! you hear the grating roar
Of pebbles which the waves draw back, and fling,
At their return, up the high strand,
Begin, and cease, and then again begin,
With tremulous cadence slow, and bring
The eternal note of sadness in.

Sophocles long ago
Heard it on the Ægean, and it brought
Into his mind the turbid ebb and flow
Of human misery: we
Find also in the sound a thought,
Hearing it by this distant northern sea.

The Sea of Faith
Was once, too, at the full, and round earth's shore
Lay like the folds of a bright girdle furled.
But now I only hear
Its melancholy, long, withdrawing roar,
Retreating, to the breath
Of the night-wind, down the vast edges drear
And shingles of the world.

Ah, love, let us be true
To one another! for the world, which seems
To lie before us like a land of dreams,
So various, so beautiful, so new,
Hath really neither joy, nor love, nor light,
Nor certitude, nor peace, nor help for pain:
And we are here as on a darkling plain
Swept with confused alarms of struggle and flight,
Where ignorant armies clash by night.

Reform begins to reach Cambridge: Sir Leslie Stephen (1832–1904), from his *Autobiography* (1903)

Stephen came from a family that was part of the 'Clapham Sect' network of philanthropic and reforming Anglican evangelicals. He resigned his fellowship at Trinity Hall, Cambridge, when his studies led him to lose his faith, and went on to have a prominent literary career in London, including editing the new Cornhill Magazine *and the* Dictionary of National Biography. *He was also a pioneer Alpinist. There is a portrait of him in the character of Mr Ramsay in* To the Lighthouse *by his daughter Virginia Woolf.*

We boast indeed of our poets at Cambridge; but if, for some mysterious reason, we have been more prolific in poets than Oxford, it is hardly because we have provided them with a more congenial atmosphere. They thrive best, perhaps, in a bracing climate. A Cambridge career induced Coleridge to become a heavy dragoon; Byron kept a bear to set a mode of manners to the dons of his day; and the one service which the place did for Wordsworth was to enable him for once in his life to drink a little more than was consistent with perfect command of his legs. Cambridge has for the last three centuries inclined to the less romantic side of things. It was for Puritans against the Cavaliers, for Whigs against Jacobites, and down to my time was favoured by 'Evangelicals' and the good 'high and dry' school which shuddered at the development of the 'Oxford Movement'. We could boast of no Newman, nor of men who, like Froude and Pattison, submitted for a time to the fascination of his genius and only broke from it with a wrench which permanently affected their mental equilibrium. 'I have never known a Cambridge man,' as a reverent disciple of the prophet lately said to me, 'who could appreciate Newman.' Our version of the remark was slightly different. We held that our common sense enabled us to appreciate him only too thoroughly by the dry light of reason and to resist the illusions of romantic sentiment. That indeed was the merit of Cambridge in the eyes of those who were responsible for my education. To have sent me to Oxford would have been to risk the contamination of what was then called 'Puseyism'. I escaped that danger pretty completely. My family – as this indicates – belonged to the second generation of the so-called 'Clapham Sect'; the 'Saints', as they were called by way of insult; the men who swore by Wilberforce [the leading Abolitionist] and fancied that they had accumulated a capital of merit by the anti-slavery crusade which entitled them for the future to live upon credit. They were, said their enemies, effete Puritans, as morose as their ancestors, but without the dignity of still militant fanaticism; Pharisees who hated innocent and artistic pleasure but found consolation in solid material comfort, blinded adherents of a dogmatic system which had long ceased to represent intellectual advance. I will not argue as to the justice of this accusation against the sect in general. I am content to say that though my childish reverence for certain members of the sect was necessarily of the instinctive variety, it does not seem misplaced to my later judgement. I have met no men in later years who seem to me to have had a higher sense of duty or deeper domestic affections. If they had obvious limitations, believed too implicitly in Noah's ark, and used language about the 'scheme of Salvation' which does not commend itself to me, they impressed me (very unintentionally) with the conviction that a man may be incomparably better than the creed which he honestly takes himself to believe. The essential Puritan may survive, as the case of Carlyle sufficiently showed, when all his dogmas have evaporated; and I confess that, rightly or wrongly, he is a person for whom I have a profound respect and much sympathy. At Cambridge, however, by my time the epithet 'Evangelical' generally connoted contempt. The 'Oxford Movement' might be altogether mistaken, but we agreed with it that the old 'low church' position had become untenable.

At Cambridge we rather shrank form all vagaries whether of high or low church. Our state, an adversary might say, was not the more gracious. If the Oxford school represented 'reaction,' it was at least, as Arnold put it, not of the Philistine variety. A mistaken or impossible idealism is better than the mere stolid indifference which chokes all speculative activity. To the radical meanwhile the two universities represented two slightly different forms of obstructiveness. They were simply Anglican seminaries; bulwarks of the establishment which was an essential part of the great conservative fortress; mediæval in their constitution and altogether behind the age in their teaching. My undergraduate career fell at a period when such criticisms were about to lead to a practical result. A Parliamentary commission began to overhaul us soon afterwards and initiated a process of reconstruction which has been going on ever since. Staunch Conservatives at that time prophesied fearful results. The English were to sink to the level of foreign universities: an awful descent! They were to be 'Germanised' – to be contaminated by 'neology,' whatever these appalling phrases might mean, generally to be trimmed and clipped in conformity with the fads of 'damned intellectuals.' In fact, the universities had somehow worked out a system which had become so thoroughly familiar to their own members and so consistently elaborated as to have the character of a natural organism, while to the outsider it appeared to be radically illogical and grotesque. …

Certainly we needed reform; and if change means reform, as I hope it does in this case, we have certainly got it. But the question occurs, Why did I love the place in spite of its admitted shortcomings? Was my conscience seared? Were not the colleges mere nests of abuses? The name 'don' may suggest visions of the indolent bigoted dullards who enraged Gray and Gibbon and Adam Smith, or the pedants whose ignorance of the world provoked the scorn of Chesterfield in the eighteenth century. Skill in writing Latin verses and solving mathematical conundrums may be compatible with intellectual torpor and devotion to port wine. When I search my memory, I can turn out a story or two to suggest that the type was not quite extinct. The peculiar position of a college fellow, for example, had its temptations. He held his post during celibacy, and after a time naturally began to feel yearnings for a domestic hearth of his own. That meant that he could not adopt teaching as a career for life, but as a stepping-stone to something else. The 'something else' was normally a college living. After a few years spent in lecturing, he could become a country parson and try how far his knowledge of the Greek drama or the planetary theory would qualify him to edify the agricultural labourer. Meanwhile waiting for a vacancy was at times demoralising. The best living of one of the colleges was held by an old gentleman, who had been described in a book of reminiscences as a specimen of the low moral standard prevalent at the end of the eighteenth century. He had the conscience to be still alive when the book appeared in the middle of the nineteenth. Meanwhile expectant successors would pay him visits and find the old cynic smoking in his kitchen and unblushingly proclaiming the intention of prolonging his existence indefinitely. They could not bear it; and the last of them, a man whom I remember, sought consolation in the college cellar. A catastrophe followed. One day the fellow came to the college hall, not only in a state of partial sobriety but with a disreputable companion who had hung about Cambridge levying contributions on some vague pretence of being a political refugee. Finding himself in respectable society, the disreputable person suddenly arose and proposed the health of the great John Bright [the radical statesman who successfully fought the Corn Laws]. In those days he might as well have proposed Beelzebub. An explosion followed. The scandal was beyond concealment; the fellow was requested to leave Cambridge, and soon afterwards fell into a canal after dinner and was drowned. A week or two later, the living for which he had been waiting became vacant, by the death of the old incumbent, and had the fellow held out a week or two longer he might have succeeded to the pastoral guidance of that bit of Arcadia. This anecdote, I must add emphatically, represents the rare exception; few of us took to drink; though now and then a man might be soured and become a crabbed, eccentric cynic of the ancient type.

Robert Browning (1812–1889), from *Bishop Blougram's Apology* (1855)

This long poem takes the form of an after-dinner conversation. The bishop attempts to disarm a sceptical young writer, over a glass of wine, with the underlying earnestness of his position, one of a worldly, charming, cynical ambivalence. Browning admitted he partly modelled his character on Cardinal Wiseman, first Roman Catholic Archbishop of Westminster.

And now what are we? unbelievers both,
Calm and complete, determinately fixed
Today, to-morrow and for ever, pray?
You'll guarantee me that? Not so, I think!
In no wise! all we've gained is, that belief,
As unbelief before, shakes us by fits,
Confounds us like its predecessor. Where's
The gain? how can we guard our unbelief,
Make it bear fruit to us – the problem here.
Just when we are safest, there's a sunset touch,

A fancy from a flower-bell, someone's death,
A chorus-ending from Euripides, –
And that's enough for fifty hopes and fears
As old and new at once as nature's self,
To rap and knock and enter in our soul,
To take hands and dance there, a fantastic ring,
Round the ancient idol, on his base again, –
The grand Perhaps! We look on helplessly.
There the old misgivings, crooked questions are –
This good God, – what he could do, if he would,
Would, if he could – then must have done long since:
If so, when, where and how? some way must be, –
Once feel about, and soon or late you hit
Some sense, in which it might be, after all.
Why not, 'The Way, the Truth, the Life'?

Gerard Manley Hopkins (1844–1889)

Hopkins grew up in Hampstead, the eldest of nine in a High Church and artistic family. At Oxford he came under the influence of John Henry Newman, who had shocked the High Church world of the Oxford Movement by leaving it for the Roman Catholic Church in 1845, and was received into it by him later that year. Hopkins's friend Robert Bridges became Poet Laureate in 1913; it was he who first found publication for some of the Jesuit priest's remarkable poems, in 1918, nearly thirty years after his death.

• An incipient Catholic to his Anglican father, from Balliol College, Oxford, 16 October 1866

My dear Father, – I must begin with a practical immediate point. The Church strictly forbids all communion in sacred things with non-Catholics. I have only just learnt this, but it prevents me going to chapel, and so yesterday I had to inform the Dean of Chapel. Today the Master sent for me and said he cd. not grant me leave of absence without an application from you. As the College last term passed a resolution admitting Catholics and took a Catholic into residence it has no right to alter its principles in my case. I wish you therefore not to give yourself the pain of making this application, even if you were willing: I am of age moreover and am alone concerned. If you refuse to make the application, the Master explains that he shall lay my case before the common-room. In this case there is very little doubt indeed that the Fellows wd. Take the reasonable course and give me leave of absence fr. chapel, and if not, I am quite contented: but in fact I am satisfied as to the course our Fellows will take and the Master will at the last hesitate to lay the matter before them perhaps even. I want you therefore to write at once, if you will, – not to the Master who has no right to ask what he does, but to me, with a refusal: no harm will follow.

The following is the position of things with me. You ask me to suspend my judgment for a long time, or at the very least more than half a year, in other words to stand still for a time. Now to stand still is not possible, thus: I must either obey the Church or disobey. If I disobey, I am not suspending judgment but deciding, namely to take backward steps fr. the grounds I have already come to. To stand still if it were possible might be justifiable, but to go back nothing can justify. I must therefore obey the Church by ceasing to attend any service of the Church of England. If I am to wait then I must either be altogether without services and sacraments, which you will of course know is impossible, or else I must attend the services of the Church – still being unreceived. But what can be more contradictory than, in order to avoid joining the Church, attending the services of that very Church? Three of my friends, whose conversions were later than mine, Garrett, Addis, and Wood, have already been received, but this is by the way. Only one thing remains to be done: I cannot fight against God Who calls me to His Church: if I were to delay and die in the meantime I shd. have no plea why my soul was not forfeit. I have no power in fact to stir a finger: it is God who makes the decision and not I. ...

You speak of the claims of the Church of England, but it is to me the strange thing that the Church of England makes no claims: it is true that Tractarians make them for her and find them faintly or only in a few instances borne out for them by her liturgy, and are strongly assailed for their extravagances while they do it. Then about applying to Mr. Liddon and the Bp. of Oxford ['Soapy Sam' Wilberforce]. Mr. Liddon writes begging me to pause: it wd. take too long to explain how I did not apply to him at first and why it wd. have been useless. If Dr. Pusey is in Oxford tomorrow I will see him, if it is any satisfaction to you. The Bishop is too much engaged to listen to individual difficulties and those who do apply to him may get such answers as young Mr. Lane Fox did, who gave up £30,000 a year just lately to become a Catholic. He wrote back about a cob which he wanted to sell to the Dean of some place and wh. Lane Fox was to put his own price on and ride over for the Bishop to the place of sale. In fact Dr. Pusey and Mr. Liddon [Liddon wrote Pusey's biography] were the only two men in the world who cd. avail to detain me: the fact that they were Anglicans kept me on, for arguments for the Church of England I had long ago felt there were none that wd. hold water, and when that influence gave way everything was gone.

You are so kind as not to forbid me your house, to which I have no claim, on condition, if I understand, that I promise not to try to convert my brothers and sisters. Before I can promise this I must get permission, wh. I have no doubt will be given. Of course this promise will not apply after they come of age. Whether after my reception you will still speak as you do now I cannot tell. ...

After writing this I feel lighter-hearted, though I still can by no means make my pen write what I shd. wish. I am your loving son,

Gerard M. Hopkins.

23 New Inn Hall Street, Oct. 17, 1866.

P.S. I am most anxious that you shd. not think of my future. It is likely that the positions you wd. like to see me in wd. have no attraction for me, and surely the happiness of my prospects depends on the happiness to me and not on intrinsic advantages. It is possible even to be very sad and very happy at once and the time I was with Bridges, when my anxiety came to its height, was I believe the happiest fortnight of my life. My only strong wish is to be independent.

• Felix Randal

This poem was written in April 1880, when Father Hopkins was a priest in Liverpool; a blacksmith parishioner of his, Felix Spencer, had recently died of tuberculosis at the age of 31. ('Sandal' is a technical name for a type of horseshoe.)

Felix Randal the farrier, O is he dead then? My duty all ended,
Who have watched his mould of man, big-boned and hardy-handsome
Pining, pining, till time when reason rambled in it and some
Fatal four disorders, fleshed there, all contended?

Sickness broke him. Impatient, he cursed at first, but mended
Being anointed and all; though a heavenlier heart began some

Months earlier, since I our sweet reprieve and ransom
Tendered to him. Ah well, God rest him all road ever he offended!

This seeing the sick endears them to us, us too it endears.
My tongue had taught thee comfort, touch had quenched thy tears,
Thy tears that touched my heart, child, Felix, poor Felix Randal;

How far from then forethought of, all thy more boisterous years,
When thou at the random grim forge, powerful amidst peers,
Didst fettle for the great grey drayhorse his bright and battering sandal!

'A Study of Two Temperaments', from Edmund Gosse (1849–1928), *Father and Son* (1907)

Gosse recalls his cloistered childhood in South Devon, soon after his mother had died, with his father Philip Gosse, a distinguished zoologist and devout member of the Plymouth Brethren, over whose local congregation he had assumed leadership. The book was initially published anonymously, at a time when Gosse was firmly established in the literary world.

[Christmas 1857]

Of our dealings with the 'Saints', a fresh assortment of whom met us on our arrival in Devonshire, I shall speak presently. My Father's austerity of behaviour was, I think, perpetually accentuated by his fear of doing anything to offend the consciences of these persons, whom he supposed, no doubt, to be more sensitive than they really were. He was fond of saying that 'a very little stain upon the conscience makes a wide breach in our communion with God,' and he counted possible errors of conduct by hundreds and by thousands. It was in this winter that his attention was particularly drawn to the festival of Christmas, which, apparently, he had scarcely noticed in London.

On the subject of all feasts of the Church he held views of an almost grotesque peculiarity. He looked upon each of them as nugatory and worthless, but the keeping of Christmas appeared to him by far the most hateful, and nothing less than an act of idolatry. 'The very word is Popish,' he used to exclaim, 'Christ's Mass!' pursing up his lips with the gesture of one who tastes assafoetida by accident. Then he would adduce the antiquity of the so-called feast, adapted from horrible heathen rites, and itself a soiled relic of the abominable Yule-Tide. He would denounce the horrors of Christmas until it almost made me blush to look at a holly-berry.

On Christmas Day of this year of 1857 our villa saw a very unusual sight. My Father had given strictest charge that no difference whatever was to be made in our meals on that day; the dinner was to be neither more copious than usual nor less so. He was obeyed, but the servants, secretly rebellious, made a small plum-pudding for themselves. (I discovered afterwards, with pain, that Miss Marks [their housekeeper] received a slice of it in her boudoir.) Early in the afternoon, the maids – of whom we were now advanced to keeping two – kindly remarked that 'the poor dear child ought to have a bit anyhow,' and wheedled me into the kitchen, where I ate a slice of plum-pudding. Shortly after I began to feel that pain inside which in my frail state was inevitable, and my conscience smote me violently. At length I could bear my spiritual anguish no longer, and bursting into the study I called out: 'Oh! Papa, Papa, I have eaten of flesh offered to idols!' It took some time, between my sobs, to explain what had happened. Then my Father sternly said: 'Where is the accursed thing?' I explained that as much as was left of it was still on the kitchen table. He took me by the hand, and ran with me into the midst of the startled servants, seized what remained of the pudding, and with the plate in one hand and me still tight in the other, ran until we reached the dust-heap, when he flung the idolatrous confectionery on the middle of the ashes, and raked it deep down into the mass. The suddenness, the violence, the velocity of this extraordinary act made an impression on my memory which nothing will ever efface.

The key is lost by which I might unlock the perverse malady from which my Father's conscience seemed to suffer during the whole of this melancholy winter. But I think that a dislocation of his intellectual system had a great deal to do with it. Up to this point in his career, he had, as we have seen, nourished the delusion that science and revelation could be mutually justified, that some sort of compromise was possible. With great and ever greater distinctness, his investigations had shown him that in all departments of organic nature there are visible the evidences of slow modification of forms, of the type developed by the pressure and practice of aeons. This conviction had been borne in upon him until it was positively irresistible. Where was his place, then, as a sincere and accurate observer? Manifestly, it was with the pioneers of the new truth, it was with Darwin, Wallace and Hooker. But did not the second chapter of 'Genesis' say that in six days the heavens and earth were finished, and the host of them, and that on the seventh day God ended his work which he had made?

Here was a dilemma! Geology certainly *seemed* to be true, but the Bible, which was God's word, *was* true. If the Bible said that all things in Heaven and

Earth were created in six days, created in six days they were – in six literal days of twenty-four hours each. The evidences of spontaneous variation of form, acting, over an immense space of time, upon ever-modifying organic structures, *seemed* overwhelming, but they must either be brought into line with the six-day labour of creation, or they must be rejected. I have already shown how my Father worked out the ingenious 'Omphalos' theory in order to justify himself as a strictly scientific observer who was also a humble slave of revelation. But the old convention and the new rebellion would alike have none of his compromise.

To a mind so acute and at the same time so narrow as that of my Father – a mind which is all logical and positive, without breadth, without suppleness and without imagination – to be subjected to a check of this kind is agony. It has not the relief of a smaller nature, which escapes from the dilemma by some foggy formula; nor the resolution of larger nature to take to its wings and surmount the obstacle. My Father, although half suffocated by the emotion of being lifted, as it were, on the great biological wave, never dreamed of letting go his clutch of the ancient tradition, but hung there, strained and buffeted. It is strange that he – an 'honest hodman of science,' as Huxley once called him – should not have been content to allow others, whose horizons were wider than his could be, to pursue those purely intellectual surveys for which he had no species of aptitude. As a collector of facts and marshaller of observations, he had not a rival in that age; his very absence of imagination aided him in this work. But he was more an attorney than a philosopher, and he lacked that sublime humility which is the crown of genius. For, this obstinate persuasion that he alone knew the mind of God, that he alone could interpret the designs of the Creator, what did it result from if not from a congenital lack of that highest modesty which replies 'I do not know' even to the questions which Faith, with menacing finger, insists on having most positively answered?

'Honour thy father and mother': Samuel Butler (1835–1902), from *The Way of All Flesh* (1903)

Many of the details of the posthumously published The Way of All Flesh *are autobiographical, even to the inclusion of actual letters written to Butler by his parents, for their unconscious self-satire. His grandfather was once headmaster of the school that both he and Darwin were to attend (Shrewsbury), later becoming a bishop; his clergyman father was a bullying figure whose grip he finally shook off by making enough money sheep-farming in New Zealand to enable him to paint, compose, and write books in London as he wanted.* Erewhon *brought him most attention, with its contemporary satire in the* Gulliver's Travels *tradition; but there was, too, much sparring with the theories of Darwin and others. The picture of* Family Prayers *that he painted on his return in 1864, which now hangs in his old Cambridge college (St John's), is an apt illustration of the suffocating orthodoxy he needed to escape.*

In Chapter 14 of The Way of All Flesh *he writes: 'Every man's work, whether it be literature or music or pictures or architecture or anything else, is always a portrait of himself, and the more he tries to conceal himself the more clearly will his character appear in spite of him. I may very likely be condemning myself, all the time that I am writing this book, for I know that whether I like it or no I am portraying myself more surely than I am portraying any of the characters whom I set before the reader.'*

From Chapter 20
The Rev. Theobald Pontifex is the Rector of Battersby. He had married Christina, to whose father he had been curate, a few years previously. Now their own children are on the way, and Ernest is the first.

Theobald had never liked children. He had always got away from them as soon as he could, and so had they from him; oh, why, he was inclined to ask himself, could not children be born into the world grown up? If Christina could have given birth to a few full-grown clergymen in priest's orders – of moderate views, but inclining rather to Evangelicism, with comfortable livings and in all respects facsimiles of Theobald himself – why, there might have been more sense in it; or if people could buy ready-made children at a shop of whatever age and sex they liked, instead of always having to make them at home and to begin at the beginning with them – that might do better, but as it was he did not like it. He felt as he had felt when he had been required to come and be married to Christina – that he had been going on for a long time quite nicely, and would much rather continue things on their present footing. In the matter of getting married he had been obliged to pretend he liked it; but times were changed, and if he did not like a thing now, he could find a hundred unexceptionable ways of making his dislike apparent.

It might have been better if Theobald in his younger days had kicked more against his father: the fact that he had not done so encouraged him to expect the most implicit obedience from his own children. He could trust himself, he said (and so did Christina), to be more lenient than perhaps his father had been to himself; his danger, he said (and so again did Christina), would be rather in the direction of being too indulgent; he must be on his guard against this, for no duty could be more important than that of teaching a child to obey its parents in all things. ...

The practical outcome of the foregoing was a conviction in Theobald's mind, and if in his, then in Christina's, that it was their duty to begin training up their children in the way they should go, even from their earliest infancy. The first signs of self-will must be carefully looked for, and plucked up by the roots at once before they had time to grow. Theobald picked up this numb serpent of a metaphor and cherished it in his bosom.

Before Ernest could well crawl he was taught to kneel; before he could well speak he was taught to lisp the Lord's prayer, and the general confession. How was it possible that these things could be taught too early? If his attention flagged or his memory failed him, here was an ill weed which would grow apace, unless it were plucked out immediately, and the only way to pluck it out was to whip him, or shut him up in a cupboard, or dock him of the small pleasures of childhood. Before he was three years old he could read and after a fashion, write. Before he was four he was learning Latin, and could do rule-of-three sums.

As for the child himself, he was naturally of an even temper; he doted upon his nurse, on kittens and puppies, and on all things that would do him the kindness of allowing him to be fond of them. He was fond of his mother, too, but as regards his father, he has told me in later life he could remember no feeling but fear and shrinking. Christina did not remonstrate with Theobald concerning the severity of the tasks imposed upon their boy, nor as yet to the continual whippings that were found necessary at lesson times. Indeed, when during any absence of Theobald's the lessons were entrusted to her, she found to her sorrow that it was the only thing to do, and she did it no less effectually than Theobald himself; nevertheless she was fond of her boy, which Theobald never was, and it was long before she could destroy all affection for herself in the mind of her first-born. But she persevered.

The archdeacon is counselled by his wife: Anthony Trollope (1815–1882), from *The Warden* (1855)

Until 1867 Trollope was an employee of the Post Office (where he was the instigator of the pillar-box), and his writing was fitted into a tightly disciplined three-hour schedule before he left for work. His Barsetshire novels proved his first big success, initially hatched, according to his Autobiography, *while wandering around Salisbury Cathedral close one summer evening.*

Many of us have often thought how severe a trial of faith must this be to wives of our great church dignitaries. To us these men are personifications of St. Paul; their very gait is a speaking sermon; their clean and sombre apparel exacts from us faith and submission, and the cardinal virtues seem to hover round their sacred hats. A dean or archbishop, in the garb of his order, is sure of our reverence, and a well-got-up bishop fills our very souls with awe. But how can this feeling be perpetuated in the bosoms of those who see the bishops without their aprons, and the archdeacons even in a lower state of dishabille?

Do we not all know some reverend, all but sacred, personage before who our tongue ceases to be loud and our step to be elastic? But were we once to see him stretch himself beneath the bed-clothes, yawn widely, and bury his face upon his pillow, we could chatter before him as glibly as before a doctor or a lawyer. From some such cause, doubtless, it arose that our archdeacon listened to the counsels of his wife, though he considered himself entitled to give counsel to every other being whom he met.

'My dear,' he said, as he adjusted the copious folds of his nightcap, 'there was that John Bold at your father's again to-day. I must say your father is very imprudent.'

'He is imprudent – he always was,' replied Mrs. Grantly, speaking from under the comfortable bedclothes. 'There's nothing new in that.'

'No, my dear, there's nothing new – I know that; but, at the present juncture of affairs, such imprudence is – is – I'll tell you what, my dear, if he does not take care what he's about, John Bold will be off with Eleanor.'

'I think he will, whether papa takes care or no. And why not?'

'Why not!' almost screamed the archdeacon, giving so rough a pull at the nightcap as almost to bring it over his nose; 'why not! – that pestilent, interfering upstart, John Bold – the most vulgar young person I ever met! Do you know that he is meddling with your father's affairs in a most uncalled-for

– most –' And being at a loss for an epithet sufficiently injurious, he finished his expressions of horror by muttering, 'Good heavens!' in a manner that had been found very efficacious in clerical meetings of the diocese. He must for the moment have forgotten where he was.

'As to his vulgarity, archdeacon' (Mrs. Grantly had never assumed a more familiar term than this in addressing her husband), 'I don't agree with you. Not that I like Mr. Bold – he is a great deal too conceited for me; but then Eleanor does, and it would be the best thing in the world for papa if they were to marry. Bold would never trouble himself about Hiram's Hospital if he were papa's son-in-law.' And the lady turned herself round under the bed-clothes, in a manner to which the doctor was well accustomed, and which told him, as plainly as words, that as far as she was concerned the subject was over for that night.

'Good heavens!' murmured the doctor again – he was evidently much put beside himself.

Dr. Grantly was by no means a bad man; he was exactly the man which such an education as his was most likely to form; his intellect being sufficient for such a place in the world, but not sufficient to put him in advance of it. He performed with a rigid constancy such of the duties of a parish clergyman as were, to his thinking, above the sphere of his curate, but it is as an archdeacon that he shines.

George Eliot (1819–1880)

From a conventionally religious background and education in the provincial Midlands, Mary Ann Evans fell out with her land-agent father over her refusal to go to church (1842), although she continued to keep house for him until his death (1849) while coming to know a circle of radical thinkers. In 1846 she translated The Life of Jesus Critically Examined *by Pastor David Strauss, the cause of shock waves to traditional belief. By 1851 she was assistant editor of the* Westminster Review.

• From the *Westminster Review*, October 1855

In an article on Dr Cumming, a highly popular Evangelical preacher, she wrote:

Pleasant to the clerical flesh under such circumstances is the arrival of Sunday! Somewhat at a disadvantage during the week, in the presence of working-day interests and lay splendours, on Sunday the preacher becomes the cynosure of a thousand eyes ... no one may hiss, no one may depart. Like the writer of imaginary conversations, he may put what imbecilities he pleases into the mouths of his antagonists, and swell with triumph when he has refuted them. He may riot in gratuitous assertions, confident that no man will contradict him; he may exercise perfect free-will in logic, and invent illustrative experience; he may give an evangelical edition of history with the inconvenient facts omitted: – all this he may do with impunity, certain that those of his hearers who are not sympathizing are not listening.

A year later, in her late thirties, with her partner G. H. Lewes's encouragement she embarked on her first attempt at fiction, 'The Sad Fortunes of the Reverend Amos Barton'. This became the first of her Scenes from Clerical Life *that Lewes persuaded Blackwood to publish under the name of George Eliot. She based her 'superlatively middling' hero on the Rev. John Gwyther, the curate whose sermons she had listened to as a girl, and who had conducted her mother's funeral in 1836.*

• 'The Sad Fortunes of the Reverend Amos Barton' (1856), from *Scenes from Clerical Life*

The Rev. Amos Barton, whose sad fortunes I have undertaken to relate, was, you perceive, in no respect an ideal or exceptional character; and perhaps I am doing a bold thing to bespeak your sympathy on behalf of a man who was so very far from remarkable, – a man whose virtues were not heroic, and who had no undetected crime within his breast; who had not the slightest mystery hanging about him, but was palpably and unmistakably commonplace; who was not even in love, but had had that complaint favourably many years ago. 'An utterly uninteresting character!' I think I hear a lady reader exclaim – Mrs. Farthingale, for example, who prefers the ideal in fiction; to whom tragedy means ermine tippets, adultery, and murder; and comedy, the adventures of some personage who is quite a 'character'.

But, my dear madam, it is so very large a majority of your fellow-countrymen that are of this insignificant stamp. At least eighty out of a hundred of your adult male fellow-Britons returned in the last census are neither extraordinarily silly, nor extraordinarily wicked, nor extraordinarily wise; their eyes are neither deep and liquid with sentiment, nor sparkling with suppressed witticisms; they have probably had no hairbreadth escapes or thrilling adventures; their brains are certainly not pregnant with genius, and their passions have not manifested themselves at all after the fashion of a volcano. They are simply men of complexions more or less muddy, whose conversation is more or less bald and disjointed. Yet these commonplace people – many of them – bear a conscience, and have felt the sublime prompting to do the painful right; they have their unspoken sorrows, and their sacred joys; their hearts have perhaps gone out towards their first-born, and they have mourned over the irreclaimable dead. Nay, is there not a pathos in their very insignificance – in our comparison of their dim and narrow existence with the glorious possibilities of that human nature which they share?

Depend upon it, you would gain unspeakably if you would learn with me to see some of the poetry and the pathos, the tragedy and the comedy, lying in the experience of a human soul that looks out through dull grey eyes, and that speaks in a voice of quite ordinary tones. In that case, I should have no fear of your not caring to know what farther befell the Rev. Amos Barton, or of your thinking the homely details I have to tell at all beneath your attention. As it is, you can, if you please, decline to pursue my story farther; and you will easily find reading more to your taste, since I learn from the newspapers that many remarkable novels, full of striking situations, thrilling incidents, and eloquent writing, have appeared only within the last season.

Meanwhile, readers who have begun to feel an interest in the Rev. Amos Barton and his wife, will be glad to learn that Mr. Oldinport lent them twenty pounds. But twenty pounds are soon exhausted when twelve are due as back payment to the butcher, and when the possession of eight extra sovereigns in February weather is an irresistible temptation to order a new greatcoat. And though Mr. Bridmain so far departed from the necessary economy entailed on him by the Countess's elegant toilette and expensive maid, as to choose a handsome black silk, as his experienced eye discerned, with the genuine strength of its own texture, and not with the factitious strength of gum, and present it to Mrs. Barton, in retrieval of the accident that had occurred at his table, yet, dear me – as every husband has heard – what is the present of a gown when you are deficiently furnished with the et-ceteras of apparel, and when, moreover, there are six children whose wear and tear of clothes is something incredible to the non-maternal mind?

Indeed, the equation of income and expenditure was offering new and constantly accumulating difficulties to Mr. and Mrs. Barton; for shortly after the birth of little Walter, Milly's aunt, who had lived with her ever since her marriage, had withdrawn herself, her furniture, and her yearly income, to the household of another niece; prompted to that step, very probably, by a slight 'tiff' with the Rev. Amos, which occurred while Milly was up-stairs, and proved one too many for the elderly lady's patience and magnanimity. Mr. Barton's temper was a little warm, but, on the other hand, elderly maiden ladies are known to be susceptible; so we will not suppose that all the blame lay on his side – the less so, as he had every motive for humouring an inmate whose presence kept the wolf from the door. It was now nearly a year since Miss Jackson's departure, and to a fine ear, the howl of the wolf was audibly approaching.

It was a sad thing, too, that when the last snow had melted, when the purple and yellow crocuses were coming up in the garden, and the old church was already half pulled down, Milly had an illness which made her lips look pale, and rendered it absolutely necessary that she should not exert herself for some time. Mr. Brand, the Shepperton doctor so obnoxious to Mr. Pilgrim, ordered her to drink port-wine, and it was quite necessary to have a char-woman very often, to assist Nanny in all the extra work that fell upon her.

Mrs. Hackit, who hardly ever paid a visit to any one but her oldest and nearest neighbour, Mrs. Patten, now took the unusual step of calling at the vicarage one morning; and the tears came into her unsentimental eyes.

'The Curate in a Populous Parish', from Anthony Trollope (1815–1882), *Clergymen of the Church of England* (1866)

From the eighth of Trollope's ten short sketches surveying the ranks of the Anglican hierarchy and their social positions.

Let us for a moment look at the life of a curate of the present day. We will suppose that he comes from some college at Cambridge or Oxford. We will so suppose because Cambridge and Oxford still give us the majority of our clergymen, though we can hardly hope that they will continue to be so bountiful. He enters the Church, moved to do so by what we call a special vocation. During the period of his education he feels himself to be warmed towards the teaching of the English Protestant Church, and as he finds the ministry easily in his way he enters it – and at about the age of twenty-four he becomes a curate. He is at first gratified at the ease with which are confided to him the duties of an assistant in the cure of souls, and does not think much of the stipend which is allotted to him. He has lived as a boy at the university upon two hundred a year without falling much into debt, and thinks that as a man he can live easily upon seventy pounds. Hitherto he has indulged himself with many things. He has smoked cigars, and had his wine parties, and been luxurious; but as a curate he will be delighted to deny himself all luxuries. His heart will be in the service of his God, and his appetites shall be to him as thorns which he will make to crackle in the fire. To eat bread without butter and to drink tea without milk is a glory to him, – and so he begins the world.

And for a year or two, if he be not weak-minded, things do not go badly with him. The parson's wife sees far into his character, and is kind to him, stirred thereto by a conviction of which she herself is unconscious, that the money payment made by her husband is insufficient. The dry bread and the brown tea are still sweetened by reminiscences of St. Paul's sufferings, and the young man consoles himself by inward whisperings of forty stripes save one five times repeated. To be persecuted is as yet sweet to him, and he knows that in doing all the rector's work for seventy pounds a year he is being persecuted. But anon there grows up within his breast a feeling in which the grievance as regards this world is brought into unpleasant contact with the persecution in which he has a pietistic delight. He still rejoices in the reflection that he cannot possibly buy for himself a much-needed half-dozen of new shirts, but is uncomfortably angry because the rector himself is not only idle, but has bought a new carriage. And then he gives way a little – the least in the world – and at the end of the year owes the butcher a small bill which he cannot settle. From that day the vision of St. Paul melts before his eyes, and he sighs for replenished fleshpots.

But he still works hard in his curacy, – perhaps harder than ever, driven thereto by certain inward furies. What will become of him, – of him, with his seventy pounds a year, and nothing further to expect as professional result, if he be deserted by his religious ecstasy? But religious ecstasy will not permit itself to be maintained on such terms, and gradually there creeps upon him the heart-breaking disappointment of a soured and injured man. In the midst of this he takes to himself a wife. It is always so. The man who is most in the dark will be the best inclined to take a leap in the dark. In the lowest period of his despondency he becomes a married man – enjoying at the moment a little fitful gleam of shortlived worldly pleasure. Then, again, he is a male saint for a few months, with a female saint beside him; and after that all collapses, and he goes down into irrevocable misery and distress. In a few years we know of him as a beggar of old clothes, as a man whom from time to time his friends are asked to lift from unutterable depths of distress by donations which no gentleman can take without a crushed spirit – as a pauper whom the poor around him know to be a pauper, and will not, therefore, respect as a minister of their religion. In all this there has been very little, we may say, nothing, of fault in the curate himself. As a young man, almost as a boy, he placed himself in a position of which he knew the old conditions rather than those then existing around him – and through that mistake he fell.

But young men are now beginning to know, and the fathers of young men also, what are at present the true conditions of the Church of England as a profession, and they who have been nurtured softly, and who have any choice, will not undergo its trials – and its injustice! For men of a lower class in life, who have come from harder antecedents, the normal seventy pounds per annum may suffice; but all modern Churchmen will understand what must be the effect on the Church if such be the recruits to which the Church must trust.

'A Street Boy', from Henry Mayhew (1812–1887), *London Labour and the London Poor*

Mayhew was a London journalist and one of the original founders of Punch *magazine (1841). He began his 'inquiries' into 'the industry, the want, and the vice of the great Metropolis' in 1849 as newspaper articles, continued them independently, and finally brought them together in four volumes (1861–62). In his Preface he wrote: 'It surely may be considered curious as being the first attempt to publish the history of a people, from the lips of the people themselves – giving a literal description of their labour, their earnings, their trials, and their sufferings, in their own "unvarnished language."'*

Another boy, perhaps a few months older, gave me his notions of men and things. He was a thick-limbed, red-cheeked fellow; answered very freely, and sometimes, when I could not help laughing at his replies, laughed loudly himself, as if he entered into the joke.

Yes, he had heer'd of God, who made the world. Couldn't exactly recollec' when he'd heer'd on him, but he had, most sartenly. Didn't know when the world was made or how anybody could do it. It must have taken a long time. It was afore his time, 'or yourn either, sir.' Knew there was a book called the Bible; didn't know what it was about; didn't mind to know; knew of such a book to a sartinty, because a young 'oman took one to pop [pawn] for an old 'oman what was on the spree – a brand new 'un – but the cove would[n?]'t have it, and the old 'oman said he might be d––d. Never heer'd tell on the deluge; of the world having been drownded, it couldn't, for there wasn't water enough to do it. He weren't a-going to fret hisself for such things as that. Didn't know what happened to people after death, only that they was buried. Had seen a body laid out; was a little afeared at first; poor Dick looked so different, and when you touched his face, he was so cold! oh, so cold! Had heer'd on another world; wouldn't mind if he was there hisself, if he could do better, for things was often queer here. Had heered on it from a tailor – such a clever cove, a stunner – as went to 'Straliar [Australia], and heer'd him say he was going into another world.

Had never heer'd of France, but had heer'd of Frenchmen; there wasn't half a quarter so many on 'em as of Italians, with their earrings like flash gals. Didn't dislike foreigners, for he never saw none. What was they? Had heer'd of Ireland. Didn't know where it was, but it couldn't be very far, or such lots wouldn't come from there to London. Should say they walked it, aye, every bit of the way, for he'd seen them come in, all covered with dust. Had heer'd of people going to sea, and had seen the ships in the river, but didn't know nothing about it, for he was very seldom that way. The sun was made of fire, or it wouldn't make you feel so warm. The stars was fire, too, or they wouldn't shine. They didn't make it warm, they was too small. Didn't know any use they was of. Didn't know how far they was off; a jolly lot higher than the gas lights some on 'em was. Was never in a church; had heer'd they worshipped God there; didn't know how it was done; had heer'd singing and playing inside when he'd passed; never was there, for he hadn't no togs to go in, and wouldn't be let in among such swells as he had seen coming out. Was a ignorant chap, for he'd never been to school, but was up to many a move and didn't do bad. Mother said he would make his fortin yet.

A fictional street-boy, from Charles Dickens (1812–1870), *Bleak House* (1852–53)

Dickens had published Sketches by Boz *in 1836 (see above, p. 233). Amongst the huge range of memorable characters in* Bleak House *the homeless crossing-sweeper Jo is seemingly the least significant until by the end he is found to be at the heart of Dickens's indictment of society's casual inhumanities and hypocrisies. Here, he has just escaped the sanctimonious clutches of the Rev. Chadband and company, and is once more having to 'move on'.*

Jo moves on, through the long vacation, down to Blackfriars bridge, where he finds a baking stony corner, wherein to settle to his repast.

And there he sits, munching and gnawing, and looking up at the great Cross on the summit of St. Paul's Cathedral, glittering above a red and violet-tinted cloud of smoke. From the boy's face one might suppose that sacred emblem to be, in his eyes, the crowning confusion of the great, confused city; so golden, so high up, so far out of his reach. There he sits, the sun going down, the river running fast, the crowd flowing by him in two streams – everything moving on to some purpose and to one end – until he is stirred up, and told to 'move on' too.

Dartmoor habits, from Cecil Torr (1857–1928), *Small Talk at Wreyland*

Apart from his regular annual travels following his antiquarian interests, Torr settled for a congenial life in the family hamlet on the edge of Dartmoor. His 'small talk' reminiscences and observations, bolstered with the evidence of family papers, paint a keen-eyed, forthright and amused picture of the local way of life over the half-century before he put them all together in 1916–23.

Writing to my father on 7 November 1852, my grandfather tells him: – 'The Lustleigh folks had a bonfire on the 5th [Guy Fawkes Day], and burnt the Pope in a white surplice: therefore the old women say it was intended for the Rector.' He writes on 15th May 1853: – 'Your mother has been to church this morning, and says there was not a score of folks there, and the Rector was looking wretched: which I do not wonder at. His congregation have left him, and now there is a chapel building.'

Lustleigh was upset by his preaching in a surplice. Most of his parishioners thought it meant a change of doctrine; and they called him a High Romish Priest. I do not know his motives; but I know the motives of another country clergyman, who did the same. His old black gown was getting so shabby that his wife was always telling him that he must have a new one. And he shelved the question by preaching in his surplice.

As a rule, a surplice meant a shorter sermon; but my friend preached on, as if he had a new black gown. A dreamy organist once played a great Amen in a slight pause in the sermon; and the choir and congregation sang it very fervently. ...

I see that I first went to Lustleigh Church on the Good Friday and Easter Sunday of 1862, while I was down here on a visit to my grandfather. In those days the service was mainly a dialogue between the parson and the clerk, the parson in very cultured tones and the clerk in resonant dialect, one saying 'As for lies, I hate and abhor them' as if it was superfluous for him to say so, and the other responding 'Seven times a day do I praise thee' as if it was a fact and he wished it generally known. The singing was confined to hymns. There was a choir of men and boys in a gallery below the tower, and a harmonium near them. But there used to be a choir of men and women, and an orchestra of bass-viol, violin and flute; and the tuning made a pleasant prelude to the service. There were three men who could play the viol; and it went by rank, not merit. One man farmed his own land, and he had first claim: next came a man who was a tenant farmer; and last a man who had no farm, but played better than the other two.

There were high pews then, and a razed three-decker – parson over clerk, with sounding-board on top, and reading-desk alongside half way up. Nearly all the windows had plain glass, so that one could see the trees and sky; and everything was whitewashed.

The whitewash was removed in 1871, and made way for much worse things – green distemper on the walls, blue paint and gilt stars in the roof, crude stencils on the side walls of the chancel, and on the eastern wall a fresco made in Germany. The trees and sky were hidden by glass that is exasperating in its colour and design. Lavatory tiles replace the granite paving of the chancel, and there is marble of the sort one sees on washstands. – It makes one crave for the French system of scheduling old churches as National Monuments, and putting them under the Ministry of Fine Arts.

'The cadences of Evensong fell rich and soothing', from George Sturt (1863–1927), *A Small Boy in the Sixties*

George Sturt, who mostly published under the name George Bourne, recalls his 1860s childhood in Surrey. His father ran the family wheelwright business, which he took over for some years.

Of more importance than the Bishop of Winchester to my childish eyes was the Archdeacon of Surrey, resident then in Farnham as rector. Archdeacons of Surrey had often been, *ex officio*, Rectors of Farnham. Of Archdeacon

Utterton I remember chiefly the clerical gaiters, they being at the right height for a child to notice. Otherwise I remember only that he annoyed my mother once by stopping a newspaper boy and trying to buy a paper, though the boy was only delivering papers to regular customers and had none to sell.

What happened to the Archdeacon? A new Bishop (Wilberforce had never come into residence; and it was Harold Browne now) was at the Castle; and by and by he appointed a new Rector of Farnham. The Archdeacon had lived sumptuously in Castle Street; but for Mr Hoste – a tall man, with a big family – the Rectory (a more obscure place) was done-up, while the ancient Vicarage across the churchyard was made ready for a relative of his.

And soon I heard for the first time in my life of church disputes. For Mr Hoste began by giving offence. His face looked kindly – if a child could look up so far; and he seemed all right when I saw him walking along the pavement past our shop. Moreover I heard him 'read himself in' at the Parish Church; and through all the Thirty-nine Articles there was nothing to dislike in his steady level voice. (Long afterwards I realized that it was sheer pleasure to hear him read.) And yet, ere long it grew all too plain that people were feeling affronted!

What was wrong? Perhaps he was a trifle 'High,' it was hinted. Or possibly the introduction into Farnham of the 'Hymns Ancient and Modern' may have been an unnecessary expense due to him. But the serious thing – somehow I hadn't noticed it, yet what cause for dismay! – was that he preached in a white surplice instead of in a black gown! At that, various citizens marked their displeasure by going elsewhere – a little ostentatiously perhaps. One became a pillar of Wrecclesham Church; while my father, as told already, chose to go to Hale. Very punctilious he was, too, in his attendances. I don't think there were any more Sunday morning walks to Frensham. My father had to testify against preaching in a white surplice, and he testified very week.

Did he really care? Or was it not rather just perversity? We children often walked to Hale Church with him; where Mr Rowe preached in black, I suppose, though I do not know that he did. At Hale Church I saw various queer things – amongst them one or two odd-looking men whom their grand-children in Farnham at this day might be willing to forget. Also there was a sexton, grim-faced, who prowled about with a cane to keep the boys in order. I liked the walk to Hale Church, along the lower side of Farnham Park. Yet I often went to Farnham Parish Church – on Sunday evenings instead of afternoons as I grew older. And very good it was. I think I have never elsewhere known such tranquility as I felt then in that quiet church on still summer evenings, listening to the swifts screaming round and round outside, and uplifted all the time by Mr Hoste's perfectly managed voice within. From him the cadences of Evensong fell rich and soothing, as if the ripeness and value they had gained in the centuries were being unlocked again for one's special behoof. Somehow his composure, echoing from the candle-lit chancel, expressed the emotion of long generations, which was renewed in one's-self, so that man's life seemed dignified by the touch of past ages. Of course other things helped to kindle that feeling – the ample cool aisles, the colours and the curves and the woodwork, the stealing on of evening shadows, the sense of old-world associations – but there is no doubt that it all took richer meaning from the stately English sentences, well-known and familiar, ringing so quiet and even through the listening church. Mr Hoste himself must have felt it, and with enthusiasm, though I am not persuaded that he knew by what mechanism – of colours and curves and voice tones and associations – the effect was produced. Perhaps he did not know. His sermons often seemed foolishness even to me, though possibly memory plays me false.

Can I really have heard him tell how all who dissented from the Church of England were doomed to perdition? or that when the wind blew open the church door Satan was at work? I once watched the south door quietly swinging ajar, but nothing happened that seemed to me unpleasant. But I probably misunderstood; and anyhow one's mind easily forgets rubbishy opinions, while one's tissues take permanent growth from feelings. Taste grows without thought and perhaps I owe some taste for serenity to Canon Hoste. He became honorary canon of Winchester; and by the time he left, worn out, for a lighter cure, and died of cancer in the throat, the very dissenters had learnt to revere him as a kindlier man – a more true-hearted man – than most, and of matchless veracity.

'Vo'k a-Comen into Church', by William Barnes (1801–1886)

Of Dorset stock, William Barnes was a schoolmaster turned clergyman, and a lifelong scholar of languages who treasured the music of his own dialect in his poetry. Francis Kilvert's Diary for 30 April 1874 records his visit to him at home in Winterbourne Came: 'I was immediately struck by the beauty and grandeur of his head. It was an Apostolic head, bald and venerable, and the long soft silvery hair flowed on his shoulders and a long white beard fell upon his breast. His face was handsome and striking, keen yet benevolent, the finely pencilled eyebrows still dark and a beautiful benevolent loving look lighted up his fine dark blue eyes when they rested on you.'

The church do zeem a touchen zight,
  When vo'k, a-comen in at door,
Do softly tread the long-ail'd vloor
Below the pillar'd arches' height,
  Wi' bells a-pealen,
  Vo'k a-kneelen,
Hearts a-healen, wi' the love
An' peäce a-zent em vrom above.

An' there, wi' mild an' thoughtvul feäce,
  Wi' downcast eyes, an' vaices dum',
  The wold an' young do slowly come,
An' teäke in stillness each his pleäce,
  A-zinken slowly,
  Kneelen lowly,
Seeken holy thoughts alwone,
In pray'r avore their Meäker's throne.

An' there be sons in youthvul pride,
  An' fathers weak wi' years an' pain,
  An' daughters in their mother's train,
The tall wi' smaller at their zide;
  Heads in murnen
  Never turnen,
Cheäks a burnen, wi' the het
O' youth, an' eyes noo tears do wet.

There friends do settle, zide by zide,
  The knower speechless to the known;
  Their vaice is there, vor God alwone,
To flesh an' blood their tongues be tied,
  Grief a-wringen,
  Jay a-zingen,
Pray'r a-bringen welcome rest
So softly to the troubled breast.

Rev. Francis Kilvert (1840–1879), from his Diary for 1870

'Why do I keep this voluminous journal? I can hardly tell. Partly because life appears to me such a curious and wonderful thing that it almost seems a pity that even such a humble and uneventful life as mine should pass altogether away without some such record as this, and partly too because I think the record may amuse and interest some who come after me.' (From his entry on 3 November 1885)

The 22 surviving notebooks of Kilvert's journals cover much of the period between 1 January 1870 and 14 March 1879, when entries abruptly end. They came the way of William Plomer at Jonathan Cape, who published three volumes of selections between 1938 and 1940. The candid and faithful accounts Kilvert gives of the countryside and people he worked among as curate and later vicar, mostly on the Welsh Border but also for a time in his father's Wiltshire parish, found instant recognition as both a wonderfully observed record and an unusually engaging read. The natural world constantly draws his eye – and feet – and his feelings for his parishioners are full of warm interest. His pleasure in the society of Hay Castle, Clyro Court (dinners, croquet, archery, attractive visitors), is there, but so too is his devoted work in the parish (of which Plomer said there was a great deal that he left out). His susceptibility for pretty young girls finds candid, almost artless expression, though he seemed to have some insight into his ability to charm ('It is a strange and terrible gift, this power of stealing hearts and exciting such love'). We have no diary for the few months leading to his marriage to Elizabeth Roland at Woodstock in August 1879, or for the five weeks following, before he suddenly died of peritonitis aged thirty-eight. There are indications that his widow was responsible for gaps in the run made available to Plomer, and even those originals were nearly all regrettably disposed of by a relative in the 1950s.

Saturday, 12 March

... Luncheon at the Vicarage with Lord and Lady Hereford, two Miss Ravenscrofts and Miss Baskerville. Afterwards they went up to the Bron and Pen y Llan to see the view as the N. wind had cleared the air. I left them at the Post Office and went to Upper Cabalva where Mrs. Dyke gave me a pocketful of golden pippins. Annie up at Llwyn Gwillim, but before she went she had gathered a glassfull of primroses from the rickyard hedge. On to Lower Cabalva. Women carrying home on their heads heavy burdens of wood from the dingle and fields where a fall of timber is going on. Mrs. Collett with a new baby to be christened at Bettws Chapel tomorrow. Mary Collett proud to show me her Whitney School prizes and all her little treasures. She is a very good girl very fond of reading and going to school and devours books. I lent her Miss Edgeworth's *Parent's Assistant.* She has good eyes but she will never match her mother's beautiful noble face. Mrs. Collett says they must have their turkey cock killed because he knocks the children down and stocks (pecks) them. Collett set one child to drive the turkey with a stick but the bird flew at her, knocked her down and stocked her too, so there were two children roaring at once and the turkey triumphant.

Sunday, 13 March

I looked out last night at 11:30 and was surprised to see snow on the ground. This morning showed a fall of 3 inches level and the snow fell straight and even as there was no wind. The mountains evidently deep in snow. Few children at school as the poor darlings could not come far through the snow. Very few people in Church. Mr. Venables preached and I went to Bettws, a lovely walk in the glorious afternoon. At Cross Fordd the great dark stone standing in a sheet of dazzling snow a solitary silent witness of some dead covenant or boundary. The shady steep hill descending to the Mill covered with snow. The Chapel field Bettws deep in snow. The clerk and two other men lounging about the W. end of the Chapel till they saw me crossing the white waste when the clerk (Wilding) disappeared round the corner and immediately after the bell pealed out over the snow. Mrs. Collett rode a pony up to Chapel on a man's saddle and was churched. The baby came in after the sermon and was baptized [*sic*] 'Alice Shelburne', an old name in Collett's family he says. The baby very good and quiet.

Climbed the ladder to see old Jones in bed who complained of a headache and nothing more. Read to him Mark ii out of his old-fashioned Bible. Went into the old blind 'Simon's' house and read to him. At the bend of the Wye between Bronydd & Cabalva the mountain clad in deep snow and tinged with rose colour was reflected in the river like Mont Blanc in the Lake of Geneva. As the sun set a lovely rose tint stole over the snowy mountains, but paled and died leaving the mountain tops cold dim blue before I reached Clyro. The silent folk lying still in their winding sheets in the churchyard. Dined at the Vicarage and read to Mr. V. the ballad of our Saviour and the Three Children which interested him much.

Wednesday, 16 March

I ate so much hare that I could hardly walk and saw stars, but at 4 went up the hill by the Bron Penllan and Little Wern y Pentre. The lane between Little

Wern y Pentre and the Tall Trees infamous, so deep and soft that it is almost impossible to feel bottom. Mrs. Williams plunging down the lane through the mud and fording the pools with a sack of swedes on her back. In the meadow between the Tall Trees and Sunny Bank was singing the first lark I have noticed this year. He was coming down, his song stopped suddenly and he dropped to his nest.

Below Tybella a bird singing unseen reminded me how the words of a good man live after he is silent and out of sight – 'He being dead yet speaketh'.

Also the scent of an unseen flower seemed like the sweet and holy influence of a good kind deed which cannot be concealed though the deed itself may be hidden. On to Cefn y Blaen where a 'King' once lived. Alas for the pretty merry yellow-haired lassie who used to make this house so bright. Three rather nice rosy black-haired grey-eyed girls. The men sitting at tea but they had finished and went out as I came in. A tall spare old man with a wild eye and a night cap rose from the chimney corner, came forward and shook me by the hand respectfully, claiming acquaintance as he had seen me at Wernnewydd. Round the corner of the Vicar's Hill to Little Twyn y Grain, passing by the Great Twyns which I am happy to see is falling into ruin, the window frames falling in. How well I remember and how short a time ago it seems though nearly five years. I never pass the house without thinking of that afternoon when after neglecting Margaret Thomas' dying son for a long time I went to call and was inexpressibly shocked to find that he had died only ten minutes before.

Faint sunshine on Bryngwyn Hill and a cold cheery gleam of water from the great peat bog below on the edge of which stands the grey cluster of buildings and the tall dark yew of Llanship. I went down there and waded across the yard to the house through a sea of mud and water. The kitchen was very dark, the bank rising steep in front of the window. Mrs. Morgan gave me some tea and cake. On the settle sat a man perfectly still, silent and in such a dark corner that I could not see his face. On a stool in the chimney corner sat little girl 'Ellen' holding a baby lately vaccinated, both sound asleep, and Mrs. Morgan very anxious lest the girl should 'fall the baby'. Morgan anxious to get out to his ewes and lambs and a tall girl strode into the kitchen crying in a peculiar strident voice that 'a ewe was going up Cae Drws alone' as if about to yean. Morgan went out with some hot milk and showed me the remains of the moat, where the Scotch pedlar was hidden after being murdered for the sake of his pack while lodging in the house and where his skeleton was found when the moat was cleared out. The moat that is left is a broad deep formidable ditch and rather a long pond at one end of the house and full of water. It extended once all round the house and had to be crossed by a bridge. Llanship a fearfully wet swampy place, almost under water and I should think very unhealthy. One of the twin yews was lately blown down and cut up into gate posts which will last twice as long as oak. The wood was so hard that Morgan said it turned many of the axes as if they were made of lead. Other axes splintered and broke upon the wood and the old yew was a crucial test of the axes. I wonder in which of these yews Gore hid the penknife before his death which made him restless as hidden iron is said to do, and caused his spirit to come back rummaging about the house and premises and frightening people out of their wits. Maria Lake used to tell me this story. It was getting dusk as I left Llanship and after I had plunged about for some time in the swampy Wern up to my ancles in water I lost my bearings and missed the way, so that I might have been belated but that I heard the welcome clank of plough chains as the team came down home and Joe the Llanship ploughman directed me up to the Holly House near which in the top of the steep bank I heard children's voices and Hannah and Aaron Gore were gathering 'chat'[catkins]. They guided me to a 'glat' which I tumbled over. I met old Williams the patriarch of Crowther's Pool coming away from the Holly House a grand old man, hale, fresh and upright, contented and dignified. I asked his age. 'Eighty-seven, if I live till the 6th of old March' (that is the day after tomorrow). Struck over the top of the Vicar's Hill and as I passed Cross Ford the frogs were croaking snoring and bubbling in the pool under the full moon.

Mellstock Parish Band, from Thomas Hardy (1840–1928), *Under the Greenwood Tree* (1872)

In aiming 'to preserve for my own satisfaction a fairly true record of a vanishing life' in this first of his 'Wessex' novels, Hardy drew on his own early life in and around Stinsford, where both father and grandfather had played in the village band. In this story, the all-male Mellstock Quire has been carol-singing late into the previous night, and are now in position in the church gallery and slightly the worse for wear. Suddenly the girls of the village add a different voice. The young vicar Mr Maybold finds that their pretty new schoolmistress Fancy Day also has organ-playing skills, and this is to threaten the future of their whole tradition: 'I see that violins are good, and that an organ is good; and when we introduce the organ it will not be that fiddles were bad, but that an organ was better.'

The music on Christmas mornings was frequently below the standard of church-performances at other times. The boys were sleepy from the heavy exertions of the night; the men were slightly wearied; and now, in addition to these constant reasons, there was a dampness in the atmosphere that still further aggravated the evil. Their strings, from the recent long exposure to the night air, rose whole semitones, and snapped with a loud twang at the most silent moment; which necessitated more retiring than ever to the back of the gallery, and made the gallery throats quite husky with the quantity of coughing and hemming required for tuning in. The vicar looked cross.

When the singing was in progress there was suddenly discovered to be a strong and shrill reinforcement from some point, ultimately found to be the schoolgirls' aisle. At every attempt it grew bolder and more distinct. At the third time of singing, these intrusive feminine voices were as mighty as those of the regular singers; in fact, the flood of sound from this quarter assumed such an individuality, that it had a time, a key, almost a tune of its own, surging upwards when the gallery plunged downwards, and the reverse.

Now this had never happened before within the memory of man. The girls, like the rest of the congregation, had always been humble and respectful followers of the gallery; singing at sixes and sevens if without gallery leaders; never interfering with the ordinances of these practised artists – having no will, union, power, or proclivity except it was given them from the established choir enthroned above them.

A good deal of desperation became noticeable in the gallery throats and strings, which continued throughout the musical portion of the service. Directly the fiddles were laid down, Mr Penny's spectacles put in their sheath, and the text had been given out, an indignant whispering began.

'Did ye hear that, souls?' Mr Penny said, in a groaning breath.

'Brazen-faced hussies!' said Bowman.

'True; why, they were every note as loud as we, fiddles and all, if not louder!'

'Fiddles and all!' echoed Bowman bitterly.

'Shall anything saucier be found than united 'ooman?' Mr Spinks murmured.

'What I want to know is,' said the tranter (as if he knew already, but that civilization required the form of words), 'what business people have to tell maidens to sing like that when they don't sit in a gallery, and never have entered one in their lives? That's the question, my sonnies.'

Shipwrecks and vicars of Morwenstow, Robert Stephen Hawker (1803–1875) and the Rev. Sabine Baring-Gould (1834–1924), from the latter's biography of the former (1876)

In 1864 a large ship was seen in distress off the coast. The Rev. A. Thynne, Rector of Kilkhampton, at once drove to Morwenstow. The vessel was riding at anchor a mile off shore, west of Hartland Race. He found Mr. Hawker in the greatest excitement, pacing his room, and shouting for some things he wanted to put in his greatcoat-pockets, and intensely impatient because his carriage was not round. With him was the Rev. W. Valentine, rector of Whixley in Yorkshire, then resident at Chapel, in the parish of Morwenstow.

'What are you going to do?' asked the rector of Kilkhampton. 'I shall drive at once to Bude for the lifeboat.'

'No good!' thundered the vicar, 'no good comes out of the west. You must go east. I shall go to Clovelly, and then, if that fails, to Appledore. I shall not stop till I have got a lifeboat to take those poor fellows off the wreck.'

'Then,' said the rector of Kilkhampton, 'I shall go to Bude, and see to the lifeboat there being brought out.'

'Do as you like; but mark my words, no good comes of turning to the west. Why,' said he, 'in the primitive church they turned to the west to renounce the Devil.'

His carriage came to the door, and he drove off with Mr. Valentine, as fast as his horses could spin him along the hilly, wretched roads.

Before he reached Clovelly, a boat had put off with the mate from the ship, which was the *Margaret Quail*, laden with salt. The captain would not leave the vessel; for, till deserted by him, no salvage could be claimed. The mate was picked up on the way, and the three reached Clovelly.

Down the street proceeded the following procession – the street of Clovelly being a flight of steps: –

First, the vicar of Morwenstow in a claret-coloured coat, with long tails flying in the gale, blue knitted jersey, and pilot-boots, his long silver locks fluttering about his head. He was appealing to the fishermen and sailors of Clovelly, to put out in their lifeboat, to rescue the crew of the *Margaret Quail*. The men stood sulky, lounging about with folded arms, or hands in their pockets, and sou'-esters slouched over their brows. The women were screaming at the tops of their voices, that they should not have their husbands and sons and sweethearts enticed away to risk their lives to save wrecked men. Above the clamour of their shrill tongues, and the sough of the wind, rose the roar of the vicar's voice: he was convulsed with indignation, and poured forth the most sacred appeals to their compassion for drowning sailors.

Second in the procession moved the Rev. W. Valentine, with purse full of gold in his hand, offering any amount of money to the Clovelly men, if they would only go forth in the lifeboat to the wreck.

Third came the mate of the *Margaret Quail*, restrained by no consideration of cloth, swearing and damning right and left, in a towering rage at the cowardice of the Clovelly men.

Fourth came John, the servant of Mr. Hawker, with bottles of whiskey under his arm, another inducement to the men to relent, and be merciful to their imperilled brethren.

The first appeal was to their love of heaven, and to their humanity; the second was to their pockets; the third to their terrors, their fear of Satan, to whom they were consigned; and the fourth to their stomachs, their love of grog.

But all appeals were in vain. Then Mr. Hawker returned to his carriage, and drove away, further east, to Appledore, where he secured the lifeboat. It was mounted on a wagon. Ten horses were harnessed to it; and as fast as possible, it was conveyed to the scene of distress.

But, in the mean while, the captain of the *Margaret Quail*, despairing of help, and thinking that his vessel would break up under him, came off in his boat, with the rest of the crew, trusting rather to a rotten boat, patched with canvas which they had tarred over, than to the tender mercies of the covetous Clovellites, in whose veins ran the too recent blood of wreckers. The only living being left on board was a poor dog.

No sooner was the captain seen to leave the ship, than the Clovelly men lost their repugnance to go to sea. They manned boats at once, gained the *Margaret Quail*, and claimed three thousand pounds for salvage.

There was an action in court, as the owners refused to pay such a sum; and it was lost by the Clovelly men, who, however, got an award of twelve hundred pounds. The case turned somewhat on the presence of the dog on the wreck; and it was argued that the vessel was not deserted, because a dog had been left on board, to keep guard for its masters. The owner of the cargo failed; and the amount actually paid to the salvors was six hundred pounds to two steam-tugs (three hundred pounds each), and three hundred pounds to the Clovelly skiff and sixteen men. The ship and cargo, minus masts, rigging, cables, and anchors, were valued at five thousand pounds.

Mr. Hawker went round the country indignantly denouncing the sailors of Clovelly, and with justice. It roused all the righteous wrath in his breast.

And, as may be believed, no love was borne him by the inhabitants of that little fishing village. They would probably have made a wreck of him, had he ventured among them.

After Hawker died, Baring-Gould stood in for him as vicar for a while.

[1875] I had got as far as this in my memoir on Saturday night, November 13th. On the following morning I went to Morwenstow, to take duty in church. The wind was blowing a hurricane from the south-west. I had to hold on to the grave-stones, to drag myself through the churchyard in the teeth of the storm, to the church porch.

There were few present that morning. No woman could have faced the wind. The roar of the ocean, the howling of the blast, the clatter of the glass in the windows, united, formed such a volume of sound that I had to shout my loudest, to be heard when reading the service.

When morning prayer was over, I went into the porch. A few men were there, holding their hats on their heads, and preparing for a battle with the wind.

'Not many at church this morning,' I said. 'No, your honour,' was the answer: 'the wind would blow the women away; and the men are most of 'em on the cliffs, looking out if there be wrecks.'

Two vessels were caught sight of between the scuds of rain, now on the top of a billow, now lost in the trough of the waves. They had been driven within the fatal line between Hartland Head and Padstow Point.

'Is there no chance for them?'

'None at all.'

That evening we sang in church the hymn for those at sea, in *Ancient & Modern*. Whilst it was being sung, one vessel foundered; but the crew, six Frenchmen, came ashore in a boat. An hour or two earlier the other went down, with all hands on board.

On Monday and Tuesday bits of the wreck came up in the coves, with *Wilhelmina* on them, but no bodies.

After a storm the corpses are fearfully mangled on the sharp rocks, and are cut to pieces by the slate as by knives, and bits of flesh come ashore. These are locally called 'gobbets'; and Mr. Hawker, after a wreck, used to send a man with a basket along the beaches of the coves in his parish, collecting these 'gobbets', which he interred in his churchyard, on top of the cliffs.

'Hunting parsons', from Sabine Baring-Gould (1834–1924), *Devonshire Characters* (1908)

Baring-Gould was both squire and from 1881 vicar ('squarson') of the small Devon parish of Lew Trenchard. He was a collector of folksongs, an antiquarian, and an immensely prolific writer. In Devonshire Characters *he turned his pen to 'hunting parsons' among others.*

At the beginning of the nineteenth century, few counties in England produced such a crop of hunting parsons as did Devonshire. They were in force for the first fifty years. In 1831 Henry Phillpotts was consecrated Bishop of Exeter. Shortly after, as he was driving with his chaplain on the way to a Confirmation, a fox-hunt passed by in full halloo.

'Dear me!' exclaimed his lordship; 'what a number of black coats among the hunters. Has there been some great bereavement in the neighbourhood?'

'My lord,' replied the chaplain, 'the only bereavement these black-coated sportsmen suffer from is not being able to appear in pink.'

There were, it was computed, in the diocese of Exeter a score of incumbents who kept their packs; there must have been over a hundred parsons who hunted regularly two or three days in the week, and as many more who would have done so had their means allowed them to keep hunters.

There is no objection to be made to a parson following the hounds occasionally; the sport is more manly than that which engrosses so many young clerics nowadays, dawdling about with ladies on lawn-tennis grounds or at croquet. But those early days of the last century hunting was with many the main pursuit of their life, and clerical duties were neglected or perfunctorily performed.

If the most famous of these was Jack Russell, the most infamous was the Rev. Froude of Knowstone.

When Froude got old he was forced by the Bishop to have a curate. 'I don't care to keep dogs to do the barking for me, no fye,' said he, 'but I can't help it. You see, I just maintains a rough boy to do the work now, and I sits in the vestry and hears 'un tell.'

Between services one Sunday, Froude gave his young curate, who was dining with him and some of his farmer friends, too much of his soft but strong ale. He disliked the young fellow, who was a bit of a clown and uncouth, and did it out of malice. The curate, quite ignorant of the headiness of the ale, inadvertently got fuddled.

The conversation turned on a monstrous pig that Froude had killed, and which was hung up in his outhouse, and he invited his guests to accompany him and view the carcase, and estimate the weight. One thought it weighed so many stone, others thought differently. Froude said it weighed just the same as his curate, who was fat. The rough farmers demurred to the rector's estimate, and finding an empty cornsack, they thrust the intoxicated ecclesiastic into it, and, hanging him up to the end of the beam, shouted with delight as the curate brought the weight down. Meanwhile the bells were ringing for evensong, but they left the curate hung up in the sack, where he slept uncomfortably. The congregation assembled for service, and waited. Froude would not officiate, and the curate was incapable of doing so.

Mr. Matthews, afterwards Prebendary of Exeter, had been dining at South Molton in Froude's company, and Froude undertook to drive him back to Knowstone in his gig, where Mr. Matthews was to sleep the night. Froude had drunk too much, but insisted on driving home himself. At the bottom of the long street the road crosses the river, and the bridge is set on at an angle to the road. The horse was a spirited animal, and was going home. So down the street they went at a spanking pace, and over the bridge with a whir. Froude had fallen asleep already, but Matthews seized the reins and guided the animal, and thus they narrowly escaped destruction.

Froude slept on, and, arriving at Knowstone, Matthews went in to prepare the young wife to get the rector to bed.

'Oh, what is the matter?' cried Mrs. Froude, when she was informed that her husband was not very well, and had better be put to bed. 'Oh, dear lamb' – Mrs. Froude was not happy in her choice of descriptive epithets – 'dear lamb, are you ill? Oh dear! dear!

'Nonsense,' retorted Froude, 'I bain't ill. I'm only drunk, my dear, that's all.'

One day he was riding on the quay at Barnstaple, and asked some question of a bargeman in his boat. The fellow gave him a rude answer. Thereupon Froude leaped his horse down into the barge, and thrashed the man.

In the end, Froude gave up doing duty, and retired into a small house in Molland, as more sheltered than Knowstone. In *The Maid of Sker*, R. D. Blackmore represents him as torn to pieces by his hounds. Actually this was not the occasion of his death.

W. H. Thornton (1830–1916), from *Reminiscences and Reflections of an Old West-Country Clergyman* (1897–99)

Thornton was a seventeen-year-old at Rugby when, the night after a glorious 'hare and hounds' cross-country chase, he was struck down by cholera. He was sent off to a family friend who was curate of Selworthy, near Porlock, and there fell in love with the Exmoor country where he would come to spend the rest of his life as a parson.

i

My life as a curate was naturally very uneventful. I was nearly ubiquitous. Nothing came amiss to me. If I could not drive, I rode, and if I could not ride, I ran; and forty miles, more or less, were nothing to me whether with a horse or without one. I was only engaged to take one Sunday service, that at Countesbury, and the clergy for many miles around took advantage of this circumstance, and of my bodily activity, to get their churches served gratuitously when they were unwell or absent from home.

I have before now taken three full services, with christenings and funerals between, have been wet to the skin before I began the first of them, and have neither changed clothes nor taken nourishment until I returned home, after riding perhaps twenty or thirty miles and experiencing three or four separate wettings, one upon the top of the other, and I have never taken a guinea from anyone in all my life.

The younger generation of clergy will think I was a fool for my pains, and few of them would care to follow my example, yet even now, in my sixty-eighth year, I am often similarly worked and greatly exposed.

Naturally my willingness in these matters made me popular, and I had the run of all the houses within some twenty miles of my residence, and could shoot or fish wherever I pleased. Two nieces, daughters of my brother Edward, who was then a Commissioner under Government in the Punjab, kept house for me in the summer months, and my parents and other relatives visited me from time to time.

ii

One day I had a letter from Mr Pike of Parracombe, to say that he would be obliged to me if I would ride over by eleven a.m. and marry a couple of his parishioners. On the day in question I rode up to the old church, which occupied a position upon a hill, and began to look about for some place in which to stable my horse. There were two cottages by the church, and in the garden of one of them an old man was at work. I asked him if he could tell me where I could put my horse, and he replied that he had a shed full of tools and a wheelbarrow, with a grey goose a-brood in it, but that we could turn out the tools, and the old goose would not mind. Only, he added, that the trouble was in vain, as there would be no wedding that day.

'But, my friend,' said I, 'I have ridden ten miles to officiate.'

'Never mind that,' he observed, 'this won't be the first young woman by many that Mr Jones will have played his tricks upon.'

Nevertheless, I trundled the wheelbarrow out, removed the tools, and putting the big blood mare into the little shed, I left her and the goose to converse with one another, while I took up my position in the churchyard. I could see all the church path down below to the village, and when my watch informed me that it was after half-past eleven, I went to the old man and told him that the law did not permit me to marry after noon, that there was no sign from below, and that I was going home; if the bridegroom should come, he was to present him with my compliments and recommend him in future to practise the virtue of punctuality.

While we were speaking, however, the wedding party emerged from the houses and came slowly up the hill. By the time they arrived at the church, it wanted only ten minutes to twelve, and the law was imperative. I went straight for the bridegroom and scolded him well, bidding him at the same time to be quick, and to get the church opened.

'Now see, sir, for yourself,' said he, 'what jealousy is capable of. The clerk of the parish wants to marry this young woman himself, and as she prefers me to him, he has gone away and taken the keys with him.'

I was desperate. I rushed at the iron gates of the churchyard, put my shoulder against one of them, heaved, and lifted it off its hinges. Down it went with a crash.

'Now then,' said I, 'for the church.'

The bridegroom made a back against the wall, the best man mounted upon him, and wrapping his pocket handkerchief round his hand smashed in a pane of glass; then he unfastened the window and disappeared head foremost into a pew. I can almost see his forked legs at this moment as he went down. The bride turned to me with a smile and said, 'This, sir, is what I do call a regular jolly lark.'

'Silence, you scandalous woman,' I cried, 'or I will see you at Jericho before I marry you.'

Then the bolt of the little belfry door was slidden back and we entered, the whole party in a titter of amusement. I hurried on my surplice, and entering the altar rails knelt down in order to steady them, but dared not remain upon my knees, as it was just upon twelve o'clock. When I reached the ring portion of the service, I bade Mr Jones put the ring upon the third finger of the woman's left hand, and say, etc. He seized the second finger and the ring would not pass.

'You stupid jackass,' said she, 'what are you up to now?'

I hurried over the service, declined to take a fee, and 'discoursed' them, as the Irish say, in the churchyard as roundly as ever newly married couple were discoursed since the world began. I blew them up sky-high, and rode off, declaring that Parracombe people might in future marry each other with whatever horrid rites they thought proper, but that I would never again be party to 'burgling' a church to oblige the best of them.

'Sunday as spent by children of the last generation', from Lewis Carroll (1832–1898), *Sylvie and Bruno* (1889)

Lewis Carroll – Charles Lutwidge Dodgson – was one of eleven children of a High Church clergyman who was a strong traditionalist; they were encouraged to create their own home-made amusements. The church in the parish where the family moved in the 1840s, St Peter, Croft-on-Tees, in North Yorkshire, has a 'Cheshire cat' on the sedilia. As a college fellow (Christ Church, Oxford, mathematics) he was necessarily in Anglican orders, but, unusually, he was granted an exemption from full ordination.

Sylvie and Bruno *grew from a 'huge unwieldy mass' of material that he had been accumulating for years. He recognised that his attempts to string it together 'upon the thread of a consecutive story' were a struggle, but it was the best he could do 'for the children whom I love'. He wrote in the Preface: 'The descriptions of Sunday as spent by children of the last generation are quoted verbatim from a speech made to me by a child-friend and a letter written to me by a lady-friend.'*

'Then you would allow children to *play* on Sunday?'

'Certainly I should. Why make the day irksome to their restless natures?'

'I have a letter somewhere,' said Lady Muriel, 'from an old friend, describing the way in which Sunday was kept in her younger days. I will fetch it for you.'

'I had a similar description, *viva voce*, years ago,' Arthur said when she had left us, 'from a little girl. It was really touching to hear the melancholy tone in which she said "On Sunday I mustn't play with my doll! On Sunday I mustn't run on the sands! On Sunday I mustn't dig in the garden!" Poor child! She had indeed abundant cause for hating Sunday!'

'Here is the letter,' said Lady Muriel, returning. 'Let me read you a piece of it.'

'When, as a child, I first opened my eyes on a Sunday morning, a feeling of dismal anticipation, which began at least on the Friday, culminated. I knew what was before me, and my wish, if not my word, was "Would God it were evening!" It was no day of rest, but a day of texts, of catechisms (Watts'), of tracts about converted swearers, godly char-women, and edifying deaths of sinners saved.

'Up with the lark, hymns and portions of Scripture had to be learnt by heart till 8 o'clock, when there were family prayers, then breakfast, which I was never able to enjoy, partly from the fast already undergone, partly from the outlook I dreaded.

'At 9 o'clock came Sunday-School; and it made me indignant to be put into the class with the village-children, as well as be alarmed lest, by some mistake of mine, I should be put below them.

'The Church-Service was a veritable Wilderness of Zin. I wandered in it, pitching the tabernacle of my thoughts on the lining of the square family-pew, the fidgets of my small brothers, and the horror of knowing that, on the Monday, I should have to write out, from memory, jottings of the rambling disconnected extempore sermon, which might have any text but its own, and to stand or fall by the results.

'This was followed by a cold dinner at 1 (servants to have no work), Sunday-School again from 2 to 4, and Evening-Service at 6. The intervals were perhaps the greatest trial of all, from the efforts I had to make, to be less than usually sinful, by reading books and sermons as barren as the Dead Sea. There was but one rosy spot, in the distance, all that day: and that was "bed-time," which never could come too early!'

'Such teaching was well meant, no doubt,' said Arthur; 'but it must have driven many of its victims into deserting the Church-Services altogether.'

The house-party launches into Sunday, from Benjamin Disraeli (1804–1881), *Lothair* (1870)

Lothair *was Disraeli's last novel, written between his two periods of serving as Prime Minister. The titled and extremely wealthy hero, after a Presbyterian upbringing with his guardian Lord Culloden, joins Garibaldi's campaign in Italy. His other guardian, the Catholic convert Grandison, now elevated to the cardinalate, aims, too, to win him for Rome. Grandison was recognised as a thinly disguised Cardinal Manning. The book went through eight editions in its first year. In this scene, Lothair's guests assemble for the day's rituals.*

There can be little doubt, generally speaking, that it is more satisfactory to pass Sunday in the country than in town. There is something in the essential stillness of country life, which blends harmoniously with the ordinance of the most divine of our divine laws. It is pleasant too, when the congregation breaks up, to greet one's neighbours; to say kind words to kind faces; to hear some rural news profitable to learn, which sometimes enables you to do some good, and sometimes prevents others from doing some harm. A quiet domestic walk too in the afternoon has its pleasures; and so numerous and so various are the sources of interest in the country, that, though it be Sunday, there is no reason why your walk should not have an object.

But Sunday in the country, with your house full of visitors, is too often an exception to this general truth. It is a trial. Your guests cannot always be at church, and, if they could, would not like it. There is nothing to interest or amuse them: no sport; no castles or factories to visit; no adventurous expeditions; no gay music in the morn, and no light dance in the evening. There is always danger of the day becoming a course of heavy meals and stupid walks, for the external scene and all its teeming circumstances, natural and human, though full of concern to you, are to your visitors an insipid blank.

How did Sunday go off at Muriel Towers?

In the first place there was a special train, which at an early hour took the Cardinal and his suite and the St. Jerome family to Grandchester where they were awaited with profound expectation. But the Anglican portion of the guests were not without their share of ecclesiastical and spiritual excitement, for the Bishop was to preach this day in the chapel of the Towers, a fine and capacious sanctuary of florid Gothic, and his Lordship was a sacerdotal orator of repute.

It had been announced that the breakfast hour was to be somewhat earlier. The ladies in general were punctual, and seemed conscious of some great event impending. The ladies Flora and Grizell entered with, each in her hand, a prayer-book of purple velvet adorned with a decided cross, the gift of the Primus. Lord Culloden, at the request of Lady Corisande, had consented to their hearing the Bishop, which he would not do himself. He passed his morning in finally examining the guardians' accounts, the investigation of which he conducted and concluded during the rest of the day with Mr. Putney Giles. Mrs. Campian did not leave her room. Lord St. Aldegonde came down late, and looked about him with an uneasy, ill-humoured air.

Whether from the absence of Theodora, or from some other cause, he was brusk, ungracious, scowling, and silent, only nodding to the Bishop who benignly saluted him, refusing every dish that was offered, then getting up and helping himself at the side table, making a great noise with the carving instruments, and flouncing down his plate when he resumed his seat. Nor was his costume correct. All the other gentlemen, though their usual morning dresses were sufficiently fantastic (trunk hose of every form, stockings as bright as paroquets, wondrous shirts, and velvet coats of every tint), habited themselves to-day, both as regards form and colour, in a style indicative of the subdued gravity of their feelings. Lord St. Aldegonde had on his shooting jacket of brown velvet and a pink shirt and no cravat, and his rich brown locks, always to a certain degree neglected, were peculiarly dishevelled.

Hugo Bohun, who was not afraid of him and was a high churchman, being in religion and in all other matters on the side of the Duchesses, said, 'Well, St. Aldegonde, are you going to chapel in that dress?' But St. Aldegonde would not answer; he gave a snort and glanced at Hugo with the eye of a gladiator.

The meal was over. The Bishop was standing near the mantelpiece talking to the ladies, who were clustered round him; the Archdeacon and the Chaplain and some other clergy in the background; Lord St. Aldegonde, who, whether there were a fire or not, always stood with his back to the fireplace with his hands in his pockets, moved discourteously among them, assumed his usual position, and listened, as it were grimly, for a few moments to their talk; then he suddenly exclaimed in a loud voice, and with the groan of a rebellious Titan, 'How I hate Sunday!'

A vicar's wife discovers her own voice, from Annie Besant (1847–1933), *An Autobiography* (1893)

Unhappily married to a clergyman in Sibsey, Lincolnshire, in 1872–73 Annie Besant reached a personal crisis. Lying ahead were her pioneering work with the Fabians and the 'freethinker' Charles Bradlaugh – organisation of trade unions, advocation of birth control, immersion in theosophy, and, beyond this autobiography, years of active support for the Indian nationalist movement.

And now came the return to Sibsey, and with it the need for definite steps as to the Church. For now I no longer doubted, I had rejected, and the time for silence was past. I was willing to attend the Church services, taking no part in any not directed to God Himself, but I could no longer attend the Holy Communion, for in that service, full of recognition of Jesus as Deity and of His atoning sacrifice, I could no longer take part without hypocrisy. This was agreed to, and well do I remember the pain and trembling wherewith on the first 'Sacrament Sunday' after my return I rose and left the church. That the vicar's wife should 'communicate' was as much a matter of course as that the vicar should 'administer'; I had never done anything in public that would draw attention to me, and a feeling of deadly sickness nearly overcame me as I made my exit, conscious that every eye was on me, and that my non-participation would be the cause of unending comment. As a matter of fact, every one naturally thought I was taken suddenly ill, and I was overwhelmed with calls and inquiries. To any direct question I answered quietly that I was unable to take part in the profession of faith required by an honest communicant, but the statement was rarely necessary, as the idea of heresy in a vicar's wife is slow to suggest itself to the ordinary bucolic mind, and I proffered no information where no question was asked.

It happened that, shortly after that (to me) memorable Christmas of 1872, a sharp epidemic of typhoid fever broke out in the village of Sibsey. The drainage there was of the most primitive type, and the contagion spread rapidly. Naturally fond of nursing, I found in this epidemic work just fitted to my hand, and I was fortunate enough to be able to lend personal help that made me welcome in the homes of the stricken poor. The mothers who slept exhausted while I watched beside their darlings' bedsides will never, I like to fancy, think over-harshly of the heretic whose hand was tender and often more skilful than their own. I think Mother Nature meant me for a nurse, for I take a sheer delight in nursing any one, provided only that there is peril in the sickness, so that there is the strange and solemn feeling of the struggle between the human skill one wields and the supreme enemy, Death. There is a strange fascination in fighting Death, step by step, and this is of course felt to the full where one fights for life as life, and not for a life one loves. When the patient is beloved the struggle is touched with agony, but where one fights with Death over the body of a stranger there is a weird enchantment in the contest without personal pain, and as one forces back the hated foe there is a curious triumph in the feeling which marks the death-grip yielding up its prey, as one snatches back to earth the life which had well-nigh perished.

The spring of 1873 brought me knowledge of a power that was to mould much of my future life. I delivered my first lecture, but delivered it to rows of empty pews in Sibsey Church. A queer whim took me that I would like to know how 'it felt' to preach, and vague fancies stirred in me that I could speak if I had the chance. I saw no platform in the distance, nor had any idea of possible speaking in the future dawned upon me. But the longing to find outlet in words came upon me, and I felt as though I had something to say and was able to say it. So locked alone in the great, silent church, whither I had gone to practise some organ exercises, I ascended the pulpit steps and delivered my first lecture on the Inspiration of the Bible. I shall never forget the feeling of power and delight – but especially of power – that came upon me as I sent my voice ringing down the aisles, and the passion in me broke into balanced sentences and never paused for musical cadence or for rhythmical expression. All I wanted then was to see the church full of upturned faces, alive with throbbing sympathy, instead of the dreary emptiness of silent pews. And as though in a dream the solitude was peopled, and I saw the listening faces and the eager eyes, and as the sentences flowed unbidden from my lips and my own tones echoed back to me from the pillars of the ancient church, I knew of a verity that the gift of speech was mine, and that if ever – and then it seemed so impossible! – if ever the chance came to me of public work, this power of melodious utterance should at least win hearing for any message I had to bring.

But the knowledge remained a secret all to my own self for many a long month, for I quickly felt ashamed of that foolish speechifying in an empty church; but, foolish as it was, I note it here, as it was the first effort of that expression in spoken words which later became to me one of the deepest delights of life. And, indeed, none can know, save they who have felt it, what joy there is in the full rush of language that moves and sways; to feel a crowd respond to the slightest touch; to see the faces brighten or darken at your bidding; to know that the sources of human emotion and human passions gush forth at the word of the speaker as the stream from the riven rock; to feel that the thought which thrills through a thousand hearers has its impulse from you, and throbs back to you the fuller from a thousand heart-beats. Is there any emotional joy in life more brilliant than this, fuller of passionate triumph, and of the very essence of intellectual delight?

In 1873 my marriage tie was broken. I took no new step, but my absence from the Communion led to some gossip, and a relative of Mr. Besant pressed on him highly-coloured views of the social and professional dangers which would accrue if my heresy became known. My health, never really restored since the autumn of 1871, grew worse and worse, serious heart trouble having arisen from the constant strain under which I lived. At last, in July or August, 1873, the crisis came. I was told that I must conform to the outward observances of the Church, and attend the Communion; I refused. Then came the distinct alternative; conformity or exclusion from home – in other words, hypocrisy or expulsion. I chose the latter.

A bitterly sad time followed.

The language of the Prayer Book, from Matthew Arnold, 'A Psychological Parallel', in *Last Essays on Church and Religion* (1877)

Almost thirty years after 'Dover Beach' (above, p. 260), Arnold's late essays show him still addressing the religious controversies of his age in their significance for a broader understanding of culture.

We can hardly conceive modern civilization breaking up as did [the civilization of the Roman world], and men beginning again as they did in the fifth century. But the improbability of this implies the improbability, too, of our seeing all the form and feature of Christianity disappear, – of the religion of Christendom. For so vast a revolution would this be, that it would involve the other.

These considerations are of force, I think, in regard to all radical change in the language of the Prayer Book. It has created sentiments deeper than we can see or measure. Our feeling does not connect itself with *any* language about righteousness and religion, but with *that* language. Very much of it we can all use in its literal acceptation. But the question is as to those parts which we cannot. Of course, those who can take them literally will still continue to use them. But for us also, who can no longer put the literal meaning on them which others do, and which we ourselves once did, they retain a power, and something in us vibrates to them. And not unjustly. For these old forms of expression were men's sincere attempt to set forth with due honour what we honour also; and the sense of the attempt gives a beauty and an emotion to the words, and makes them poetry.

Alfred North Whitehead (1861–1947) discusses emotional appeal in religion

Whitehead was the son of a Kent clergyman and schoolmaster, and wrote Principia Mathematica *with Bertrand Russell. He became influential in educational reform and 'process philosophy', and in his sixties took up a position at Harvard, where in his retirement the 'Sunday evenings' he held with his wife were very popular with students. His friend Lucien Price recorded some of his conversations (*Dialogues of Alfred North Whitehead*), and this extract comes from 1945, the year in which he was awarded the Order of Merit. He is recalling his childhood.*

'I am standing now at a window of my grandmother's house,' he mused.

'Eighty-one Piccadilly?' supplied Mrs. Whitehead, wistfully.

'Looking out over Green Park,' he continued, 'and there is Queen Victoria going by –'

'You would have seen her?...'

'Bless you, yes; and not once or twice but every day or so.'

'Imagine your having seen the old queen as often as the grocer's delivery wagon!'

'She wasn't "old" then; she was in the prime of life, and not very popular. It was only after the 1870's that she began to be popular, and she ended by becoming such an institution that when she died, we couldn't believe it.'

'Even the poor went into mourning,' said Mrs. Whitehead. 'If they couldn't afford to buy black clothes, they died their ordinary clothes black. They were in mourning for the Victorian Age – though they didn't know that then,' she added sombrely.

'We had grave apprehensions about Edward VII,' continued Whitehead, 'and he was far from popular when he came to the throne, but by the end of his reign he was well liked. The two Georges since (I think) have paid their way.'

'Though George VI seems to me a somewhat colourless figure,' said she, 'after his father. George V had a temper.'

'It's amazing that the monarchy has lasted until 1945,' said I.

'Oh, no, it isn't,' said Whitehead. 'The English never abolish anything. They put it in cold storage. That has its advantages. If they should want it again, there it is!'

'If you will permit me to say so, sir, that also goes for their Established Church.'

'As I have said to you before,' remarked Whitehead, 'the Reformation seems to me one of the calamities of history. If given more time, I think the Church would have reformed from within. Erasmus had about the right ideas and he was offered a cardinal's hat before his death, though he refused it. But the revolt of the Protestants hardened the Church's resistance; and the Protestants threw out precisely that part of the Church which makes it gracious and tolerable; namely, its aesthetic and emotional appeal. If I were to choose among present-day Christians, I would prefer the Unitarians, but I wish they had more influence. They are, I realize, close to the Congregationalists, and I think it would be well if they were closer, for it would not surprise me if in another hundred years the United States were predominantly Catholic.'

'The one aesthetic and emotional appeal which the Protestants didn't throw overboard,' I remarked, 'was music.'

'Religion,' said Whitehead, 'cannot exist without music. It is too abstract.'

'That's so! Even the New England Puritans, who did away with church organs and instruments, kept their psalmody!'

'Music comes before religion,' said he, 'as emotion comes before thought, and sound before sense. What is the first thing you hear when you go into a church? The organ playing. What is the last thing you hear as you come out? The organ. And in the Catholic service, the mass itself is sung. Music comes aeons before religion. You can't tell me that the nightingale is singing to its mate out of anything but the joy of life, for the love of singing. These things lie deeper than thought, as sound strikes deeper in us than sight. When we were savages, I venture to suppose, we were much more impressed by the sound of thunder than by the flash of lightning.'

William Hale White (1831–1913) as 'Mark Rutherford', from *The Revolution in Tanner's Lane* (1887)

From a Dissenting background, White trained as a minister and practised as a Unitarian preacher before turning to publishing and then the Civil Service. In his fifties he began writing essays and novels under the name Mark Rutherford.

COWFOLD, half village, half town, lies about three miles to the west of the Great North Road from London to York. As you go from London, about fifty miles from the Post Office in St. Martin's-le-Grand – the fiftieth milestone is just beyond the turning – you will see a hand-post with three arms on it; on one is written in large letters, 'TO LONDON'; on the second, in equally large letters, 'TO YORK'; and on the third, in small italic letters, '*To Cowfold*.'

Cowfold had four streets, or more correctly, only two, which crossed one another at right angles in the middle of the town, and formed there a kind of square or open place, in which, on Saturdays, a market was held. The 'Angel' was in this square, and the shops grouped themselves round it. In the centre was a large pump with a great leaden spout that had a hole bored in it at the side. By stopping up the mouth of the spout with the hand it was possible through this hole to get a good drink, if a friend was willing to work the handle; and as the square was a public playground, the pump did good service, especially amongst the boys, all of whom preferred it greatly to a commonplace mug. On Sundays it was invariably chained up; for although it was no breach of the Sabbath to use the pump in the backyard, the line was drawn there, and it would have been voted by nine-tenths of Cowfold as decidedly immoral to get water from the one outside. The shops were a draper's, a grocer's, an ironmonger's, a butcher's, and a baker's. All these were regular shops, with shop-windows, and were within sight of one another. There were also other houses where things were sold; but these were mere dwelling-houses, and were at the poorer and more remote ends of Cowfold. None of the regular shops aforesaid were strictly what they professed to be. Each of them diverged towards 'the general.' The draper sold boots and shoes; the grocer sold drugs, stationery, horse and cow medicines, and sheep ointment; and the ironmonger dealt in crockery. Even the butcher was more than a butcher, for he was never to be seen at his chopping-block, and his wife did all the retail work. He himself was in the 'jobbing' line, and was always jogging about in a cart, in the hind part of which, covered with a net, was a calf or a couple of pigs. Three out of the four streets ran out in cottages; but one was more aristocratic. This was Church Street, which contained the church and the parsonage. It also had in it four red-brick houses, each surrounded with large gardens. In one lived a brewer who had a brewery in Cowfold, and owned a dozen beer shops in the neighbourhood; another was a seminary for young ladies; in the third lived the doctor; and in the fourth old Mr. and Mrs. Muston, who had no children, had been there for fifty years, and this, so far as Cowfold was aware, was all their history. Mr. and Mrs. Muston and the seminary were the main strength of the church. To be sure, the doctor and the landlord of the 'Angel' professed devotion to the Establishment, but they were never inside the church, except just now and then, and were charitably excused because of their peculiar callings. The rest of Cowfold was Dissenting or 'went nowhere.' There were three chapels; one, *the* chapel, orthodox, Independent, holding about seven hundred persons, and more particularly to be described presently; the second, Wesleyan, new, stuccoed, with grained doors and cast-iron railing; the third, Strict Baptist, ultra-Calvinistic, Antinomean, surrounded by a small long-grassed graveyard, and named ZOAR in large letters over the long window in front. The 'went nowhere' class was apparently not very considerable. On Sunday morning at twelve o'clock Cowfold looked as if it had been swept clean. It was only by comparison between the total number of church-goers and chapel-goers and the total population that it could be believed that there was anybody absent from the means of grace; but if a view could have been taken of the back premises an explanation would have been discovered. Men and women 'did up their gardens,' or found, for a variety of reasons, that they were forced to stay at home. In the evening they grew bolder, and strolled through the meadows. It is, however, only fair to respectable Cowfold to say that it knew nothing of these creatures, except by employing them on week-days.

With regard to the Wesleyan Chapel, nothing much need be said. Its creed was imported, and it had no roots in the town. The Church disliked it because it was Dissenting, and the Dissenters disliked it because it was half-Church and, above all, Tory. It was supported mainly by the brewer, who was drawn thither for many reasons, one of which was political. Another was that he was not in trade, and although he objected to be confounded with his neighbours who stood behind counters, the church did not altogether suit him, because there Mr. and Mrs. Muston and the seminary stood in the way. Lastly, as he owned beer-shops, supplied liquor which was a proverb throughout the county, and did a somewhat doubtful business according to the more pious of the Cowfold Christians, he preferred to be accredited as a religious person by Methodism than by any other sect, the stamp of Methodism standing out in somewhat higher relief.

As for Zoar, it was a place apart. Its minister was a big, large-jawed, heavy-eyed man who lived in a little cottage hard by. His wife was a very plain-looking person, who wore, even on Sundays, a cotton gown without any ornament, and who took her husband's arm as they walked down the lane to the chapel. The Independent minister, the Wesleyan minister, and, of course, the rector, had nothing to do with the minister of Zoar. This was not because of any heresy or difference of doctrine, but because he was a poor man, and poor persons sat under him. Nevertheless, he was not in any way a characteristic Calvinist. The Calvinistic creed was stuck in him as in a lump of fat, and had no organizing influence upon him whatever. He had no weight in Cowfold, took part in none of its affairs, and his ministrations were confined to about fifty sullen, half-stupid, wholly ignorant people who found in the Zoar services something sleepier and requiring less mental exertion than they needed elsewhere; although it must be said that the demands made upon the intellect in none of the places of worship were very extensive.

Christina Rossetti (1830–1894)

The youngest of three children of Italian political exiles, much of her poetry was of a devotional, High Anglican cast. Her brother, the Pre-Raphaelite painter Dante Gabriel Rossetti, died in Birchington, on the Kent coast, on 9 April 1882, and was buried in the churchyard. Her commemorative poem was published in the Athenaeum *on 25 April.*

Birchington Churchyard

A lowly hill which overlooks a flat,
  Half sea, half countryside;
A flat-shored sea of low-voice creeping tide
  Over a chalky weedy mat.

A hill of hillocks, flowery and kept green
  Round Crosses raised for hope,
With many-tinted sunsets where the slope
  Faces the lingering western sheen.

A lowly hope, a height that is but low,
  While Time sets solemnly,
While the tide rises of Eternity,
  Silent and neither swift not low.

William Morris (1834–1896), letter to *The Times*, 15 August 1890

Writer, designer, leading figure in British socialism and the Arts and Crafts movement. He had founded the Society for the Protection of Ancient Buildings (SPAB) in 1877 to promote the sensitive conservation of buildings and their contents.

Sir,
My attention has been called to a letter from the vicar of Stratford-on-Avon appearing in your issue of July 28th, and appealing for funds generally towards the completion of the restoration. In this letter occurs the following sentence: 'Under the stalls sufficient of the ancient reredos has been found to make Mr. Garner think he can give us a drawing of what it was when the church was built. We shall hope, then, that somebody will provide the funds to erect a copy of it in the old place.'

I am glad that the vicar talks about a 'copy' of the reredos, and not a 'restoration' of it: but may I ask why a copy of it should be 'erected in the old place'? Will not every fresh piece of modern work make 'the old place' (the church, I mean) look less old and more like a nineteenth-century mediaeval furniture-dealer's warehouse? There has been a great deal too much modernization of this fine church of Stratford-on-Avon already, and it is more than time that it should come to an end. Once for all I protest against the trick which clergymen and restoration committees have of using an illustrious name as a bait wherewith to catch subscriptions. Shakespeare's memory is best honoured by reading his works intelligently; and it is no honour to him to spend money in loading the handsome mediaeval church which contains his monument with trash which can claim none of the respect due to either an ancient or a modern work of art.

'To Church on Sunday', from Flora Thompson (1876–1947), *Lark Rise* (1939)

Flora Thompson, whose working life as a Post Office clerk began at the age of fourteen, had written poems and pieces for magazines before she turned in Lark Rise *to a fuller evocation of the rural culture in which she grew up on the Oxfordshire–Buckinghamshire border. Her own village of Juniper Hill (Lark Rise) and its set old ways, and the 'mother village' with the church, Cottisford, are seen through the eyes of 'Laura,' a version of her childhood self.*

If the Lark Rise people had been asked their religion, the answer of nine out of ten would have been 'Church of England', for practically all of them were christened, married, and buried as such, although, in adult life, few went to church between the baptisms of their offspring. The children were shepherded there after Sunday school and about a dozen of their elders attended regularly; the rest stayed at home, the women cooking and nursing, and the men, after an elaborate Sunday toilet, which included shaving and cutting each other's hair and much puffing and splashing with buckets of water, but stopped short before lacing up boots or putting on a collar and tie, spent the rest of the day eating, sleeping, reading the newspaper, and strolling round to see how their neighbours' pigs and gardens were looking.

There were a few keener spirits. The family at the inn was Catholic and was up and off to early Mass in the next village before others had turned over in bed for an extra Sunday morning snooze. There were also three Methodist families which met in one of their cottages on Sunday evenings for prayer and praise; but most of these attended church as well, thus earning for themselves the name of 'Devil dodgers'.

Every Sunday, morning and afternoon, the two cracked, flat-toned bells at the church in the mother village called the faithful to worship. *Ding-dong, Ding-dong, Ding-dong,* they went, and, when they heard them, the hamlet churchgoers hurried across fields and over stiles, for the Parish Clerk was always threatening to lock the church door when the bells stopped and those outside might stop outside for all he cared.

With the Fordlow cottagers, the Squire's and farmer's families and maids, the Rectory people and the hamlet contingent, the congregation averaged about thirty. Even with this small number, the church was fairly well filled, for it was a tiny place, about the size of a barn, with nave and chancel only, its grey, roughcast walls, plain-glass windows, and flagstone floor. The cold, damp, earthy odour common to old and unheated churches pervaded the atmosphere, with occasional whiffs of a more unpleasant nature said to proceed from the stacks of mouldering bones in the vault beneath. Who had been buried there, or when, was unknown, for, excepting one ancient and mutilated brass in the wall by the font, there were but two memorial tablets, both of comparatively recent date. The church, like the village, was old and forgotten, and those buried in the vault, who must have been people of importance, had not left even a name. Only the stained glass window over the altar, glowing jewel-like amidst the cold greyness, the broken piscina within the altar rails, and a tall broken shaft of what had been a cross in the churchyard, remained to witness mutely to what once had been.

The Squire's and clergyman's families had pews in the chancel, with backs to the wall on either side, and between them stood two long benches for the school-children, well under the eyes of authority. Below the steps down into the nave stood the harmonium, played by the clergyman's daughter, and round it was ranged the choir of small school-girls. Then came the rank and file of the congregation, nicely graded, with the farmer's family in the front row, then the Squire's gardener and coachman, the schoolmistress, the maid-servants, and the cottagers, with the Parish Clerk at the back to keep order.

'Clerk Tom', as he was called, was an important man in the parish. Not only did he dig the graves, record the banns of marriage, take the chill off the water for winter baptisms, and stoke the coke stove which stood in the nave at the end of his seat; but he also took an active and official part in the services. It was his duty to lead the congregation in the responses and to intone the 'Amens'. The psalms were not sung or chanted, but read, verse and verse about, by the Rector and people, and in these especially Tom's voice so drowned the subdued murmur of his fellow worshippers that it sounded like a duet between him and the clergyman – a duet in which Tom won easily, for his much louder voice would often trip up the Rector before he had quite finished his portion, while he prolonged his own final syllables at will.

The afternoon service, with not a prayer left out or a creed spared, seemed to the children everlasting. The school-children, under the stern eye of the Manor House, dared not so much as wriggle; they sat in their stiff, stuffy best clothes, their stomachs lined with heavy Sunday dinner, in a kind of waking doze, through which Tom's 'Amens' rang like a bell and the Rector's voice buzzed beelike. Only on the rare occasions when a bat fluttered down from the roof, or a butterfly drifted in at a window, or the Rector's little fox terrier looked in at the door and sidled up the nave, was the tedium lightened.

Edmund and Laura, alone in their grandfather's seat, modestly situated exactly half-way down the nave, were more fortunate, for they sat opposite the church door and, in summer, when it was left open, they could at least watch the birds and the bees and the butterflies crossing the opening and the breezes shaking the boughs of the trees and ruffling the long grass on the graves. It was interesting, too, to observe some woman in the congregation fussing with her back hair, or a man easing his tight collar, or old Dave Pridham, who had a bad bunion, shuffling off a shoe before the sermon began, with one eye all the time upon the clergyman; or to note how closely together some newly married couple were sitting, or to see Clerk Tom's young wife suckling her baby. She wore a fur tippet in winter and her breast hung like a white heather bell between the soft blackness until it was covered up with a white handkerchief, 'for modesty'.

Mr. Ellison in the pulpit was the Mr. Ellison of the Scripture lessons, plus a white surplice. To him, his congregation were but children of a larger growth, and he preached as he taught. A favourite theme was the duty of regular churchgoing. He would hammer away at that for forty-five minutes, never seeming to realize that he was preaching to the absent, that all those present were regular attendants, and that the stray sheep of his flock were snoring upon their beds a mile and a half away.

Another favourite subject was the supreme rightness of the social order as it then existed. God, in His infinite wisdom, had appointed a place for every man, woman, and child on this earth and it was their bounden duty to remain contentedly in their niches. A gentleman might seem to some of his listeners to have a pleasant, easy life, compared to theirs at field labour; but he had his duties and responsibilities, which would be far beyond their capabilities. He had to pay taxes, sit on the Bench of Magistrates, oversee his estate, and keep up his position by entertaining. Could they do these things? No. Of course they could not; and he did not suppose that a gentleman could cut as straight a furrow or mow or thatch a rick as expertly as they could. So let them be thankful and rejoice in their physical strength and the bounty of the farmer, who found them work on his land and paid them wages with his money.

Less frequently, he would preach eternal punishment for sin, and touch, more lightly, upon the bliss reserved for those who worked hard, were contented with their lot and showed proper respect to their superiors. The Holy Name was seldom mentioned, nor were human griefs or joys, or the kindly human feelings which bind man to man. It was not religion he preached, but a narrow code of ethics, imposed from above upon the lower orders, which, even in those days, was out of date.

Once and once only did inspiration move him. It was the Sunday after the polling for the General Election of 1886, and he had begun preaching one of his usual sermons on the duty to social superiors, when, suddenly something, perhaps the memory of the events of the past week, seemed to boil up within him. Flushed with anger – 'righteous anger', he would have called it – and his frosty blue eyes flashing like swords, he cast himself forward across the ledge of his pulpit and roared: 'There are some among you who have lately forgotten that duty, and we know the cause, the *bloody* cause!'

Laura shivered. Bad language in church! And from the Rector! But, later in life, she liked to think that she had lived early enough to have heard a mild and orthodox Liberalism denounced from the pulpit as 'a bloody cause'. It lent her the dignity of an historic survival.

The sermon over, the people sprang to their feet like Jacks-in-a-box. With what gusto they sang the evening hymn, and how their lungs expanded and their tongues wagged as they poured out of the churchyard! Not that they resented anything that was said in the Rector's sermons. They did not listen to them. After the Bloody Cause sermon Laura tried to find out how her elders had reacted to it; but all she could learn was: 'I seems to have lost the thread just then,' or, more frankly, 'I must've been nodding'; the most she could get was one woman's, 'My! Didn't th'old parson get worked up to-day!'

Some of them went to church to show off their best clothes and to see and criticize those of their neighbours; some because they loved to hear their own voices raised in the hymns, or because churchgoing qualified them for the Christmas blankets and coals; and a few to worship. There was at least one saint and mystic in that parish and there were several good Christian men and women, but the majority regarded religion as something proper to extreme old age, for which they themselves had as yet no use.

'About time he wer' thinkin' about his latter end,' they would say of one who showed levity when his head and beard were white, or of anybody who was ill or afflicted. Once a hunch-back from another village came to a pig feast and distinguished himself by getting drunk and using bad language, and, because he was a cripple, his conduct was looked upon with horror. Laura's mother was distressed when she heard about it. 'To think of a poor afflicted creature like that cursing and swearing,' she sighed. 'Terrible! Terrible!' And when Edmund, then about ten, looked up from his book and said calmly, 'I should think if anybody's got a right to swear it's a man with a back like that,' she told him he was nearly as bad to say such a thing.

The Catholic minority at the inn was treated with respect, for a landlord could do no wrong, especially the landlord of a free house where such excellent beer was on tap. On Catholicism at large, the Lark Rise people looked with contemptuous intolerance, for they regarded it as a kind of heathenism, and what excuse could there be for that in a Christian country? When, early in life, the end house children asked what Roman Catholics were, they were told they were 'folks as prays to images', and further inquiries elicited the information that they also worshipped the Pope, a bad old man, some said in league with the Devil. Their genuflexions in church and their 'playin' wi' beads' were described as 'monkey tricks'. People who openly said they had no use for religion themselves became quite heated when the Catholics were mentioned. Yet the children's grandfather, when the sound of the Angelus bell was borne on the wind from the chapel in the next village, would take off his hat and, after a moment's silence, murmur, 'In my Father's house are many mansions.' It was all very puzzling.

Later on, when they came to associate more with the other children, on the way to Sunday school they would see horses and traps loaded with families from many miles around on their way to the Catholic Church in the next village. 'There go the old Catholics!' The children would cry, and run after the vehicles shouting: 'Old Catholics! Old lick the cats!' until they had to fall behind for want of breath. Sometimes a lady in one of the high dogcarts would smile at them forbearingly, otherwise no notice was taken.

The horse and traps were followed at a distance by the young men and big boys of the families on foot. Always late in starting, yet always in time for the service, how they legged it! The children took good care not to call out after them, for they knew, whatever their haste, the boy Catholics would have time to turn back and cuff them. It had happened before. So they let them get on for quite a distance before they started to mock their gait and recite in a snuffling sing-song:

'O dear Father, I've come to confess.'
'Well, my child, and what have you done?'
'O dear Father, I've killed the cat.'
'Well, my child, and what about that?'
'O dear Father, what shall I do?'
'You kiss me and I'll kiss you.'

'A supreme bore', from Gwen Raverat (1885–1957), *Period Piece – A Cambridge Childhood* (1952)

Gwen Raverat was the granddaughter of Charles Darwin, and a wood engraver. Her father was Professor of Astronomy at Cambridge; her mother was an American socialite. Her childhood home on the River Cam now houses Darwin College.

It was unfortunate that my mother insisted on giving us Bible lessons herself, for they bored us dreadfully, and there was always trouble about them. She had little gift for teaching; but I do not now think that she was insincere about it, though I am afraid I thought so then. The fact was that she was far simpler in her views on religion than I would have thought possible in anyone grown-up. She was a warm-hearted, innocently pleasure-loving person who, to the end of her life, enjoyed the things of this world in a fresh and youthful way, which was very attractive, though we superior children sometimes found it rather exasperating. She loved engagements and weddings and babies and food and games and dress and riddles and auction-sales; and above all she simply adored parties and picnics and sprees of any kind. But she also truly wished to be good and to do right, and so she took us to church and taught us about religion, just as she had been taught herself when she was young. For the vestiges of her early-American puritanism still clung about her; rather oddly combined with the axiom that what my father thought was always right; however the demands of logic never troubled her at any time, She was not a bit worldly, like Aunt Cara, but she had not got a religious nature, and religion, as taught by her, made no sense at all to us. Perhaps it wouldn't anyhow, but we should have respected it more if we had been taught by someone with a natural feeling for spiritual matters. As it was, it was hopeless.

There was a certain grey Sunday-school book which seemed to us beyond bearing; and so, after a good deal of plotting and counter-plotting, we hid it in a very good place, between the rafters and ceiling of the attic. It fell down into the hollow of the wall, and we thought we were safe. But after a time suspicion fell on us, and there was a dreadful fuss. We were sent up before the highest tribunal, and at last obliged to confess. Then my father took the fire-tongs and led a very solemn procession upstairs, and there was a ceremonial fishing in the wall with the tongs. Unfortunately the book was hooked and landed; and we were immediately given a lesson out of it. This we received very meekly, for we were much impressed by my father's intervention. After that the book tactfully disappeared of its own accord, and we never saw it again; I suppose my father had recommended its eclipse. It would have been better if he had intervened more often in our affairs – he hardly ever did – for things went very smoothly when he took a hand, and we grew reasonable and calm.

There were always difficulties about going to church, too, because it was such a supreme bore. It was not quite as bad as dancing class, though in the same category, because it only required passive endurance, not active participation. Still it made us very cross to have to spend all that time keeping still and thinking about nothing at all; especially when there were so many thousands of things we were simply dying to do at home. Boredom was to me an active torment, not a passive one, and I just raged and seethed with impatience, all through the service, waiting for the moment when I could rush home, tear off my horrible hat and gloves, and get on with whatever I had been doing, when I had been shanghaied by the Press Gang (my mother). I remember how once the congregation stared at me when I leapt enthusiastically to my feet at the sound of a premature '*And Now*' from the parson; and how miserably I sank back into my place as he went droning on again. I believe my poor mother felt that if only she could get us into church, some of the meaning of it might sink into us unconsciously; but I don't see how it could, with anyone in my usual church-going mood of white-hot indignation.

College chapels usually have the Litany instead of a sermon; this seemed to me the lowest layer of the dust-and-ashes of boredom and misery. I never listened to any part of the service except the Psalms; I liked them because I always liked poetry. For the same reason I did not like the hymns. I lived through the Litany by thinking what horrid words *Vouchsafe* and *Beseech* were, and wondering if they meant something frightfully improper; or by hoping that the pigeons would get inside the roof again.

For it was to King's College Chapel that we were usually taken; and that was another trouble: I couldn't bear the music there! I don't expect anyone to understand about this, but I simply hated the unfair, juicy way in which the organ notes oozed round inside the roof, and sapped your vitals, and made you want to cry about nothing at all. I liked my music dry, not wet, in those days, just as I still do. Dr. Mann was organist then, and I dare say that he was rather soulful; at any rate, I have never yet been able to dissociate music at King's Chapel from the kind of emotional appeal which I find most antipathetic of all.

Nor were other churches more congenial to me. For one thing, I was quite Oliver-Cromwellian in my distaste for all kinds of ritual and ceremony. They told you that God was a spirit; that seemed to me a good idea, and I understood it and liked it; and then they spoilt it altogether by doing all sorts of mumbo-jumbo, which could not possibly have anything to do with a God who was a spirit. This shocked me unspeakably; for I was very high-minded and pure in those days; not to say arrogant. I was really far more anti-clerical than anti-religious; I might conceivably have made quite a decent Quaker.

As it was, I went to church cross, and got crosser all the time; I grew to distrust the very church bells, and honestly believed that nine-tenths of the congregation were hypocrites, and the remaining tenth, sentimental fools. My only excuse is that I really did not know anyone of a religious temperament whom I could love and admire; and occasional pious governesses made it much worse.

Winifred Spence (b. 1891), recorded in George Ewart Evans, *The Days that We have Seen* (1975)

In a series of books that started in 1956 the oral historian Evans (1909–1988) sympathetically captured voices and stories from the traditional world of rural Suffolk with his tape recorder just before social changes eclipsed them. Here, Winifred Spence at eighty-one recalls her childhood.

'My sister and I were twins: I came seventh in the family. Mother had two sets of twins. There were eighteen girls and four boys in the family. But she brought up sixteen to live. Well then – of course my father worked on the farm at Flixton near Lowestoft in Suffolk; after he married he did. But before he married he worked at Blundeston Hall which is now where the prison is. And his father had worked there with his father. Then he worked on different farms; then he was a farm-steward; and after that he was a groom-gardener; he finished up as a chauffeur. He was in Norfolk when he finished up as a chauffeur – Widacre Hall.

'Mother used to make – she had seven dinners to pack up every day for school; seven! And she used to make eighteen two-pound loaves of bread at once, in the brick oven. She used to heat it with faggots on Fridays and Wednesdays – two bakes a week. Well, being all girls, we went out to service. As we reached twelve years old we were packed up to go. in the first place I was, there was a housekeeper and a butler there. I did all the rough scrubbing up; and it *was* scrubbing in them days: scrub right through the house once a week. In the evenings I helped mother when I went home – sit and do some sewing or something like that. Mother would make all our clothes: coats, dresses and everything. Of course, we had to do the finishing off, sew the buttons on. We had to help quite a lot. We went to church – Church of England. We used to go off to Sunday school and from Sunday school to church. My father was very strict. He tested each of us every Sunday morning on the *collect* for the day. He used to come to church to see that we behaved ourselves. Most of the family went. We've all been Church of England. I still go, like to go, every Sunday.

'Yes, I liked it when I was young. It was a jolly sight better than it is today. (People say: *the bad old times*: I always say *the good old times*.) Yes, Mother had ten girls before she had a boy. Ten girls! And, of course, when my brother came along, the one who came to see me yesterday, well! people put their flags out; and they made such a fuss! There were only four boys: eighteen girls and four boys. Twenty-two, all born and christened. She had them christened, them that died early. She brought sixteen to grow up. I used to look forward to my birthday because my father always gave me tuppence: I was able to spend that and do what I liked with it. That was great! I used to get a hap'orth of this and a farthing's worth of that, and I made it last as long as ever it would. We never had any pocket-money. We didn't know what pocket-money was in those days – not until you got out to work. I mean, they didn't have it to give. When there was ten of us at home. And I don't think my father was earning more than about eighteen shillings a week. He used – always used to have rent free. But if there was sixpence to be earned anywhere he would earn it. He used to do all sorts of things: cut people's hair, *clip* horses: he was always at work. He had a large garden, and always grew potatoes and things for us. He used to have a piece of field as well, to grow his potatoes on, off the farm. He started on the farm as a horseman, finished up there as farm-steward; and we lived in the farmhouse which was plenty of room. That also was at Oulton Broad. We were a happy family. Of course, Christmas time was very exciting. We used to hang our stockings downstairs. Mother used to put a line up. She couldn't very well do them up in the cold upstairs. We didn't know any different. But we always used to get the things. How she used – oh, she used to sit up night after night making rag-dolls and dressing them, all sorts of things for our stockings; and we were happy – happier than they are today with all they have!

'We used to sing on Sunday nights. Father used to play the violin; and we always had hymns on Sunday night. And the boss came one Sunday night to ask him to take him to the Station on Monday morning. And he said he'd been standing outside quite ten minutes listening to us singing: "That put you in mind of Sunday school!" We were all singing and Father was playing the violin. No, really we were very happy, all of us. We had a good father and mother, and they made us happy; and we *were* happy. My father was a very colourful man: he always had something funny to come up with; and he knew one or two comical songs. He always kept us alive.'

Rudyard Kipling (1865–1936): 'Natural Theology' (1919)

Kipling's poems and stories from his life in India helped create his reputation as the 'Poet of Empire', and he was the first English recipient of the Nobel Prize for Literature (1907). From 1896 on, he and his family lived in England, mainly at Bateman's, in Sussex. His son John was killed in the First World War aged eighteen at the battle of Loos in 1915. After the war Kipling became a member of the Imperial War Graves Commission, whose motto 'Their Name Liveth for Evermore' he proposed from Ecclesiasticus. A body recovered in 1992 has been identified by the (now) Commonwealth Graves Commission as belonging to John.

PRIMITIVE

I ate my fill of a whale that died
　And stranded after a month at sea...
There is a pain in my inside.
　Why have the Gods afflicted me?
Ow! I am purged till I am a wraith!
　Wow! I am sick till I cannot see!
What is the sense of Religion and Faith?
　Look how the Gods have afflicted me!

PAGAN

How can the skin of rat or mouse hold
　Anything more than a harmless flea?...
The burning plague has taken my household.
　Why have the Gods afflicted me?

All my kith and kin are deceased,
  Though they were as good as good could be.
I will out and batter the family priest,
  Because my Gods have afflicted me!

MEDIAEVAL

My privy and well drain into each other
  After the custom of Christendie...
Fevers and fluxes are wasting my mother.
  Why has the Lord afflicted me?
The Saints are helpless for all I offer –
  So are the clergy I used to fee.
Henceforward I keep my cash in my coffer,
  Because the Lord has afflicted me.

MATERIAL

I run eight hundred hens to the acre.
  They die by dozens mysteriously...
I am more than doubtful concerning my Maker.
  Why has the Lord afflicted me?
What a return for all my endeavour –
  Not to mention the £. s. d.!
I am an atheist now and forever,
  Because this God has afflicted me!

PROGRESSIVE

Money spent on an Army or Fleet
  Is homicidal lunacy...
My son has been killed in the Mons retreat.
  Why is the Lord afflicting me?
Why are murder, pillage and arson
  And rape allowed by the Deity?
I will write to the *Times*, deriding our parson,
  Because my God has afflicted me.

CHORUS

We had a kettle: we let it leak:
  Our not repairing it made it worse.
We haven't had any tea for a week…
  The bottom is out of the Universe!

CONCLUSION

This was none of the good Lord's pleasure,
  For the Spirit He breathed in Man is free;
But what comes after is measure for measure
  And not a God that afflicteth thee.
As was the sowing so the reaping
  Is now and evermore shall be.
Thou art delivered to thine own keeping.
  Only thyself hath afflicted thee!

Siegfried Sassoon (1886–1967), from *Memoirs of a Fox-Hunting Man* (1928)

Sassoon's Memoirs of a Fox-Hunting Man *evokes the as yet unscarred world – in his case, rural Kent – that his gilded generation was about to lose in the Great War; it was the first volume of what became his 'George Sherston' trilogy,* Memoirs of an Infantry Officer *being the second. He was sent to France as a second lieutenant in the Royal Welch Fusiliers in 1915. He was awarded the Military Cross, but in 1917 he sent a statement to his commanding officer: 'Finished with the War: A Soldier's Declaration'. It was decided that he was suffering from 'shell shock', and he was sent to Craiglockhart, a mental hospital in Edinburgh. By then he was known as a war poet, and there he met and encouraged Wilfred Owen. He became a Catholic ten years before his death.*

The Rev. Harry Colwood, as I remember him, was a composite portrait of Charles Kingsley and Matthew Arnold. This fanciful resemblance has no connection with literature, toward which Mr. Colwood's disposition was respectful but tepid. My mental semi-association of him with Arnold is probably due to the fact that he had been in the Rugby eleven somewhere in the 'sixties'. And I have, indeed, heard him speak of Arnold's poem, *Rugby*

Chapel. But the Kingsley affinity was more clearly recognizable. Like Kingsley, Mr. Colwood loved riding, shooting, and fishing, and believed that such sports were congruous with the Christian creed which he unobtrusively accepted and lived up to. It is questionable, however, whether he would have agreed with Kingsley's Christian Socialism. One of his maxims was 'Don't marry for money but marry where money is', and he had carried this into effect by marrying, when he was over forty, a sensible Scotch lady with a fortune of £1,500 a year, thereby enabling his three sons to be brought up as keen fox-hunters, game-shooters, and salmon-fishers. And however strongly the Author of his religion might have condemned these sports, no one could deny him the Christian adjectives gentle, patient, and just.

At first I had been intimidated by him, for the scrutinizing look that he gave me was both earnest and stern. His were eyes which looked straight at the world from under level brows, and there was strictness in the lines of his mouth. But the kindliness of his nature emerged in the tone of his voice, which was pitched moderately low. In his voice a desire for gaiety seemed to be striving to overmaster an inherent sadness. This undertone of sadness may have been accentuated as the result of his ripened understanding of a world which was not all skylarking and sport, but Stephen (who was a lankier and less regular-featured edition of his father) had inherited the same quality of voice. Mr. Colwood was a naturally nervous man with strong emotions, which he rigidly repressed.

When I arrived that afternoon both the Rector and his wife were attending some parochial function in the village. So Stephen took me up to the schoolroom, where we had our tea and he jawed to me about horses and hunting to his heart's content. He ended by asserting that he'd 'sooner cheer a pack of Pomeranians after a weasel from a bath-chair than waste his life making money in a blinking office'.

A tenor bell in Hoadley Church tower was making its ultimate appeal to those who were still on their way to morning service. While Stephen and I hurried hatless across the sloping cricket-field which divided the Rectory garden from the churchyard I sniffed the quiet wintry-smelling air and wondered how long Mr. Colwood's sermon would last. I had never been to his church before; there was a suggestion of embarrassment in the idea of seeing him in a long white surplice – almost as if one were taking an unfair advantage of him. Also, since I hadn't been to church with Aunt Evelyn for Heaven knew how long, I felt a bit of an outsider as I followed Stephen up the aisle to the Rectory pew where his matronly mother was awaiting us with the solemnly cheerful face of one who never mumbled the responses but made them as though she meant every word. Stephen, too, had the serene sobriety of an habitual public-worshipper. No likelihood of his standing up at one of those awkward places when everyone kneels down when you don't expect them to.

As the service proceeded I glanced furtively around me at the prudent Sunday-like faces of the congregation. I thought of the world outside, and the comparison made life out there seem queer and unreal. I felt as if we were all on our way to next week in a ship. But who was I, and what on earth had I been doing? My very name suddenly seemed as though it scarcely belonged to me. Stephen was sitting there beside me, anyhow; there was no doubt about his identity, and I thought what a nice face he had, gentle and humorous and alight with natural intelligence. I looked from him to this father, who had been in the background, so far, since the curate had been reading the service (in an unemphatic businesslike voice). But the Rector's eye met mine, which shied guiltily away, and my wool-gathering was interrupted. Even so might his gaze have alighted on one of the coughing village children at the back of the church.

My sense of unfamiliarity with what was going on was renewed when Colonel Hesmon's wizened face and bushy grey eyebrows appeared above the shiny brass eagle to read the First Lesson. This was not quite the same Colonel who had been in such a frenzy of excitement over the point-to-point race eight months ago, when he had exclaimed, over and over again, 'I've told the boy that if he wins *I'll give him the horse!*'

The Colonel's voice was on church parade now, and he was every inch a churchwarden as well. He went through the lesson with dispassionate distinctness and extreme rapidity. Since it was a long passage from Isaiah, he went, as he would have said, 'a rattling good gallop'. But the words, I thought, were incongruous ones when uttered by the Colonel.

'And he will lift up an ensign to the nations from far, and will hiss unto them from the end of the earth: and, behold, they shall come with speed swiftly: none shall be weary nor stumble among them; none shall slumber nor sleep; neither shall the girdle of their loins be loosed, nor the latchet of their shoes be broken: whose arrows are sharp, and all their bows bent, their horses' hoofs shall be counted like flint, and their wheels like a whirlwind: their roaring shall be like a lion, they shall roar like young lions: yea, they shall roar, and lay hold of the prey, and shall carry it away safe, and none shall deliver it. And in that day they shall war against them like the roaring of the sea: and if one look unto the land, behold darkness and sorrow, and the light is darkened in the heavens thereof. Here endeth the First Lesson.' And the brisk little man turned over the leaves to a passage from Peter, arranged the gold-embroidered marker, and returned to his pew with erect and decorous demeanour.

Twenty minutes later Mr. Colwood climbed the pulpit steps to the strains of 'O God our help in ages past'. My own vocal contribution was inconspicuous, but I had a stealthy look at my watch, which caused Stephen, who was giving a creditable performance of the hymn, to nudge me with his elbow. The sermon lasted a laborious twelve minutes. The Rector had a nervous mannerism which consisted in his continually gathering up his surplice with his left hand, as if he were testing the quality of the linen with his fingers. The offertory was for a missionary society, and he took as his text: '*He that hath two coats, let him impart to him that hath none; and he that hath meat, let him do likewise*'. The results of the collection were handed to him on a wooden plate by the Colonel, who remarked afterwards at lunch that he 'didn't mind saying that with the best will in the world he'd have preferred to give his half-sovereign to someone nearer home' – Stephen having already made his rather obvious joke – 'Whatever the Guv'nor may say in his sermon about "imparting," if I ever get a new hunting-coat I'm going to ruddy well keep my old one for wet days!'

Robert Roberts (1905–1974), from *A Ragged Schooling – Growing Up in the Classic Slum* (1976)

Roberts was an English teacher and autobiographer. His The Classic Slum: Salford Life in the First Quarter of the Century *(1971) has become a classic of its own.*

In our village about one fifth of the inhabitants were Roman Catholic and the rest Protestants of some sort, shopkeepers and artisans, of course, tending to support Dissenting chapels. The great majority of Protestants, however, did not 'practise' themselves, but saw to it, perhaps as a conscience salver, that their children went regularly to Sunday school. In our home, though, it was a matter of indifference whether we attended or not. But I enjoyed going; discipline was slack, instruction vapid but short, and opportunity for minor mischief frequent. We often had speakers from other chapels who gave us little lectures on each of the virtues, pointed with parables out of their experience, but only one homilist, unfortunately, ever stirred me positively. His theme for the day was 'Perseverance'. Whenever we sinned, he told us, we must ask the Lord's forgiveness, then get up off our knees and go on fighting to follow God's will – never ever give up trying to do good every day, no matter how small the deed. That was Perseverance! Now, however irreproachable the sentiment, we had heard it all before, and I, for one, was drifting into reverie, when the speaker offered such a signal example from life itself of the rewards of resolution that I jerked to attention at once. 'Matchsticks!' he said dramatically. In the year 1880 a friend of his had begun to collect used matchsticks from all over Manchester, persuading others to help him. Then, slowly, steadily, *persevering all the time*, he started to build with them, and after twelve years' work the gentleman had completed his erection – a perfect model, three feet high, of Manchester cathedral! And underneath it was a little notice in golden letters which read:

PERSEVERANCE, STICKS AND GLUE – 1892.

This tale much impressed us. Here was a man, we felt, who had really put his time to valuable use, and in a way that any determined boy could copy. I ran home, alight with enthusiasm, to tell them all about it. And more, I *too*, I announced would build to the greater glory of the Lord – to wit, one Congregationalist chapel in matchsticks which, on completion, would be presented to Mr. Waters, the minister, before a large audience! At home Ellie and Ada, who had heard the story, quite thrilled to my idea and offered their assistance; but the whole thing, for some reason, made Jane giggle. 'Imbecility, sticks and glue,' she chanted, '1892!' Then for the next few days she kept rushing up from all parts of the house and presenting me with a spent match. In face of this my perseverance petered out.

A few weeks before Whitsuntide, Sunday schools had a temporary influx of small recruits, all sent by mothers who wanted to see their children walk in new clothes with the religious processions. In one family we knew of, the desire to testify openly for the Lord was so strong that an elder son sneaked out at night and 'did a job' to provide the wherewithal for his sisters' white dresses.

Protestants 'witnessed' publicly on Monday, the Roman Catholics Friday, in acrid competition with each other. 'God knows his own!' some Christians would say smugly if it rained on their rivals but stayed fine for the 'one true faith'. In our immediate district, however, several sects walked – separately, of course – on White Sunday, a practice which led to a certain acrimony at home and embittered the Old Man on one religion at least.

A pawnbroker's stood a few yards from us, and at weekends our shop functioned as an extension of its services. Many women on Saturday evenings, waiting for husbands to come home with wages, hadn't the money to redeem their pledges before 'Uncle's' closed. To overcome this difficulty Tom Arnott, the broker, paid my mother a fee, and every weekend I transferred from his premises to ours a consignment of up to twenty bundles of clothes. These were now available for redemption until 11 p.m. and also on Sunday. Best clothes taken out at the last minute could then be worn on the holy day and social status maintained. Bundles would, of course, be hocked again early on Monday morning. When our service first began, a few tick [credit] customers saw it as an excellent means of retrieving their apparel without spot cash, but Mother disagreed. 'We're agents,' she said, 'and hold the stuff on trust. No money, no clothes!' Each bundle in pawn had a small white ticket pinned on it denoting the owner. This gave rise to a pretty euphemism. 'Where's that nice brown suit?' one might ask a friend not looking his sartorial best at the Saturday hop. 'It's still got a "butterfly" on!' he would say sadly.

Among the load I collected from the pawnshop there was occasionally a bundle my father called a 'dead'un'. It could, at times, be very much alive, a sort of social 'bomb' that duly exploded. Some woman would arrange to do a neighbour's weekly wash on condition that she be allowed, afterwards, to pawn the clean clothes until week end. All would go well, perhaps, for a month or so, then one Saturday night the 'contractor' might find herself without money to redeem her pledge. Afraid to face the music, she would come quietly and slip the pawn ticket on to our counter and vanish. I then had the job of going to tell the owner that a 'butterfly' had landed. If money was available she would follow me back to the shop and, raging, bail out her own clothes. Later high words might be heard in the street, or even the sound of breaking glass. 'Pushin' her windows in' was a frequent form of reprisal in public dispute. Any bundles unredeemed over the weekend I returned on Monday morning. These sometimes acted as pointers to those of our credit customers who had begun to fall on hard times. My mother, thinking anxiously of her own solvency, might then start to limit the extent of their tick 'shots'.

One Saturday night before Whitsuntide Father, in a merry mood, let Kate Sweeney, a good Irish customer, borrow a pledge containing 'our little Patrick's sailor suit – just so he can walk proud, God bless him, with St. Joseph's tomorrer.' She swore on the grave of several relatives and the Holy

Mother of God to return it the minute the procession was over. Father fell for her blarney. But the news got around and set up a chain reaction. Others made Christian appeal for their children's clothes and, wanting to be fair to all faiths, he allowed bundles to go out without payment to two Primitive Methodists, a Congregationalist and a couple of Church of Englanders. Mother disapproved of it all. 'Nothin' to worry about,' he told her. 'Special occasion. Wouldn't do it regular, of course. And they've got to bring them back, else how could they use the pop shop again?' And that seemed sound sense. So their children walked the parish and looked in 'borrowed' finery as beautiful as any others. Later in the day all duly turned up with their bundles, save one – Mrs. Sweeney. On Monday night after work Father went round to get the clothes, cash, or 'knock hell out of their Mick!' But the Sweeney menage had migrated! Deeply in debt to shops around, the family had done a 'moonlight' to somewhere, neighbours said, 'up Harpurhey.' This shook Father on Catholics. He never had a good word for the Pope after.

Surprisingly for those times, when 'atheist' was still a sinister word, neither of my parents accepted Christianity. Perhaps they felt that the Church of England especially had little to offer shorn lambs beyond preaching acceptance of the wind. This was an era in which the Archbishop of Canterbury could organise a luncheon party 'exclusively for dowager duchesses'. Every morning at school we got the usual long and, to me, tedious doses of 'scripture'. Fifty years after, looking in the school log book, I was astonished to read that the 'Bishop's Examiners' had singled out my knowledge for special praise. They didn't know that at the time I was avid to absorb anything, even the 'begatting' of Old Testament genealogy. But belief was something else again. My mother, an open sceptic, had issued an admonition to us all. 'In religion,' she used to say, 'they often tell you they *know* things when in fact they only *believe* them. Just bear that in mind.'

The parish church, 'incumbered' in our time by a large and arrogant Rector, ran three day schools and a religious outpost. This last, a corrugated iron structure, stood in darkest Salford about a hundred yards from the shop. On summer evenings a band of missionaries, backed by two curates and a harmonium, made sallies to our street corners, where with hymn and sermonette they tried to evangelize the natives. Friendly people, whenever one of them came into the shop Mother always bought his offering. Once, however, clearly showing them how to do it, came our Rector in person. Bland and booming, he went among the lowly, spreading the Good News himself, and arrived, all condescension, at our counter.

'Now, young woman, the Magazine!'
'No, thank you,' said my mother civilly.
'It's the church periodical!' he reproved her.
'No, thank you,' she repeated.
'Humph!' he said, turning to go. 'It's easy to see *you* don't attend church!'
'And it's easy,' she told him, 'to see why!' The Rector didn't call again.

Thomas Hardy (1840–1928): 'Channel Firing' (1914)

The Royal Navy's gunnery practice off the Dorset coast in April 1914 foreshadowed the war that was to break out just a few months later, on 4 August. Stourton Tower is the 1770s folly that commemorates both the end of the Seven Years' War against France (1756–63) and King Alfred's stand against the Danes.

That night your great guns, unawares,
Shook all our coffins as we lay,
And broke the chancel window-squares,
We thought it was the Judgment-day

And sat upright. While drearisome
Arose the howl of wakened hounds:
The mouse let fall the altar-crumb,
The worms drew back into their mounds,

The glebe cow drooled. Till God called, 'No;
It's gunnery practice out at sea
Just as before you went below;
The world is as it used to be:

'All nations striving strong to make
Red war yet redder. Mad as hatters
They do no more for Christès sake
Than you who are helpless in such matters.

'That this is not the judgement-hour
For some of them's a blessed thing,
For if it were they'd have to scour
Hell's floor for so much threatening ...

'Ha, ha. It will be warmer when
I blow the trumpet (if indeed
I ever do; for you are men,
And rest eternal sorely need).'

So down we lay again. 'I wonder,
Will the world ever saner be,'
Said one, 'than when He sent us under
In our indifferent century!'

And many a skeleton shook his head.
'Instead of preaching forty year,'
My neighbour Parson Thirdly said,
'I wish I had stuck to pipes and beer.'

Again the guns disturbed the hour,
Roaring their readiness to avenge,
As far inland as Stourton Tower,
And Camelot, and starlit Stonehenge.

Wilfred Owen (1893–1918): 'The Parable of the Old Man and the Young,' 1918

Before he was twenty, Owen spent nearly two years as lay assistant and theological pupil with the vicar of Dunsden in Oxfordshire. His youthful ideals were badly shaken by the harsh realities of the lives to which he was supposed to bring comfort, and in a letter to his mother (on 4 January 1913) he wrote: 'I have murdered my false creed. If a true one exists, I shall find it. If not, adieu to the still falser creeds that hold the hearts of nearly all my fellow men.'

As the world of his generation was overtaken by the Great War, he began to find his voice in the poems that forged expression of that experience. A draft Preface he was preparing for them, found among his papers after his death, states: 'Above all I am not concerned with Poetry. My subject is War, and the pity of War. The Poetry is in the pity.'

He found important encouragement in the time spent with Siegfried Sassoon when fellow trauma patients at Craiglockhart in Edinburgh; in a letter to him in November 1917 he wrote: 'Know that since mid-September, when you still regarded me as a tiresome little knocker on your door, I held you as Keats + Christ + Elijah + my Colonel + my father-confessor + Amenophis IV in profile.'

He was killed in the last week of the war.

'Parable', his re-casting of the Abraham and Isaac story in Genesis 22, is one of nine Owen poems set by Britten in his War Requiem, *first performed in 1962 at the consecration of the new Coventry Cathedral.*

So Abram rose, and clave the wood, and went,
And took the fire with him, and a knife.
And as they sojourned both of them together,
Isaac the first-born spake and said, My Father,
Behold the preparations, fire and iron,
But where the lamb for this burnt-offering?
Then Abram bound the youth with belts and straps,
And builded parapets and trenches there,
And stretchèd forth the knife to slay his son.
When lo! an angel called him out of heaven,
Saying, Lay not thy hand upon the lad,
Neither do anything to him. Behold,
A ram, caught in a thicket by its horns;
Offer the Ram of Pride instead of him.
But the old man would not so, but slew his son,
And half the seed of Europe, one by one.

Siegfried Sassoon: 'They' (1917)

For Sassoon *see above, p. 322.*

The Bishop tells us: "When the boys come back
'They will not be the same; for they'll have fought
'In a just cause: they lead the last attack
'On Anti-Christ; their comrades' blood has bought
'New right to breed an honourable race,
'They have challenged Death and dared him face to face.'

'We're none of us the same!' the boys reply.
'For George lost both his legs; and Bill's stone blind;
'Poor Jim's shot through the lungs and like to die;
'And Bert's gone syphilitic: you'll not find

'A chap who's served who hasn't found *some* change.'
And the Bishop said: 'The ways of God are strange!'

Adrian Bell (1901–1980), from *Corduroy* (1930)

In Corduroy *Bell recounts how as a very young man he left his London background of Left-inclined journalism and apprenticed himself to a life of farming in rural Suffolk.*

Our Sunday dress in winter was breeches of a smarter cut than those of every day, and clean leggings and boots. My original brown boots had been polished up, and seemed now the thing for Sunday wear. Mr. Colville had a pair like them. They felt light as dancing-shoes after the working-boots.

Mr. Colville rode across the fields to church. I lay in a horsehair armchair in the breakfast-room with pipe and book, and for once the bustling Millicent failed to stir me. One of the first questions put to me on my arrival at Farley Hall had been (*in camera*), 'Are you Church of England?' The object of it had been merely to inform me of the nearest place of worship of those of my creed. It was a question that had caused me some confusion in the past. Religion, in fact, had been full of perplexities, beginning with my first encounter – a painful scene with my nurse who refused to allow me to rise from table before I had said, 'Thank God for a good dinner.' I had not the vaguest idea who or what God was, nor, since the dinner had included rice pudding, was I feeling particularly thankful for it. Then there had been the first day at kindergarten school, which had begun with us all kneeling down (a new game, I thought) and muttering. 'Harold be Thy name,' I thought they said, and wondered. In any case, what could the word 'hallowed' mean to a child of six? My parents had been reticent about established religion – wisely so, I think; for how can the idea of God be conveyed to a child's mind in words, a Being about whom the adult world differs so furiously? How, without at the same time creating unnameable fears which cause children much private suffering?

Then there had been an interview with the headmaster of my public school on the first day of term. 'Are you Church of England?' 'Yes,' I faltered. But that was not enough. 'What church do you attend at home?' I sought wildly for a name. The memory of a visitor's conversation saved me. 'St. Leonard's,' I answered.

But at school there was a short period of religious fervour, owing really to the persecutions of larger boys, from whom one was only safe in chapel. Then becoming a larger boy oneself and insufferably knowing, atheism was the only possible attitude to the unknown. My housemaster – blessings on his memory! – hearing of this, laughed at me. Just when I was prepared, martyr-like, to suffer expulsion for my non-belief, he said in passing, 'So you are the young man who believes we go out like a candle?' 'Yes, sir,' I said. His answer was, 'Ha, ha, ha!'

From this I had drifted to the modern attitude of open-minded doubt which awaits, as it were, the next mystico-scientific discovery for light. So again the question, 'Are you Church of England?' was a poser. I made an inadequate reply, indicating that I was not a regular churchgoer. This left an unsatisfied silence, and a few days later Mrs. Colville returned to the attack.

'If you don't go to church, what makes you do good?'

My behaviour was instinctive and hereditary, not the result of reason.

'I suppose because it is usually less dangerous than doing ill,' I answered.

'But if you are not afraid of going to hell?'

I mumbled my way unsatisfactorily through these inquisitions. But to Mrs. Colville and the ladies of the family I became 'a case'; they looked upon me curiously. The young man who behaved in an ordinary way, yet did not believe in heaven or hell! They saw nothing to restrain me from diabolical crimes, and for a while they regarded me much as a tiger cub, gentle and playful until one day it should taste blood. I mention this to show that here a pre-Darwinian faith still held good. It was the simple affair of the days of Tusser:*

> Tithe duly and well, with hearty goodwill,
> That God and His blessing may dwell with thee still.
> Though parson neglecteth his duty for this,
> Thank thou thy Lord God, and give every man his.

Mr. Colville, believing that every man knew his own business, kept religion a personal matter. But once when his brother Arnold was going to sell me a gun, and I, meeting him on a Sunday, enquired of him his price, said, 'I shouldn't do a deal on a Sunday, if I were you. It may be my fancy, but it don't ever seem to turn out right. Once when I was a boy I bought some ferrets on a Sunday, and dash me if they didn't all die.'

The infallibility of parsons was no more an illusion here and now than in the time of Tusser. In fact, the inhabitants of Benfield *liked* a parson for his humanity rather than his godliness. The present one's predecessor had been a keen sportsman, who had boxed the local publican for a wager and beaten him, spending the stake money on drinks all round. He used to ride to hounds twice a week, and legend has it that, seeing a fox cross the churchyard, he paused in his sermon to shout 'Tally-ho!'

On Mr. Colville's return from church, we motored down to Benfield to his father's for lunch. This, I learned, was a weekly function, a gathering of the clan.

* Thomas Tusser (d. 1580) spent most of his life farming in Essex and Suffolk, and wrote an often-reprinted poem-cum-manual on the Five Hundred Points of Good Husbandry. He also had periods of employment as a chorister, at St Paul's Cathedral and elsewhere.

D. H. Lawrence (1885–1930), 'Hymns in a Man's Life' (*Evening News*, London, 13 October 1928)

Lawrence wrote this newspaper article in the same year as Lady Chatterley's Lover, *two years before his death from TB. One of the vivid threads of his autobiographical novel* Sons and Lovers *(1913) is the force of Nonconformist life in turn-of-the-century Nottinghamshire where he grew up. Exploring the religious impulse remained a consuming theme in his writing.*

Nothing is more difficult than to determine what a child takes in, and does not take in, of its environment and its teaching. This fact is brought home to me by the hymns which I learned as a child, and never forgot. They mean to me almost more than the finest poetry, and they have for me a more permanent value, somehow or other.

It is almost shameful to confess that the poems which have meant most to me, like Wordsworth's *Ode to Immortality* and Keats' *Odes*, and pieces of *Macbeth* or *As You Like It* or *Midsummer Night's Dream*, and Goethe's lyrics such as *Über allen Gipfeln ist Ruh*, and Verlaine's *Ayant poussé la porte qui chancelle* – all these lovely poems which after all give the ultimate shape to one's life; all these lovely poems woven deep into a man's consciousness, are still not woven so deep in me as the rather banal Nonconformist hymns that penetrated through and through my childhood.

Each gentle dove
And sighing bough
That makes the eve

So fair to me
Has something far
Diviner now
To draw me back
To Galilee
O Galilee, sweet Galilee,
Where Jesus loved so much to be,
O Galilee, sweet Galilee,
Come sing thy songs again to me!

To me the word Galilee has a wonderful sound. The Lake of Galilee! I don't want to know where it is. I never want to go to Palestine. Galilee is one of those lovely, glamorous worlds, not places, that exist in the golden haze of a child's half-formed imagination. And in my man's imagination it is just the same. It has been left untouched. With regard to the hymns which had such a profound influence on my childish consciousness, there has been no crystallising out, no dwindling into actuality, no hardening into the common place. They are the same to my man's experience as they were to me nearly forty years ago. ...

When all comes to all, the most precious element in life is wonder. Love is a great emotion, and power is power. But both love and power are based on wonder. Love without wonder is a sensational affair, and power without wonder is mere force and compulsion. The one universal element in consciousness which is fundamental to life is the element of wonder. You cannot help feeling it in a bean as it starts to grow and pulls itself out of its jacket. You cannot help feeling it in the glisten of the nucleus of the amoeba. You recognize it, willy-nilly, in an ant busily tugging at a straw; in a rook, as it walks the frosty grass.

They all have their own obstinate will. But also they all live with a sense of wonder. Plant consciousnsess, insect consciousness, fish consciousness, animal consciousness, all are related by one permanent element, which we may call the religious element inherent in all life, even in a flea: the sense of wonder. That is our sixth sense. And it is the natural religious sense.

Somebody says that mystery is nothing, because mystery is something you don't know, and what you don't know is nothing to you. But there is more than one way of knowing.

Even the real scientist works in the sense of wonder. The pity is, when he comes out of his laboratory he puts aside his wonder along with his apparatus, and tries to make it all perfectly didactic. Science in its true condition of wonder is as religious as any religion. But didactic science is as dead and boring as dogmatic religion. Both are wonderless and productive of boredom, endless boredom.

Now we come back to the hymns. They live and glisten in the depths of the man's consciousness in undimmed wonder, because they have not been subjected to any criticism or analysis. By the time I was sixteen I had criticized and got over the Christian dogma.

It was quite easy for me; my immediate forebears had already done it for me. Salvation, heaven, Virgin birth, miracles, even the Christian dogmas of right and wrong – one soon got them adjusted. I never could really worry about them. Heaven is one of the instinctive dreams. Right and wrong is something you can't dogmatize about; it's not so easy. As for my soul, I simply don't and never did understand how I could 'save' it. One can save one's pennies. But how can one save one's soul? One can only *live* one's soul. The business is to live, really alive. And this needs wonder.

So that the miracle of the loaves and fishes is just as good to me now as when I was a child. I don't care whether it is historically a fact or not. What does it matter? It is part of the genuine wonder. The same with all the religious teaching I had as a child, apart from the didacticism and sentimentalism. I am eternally grateful for the wonder with which it filled my childhood.

Sun of my soul, thou Saviour dear,
It is not night if Thou be near –

That was the last hymn at the board school. It did not mean to me any Christian dogma or any salvation. Just the words, 'Sun of my soul, thou Saviour dear' penetrated me with wonder and the mystery of twilight. At another time the last hymn was:

Fair waved the golden corn
In Canaan's pleasant land –

And again I loved 'Canaan's pleasant land'. The wonder of 'Canaan', which could never be localised.

I think it was good to be brought up a Protestant: and among Protestants, a Nonconformist, and among Nonconformists, a Congregationalist. Which sounds pharisaic. But I should have missed bitterly a direct knowledge of the Bible, and a direct relation to Galilee and Canaan, Moab and Kedron, those places that never existed on earth. And in the Church of England one would hardly have escaped those snobbish hierarchies of class, which spoil so much for a child. And the Primitive Methodists, when I was a boy, were always having 'revivals' and being 'saved', and I always had a horror of being saved.

So, altogether, I am grateful to my 'Congregational' upbringing. The Congregationalists are the oldest Nonconformists, descendants of the Oliver Cromwell Independents. They still had the Puritan tradition of no ritual. But they avoided the personal emotionalism which one found among the Methodists when I was a boy.

I liked our chapel, which was tall and full of light, and yet still; and colour-washed pale green and blue, with a bit of lotus pattern. And over the organ-loft, 'O worship the Lord in the beauty of holiness,' in big letters. That was a favourite hymn, too:

O worship the Lord, in the beauty of holiness,
Bow down before Him, His glory proclaim;
With gold of obedience and incense of lowliness
Kneel and adore Him, the Lord is His name.

I don't know what the 'beauty of holiness' is exactly. It easily becomes cant, or nonsense. But if you don't think about it – and why should you? – it has a magic. The same with the whole verse. It is rather bad, really, 'gold of obedience' and 'incense of lowliness'. But in me, to the music, it still produces a sense of splendour.

I am always glad we had the Bristol hymn-book, not Moody and Sankey. And I am glad our Scotch minister on the whole avoided sentimental messes such as *Lead, Kindly Light*, or even *Abide With Me*. He had a healthy preference for healthy hymns.

At even, ere the sun was set,
The sick, O Lord, around Thee lay.
Oh, in what divers pains they met!
Oh, in what joy they went away!

And often we had 'Fight the good fight with all thy might.'

In Sunday School I am eternally grateful to old Mr. Remington, with his round white beard and his ferocity. He made us sing! And he loved the martial hymns:

Sound the battle-cry,
See, the foe is nigh.

Raise the standard high
For the Lord.

The ghastly sentimentalism that came like a leprosy over religion had not yet got hold of our colliery village. I remember when I was in Class II in the Sunday School, when I was about seven, a woman teacher trying to harrow us about the Crucifixion. And she kept saying: 'And aren't you sorry for Jesus? Aren't you sorry?' And most of the children wept. I believe I shed a crocodile tear or two, but very vivid is my memory of saying to myself: 'I don't *really* care a bit.' And I could never go back on it. I never *cared* about the Crucifixion, one way or another. Yet the *wonder* of it penetrated very deep in me.

Thirty-six years ago men, even Sunday School teachers still believed in the fight for life and the fun of it. 'Hold the fort, for I am coming.' It was far, far from any militarism or gunfighting. But it was the battle-cry of a stout soul, and a fine thing too.

Stand up, stand up for Jesus,
Ye Soldiers of the Lord.

Here is the clue to the ordinary Englishman – in the Nonconformist hymns.

Alfred Noyes (1880–1958): 'The Bee in Church' from *Ballads and Poems* (1928)

Noyes was a poet, novelist, and lecturer; he converted to Catholicism in 1927, the year after his first wife's death. This poem was published in 1928.

The small Norman flint church of St Wulfran at Ovingdean lies on the Sussex coast near Brighton, and Noyes lived nearby for a while. It has much decoration by the Victorian stained-glass designer Charles Kempe, who was born and buried in Ovingdean.

John Chrystostom, 'Golden-Mouth', was a prolific Early Church Father in Constantinople.

The nestling church at Ovingdean
Was fragrant as a hive in May;
And there was nobody within
To preach, or praise, or pray.

The sunlight slanted through the door,
 And through the panes of painted glass,
When I stole in, alone, once more
 To feel the ages pass.

Then, through the dim grey hush there droned
 An echoing plain-song on the air,
As if some ghostly priest intoned
 An old Gregorian there.

Saint Chrysostom could never lend
 More honey to the heavenly Spring
Than seemed to murmur and ascend
 On that invisible wing.

So small he was, I scarce could see
 My girdled brown hierophant;
But only a Franciscan bee
 In such a bass could chant.

His golden Latin rolled and boomed.
 It swayed the altar flowers anew,
Till all that hive of worship bloomed
 With dreams of sun and dew.

Ah, sweet Franciscan of the May,
 Dear chaplain of the fairy queen,
You sent a singing heart away
 That day from Ovingdean.

T. F. Powys (1875–1953): 'The Hassock and the Psalter', from *Fables* (1929)

Powys was the second of eleven children of the rectory, all to make their mark in different ways. His son Francis wrote of him in 1954: 'Deeply religious in his unorthodox way, Theodore did not go to church on Sunday. He went on Monday, Tuesday, Wednesday, Thursday, Friday and Saturday, ringing the church bell and sitting in his pew for Compline. An old man, he had found what he sought so long, in men's hearts, on the bare hills or by the sea waves.' Dorset village life is evoked in this short story.

In the church of St. Nicholas at Madder there is a pew that, though it has a rightful owner, is nearly always unoccupied. This pew is neither the first nor the last, but is the second highest in the aisle.

It is commonly known that the seats in a village church, that is to say the forwardest of them, are, by right of custom – though no rent is charged – the property of the richest householders. The first gentleman is the landowner, who sometimes, when the church is large enough, has a whole transept for himself, his family and his servants, but, generally speaking, in the smaller churches, such as St. Nicholas at Madder, the squire sits in the front seat, and a little lower down are the pews of the larger occupiers of land.

When the quality and the chief tradesmen are satisfactorily seated as near to God as they can get, then the commonalty may have the lower or side pews. These are also allotted by custom, and are as jealously guarded as the uppermost, even though they may be as far back as you can go, in a direct draught from the door, or where the dead bees are forgotten by the church cleaner and lie about until they rot away.

But people make no long stay upon earth, and the church seats only give an honour to the name of the occupier during each his lifetime. The house or farm, or even the trade, gives the lasting right to a church seat. The blacksmith has always sat in a certain corner, and so he will sit until the end of time – or the end of Christianity – though his name may be changed.

Whoever comes to the Madder Manor Farm in a hundred years will partake – along with many a strange ghost – of the bench that belongs to the farm.

Sometimes, maybe, a foolish clergyman who has read, though without understanding, that God is no respecter of persons, has endeavoured to place the poorest in the uppermost seats, but has, in a very little while, discovered wiser behaviour by the lesson of an empty church.

In a small parish church every one is counted by either the clerk or the priest or – at the time we are writing of – by little Nellie Biss. But neither Nellie, nor the clerk, nor the Reverend Thomas Tucker, were the only ones who had the right to be interested in the people who came, for God counts them too. And though, sometimes – as when Mr. Tucker's little dog, Toby, wandered into church and God made one soul too many – a mistake is made, 'tis not a common one.

Though the clerk and the clergyman have an eye to the money-bag in this sum, God and Nellie Biss are more interested in the reasons that prevent so many from coming to the pews that belong to them. Nellie can only guess, but God, who knows everything, is well aware – perhaps upon an Easter morning – that Mrs. Jane Shore was not there because her husband had taken the shilling that Jane had laid upon her prayer-book, and had departed with it to the tavern.

As a rule the reasons that kept people away were sound and proper, for God never wished Mrs. Biss – Nellie's grandmother – to come through the mire when He knew all about her bad leg.

The second pew, counting of course from the altar end of the church, had belonged, since the church was first built, to Wiscoomb Farm, situated upon the Shelton Heath two miles away from Madder, though in Madder parish. The farmer who abode there was one Mr. Spurdle, a good churchgoer – as he always said he was – though only upon one or two occasions had he reached that building. It was necessary for him to go – when he wished to be devout, which happened every Sunday – through his own farm before he reached the green hill, over which he must climb or ever he came to Madder.

As each Sunday came there were the properest preparations made for this journey. Mr. Spurdle would rise early, he would eat his breakfast Christianly, knowing that Mrs. Spurdle had laid his best clothes ready upon the bed upstairs, and he would be sure to be dressed at the proper time to start to the church.

He spoke in the same manner every Sunday morning, telling Mrs. Spurdle, who was not a good walker, that he mistrusted the weather, and also that the distance was too far for her.

'But I will go,' Mr. Spurdle used to say, holding the front door open, as if he supposed Mr. Tucker the clergyman to be within hearing, 'I will go to church and sit in the Wiscoomb pew.'

Mr. Spurdle would walk with a religious tread until he reached the end of the drive and entered the first of his fields. Once in the fields his manners would change, and though it was a Sunday he would look about him as if it were a working day. He would begin to go a few steps to one side or the other, moving at all times a little further into the field through which he was passing. He could never see a thistle or a dock, even at a distance, without going to pull it up, and so in the spring or summer he was never known to reach even the little hill from which the Madder church could be easily seen.

In the winter, too – though there would not be the weeds to go after – there would be always something to prevent Mr. Spurdle from continuing his holy journey. When the farmer entered the grassy lane an ox would low, which sound would always cause him to return at once to the stalls, for he would fancy that the careless cowboy had forgotten to fodder the bullocks. And again, as he would perhaps be near to coming to the hill, he might stop to look for a few moments into the sheepfold, turning up the legs of his Sunday trousers so as not to dirty them. Once there, he would be sure to find a lame sheep that needed attention or another that he feared might be scabby, and when he had done looking after them, an hour or two had gone by.

Thus it aways happened that something or other never failed to keep Mr. Spurdle at home, and however much he wished to go there the Wiscoomb pew was always deserted. …

God loveth prayer. He is not particular what the prayer is, and though some prayers may not exactly please Him, all are sure to amuse Him.

God always has the wish to listen when any one has the wish to talk to Him, and He always felt sure that Mr. Spurdle, who was an honest fellow at heart, would be able to invent a pretty word or two, did he come to church, about the weather.

As everyone knows, God moves through each church in the land both during matins and evensong, and is sometimes seen, as He once was – with trepidation – by little Nellie Biss, when He took the form of a mouse and jumped upon her knee. But, as a rule, He is not beheld so easily, and the only token that He is moving there is usually a little extra thickness or a movement of the air.

There is no need for God to pray or to preach in a church, for He can take no part in a service that is the worship of Himself. What king drinks his own health when it is proposed by his servants?

One Sunday God sauntered into Madder church, being guided there by St. Nicholas and left at the door – for the saint had to return to a little cottage where his duty was to scare away the Devil from an old woman who was dying.

God waited for a few moments beside Farmer Shore's pew to hear what he was saying. Farmer Shore was praying that all the corn in the country, except his own, should be eaten by rats, worms and birds, spoilt by rain, or left to rot in the fields. God smiled to Himself and moved to the deserted pew.

At that very moment Mr. Spurdle, with his coat off and his trousers all muddy, was pulling a young heifer out of a ditch into which it had been unlucky enough to fall.

God looked into the empty seat. Something ought to be there, He felt, to speak and to pray for Mr. Spurdle – something that would take the farmer's place and be Mr. Spurdle.

God saw the hassock and the psalter.

'I give you speech,' He said to these two, 'and you must do your best for honest Mr. Spurdle to save his soul alive.'

The service closed with a pious hymn, and after that was over God joined the little throng that moved silently out of the church, for the organ had ceased to play.

Walking next to Nellie, God tried his best to stifle her laughter that He considered a little unbecoming, by treading on her toes, and succeeded so well that Nellie only burst out a-laughing when she reached the door.

Upon the Monday, when the afternoon came and the great hand in the church clock had begun to move towards the hour of four, the hassock in Mr. Spurdle's pew began to speak.

It was winter, and the church, that had been dim all that day, began to turn to real darkness, that gave a good cover to strange and unusual voices.

'Alas! alas!' cried the hassock, 'I fear me that true piety has left our land, for never does the owner of this seat, Farmer Spurdle, come to church.'

'And if he did,' said the psalter, in a much gayer tone than that used by the hassock, 'he would certainly not kneel down.'

'You say truly, noble book,' observed the hassock, 'for only those who come here with a load of grief to carry kneel down upon their knees, and some of these do not seem to wish ever to rise again.'

'You are thinking of funerals,' said the psalter gaily, 'but I prefer to think of a wedding, for then I am usually held upside down, or else I am pressed against the lips of some young woman to hide her amusement.'

'Do not jest, sir,' said the hassock, 'for you know well enough that our voices are only given to us for the sake of Mr. Spurdle. We have taken upon us a truly serious responsibility.'

'Nothing of the kind,' replied the psalter, 'our consciousness is given to us for our own entertainment. Because Mr. Spurdle does not often come, we have to be merry in his stead. All that I have a mind to do is to look about me and be happy with the girls.'

'You speak as a fool,' said the hassock, 'for it is not upon the present that our responsibility rests – it is about the future life of Mr. Spurdle that we must be troubled. Mr. Spurdle's good or ill in eternity is in our keeping. Were he here he would pray for his own salvation, and might, at last, get to heaven, but as he is prevented from doing so, by reasons that God Himself considers proper, it is our duty to so manage His worship and adoration by humilitude and holiness, that Farmer Spurdle may enter happily into God's heavenly kingdom.'

'It is all very well for you to say that, who art but a poor and worn hassock,' remarked the psalter haughtily, 'but I take the commands of God in quite a different manner, and though I have been given a voice because of Mr. Spurdle I care not a snap about him. I belong to the highest order in literature – the Holy Scriptures – and therefore I have a right to do as I choose.

'I have a gold clasp, and I am bound in the best cloth. Why should I concern myself about the future of a stupid farmer? A holy book can do no ill, and I have a mind to invite Nellie Biss to sit in this pew so that when no one is looking we may be merry together.

'As I am written by one of God's favourites, I know well enough the only way in which a creature can be saved, and that it is neither goodness nor virtue that brings salvation, but only an immortal act, and Mr. Spurdle must look to himself. God only means to be kind to him in a jest.'

'Though I am not beautiful and have no golden clasp,' said the hassock – who was, indeed, very old and ragged – 'I will do my best not to disgrace Mr. Spurdle. I have always listened to the worship through the knees of some of the worshippers, and, by my so doing, the religion of many a good old woman has entered into my body.

'Do you remember the last occupier of Wiscoomb Farm – Widow Rust? She would always kneel upon me, and the joy she had in her prayers was very great. She came to church in a bonnet that was tied under her chin with a black ribbon, and whenever her granddaughter Mary came with her and happened to be naughty, Mrs. Rust would pinch the girl's legs until they were black and blue.'

'I was extremely angry with the old witch,' said the psalter, 'for sometimes Mary would place me upon her lap and turn over my pages during sermon time.'

'Mary was a naughty child,' observed the hassock, 'and deserved the many beatings that she had at home for behaving ill in church. You may be sure that I learned a great deal of religion from Widow Rust, who was never tired of thanking God for the death of her husband, for which event she had prayed for a great while.'

'I do not doubt it,' laughed the psalter. ...

'Mr. Spurdle,' continued the hassock, 'is as good a man as Widow Rust was a woman. I shall pray for him most kindly – indeed, I shall pray as if I were him. And I believe I shall have my reward.'

'That was,' said the psalter, 'what Widow Rust always expected from her devotions, and from the way she pinched and prodded Mary – for she sometimes used her knuckles; she was always praying that God would take her to live with Him, where there would be nothing else to do but talk of her friends who were damned.'

'The pious lady hoped for the best,' said the hassock, 'and I, too, certainly deserve the very greatest care and attention from Mr. Spurdle because I have already done his family so much good. If it had not been for me, Mr. Spurdle's grandfather, who lived at Fiddleford – a hamlet that is but a short distance from here – might have been hanged. The poor man had stolen a sheep, and, as the shepherds were after him, he carried the sheep into the church, stuck a knife into its throat, and hid it in the pulpit. The shepherds entered the church and, seeing only a poor man devoutly praying, they let him alone.

'And that is not all that I have done for Mr. Spurdle, for when he wished to marry the rich lady who is his wife, I guided her into this pew and Mr. Spurdle was brave enough to follow, and their knees met upon me. I have a true love for Mr. Spurdle and wish him well, most heartily.'

'And much good your love will do him, or yourself either,' retorted the psalter. 'It is now twenty years ago since he came into the church, and that was when he was married. You had much better love the young women, who are willing to adore anything that a young spark has knelt upon – even an old worn footstool, only fit to be burnt.'

'Say rather,' replied the hassock, 'fit to be preserved in the highest honour. I am religiously minded and enjoy my prayers; I am humble because I am sometimes knelt upon, and I feel myself filled with virtue, that is itself a grand reward. I do exactly as God tells me.'

'And I do a great deal more,' cried the psalter, 'for when any woman holds me in her hands I ask her a question.'

'I hope a proper one,' sighed the hassock.

'All things are proper to him that believeth,' answered the psalter, with a smile.

'It is time that we prayed,' murmured the hassock, 'and I am sure, as a reward for my prayers, either God or Mr. Spurdle will give me a new cover.'

'You certainly need one,' said the psalter, 'for at the funeral of old John Shore, when his weeping widow had the impertinence to enter our seat, she knelt upon you, and though I kept my clasp tightly shut the whole time so that she could not open me, I know that her knees were none of the cleanest.'

'It is worship and not dirt that matters in God's house,' observed the hassock reprovingly.

'That may be so,' cried the psalter, 'but all the same it's nicer to be touched by pretty hands than by an old woman's swollen knees.'

'Cease your mockery,' answered the other, 'but know that however you choose to behave in this holy building, I, at least, know my duty to God and my duty to Mr. Spurdle. I will pray for Mr. Spurdle. I will do him all the good in my power. I will correct all the wickedness of the flesh; I will shut my eyes tight if, by an unlucky chance, Nellie were to enter here for a churching. I will become the virtuous right knee of Mr. Spurdle so that he may be exalted.'

'Have you not heard,' said the psalter, who, being of a flighty nature, liked a little gossip, 'that at the last vestry meeting held here Mr. Spurdle was appointed churchwarden, and that there is a balance of thirty pounds in the churchwardens' accounts, which, as he is the premier churchwarden, is as good as his own, and that, this very day, he is coming here in order to see what should be renewed and what retained of the church furniture?'

The psalter had hardly spoken these words when Mr. Spurdle entered the church.

As money had come with it, the church of St. Nicholas had now become like a field of profit, so Mr. Spurdle willingly crossed over the grassy hill, passing by his little pigs, who were searching for acorns under a large tree, and stepped briskly into the church.

The first pew that Mr. Spurdle entered – in order to see if anything was required to make it more comfortable – was his own.

As it happened, that day Mr. Spurdle had nothing for his farm hands to do at home, and so he was employing two of them to clean up the nettles and rubbish that lay about in the churchyard, rake it into a heap and set it afire.

In his pew Mr. Spurdle saw the hassock and the psalter. He took up the psalter and noticed, with pride and pleasure, its golden clasp. But the hassock, that was worn and only stuffed with straw, he carried out of the church and cast upon the fire.

A lift from a bishop, from Sir John Squire (1884–1958), *The Honeysuckle and the Bee* (1937)

The gregarious Squire was a leading and prolific literary figure among the 'Georgian' circle of writers (dubbed the 'Squirearchy' by the Modernists). As a young man he had regularly walked the distance between the West Country and Cambridge. He rose to his wife's bait to make a similar journey in middle age: this is from the fifth day of his eleven-day walk from London to Devon.

'If it rains': I had just, at about eleven-thirty, got to the parting of the ways before Wilton and the gates of the great house when a heavy drop fell on my nose and another on my neck. It began to pelt, and cursing at having to undo my neatly-strapped bundle in order to get at my mackintosh cape, I was just getting my arms out of the straps when a car stopped in front of me. It was the most dilapidated Austin Seven I had ever seen. The front door was pushed open and an elderly weather-beaten parson's face was pushed out.

'Wouldn't you like to come in out of the rain?'

'Thank you very much--' – and I did.

'Which way are you going?'

'I really don't know. Almost anywhere – really.'

'Can I give you a lift?'

'That would be extraordinarily kind of you, so long as you aren't going due east.'

'Would it help you if I dropped you in the middle of the Plain?'

The rain was coming down in sheets. I thought I'd stick to the temporary shelter and find out later where I was to be deposited; the sideboard [the 'largest sideboard in England', in the dining room of the Grosvenor Hotel, Shaftesbury], the Cerne Abbas Giant, Portland Bill, Egdon Heath and all the other temptations in the south-westerly direction could wait to see me another time. Several flashes of lightning, more torrents, and with the water pouring down the wind-screen we set off on the road that leads north-west up the Wylye valley: a new road to me, though I knew both ends of it.

By this time I had noticed three things about my companion. One was that his rugged face had known tropic suns. Another was that his pipe had seen long service. And the third was that on his ancient hat were those strings which are worn only by the upper ranks of the ecclesiastical profession. We were both of us rather shy for the first minutes, and after we had both acutely observed that it was very wet, silence fell upon us, as we sped away from the English Channel, my destination, towards the Bristol Channel, which was once apostrophized by Mrs. Yearsley, the Bristol milkwoman poet, with 'Hail, useful channel!' After a while I felt it would be mannerly of me to break the ice, so I said: 'Excuse me, sir, but are you a bishop?'

'Yes,' he replied, 'that is to say, I was.'

'Colonial?'

'British Bongoland.'

'Is there a nice cathedral there?'

'Not at all bad.'

'It's in Edwardstown, isn't it?'

'Yes.'

'Very few white people there, I imagine?'

'About seventy.'

'Were all your choristers negroes?'

'Yes.'

'Many earthquakes when you were there?'

'Some.'

'How's mahogany?'

'Bad.'

'How's coffee?'

'Bad.'

'Rubber down, too?'

'Yes.'

We rattled on through the moisture; I could remember nothing further about the industries of Bongoland, and my thoughts strayed to the Monosyllabic Friars in Rabelais. Suddenly we slowed up. There was a little inn with no other houses near; it bore the name of some unusual bird, as it might be the Dodo. 'Visiting the sick,' I thought to myself, and I said: 'Parishioner?' 'No,' replied the bishop, shutting off the engines, 'but I never pass this place without going in for a Guinness. Do you mind?'

'I think I'll join you,' I answered, rejoicing in the rare opportunity of being led astray by a bishop. We went into the bar, the bishop hailed the landlord, who was discussing with two shepherds the effect of too much rain on potatoes, two Guinnesses were ordered, the right reverend gentleman refilled his pipe, and then, noticing the bandage on my hand, he said: 'Hullo, cut your finger?' I told him that I had been damaged by a fast bowler and that my finger felt as though it would always be swollen and crooked. 'I expect it will,' said the bishop cheerfully; then, holding out a gnarled handful of fingers, added: 'Wicket-keeping.'

'Bongoland?' 'No,' said he, 'Tasmania and Saskatchewan'; then, before I had time to enquire about the chronological side of his travels, he surprisingly asked me if I knew anything about church plate, proceeding to inform me about Diocesan Surveys of such things now in process. Patens and chalices at one corner of the bar, potatoes at the other; Hudson's Bay and Australia at one corner, at the other, Wiltshire.

The bishop looked at his watch. 'Would it be all right if I dropped you at Wylye?' he enquired. 'Perfect,' I said. 'You see,' he explained, 'when I get there

I have to turn east towards Amesbury.' 'That's all right, thanks very much,' I said, and we resumed our drive. It poured incessantly, and it was still pouring when he drew up at the 'Bell' at Wylye, the capital of the Plain, shook hands, raised his hat and left me.

The rector and the congregation, from Francis Brett Young (1884–1954), *Portrait of a Village* (1937)

Young served in the Medical Corps in East Africa during the First World War until he was invalided out in 1918. When ill health prevented him from practising as a doctor again, he turned to writing fiction and poetry. Portrait *is set in Worcestershire, where he lived for several years.*

Clad in his cassock, a lanky, black, tubular figure, with his slightly stooping shoulders and his puzzled mystic's eyes, he steps across the road from his monstrous rectory and threads his way over the winding path that is flagged with forgotten memorials of mortality, between the great carnivorous yews, whose wet bark is the colour of blood, and the broken tombs whose lids bird-sown elder has shifted, and enters the base of the tower where the choirboys are chattering. The cracked treble bell ringing pursues him as he follows, with bowed head and folded hands, the humble procession that shuffles so slowly up the aisle and mounts the steps where the coloured encaustic preserves the achievements of Clare, and Beauchamp, and Cantilupe, and Sheldon, and d'Abitot; as he kneels and rises again and lets his mild gaze survey, with some personal pride as well as approval, the Sunday's congregation; as he opens his lips and hears his own refined voice, with its Oxford vowels, intoning:

'Dearly beloved brethren ...'

And he really means it. But when he ascends the pulpit, the sermon he preaches is the paraphrase of a biblical text for the schoolchildren or some definition of doctrine for their elders – not a confession of the doubts that are burning in his heart. And perhaps this is just as well, besides being much easier; for old Miss Abberley is there in her pew, and possibly awake.

For so small a village, the congregation is a large one. It is one of the feathers in Mr. Follows' biretta that he has never, like some neighbouring parsons, frightened it away. In Monk's Norton there has never as yet been a chapel to compete with his service by providing a more homely, if less brightly-coloured, form of free entertainment on a day when none other is to be found. A few of his congregation go to the parish church to worship. Such is Mrs. Bentley, the postmistress, and such, perhaps, Mrs. Hawley; for Mrs. Bentley, kneeling in church or listening to Miss Martin's music, feels nearer to 'Father,' and Mrs. Hawley needs some mystical consolation for her husband's carnal infidelities, though the offender, who has always been a regular churchgoer, sits at her side. There is also Miss Coningsby, most pious and steadfast defender of the faith, who has, somehow or other, escaped notice in this perambulation: not entirely without excuse, for her minute spinsterly cottage, next door to the Rectory, is, appropriately, a mere appanage, attached to and overshadowed by that building; and she herself is equally inconspicuous – a frail, tiny creature, with scanty grey hair dragged back into an exiguous bun beneath a black hat, resembling, in her hunched figure and darting movements (which are limited to a furtive 'run' from her dwelling to the church and back again) a mouse, or one of the heraldic rabbits which decorate her family coat-of-arms. The Coningsbys, in their time, Mr. Jagger will explain, were considerable people with extensive lands in the north of the country, entitled to bear: *Gules, three sitting conies argent in a border engrailed sable*; but Miss Julia Coningsby, though she still possesses a few pieces of silver with these grandeurs engraved on them, does not concern herself with temporal pomps. Why she came to Monk's Norton or how she contrives to live there, nobody knows. From august names casually mentioned and certain faded photographs of young ladies in court-dress displayed on the mantlepiece of her little parlour, it is supposed that, in her youth, she was probably engaged as a governess in some noble family; her precise speech, too, has a suggestion of prunes and prisms; but whatever her avocation may have been in her prime, she is now the perfect church mouse, innocuous and obscure, with no other desire or ambition than to creep to and fro between her cottage and the altar-steps, and no other spiritual sustenance than the crumbs that fall from her hero the rector's table.

Apart from the service of the church she has no activities; but in such matters as the cleaning of the communion-plate and the altar-vases and provision for these of flowers which she piously cultivates all the year round in her garden and greenhouse, she is endlessly useful. She is useful to Mr. Follows in another way. Whenever it snows, blows, rains or hails, Miss Coningsby has never yet missed a celebration of the Holy Communion; and when, mounting the pulpit, doubtful of himself and conscious of the impenetrable reservations of the faces beneath him, he sees, up-turned in its accustomed place, Miss Coningsby's rapt countenance, he takes heart from the knowledge that here, at least, amid the indifferent or critical, is one humble soul who takes no count of his personal imperfections and sees in him only the anointed minister and instrument of Christ.

No other member of the morning congregation is quite so whole-hearted or single-minded as little Miss Coningsby; yet it includes, to the rector's satisfaction, the village's most substantial inhabitants. The Collinses are always there in full force, and so, naturally, is the people's warden, Mr. Cantlow. The Sheldon-Smiths are regular in their attendance; for they know that it is part of the 'county's' duty to set an example, and that the established Church is one of the main props of the state of society they desire to maintain. The captain is there, for much the same reason, and because he enjoys singing hymns; and the gnarled ancients with their shrivelled old women from 'down the road' hobble up in their Sunday broadcloth, when the weather is fair, because they have always reckoned to go to church and enjoy a good gossip outside when the service is over. Dr. Hemming rarely attends, except at the major festivals at Christmas and Easter: the rector, although he mistrusts these evidences of a nominal conformance, excuses his absence on the grounds of a wider humanity, and has never yet dared to examine the doctor on his beliefs, while the reputation of his household is sustained in any case by the regular presence of his wife.

The Perrys, too, are usually in evidence, subconsciously anxious to make amends for their calling's questionable morality [they run the Sheldon Arms]; and besides all these, more or less filling the narrow nave, there sits, pew behind pew, a mixed congregation comprising most of the children and, perhaps, a third of the adult population of the village, which, indeed, in these days of faith's decadence, is by no means bad. Mr. Follows knows every face and every name. He, himself, has catechized and prepared for confirmation most of these strapping red-faced lads in their Sunday serge, and the buxom girls in their summer silks and muslins. He is aware, as he gazes down at them, that what has brought them here is not so much the desire to worship (or even the enjoyment of his eloquence) as an established habit of 'going to church' on Sundays, and wearing their best clothes and seeing what others are wearing, and showing themselves at their best to members of the opposite sex; and this knowledge does not offend him, for he has been young himself, and considers it far better that they should come to church for these reasons than not at all. He is also not so young as he was, and feels, therefore, wistfully benevolent to all these young folk who are falling or have fallen in love, for he knows now that there is nothing in human experience so sweet as that early bemusement, and that life is shorter than they can guess, and these fleeting raptures more precious. There is something infinitely hopeful and infinitely pathetic to him in their very youth, and their confident carelessness of what the future may hold for them. His tender heart prays, as he sees them, that the village which has grown so dear to him and which, in spite of his aspirations, he is conscious of serving so inadequately, may not be decimated by another war; but when the spirit moves him to speak his mind on Armaments or Pacifism or International Relations, he realizes that these subjects are almost as contentious as Birth Control, so that the hot words die on his lips, and he rehearses instead the morals that may be drawn from the story of Daniel in the Den of the Lions.

The young people, on the whole, are more interested in the evening service, which is shorter and brighter and includes neither sermon nor Litany. It is sweet, in late cuckoo-time, to emerge from the church's atmosphere of faint repression into the golden air of evening, so fair and so free, and to linger a short while talking under the lengthening shadows of the elms. This is the hour and season of lovers. In its quiet release there is no sense of the stresses and preoccupations of the workaday world. So, when Miss Martin has finished her voluntary and shut the organ, and the rector, in his long cassock, has slowly crossed the street, and their elders stand talking in hesitant little groups at the Cross or move slowly down the road or the lane in a straggling trail, the young folk who are 'walking out' discreetly sort themselves into couples and link arms and unobtrusively steal away.

John Betjeman (1906–1984): 'In Westminster Abbey' (1940)

In 1937, the year his second collection of poems came out, Betjeman wrote to his friend Alan Pryce-Jones: 'The thing that has happened to me is that after years of sermon-tasting, I am now a member of the C. of E. and a communicant. I regard it as the only salvation against progress and Fascists on the one side and Marxists of Bloomsbury on the other.' This poem comes from his first wartime collection.

Let me take this other glove off
As the *vox humana* swells,
And the beauteous fields of Eden
Bask beneath the Abbey bells.

Here, where England's statesmen lie,
Listen to a lady's cry.

Gracious Lord, oh bomb the Germans.
   Spare their women for Thy Sake,
And if that is not too easy
   We will pardon Thy Mistake.
But, gracious Lord, whate'er shall be,
Don't let anyone bomb me.

Keep our Empire undismembered,
   Guide our Forces by Thy Hand,
Gallant blacks from far Jamaica,
   Honduras and Togoland;
Protect them Lord in all their fights,
And even more protect the whites.

Think of what our Nation stands for,
   Books from Boots' and country lanes,
Free speech, free passes, class distinction,
   Democracy and proper drains.
Lord, put beneath Thy special care
One-eighty-nine Cadogan Square.

Although dear Lord I am a sinner,
   I have done no major crime;
Now I'll come to Evening Service
   Whensoever I have the time.
So, Lord, reserve for me a crown,
And do not let my shares go down.

I will labour for Thy Kingdom,
   Help our lads to win the war,
Send white feathers to the cowards,
   Join the Women's Army Corps,
Then wash the Steps around Thy Throne
In the Eternal Safety Zone.

Now I feel a little better,
   What a treat to hear Thy Word,
Where the bones of leading statesmen
   Have so often been interr'd.

And now, dear Lord, I cannot wait
Because I have a luncheon date.

C. S. Lewis (1898–1963), from *The Screwtape Letters* (1942)

Besides his scholarly work on literature, Lewis is probably best known for his fiction for children, which he infused with his rediscovered Christian faith. His radio talks ('Mere Christianity') and The Screwtape Letters *won him wide audiences during the Second World War.*

Screwtape is a Devil's advocate, bent, in this sequence of letters, on instructing his nephew Wormwood in the art and practice of saving the human 'patient' from commitment to God ('the Enemy'). On the question of whether he believed in devils, Lewis wrote: 'I do. That is to say, I believe in angels and I believe that some of these, by the abuse of their own free will, have become enemies to God and, as a corollary, to us. These we may call devils. They do not differ in nature from good angels, but their nature is depraved. Devil *is the opposite of* angel *only as Bad Man is the opposite of Good Man. Satan, the leader or dictator of devils, is the opposite not of God but of Michael. ... These forms are not only symbolical but were always known to be symbolical by reflective people.'*

My dear Wormwood,

I note with grave displeasure that your patient has become a Christian. Do not indulge the hope that you will escape the usual penalties; indeed, in your better moments, I trust you would hardly even wish to do so. In the meantime we must make the best of the situation. There is no need to despair; hundreds of these adult converts have been reclaimed after a brief sojourn in the Enemy's camp and are now with us. All the *habits* of the patient, both mental and bodily, are still in our favour.

One of our greatest allies at present is the Church itself. Do not misunderstand me. I do not mean the Church as we see her spread out through all time and space and rooted in eternity, terrible as an army with banners. That, I confess, is a spectacle which makes our boldest tempters uneasy. But fortunately it is quite invisible to these humans. All your patient sees is the half-finished, sham Gothic erection on the new building estate. When he goes inside, he sees the local grocer with rather an oily expression on his face bustling up to offer him one shiny little book containing a liturgy which neither of them understands, and one shabby little book containing corrupt texts of a number of religious lyrics, mostly bad, and in very small print. When he gets to his pew and looks round him he sees just that selection of his neighbours whom he has hitherto avoided. You want to lean pretty heavily on those neighbours. Make his mind flit to and fro between an expression like 'the body of Christ' and the actual faces in the next pew. It matters very little, of course, what kind of people that next pew really contains. You may know one of them to be a great warrior on the Enemy's side. No matter. Your patient, thanks to Our Father below, is a fool. Provided any of those neighbours sing out of tune, or have boots that squeak, or double chins, or odd clothes, the patient will quite easily believe that their religion must therefore be somehow ridiculous. At his present stage, you see, he has an idea of 'Christians' in his mind which he supposes to be spiritual but which, in fact, is largely pictorial. His mind is full of togas and sandals and armour and bare legs and the mere fact that the other people in church wear modern clothes is a real – though of course an unconscious – difficulty to him. Never let it come to the surface; never let him ask what he expected them to look like. Keep everything hazy in his mind now, and you will have all eternity wherein to amuse yourself by producing in him the peculiar kind of clarity which Hell affords.

Work hard, then, on the disappointment or anti-climax which is certainly coming to the patient during his first few weeks as a churchman. The Enemy allows this disappointment to occur on the threshold of every human endeavour. It occurs when the boy who has been enchanted in the nursery by *Stories from the Odyssey* buckles down to really learning Greek. It occurs when lovers have got married and begin the real task of learning to live together. In every other department of life it marks the transition from dreaming aspiration to laborious doing. The Enemy takes this risk because He has acurious fantasy of making all these disgusting little human vermin into what He calls His 'free' lovers and servants – 'sons' is the word He uses, with His inveterate love of degrading the whole spiritual world by unnatural liaisons with the two-legged animals. Desiring their freedom, He therefore refuses to carry them, by their mere affections and habits, to any of the goals which He sets before them: He leaves them to 'do it on their own'. And therein lies our opportunity. But also, remember, there lies our danger. If once they get through this initial dryness successfully, they become much less dependent on emotion, and therefore much harder to tempt.

I have been writing hitherto on the assumption that the people in the next pew afford no *rational* ground for disappointment. Of course if they do – if the patient knows that the woman with the absurd hat is a fanatical bridge-player or the man with squeaky boots a miser and an extortioner – then your task is so much the easier. All you then have to do is to keep out of his mind the question 'If I, being what I am, can consider that I am in some sense a Christian, why should the different vices of those people in the next pew prove that their religion is mere hypocrisy and convention?' You may ask whether it is possible to keep such an obvious thought from occurring even to a human mind. It is, Wormwood, it is! Handle him properly and it simply won't come into his head. He has not been anything like long enough with the Enemy to have any real humility yet. What he says, even on his knees, about sinfulness is all parrot talk. At bottom, he still believes he has run up a very favourable credit-balance in the Enemy's ledger by allowing himself to be converted, and thinks that he is showing great humility and condescension in going to church with these 'smug', commonplace neighbours at all. Keep him in that state as long as you can,

Your affectionate uncle,

Screwtape

T. S. Eliot (1888–1965), from *Little Gidding* (1942)

The title of the last of Eliot's Four Quartets *refers to the remote parish in Huntingdonshire where Nicholas Ferrar founded a High Church Anglican religious community in 1626; George Herbert had asked for his poems to be given to Ferrar* *(see p. 120)**. Eliot first visited it in 1936. In his essay 'Thoughts after Lambeth' he wrote in conclusion: 'The World is trying the experiment of attempting to form a civilized but non-Christian mentality. The experiment will fail; but we must be very patient in awaiting its collapse; meanwhile redeeming the time; so that the Faith may be preserved alive through the dark ages before us; to renew and rebuild civilization, and save the World from suicide.'*

If you came this way,
Taking the route you would be likely to take,
From the place you would be likely to come from,
If you came this way in May time, you would find the hedges
White again, in May, with voluptuary sweetness.
It would be the same at the end of the journey,
If you came at night like a broken king,
If you came by day not knowing what you came for,

It would be the same, when you leave the rough road
And turn behind the pig-sty to the dull façade
And tombstone. And what you thought you came for
Is only a shell, a husk of meaning
From which the purpose breaks only when it is fulfilled
If at all. Either you had no purpose
Or the purpose is beyond the end you figured
And is altered in fulfilment. There are other places
Which also are the world's end, some at the sea jaws,
Or over a dark lake, in a desert or a city –
But this is the nearest, in place and time,
Now and in England.

If you came this way,
Taking any route, starting from anywhere,
At any time or at any season,
It would always be the same: you would have to put off
Sense and notion. You are not here to verify,
Instruct yourself, or inform curiosity
Or carry report. You are here to kneel
Where prayer has been valid. And prayer is more
Than an order of words, the conscious occupation
Of the praying mind, or the sound of the voice praying.
And what the dead had no speech for, when living,
They can tell you, being dead: the communication
Of the dead is tongued with fire beyond the language of the living.
Here, the intersection of the timeless moment
Is England and nowhere. Never and always.

John Moore (1907–1967), from *Brensham Village* (1946)

John Moore's writing about village life and the countryside around Tewkesbury in Gloucestershire became a trilogy. He was one of the founders of the Cheltenham Literary Festival.

Death of the Rector

For a long while Mr. Mountjoy had been growing more frail, more forgetful, and more haphazard in the performance of his parish duties. I believe there was no truth in the story that, having stored some live-bait in his font in anticipation of a day's pike-fishing, he forgot to remove them before the next christening; so that the infant was sprinkled with minnows and baptised with bleak. But it was certainly true that he took snuff in his pulpit, pausing in the middle of his sermon to help himself from a silver snuff-box with a small silver spoon. And I know that he went fishing, not only in his biretta, but in his cassock as well; for the last time I saw him he was worming for perch, in this rather unsuitable dress, from the landing-stage below Sammy Hunt's cottage. He had found a shoal of these confiding fishes, and was happily engaged in pulling them out one after another.

'Truly,' he said to me, 'old Izaak Walton accurately described them when he said they were like the wicked of this world, not afraid, though their friends and companions perish in their sight!'

It was a paradox that the more eccentric the Rector became and the more outrageous his behaviour grew, the better the village liked him; so that at the end even his churchwardens, who had frequently complained to the Bishop about his scandalous conduct, were heard to declare that for all his faults he was the best parson the village had ever had. He died, from a failing heart, in late November. He had never, in all his long cure, made any special effort to persuade his parishioners to go to church, and for thirty years he had preached, rather badly, to half-empty pews. He might have smiled, therefore, if he could have seen the crowd at his funeral, which overflowed into the churchyard because there was not enough room for it. But he was one of the gentlest Christians I ever knew; and there would have been no bitterness in his smile.

He was succeeded by a man called Wilkinson who immediately astonished the villagers by smiting them powerfully upon their backs and shoulders and addressing them by such terms of affection as 'Dear boy,' 'Old fellow' and even 'Gaffer.' In his conversation, and sometimes in his sermons, he frequently used such expressions as 'scrumptious,' 'ripping,' and 'awfully jolly.'

He spoke with a slight lisp, and his Christian name was Cecil. When I asked Mr. Chorlton [a retired Classics master] what he thought of him, he hesitated before answering and eventually said:

'What can one think about an overgrown Boy Scout who obviously means well? I suggest, however, that William Wordsworth described him beautifully in the worst line ever written by a great poet.'

'And what is the line?' I asked.

'"A Mr. Wilkinson, a clergyman." Simply that.'

The Groupers Arrive

Brensham had to put up with the Rector's back-slappings, shoulder-thumpings, and schoolboyish endearments for about three months when he held his first 'house-party' and let loose upon the astonished village some two-score members of the Oxford Group.

There wasn't room for them all at the Rectory, so the overflows were boarded out at the Horse Narrow, the Trumpet, and the Adam and Eve. The landlords of all three had had a bad winter, and they were very glad to make a few pounds by letting their rooms so early in the season. 'Whatever you says about the Parson,' said Joe Trentfield, 'he's the first parson I've ever heard of who was good for trade.' However, I don't think even Joe bargained for the remarkable assortment of visitors who arrived at the Horse Narrow on Friday evening. He didn't know much about the Oxford Group, but he had vaguely expected some sort of grave ecclesiastical conclave: if not of clergymen, at any rate lay brothers or foreign missioners or the kind of prim elderly ladies who organise Scripture readings or arrange for copies of the Bible to be placed in the bedrooms of commercial hotels. He was somewhat taken aback, therefore, when he discovered that his quota of guests included two bouncing gym-mistresses, a Lett who spoke little English and a Lithuanian who spoke none, and a middle-aged American lady who talked about Gard with ease and assurance but rather in the way she would speak of a President of the United States.

After closing time Joe took a walk up the village street and called on Jim Hartley at the Adam and Eve.

'What kind of queer fish has the Rector sent *you*?' he enquired.

'Rum 'uns,' said Jim. 'They may be very religious but they're certainly rum. I've got a Frog and a couple of Huns, and a pretty little piece who looks like an actress, and one of those huntin' shootin' women, and – Joe – '

'Yes, Jim?'

'I've got a bloke with his head close-cropped who always talks out of the corner of his mouth. What'd you say about him?'

'I'd say he'd probably just come out of jug.'

'And I should say,' says Jim with awe, 'that it won't be very long before he goes back there.'

Next day, as it happened, we played the first cricket match of the season; and after the match we went to the Adam and Eve for our usual game of darts. The bar, however, was so full of the Rector's guests that there was no room for us, and we went on to the Horse Narrow. Joe's bar was crowded too, but we decided to make the best of a bad job and stay there. Before we knew what was happening we found ourselves in conversation with a number of hearty young men and women who told us that their Christian names were Alan, Mabel, Betty, Ernest, Sigrid and Harry, and asked us to tell them ours.

Within a few moments Mr. Chorlton had been captured by an attractive-looking if slightly hysterical girl who discoursed to him on the subject of Absolute Truth; another girl was talking earnestly to Alfie upon some matter which seemed to cause him the profoundest embarrassment; Sir Gerald listened courteously to a blond youth who told him gravely 'I assure you, sir, even my lawn-tennis has improved since I brought religion into it.' As for me, I was cornered by the Lett whose English appeared to be limited to a single and ambiguous phrase. 'Yes, by damn no!' he shouted enthusiastically, in answer to every question; 'No, by damn, yes?' he would interrogate me by way of variation if for a few moments through sheer exhaustion I fell silent.

There was such a great deal of chatter, so much high shrill laughter, so many boisterous cries of 'Old Boy' and 'Dear Fellow' that you could hardly hear Mimi's strumming upon the piano at the other end of the room. When Joe passed me a beer across the counter he whispered:

'I likes to see 'em enjoying 'emselves, but 'tis a wonder to me how they does it, on ginger-pop.'

I now perceived that none of the Groupers drank beer, but consumed numerous fizzy drinks such as lemonade, Cydrax, or raspberry squash.

'Tell me,' I said to the Lett, 'are you all teetotallers?'

He clicked his heels and bowed.

'Yes, by damn, no!' he yelled.

Over his shoulder the blond tennis player spoke up to inform me:

'It's not a matter of principle, old fellow; nothing priggish or Blue Ribbon about it; but if God tells you, in your Q.T., to give it up, well, you give it up, that's all. He told me to stop smoking, too.'

'Q.T.?' I asked, bewildered. 'What's Q.T.?'

'Quiet Times, old man. After breakfast.'

'It's like being on the transatlantic telephone,' said the American lady, but you never get a wrong number from Gard.'

I glanced at Billy Butcher, who was standing next to her and he gave me a slow wink. He was in one of his clowning moods and I watched him put on his rather vacuous Andrew-Aguecheek look before he announced innocently:

'Really, I ought to try it. I'm the most frightful hopeless drunkard that ever was.'

They gathered round him at once like wasps round a pot of honey.

'No, honestly, you aren't *really*?' said the attractive girl who had been talking to Mr. Chorlton.

'Honestly, I'm afraid, incurable,' said Billy. 'No medicine in the world can do me good.' (I thought: By God, that's true, and I wonder if he really knows it.)

'But *our* medicine,' said the American lady, her eyes shining, 'is not of this world at all, it comes from Gard.'

I edged away, and left Billy to his fooling. It was his own business, I thought, if he liked to pull their legs; but I found it, somehow, a trifle embarrassing and I was glad of the opportunity to slip away into a corner and talk to Dick Groves about the plague of rabbits in the railway-cutting. The Groupers, no doubt, were just silly and adolescent and probably harmless; but they were alien to Brensham and to the Horse Narrow and our pub wasn't the same, our cricket-evening was utterly spoiled, because of their presence. Almost everybody, except the Groupers, looked a bit uncomfortable and constrained; and only Sammy was entirely happy, for he had got hold of the Lithuanian who couldn't speak English and was telling him, without the least risk of interruption, the story of the geisha-girl at Yokohama.

(On Sunday afternoon the Rector and his wife gave a garden-party...)

Herbert Butterfield (1900–1979), *Christianity and History* (1949)

Butterfield was Professor of Modern History at Cambridge when he gave a series of lectures at the Faculty of Divinity that became widely read at the time. He had become an Anglican after a Methodist upbringing.

Indeed after a period of fifteen hundred years or so we can just about begin to say that at last no man is now a Christian because of government compulsion, or because it is the way to procure favour at court, or because it is necessary in order to qualify for public office, or because public opinion demands conformity, or because he would lose customers if he did not go to church, or even because habit and intellectual indolence keep the mind in the appointed groove. This fact makes the present day the most important and the most exhilarating period in the history of Christianity for fifteen hundred years.

John Betjeman, from 'The Persecution of Country Clergy' (published in *Time and Tide*, 17 March 1951)

Betjeman (see above, p. 352) expressed his affectionate concern for the Church and its buildings in numerous articles, broadcasts and poems. His Collins Guide to English Parish Churches, *covering more than four thousand buildings, was first issued in 1958.*

... Let us imagine a parson, young or old, coming with perfectly definite views, Catholic or Evangelical, to an English village. Let him be a man with a real love of souls, courageously uncompromising about Truth and not prepared to water it down to suit the consciences of his flock on the off-chance of filling an empty pew.

Let us imagine a village of the usual modern structure: the large house a ruin or a Government office, the late squire's unmarried daughter living in a cottage, two or three immensely prosperous farmers, a few weekenders, a few farm workers to drive tractors, a bus collecting most able-bodied people to a factory outside the nearest town, a bus collecting the men, women and children to the cinema once or twice a week in the evening. Other nights are occupied by dances and whist drives. The rulers of the village are the innkeeper at one end and the schoolteacher at the other. The farmers live their own lives among other farmers' families. Their womenfolk take only a sporadic interest in the

Women's Institute, which is run by a schoolmistress or the squire's daughter (rarely by both) for the wives of the farm workers. The young men and the young girls think they are film stars and talk with American accents, go away on bicycles and buses every evening or else play together in the social club.

The wireless is on in every cottage as the remover's van arrives at the parsonage. Curtains are drawn aside, invalids peep with malevolent eyes from leaded windows, gossips lean on gates, young men and old happen to be casually walking by. What will the new parson be like?

On that first Sunday his church, for the first and last time in his incumbency, will be nearly full.

After the service the village will be agreed upon one point only – that his predecessor was much better. Some will think him too 'high', others too 'low'. What most of them will mean is that he is different from the man before. Villagers are notoriously ignorant of theology but conservative about ritual.

The people who may continue going to church are the following. The late squire's daughter because of Church and State and her late father's views – but woe betide the parson if he tries to change anything or teach anything except vague morality. This means that no Labour people will go – that is to say, no farm workers because going to church means you are Conservative. The bell-ringers may continue because of the pleasure of ringing and because they admire Winston Churchill. The schoolmistress will not go, even if it is a church school she is teaching in, because, being semi-educated and class conscious, she has 'theories' about religion and regards the parson as too dogmatic. She will attempt to disaffect the children and their mothers. A young girl and her friend will go for a week or two because she has fallen in love with the new parson. The innkeeper will not go because if he is to please his employers the brewers, he must not seem to take sides. The farmers will not go except at Harvest Festival because the collections are for the Farmers' Benevolent, the only charity they allow themselves to notice. Everyone feels there is no need to please any landlord any more. The village is independent, materialistic and, like all villages, a bit out of date compared with the towns where people are coming back to church.

Kathleen Raine (1908–2003): 'Returning from Church' (1980)

Poet, scholar, and co-founder of Temenos *(journal, and later Academy, exploring the great spiritual traditions), she alludes to the subject of Samuel Palmer's 1830 painting (in Tate Britain)* Coming from Evening Church.

That country spire – Samuel Palmer knew
What world they entered, who,
Kneeling in English village pew,
Were near those angels whose golden effigies looked down
From Gothic vault or hammer-beam.
Grave sweet ancestral faces
Beheld, Sunday by Sunday, a holy place
Few find who, pausing now
In empty churches, cannot guess
At those deep simple states of grace.

R. S. Thomas (1913–2000)

A minister in the Anglican Church of Wales, and of a fiercely Welsh disposition, he was nominated for the Nobel Prize in Literature in 1996.

The Country Clergy (1958)

I see them working in old rectories
By the sun's light, by candlelight,
Venerable men, their black cloth
A little dusty, a little green
With holy mildew. And yet their skulls,
Ripening over so many prayers,
Toppled into the same grave
With oafs and yokels. They left no books,
Memorial to their lonely thought
In grey parishes; rather they wrote
On men's hearts and in the minds
Of young children sublime words
Too soon forgotten. God in his time
Or out of time will correct this.

In Church (1963)

Often I try
To analyse the quality
Of its silences. Is this where God hides
From my searching? I have stopped to listen,
After the few people have gone,
To the air recomposing itself
For vigil. It has waited like this
Since the stones grouped themselves about it.
These are the hard ribs
Of a body that our prayers have failed
To animate. Shadows advance
From their corners to take possession
Of places the light held
For an hour. The bats resume
Their business. The uneasiness of the pews
Ceases. There is no other sound
In the darkness but the sound of a man
Breathing, testing his faith
On emptiness, nailing his questions
One by one to an untenanted cross.

The Priest (1968)

The priest picks his way
Through the parish. Eyes watch him
From windows, from the farms;
Hearts wanting him to come near,
The flesh rejects him.

Women, pouring from the black kettle,
Stir up the whirling tea-grounds
Of their thoughts; offer him a dark
Filling in their smiling sandwich.

Priests have a long way to go.
The people wait for them to come
To them over the broken glass

Of their vows, making them pay
With their sweat's coinage for their correction.

He goes up a green lane
Through growing birches; lambs cushion
His vision. He comes slowly down
In the dark, feeling the cross warp
In his hands; hanging on it his thought's icicles.

'Crippled soul,' do you say? looking at him
From the mind's height; 'limping through life
On his prayers. There are other people
In the world, sitting at table
Contented, though the broken body
And the shed blood are not on the menu.'

'Let it be so,' I say. 'Amen and amen.'

John Press (1920–2007): 'Narborough Church'

Press was a poet and writer about poets (including John Betjeman). His career was in the British Council. He was born in Norwich; Narborough is in Norfolk.

I stroll across the railway bridge,
Past cottages with pink-wash walls;
My sentimental pilgrimage
Deposits me inside the church
As the chill autumn evening falls.

A seventeenth-century gentleman
Leans nonchalantly on his side;
His cold stone eyes appear to scan
The casual visitor who admires
The face that art has petrified.

A snapshot of the football team
Of nineteen-ten slants on a nail.
Some of these gawky youths who seem
Fit only for a rustic farce
Found graver parts at Passchendaele.

This yellowing print, that crumbling stone,
Commemorating buried lives,
Might tell a saint that love alone,
When pride of art and body's strength
Grow dull and pitiable, survives.

But, standing here, I find it hard
To bandy such a word about.
Whatever flames grow cold and charred,
All self-consuming passion dies
And time stamps the last embers out.

My parents, married in this place,
I, baptized in this angel font,
Have left here not a single trace –
My father dead, my mother old
And I a mourning revenant.

The rags of flesh, the splintered bone,
Put off their lustre in the shade
Sooner than print or chiselled stone,
Though in the end time mars the bust
And the weak tints of sepia fade.

I walk in darkness to my car,
And drive along the narrow lane
That scores the landscape like a scar
To where my oblivious children lie
Cocooned by sleep from wind and rain.

Philip Larkin (1922–2005): 'Church Going' (July 1954)

Poet, novelist, essayist, and librarian. This is from his 1955 collection, The Less Deceived.

Once I am sure there's nothing going on
I step inside, letting the door thud shut.
Another church: matting, seats, and stone,
And little books; sprawlings of flowers, cut

For Sunday, brownish now; some brass and stuff
Up at the holy end; the small neat organ;
And a tense, musty, unignorable silence,
Brewed God know how long. Hatless, I take off
My cycle-clips in awkward reverence,

Move forward, run my hand around the font.
From where I stand the roof looks almost new –
Cleaned, or restored? Someone would know: I don't.
Mounting the lectern, I peruse a few
Hectoring large-scale verses, and pronounce
'Here endeth' much more loudly than I'd meant.
The echoes snigger briefly. Back at the door
I sign the book, donate an Irish sixpence,
Reflect the place was not worth stopping for.

Yet stop I did: in fact I often do,
And always end much at a loss like this,
Wondering what to look for; wondering, too,
When churches fall completely out of use
What we shall turn them into, if we shall keep
A few cathedrals chronically on show,
Their parchment, plate and pyx in locked cases,
And let the rest rent-free to rain and sheep.
Shall we avoid them as unlucky places?

Or, after dark, will dubious women come
To make their children touch a particular stone;
Pick simples for a cancer; or on some
Advised night see walking a dead one?
Power of some sort or other will go on
In games, in riddles, seemingly at random;
But superstition, like belief, must die,
And what remains when disbelief has gone?
Grass, weedy pavement, brambles, buttress, sky,

A shape less recognisable each week,
A purpose more obscure. I wonder who
Will be the last, the very last, to seek
This place for what it was; one of the crew

That tap and jot and know what rood-lofts were?
Some ruin-bibber, randy for antique,
Or Christmas-addict, counting on a whiff
Of gown-and-bands and organ-pipes and myrrh?
Or will he be my representative,

Bored, uninformed, knowing the ghostly silt
Dispersed, yet tending to this cross of ground
Through suburb scrub because it held unspilt
So long and equably what since is found
Only in separation – marriage, and birth,
And death, and thoughts of these – for whom was built
This special shell? For, though I've no idea
What this accoutred frowsty barn is worth,
It pleases me to stand in silence here;

A serious house on serious earth it is,
In whose blent air all our compulsions meet,
Are recognised, and robed as destinies.
And that much never can be obsolete,
Since someone will forever be surprising
A hunger in himself to be more serious,
And gravitating with it to this ground,
Which, he once heard, was proper to grow wise in,
If only that so many dead lie round.

Ronald Blythe (b. 1922), from *Akenfield* (1969)

Author, and lay reader in the Church of England. Akenfield *was the fruit of what he called 'a kind of natural conversation' with his Suffolk neighbours over the winter of 1966–67 – interviews that he transcribed and linked.*

The Rev. Gethyn Owen – aged sixty-three – Rural Dean
I arrived in the village immediately after the last war and so I have seen the 'revolution' – I think you can call it that. I came from the Welsh valleys, where my father was also a clergyman, and where the industrial dereliction of the 1930s sprawled for as far as one could see, to a part of Suffolk where the old feudal system was dying hard. The men had not as yet come back

from fighting and those who remained in the village seemed to be as they had been for all time. Many were still drinking the pond-water and were goitrous because of it The old dialect was pretty much undisturbed, horses worked the land and the 'big people', as the landowners were called, still ruled it.

I have been very happy here and what I have to say about the people mustn't be taken for negative criticism. They are the children of dissent; Unitarianism, radicalism, Anabaptism, these are the forces which have moulded them. I came to them when they had, for several generations, been literally worked to death. There was scarcely a moment they could call their own, a time when they could stop toiling and ask, 'Who am I?' Yet so were the miners in my father's parish – I mean it was even worse for them – yet nothing made them indifferent to colour and beauty. If you can measure the spiritual nature of men by these things, then the nature of the people of Akenfield strikes me as being uncultivated and neglected. The church was abysmally dull when I came here and there was no parish communion. No warmth of feeling. It was very noticeable after Wales.

I came to live in friendship and understanding with most of the inhabitants but I found that to talk on any deep level about their Christianity was intensely difficult – even when death was round the corner! It could have been me, of course! I don't think that the ordinary villager, who is linked to deeper propitiatory practices in the fields than he is aware of, has either the energy or feels the need to enquire what the Church is all about. Where it might have touched him – at the imaginative or creative level – all this side of his personality has been blunted and crushed by toil. I am talking about the older folk now, although a man doesn't have to be much over forty to have the results of the bad times marked on his heart.

I have sometimes dared to question the incredible perfection attached to certain tasks – this is heresy, if you like! Take ploughing or ricking, why should these jobs have had such a tremendous finesse attached to them? The harvest would not have been the less if the furrows wavered a little. But, of course, a straight furrow was all that a man was left with. It was his signature, not only on the field but on life. Yet it seems wrong to me that a man's achievement should be reduced to this. It was a form of bondage if he did but know it. The wives had their part to play in this; a woman was admired if she scrubbed and polished until she dropped. In my father's Welsh parish it was the doorsteps.

One of my most difficult tasks has been to persuade little groups of people to get together and, in a very simple and friendly way, to discuss the meaning of their Faith. But no one would come to a meeting if he thought he had to say something. When they have said something, one often finds that it is something quite irrelevant to what is being discussed. Religion has a lot to do with where their families and ancestors are buried. They spend hours tending graves and they are also very concerned about the state of the churchyard. Television is now breaking down their silences. They are getting accustomed to the idea of dialogue. The older villager was very different: he accepted or he rejected but he did nothing. There was no debate, or argument, as he called it. One discovered saints, of course, people of prayer and worship, men of a profound simplicity and to whose natural conception of the divine one could neither add nor subtract a thing. But generally speaking, the God of the Suffolk countryman tended to live outside the church, which was a building near the graves, and thus holy. It was all very vague. One could never really get near to them where such matters were concerned, as one could get near to the Celt.

I remember an example of the importance attached to church burial. When old Thrussel died, his widow came to me and said that he wished to be buried in the churchyard. I was very surprised to hear this because he'd been a Strict Baptist all his life and had been far from friendly towards the church. The Baptists, of course, have got their own burial ground behind the chapel. Why shouldn't he be buried there? 'He fancied the churchyard,' stated his wife – 'that bit up by the top there.' The penny now dropped. I recalled great battles with Mr. Thrussel about a scrap of his land which we had had to take in order to extend the churchyard. He had fought us all along the line but lost. Now he was getting his own back by being buried, as he believed, on his own farm! I always liked this old man. He and his family were all out of the common run, vital and clever. In the early days they had to struggle in a way you never see now. It made him tough and acquisitive. Whatever he gained he held. Bitterly. He was like the rest of the working farmers here. They didn't see this attitude as meanness but as strength. Life had taught Mr. Thrussel to hang on tight!

I am not really close to them. When I first came they said, 'You'll have to winter us and summer us, sir', and twenty years later I'm still doing this, if the truth be known. Newcomers have broken down many of the old community ideas and people have become sentimental about the passing of ways and customs, although many of them were narrow, limiting and bad. The church has been improved out of all recognition by the new inhabitants, who have brought fresh life and leadership to it. All the young people are mobile-minded, and that is a good thing. But men are still leaving the land and the land itself has less and less place in the mind and emotions. The power of the gentry has gone. Nobody takes any notice of such people nowadays. But behind the progress there lies the great imponderable of the East Anglian character, something to which I now know I shall never have the key. I have spent most of my time searching for the point of contact. They are hard people. Their lives at the higher level – and make no mistake, there *is* a higher level: I have seen it, a fugitive glimpse into a country where I cannot belong – present an imponderable. It is the only word I have for it. Fatalism is the real controlling force, this and the nature gods, the spirits of the trees and water and sky and plants. These beliefs seem to have no language, but they rule.

The more one visited the homes (which are improved out of all recognition since I came here) the less one bridged the gulf. No one likes to think that after so many years of genuine love and caring one is defeated, so I don't think of defeat. They have been awfully welcoming... helpful. Yet I don't know. It makes one wonder. The young are different. They have common communications with the world. The old look inward at things we cannot see. The young have a common image. The past is boring and shabby to them. They don't want to know about it.

There is another thing which is better now – morality. There were people living in the cottages near here who were like – well, I hardly like to say it – like animals. They had a sort of code but all the natural human relations were covered by cruel and ugly taboos which obsessed some of them. They loved children. Every child was 'the little dear' except if it was born out of wedlock. This was regarded as a terrible thing and never forgiven. The village would remember such a thing for ever.

The people who do best are those who leave the village for a spell and then return. Such people are quite astonishing. They have usually lowered their defences and the effect on their friends and family is extraordinary.

U. A. Fanthorpe (1929–2009): 'Soothing and Awful' (1984)

On a visit to Montacute Church in Somerset, the poet contemplates the comments that have been left in the Visitors' Book.

You are meant to exclaim. The church
Expects it of you. Bedding plants
And polished brass anticipate a word.

Visitors jot a name,
A nationality, briskly enough,
But find *Remarks* beyond them.

I love English churches!
Says Friederichshafen expansively.
The English are more backward. They come,

Certainly, from Spalding, Westbury-on-Trym,
The Isle of Wight; but all the words
They know are: *Very Lovely; Very Peaceful; Nice.*

A giggling gaggle from Torquay Grammar,
All pretending they can't spell *beautiful*, concoct
A private joke about the invisible organ.

A civilised voice from Cambridge
Especially noticed the well-kept churchyard.
Someone from Dudley, whose writing suggests tight shoes,

Reported *Nice and Cool.* The young entry
Yelp their staccato approval:
Super! Fantastic! Jesus Lives! Ace!

But what they found,
Whatever it was, it wasn't what
They say. In the beginning,

We know, the word, but not here,
Land of the perpetually-flowering cliché,
The rigid lip. Our fathers, who piled

Stone upon stone, our mothers
Who stitched the hassocks, our cousins
Whose bones lie smooth, harmonious around –

However majestic their gifts, comely their living,
Their words would be thin like ours; they would join
In our inarticulate anthem: *Very Cosy.*

Alan Bennett (b. 1934) on the Prayer Book, from 'Comfortable Words' (1990, published in *Writing Home*, 1994)

Playwright and actor of northern roots; author of 'The Sermon' sketch in the 1961 revue Beyond the Fringe. *This is part of an address Bennett gave to the Prayer Book Society in Blackburn Cathedral on 12 May 1990. He opened with Stevie Smith and her poem, 'Why are the clergy of the Church of England / Always changing the words of the prayers in the Prayer Book?'*

I'm not sure that I do believe in God. If I don't, it could reasonably be objected that I shouldn't be talking about the Prayer Book at all. Those who rewrote the Prayer Book complained very much at the time – and understandably – that many of the protests came from those, such as myself, whose connection with the Church was tenuous, the argument implicit in this being that the clergy know what is best for their congregations. This is the same argument that is advanced by farmers in answer to protests about the grubbing-up of hedges and the destructions of field patterns. The land is the farmer's bread and butter, the argument goes, and so he must therefore have its welfare more at heart than the occasional visitor. So in their own field the liturgical reformers grub up the awkward thickets of language that make the harvest of souls more difficult, plough in the sixteenth-century hedges that are hard to penetrate but for that reason shelter all manner of rare creatures: poetry, mystery, transcendence. All must be flat, dull, accessible and rational. Fields and worship.

The folly in the reform of institutions is to fix on an essential or a primary function. The land is there to produce food. The Prayer Book is there to net souls. Once one function has been given priority, all other considerations go by the board. But there is an ecology of belief as well as of nature. Poetry, mystery, the beauty of language – these may be incidental to the primary purpose of the Church, which is there to bring people to God, but one doesn't have to be Archbishop Laud to see that these incidental virtues of the Prayer Book are not irrelevant or dispensable. If they were, architecture would be irrelevant too; the logical end of rewriting the Prayer Book being that serious-minded congregations would worship in Nissen huts. And a small voice says, 'Well, perhaps that is what they do.'

Of course in the Anglican Church whether or not one believes in God tends to get sidestepped. It's not quite in good taste. Someone said that the Church of England is so constituted that its members can really believe anything, but of course almost none of them do.

One of the aims of the liturgical reformers was to make God more accessible; but that didn't mean that they weren't also a little embarrassed by Him, and I think it's this embarrassment that has got into their language. God is like an aged father taken in by his well-intentioned children. They want to keep him presentable and a useful member of society, so they scrap his old three-piece suit, in which he looked a little old-fashioned (though rather distinguished) and kit him out instead in pastel-coloured leisurewear in which he looks like everybody else. The trouble is, though, they can't change the habits of a lifetime. It's not so much that he spits in the fire or takes his teeth out at the table but that, given the chance, he is so forthright. He's always laying down the law and seems to think no one else exists, and his family might be servants the way he treats them. It's a bit embarrassing – particularly when those warm, friendly people from the religion next door come round. Still, it's only a matter of time. Father's old. He may die soon.

But before we adherents (I almost said fans) of the old Prayer Book congratulate ourselves on not being so silly, or trendy or however else the reformers are characterized, it's worth remembering that we have a corresponding dilemma. They are dodging God in one way, we in another. The majesty of the Prayer Book, the resonance of its language and the grandeur of its architecture, might seem to echo the qualities we attribute to the deity. But centuries of use have made it an accommodating majesty, a familiar grandeur; the sonority does not intimidate. W. H. Auden made the same point [in *Secondary Worlds* (1968)]: 'Those of us who are Anglicans know well that the language of the Book of Common Prayer, its extraordinary beauties of sound and rhythm, can all too easily tempt us to delight in the sheer sound without thinking what the words mean or whether we mean them. In the General Confession, for example, what a delight to the tongue and ear it is to recite "We do earnestly repent and are heartily sorry for these our misdoings; the remembrance of them is grievous unto us; the burden of them is intolerable." Is it really intolerable? Not very often.'

Moreover, the Prayer Book is so bound up, as P. D. James said here a couple of years ago, with memories – memories of childhood, of marriages and baptisms, births and deaths. And that is as it should be; but its very familiarity enables congregations to domesticate God. So when we hear what comfortable words Cranmer wrote, should we (and I am saying 'we' I suppose out of politeness, lest I seem to be lecturing you), should we not consider whether these well-worn liturgical paths down which we tread, the aisles and cloisters of this great cathedral of a book, while they are a way of praising God might also be a way of evading Him?

I suppose what I'm saying is that the Prayer Book gives pleasure, is enjoyable, satisfies, in a way that the Alternative Service Book doesn't. But whether that's anything to do with true religion I'm not sure. But it does give pleasure. Even at a funeral it's hard not to feel a quickening of the heart as the coffin passes into the churchyard and the great tolling words of 'I am the resurrection and the life' begin the stately ritual progress that will end in the grave. I think too of services caught by chance, sitting on winter afternoons in the nave of Ely or Lincoln and hearing from the (so-called) loudspeaker a dry, reedy, unfleshed voice taking evensong. And one was grateful that the voice was without feeling – no more emotion than from an announcer giving the times of the departure of trains: the words themselves so powerful that they do not need feeling injected into them, any more than poetry does. Or, as T. S. Eliot said, who had that style of delivery himself, 'Speak the word, speak the word only.'

Jeanette Winterson (b. 1959), from *Why Be Happy When You Could Be Normal?* (2011)

Her memoir of growing up as an adopted child in an evangelical household.

Elim Pentecostal Church, Blackburn Road, Accrington, was the centre of my life for sixteen years. It had no pews, no altar, no nave or chancel, no stained glass, no candles, no organ.

It had fold-up wooden chairs, a long low pulpit – more like a stage than the traditional box on stilts – a pub piano and a pit.

The pit could be filled with water for our baptismal services. Just as Jesus had baptised his disciples in the River Jordan, we too fully immersed ourselves in a deep warm plunge pool which had to be slowly heated up the day before the service. ...

Baptismal candidates wore a white sheet, either sheepishly or rakishly, and were asked this simple question by the pastor: 'Do you accept the Lord Jesus Christ as your saviour?'

The answer was: 'I do.' At this point the candidate waded into the water and, while held on either side by two strong men, was fully submerged – dying to the old life, surfacing into the new day. Once upright again and soaked through, they were given back their teeth and glasses and sent to dry off in the kitchen.

Baptismal services were very popular and were always followed by a supper of potato pie and mincemeat.

The Elim Church does not baptise children. Baptism is for adults, or those somewhere near adulthood – I was thirteen. No one can be baptised by Elim unless they have given their lives to Jesus and understand what that means. Christ's injunction that his followers must be twice-born, the natural birth and the spiritual birth, is in keeping with religious initiation ceremonies both pagan and tribal. There has to be a rite of passage, and a conscious one, between the life given by chance and circumstance and the life that is chosen.

There are psychological advantages to choosing life and a way of life consciously – and not just accepting life as an animal gift lived according to the haphazard of nature and chance. The 'second birth' protects the psyche by prompting both self-reflection and meaning.

I know that the whole process very easily becomes another kind of rote learning, where nothing is chosen at all, and any answers, however daft, are preferred to honest questioning. But the principle remains good. I saw a lot of working-class men and women – myself included – living a deeper, more thoughtful life than would have been possible without the Church. These were not educated people; Bible study worked their brains. They met after work in noisy discussion. The sense of belonging to something big, something important, lent unity and meaning.

A meaningless life for a human being has none of the dignity of animal unselfconsciousness; we cannot simply eat, sleep, hunt and reproduce – we are meaning-seeking creatures. The Western world has done away with religion but not with our religious impulses; we seem to need some higher purpose, some point to our lives – money and leisure, social progress, are just not enough.

We shall have to find new ways of finding meaning – it is not yet clear how this will happen.

John Rogers (1936–2018), from *The Undelivered Mardle* (2012)

John Rogers was a son of the rectory; initially training for the church, he became a teacher, tree planter, garden creator and environmentalist. In 2007 he had accepted an invitation from the people of Letheringham to give one of their 'mardles' (a Suffolk word for a gossip or a chat) in aid of their ancient church, but on the morning he was to deliver it he suffered a heart attack. This book emerged five years later from his researches and encounters and reflections.

Credo

A good friend of mine, a non-believer, agreed to visit the church with me and discuss the creeds to see what could be found in them, if anything, which was of use to the outsider. As we opened the door a sepulchral voice called out, 'Come in, come in... welcome!' We were looking down at a small man with a bicycle in the porch, plastic bags slung from the handlebars bulging with his belongings. He wore tired leather shoes, pinstriped trousers gathered around his slim waist and a black T-shirt. He had a serious but youthful face, fine-lined, with wide open eyes, bright and searching, and vigorous cropped hair. We stepped down into the little porch and we all three started talking, talking about almost everything, and my friend and I sat down on the cold stone sill, wrapped in the man's enthusiasm. His name was Albert. He lived 'for the time being' in a caravan. He said he loved lonely country churches and particularly this one. I asked if he was a Christian and he swallowed and licked his lips and said, well, he wasn't sure. 'I see angels,' he said, 'and I hear them when I pray. They're just there,' he said, 'up there,' and he pointed with his hand cupped with respect. 'I prayed not long ago for a woman who was ill. They said I needn't worry. Later I prayed again. They said there's nothing more can be done. You see? I seem to know things before they happen. That's how I am. People think I'm strange. There.'

My friend asked, 'And what do you believe?' and he spoke out at once. 'Ah! There you have it! It's how I live that's what I believe.' Those were his very words. At seventeen he had made 'a big decision' not to live 'like normal people' but to be different, independent, and to 'see things as they really are'.

Suddenly he sat on the floor, upright and with legs straight out before him. He put the tips of his two forefingers and his two thumbs to the floor either side of him at the centre of his gravity and raised his body so that it swung gently from the elbows like a fairground swingboat. After a few moments he lowered himself to the floor again, jumped up and said 'There!' meaning that's what I believe, that says it all. We were dumbfounded. I was reminded of a Roman Catholic bedtime story book long ago in which a clown crept into a church one day and started to juggle before a statue of the Blessed Virgin Mary. When a priest bustled forward to stop him she stepped down from her pedestal smiling and blessed the clown, her hand touching his head. The priest melted back into the shadows.

I cannot remember how this meeting with Albert ended but I do remember shaking hands and resolving to meet again. His hand was strong, the leathery hand of a gardener, for that is how he said he earned his living. When we left the church that day the creeds had not been mentioned. ...

Perhaps it was presumptuous of me to attempt a summary of what people believe in this building. Perhaps Jean Clarke was right: 'Different things at different times' may be as close as we can hope to get. Or, if Albert is right, I might have done better to scrutinize the churchmongers' private lives. But, as they say, only God can do that.

I met Albert again long after all this. He was cycling fast to Benhall early in the morning with a thermos in a small canvas bag over his shoulder. I asked if I could quote what he had said about belief. He looked puzzled.

'What did I say?'

'You said, "It's how I live that's what I believe."'

'Did I say that?'

'Yes, you did!'

'Really?'

'Yes, you did, Albert, and it's exactly what Jesus used to say.'

His blue eyes opened as wide as wide can be and he uttered, 'Did he?... Did he really?... Well!' and, smiling to himself, he prepared to hurry away.

'Yes, yes!' I called as he pedalled off, 'and can I put it in my book?'

'Oh yes!' he shouted and disappeared into the trees round Bigsby's Corner.

The Calendar and the Ritual Year

Quarter Days

(for settling accounts, rents, and debts, and for hiring labour)

Old style
Lady Day (Feast of the Annunciation): 6 April. This was also New Year's Day until 1752, and remains the start of the new financial year
Midsummer Day, Nativity of St John the Baptist: 6 July
Michaelmas: 11 October
Christmas: 6 January

New style
Lady Day is 25 March
Midsummer is 24 June
Michaelmas is 29 September (the traditional date for new terms to commence, and for goose to be eaten)
Christmas is 25 December

'Cross-Quarter' holidays

Candlemas, 2 February, celebrates the Presentation of Jesus to the Temple and the Purification of the Virgin Mary (40 days after the birth)
May Day
Lammas, 1 August, 'Loaf Mass': the blessing of the first fruits of the harvest
All Hallows, 1 November

Feast Days (immovable)

1 January, Feast of the Circumcision
6 January, Epiphany
the Apostles' Days

Feast Days (movable)

Reckoned from the date calculated for Easter, which was settled by the Council of Nicaea in AD 325 to fall on the first Sunday after the first full moon after the Spring equinox (therefore between 21 March and 25 April) – so:
Septuagesima precedes Easter by 70 days, ending in Shrove Tide
Ash Wednesday begins the 40-day period of Lent
Palm Sunday begins Holy Week, with Maundy Thursday leading to Good Friday, culminating with Easter Day
Ascension falls on the 6th Thursday after Easter
Whitsun (or Pentecost) on the 7th Sunday after Easter
Trinity Sunday the following week

The Ritual Year

- 6 December, St Nicholas's Day. The custom of boy bishops being elected from the choir and granted 3 weeks of episcopal honours (abolished by Henry VIII)
- 25 December: beginning of the Twelve Days of Christmas, with mummers, wassailing, the Lord of Misrule, etc., culminating in Epiphany, followed by a return to work on Plough Monday that could include 'ploughing' from door to door for money
- 2 February: Candlemas, and consecration of candles for the year
- 14 February, St Valentine's Day: the traditional date for birds to begin to pair began to become a celebration among the gentry in the fourteenth century
- Shrovetide: 3 days of preparing for Lent, commencing with confession, followed by eating provisions (Shrove Tuesday), before Ash Wednesday, when the ashes of last year's palms were sprinkled on penitents
- Palm Sunday: the drapes over the Rood were removed, and the west doors of churches were opened for the entry of processions.
- Maundy Thursday: washing of the feet
- Good Friday: vigil at the Sepulchre, 'Creeping to the Cross'
- Easter Day: egg-blessing, feasting, sports (especially archery), spring-cleaning
- Hock Tide, the Monday and Tuesday of the week after Easter: festivals and sports (e.g. fund-raising by women, rounding up men and 'ransoming' them)
- 23 April, St George's Day: a growing cult with the guilds
- May Day: maypole, fund-raising ales, and some licence
- Rogation or Gang Days, on the 3 days before Ascension: beating of the parish bounds
- Ascension Day, 6th Thursday after Easter
- Whitsun, 7th Sunday after Easter, with processions and pageants on the Monday
- Midsummer Day: 'bone-fires' (their stench purifying the air)
- Corpus Christi, Thursday after Trinity Sunday (instituted in 1317): crowds kneel before a procession carrying the Host; guilds perform plays
- 1 August, Lammas Tide: offering of first fruits, harvest season, and rush-bearing (to sweeten the smell of the church)
- 29 August–31 December, 'Pannage': commons have the right to pasture swine in the woods
- 1 November, All Hallows: the formal start of winter
- 11 November, Martinmas: slaughter of surplus stock in preparation for winter

TEXT CREDITS

Bede concludes his *History of the English Church and People* (transl. Sherley-Price, Penguin 1990)

Alfred the Great, Preface to his translation of Gregory's *Pastoral Care* (from Keynes and Lapidge, *Alfred the Great— Contemporary Sources*, Penguin 1983)

Henry of Huntingdon, from *History of the English People* (edited and translated by Diana Greenway, Clarendon Press 1996)

Exeter Book of Riddles, No. 26 (translated by Kevin Crossley-Holland – verse)

From *The Colloquies of Aelfric Bata* (*Anglo-Saxon Conversations*, ed. Gawara & Porter, Boydell 1997)

Wulfstan, from 'Sermon of the Wolf to the English' (Joyce Tally Lionarous, *The Homiletic Writings of Abbot Wulfstan*, D. S. Brewer 2010)

Eadmer, from *Life of Anselm* (quoted in Jacques Le Goff, *Medieval Civilisation*, transl. Julia Barrow, fol. 2011)

Bishop Hugh of Lincoln performs a miracle (Adam of Eynsham's *The Life of St. Hugh of Lincoln*, ed. Douie & Farmer, Clarendon Press 1985)

Walter Map, from *Courtiers' Trifles* (*De Nugis Curialium*, i.24, transl. M. R. James, rev. C. N. L. Brooks and R. A. B. Mynors, Clarendon Press 1983)

Matthew Paris, Murder of the Prior of Thetford (*The Illustrated Chronicles of Matthew Paris* ed Richard Vaughan, Stroud 1993)

The death of the priest John Ball from Thomas Walsingham, *Chronica Maiora* (transl. David Preest, 2005)

Chaucer, from the *General Prologue to the Canterbury Tales* – The Parson and his Ploughman brother (transl. Nevill Coghill)

Last will and testament, from the *Hundred Tales* (later C15), no. 96 (Rossell Hope Robbins, Bonanza Books, N.Y. 1960)

From William Tyndale, *The Obedience of a Christian Man* (ed. G. E. Duffield, Sutton Courtenay Press, 1964)

Roger Martin: Memoir of Long Melford, Suffolk, in its Catholic days (R. S. Mida, *Early Modern Catholicism*, OUP 2007)

Gwen Raverat (1885–1957) from *Period Piece – A Cambridge Childhood* (1952)

Rudyard Kipling (1865–1936): 'Natural Theology' (poem)

George Ewart Evans (1909–88). *The Days that We have Seen*

Siegfried Sassoon (1886–1967)
- from *Memoirs of a Fox-Hunting Man* (1928)
- 'They' (poem)

Robert Roberts (1905–1974), A Ragged Schooling

Thomas Hardy (1840–1928)
- "Ah, are you digging on my grave?" (poem)
- Channel firing (poem)

Adrian Bell (1901–1980), from *Corduroy*

D. H. Lawrence (1885–1930): *Hymns in a Man's Life* (*The Evening News*, London, 13 October 1928)

Alfred Noyes (1880–1958), The Bee in Church (poem)

T. F. Powys (1875–1953): The Hassock and the Psalter (from *Fables*, Chatto & Windus 1929)

Sir John Squire (1884–1958) *The Honeysuckle and the Bee* (1937)

Francis Brett Young (1884–1954) *Portrait of a Village* (1937)

John Betjeman (1906–1984)
- In Westminster Abbey (poem)
- The Persecution of Country Clergy (1951)
- Blame the vicar (*Poems in the Porch*, 1954)

C. S. Lewis (1898–1963): *The Screwtape Letters* (1942)

T. S. Eliot (1888–1965), from *Little Gidding* (Section 1)

John Moore (1907–1967) *Brensham Village* (1946)

Kathleen Raine (1908–2003) Returning from Church (poem)

R. S. Thomas (1913–2000)
- The country clergy (poem, 1958)
- The dark well (poem, 1961)
- In church (poem, 1963)
- The priest (poem, 1968)

John Press (1920–007) Narborough church (poem)

Philip Larkin (1922–2005) Church going (poem)

Ronald Blythe (1922–), *Akenfield* (1969)

U. A. Fanthorpe (1929–2009) 'Soothing and Awful' (poem)

Alan Bennett (1934–), from 'Comfortable Words'

Jeanette Winterson (1959–), from *Why Be Happy When You Could Be Normal?* (2011)

John Rogers (1936–2018), *The Undelivered Mardle* (Darton, Longman & Todd, 2012)